CARROLL, HENRY KING. Religious forces of
the United States enumerated, classified,
and described; returns for 1900 and 1910
compared with the government census of
18'0: condition and characteristics of Christianity in the United States, rev. and
brought down to 1910. il *$2 Scribner

12-25100

A work based on the 11th census of the
United States prepared by the man who had
charge of the division of churches. "The volume is given for the most part to exhibiting
the numerical increase or decrease of the different religious organizations in the United
States, but the first section, which is an introduction, takes into consideration other elements
than that of number. . . . The plan of the
second section is to take each denomination,
describe its doctrines and polity, give a brief
outline of its history and exhibit its numerical strength. The non-Christian religions are
not noticed here, except a very few. . . . The
last section gives the general statistical summaries from eight different standpoints."
(Boston Transcript)

"A most serviceable volume."
+ Bib World 41:143 F '13 200w

"This book is full of valuable information
which is indispensable to every one who means
to keep informed as to the beliefs, polity, and
numerical strength of the different religious
bodies in the United States. It should be in
every preacher's library."
+ Boston Transcript p18 D 24 '13 500w

"So far as the volume fails it will be in not
incorporating the later results into the chapters which describe the several denominations,
when we find tables not agreeing with the
figures in the statistics of the appendix."
+ — Ind 74:703 Mr 27 '13 100w

THE RELIGIOUS FORCES

OF THE

UNITED STATES

ENUMERATED, CLASSIFIED, AND DESCRIBED

RETURNS FOR 1900 AND 1910 COMPARED WITH THE GOVERNMENT
CENSUS OF 1890

CONDITION AND CHARACTERISTICS
OF CHRISTIANITY IN THE UNITED STATES

BY

H. K. CARROLL, LL.D.

IN CHARGE OF THE DIVISION OF CHURCHES, ELEVENTH CENSUS

REVISED AND BROUGHT DOWN TO 1910

NEW YORK
CHARLES SCRIBNER'S SONS
1912

CONTENTS.

INTRODUCTION

PART I.—RESULTS OF THE CENSUS OF 1890.

SECTION		PAGE
1.	THE SOURCES OF INFORMATION AND THE PLAN..............	ix
2.	THE SCOPE AND METHOD OF THE CENSUS...................	xi
3.	VARIETY IN RELIGION.....................................	xiii
4.	CLASSIFICATION OF THE CHURCHES........................	xv
5.	DENOMINATIONAL TITLES.................................	xviii
6.	THE CAUSES OF DIVISION................................	xxiii
7.	ANALYSIS OF RELIGIOUS FORCES OF THE UNITED STATES......	xxviii
8.	RELIGIOUS POPULATION..................................	xxxiii
9.	THE GROWTH OF THE CHURCHES...........................	xxxv
10.	HOW THE RELIGIOUS FORCES ARE DISTRIBUTED.............	xxxviii
11.	THE EVANGELICAL AND NON-EVANGELICAL ELEMENTS.......	xliii
12.	THE GENERAL STATISTICAL SUMMARIES....................	xlvi
13.	THE NEGRO IN HIS RELATIONS TO THE CHURCH.............	l

PART II.—THE GOVERNMENT CENSUS OF 1906.

1.	SEX IN MEMBERSHIP.....................................	lvii
2.	VALUE OF CHURCH PROPERTY.............................	lix
3.	AVERAGE OF MEMBERS TO CHURCH EDIFICES...............	lxi
4.	TENDENCY OF POPULATION TO THE CITIES.................	lxi
5.	COMMUNICANTS IN THE CITIES............................	lxii
6.	VALUE OF CHURCH PROPERTY IN THE CITIES...............	lxiii
7.	GROWTH BY STATES IN COMMUNICANTS.....................	lxiv

iii

iv   *CONTENTS.*

SECTION   PAGE
  8. THE RATE OF GROWTH IN THE SOUTH....................... lxv
  9. THE LARGEST ABSOLUTE INCREASES....................... lxvii
 10. EFFECT OF MIGRATION.................................. lxxiii

PART III.—THE RETURNS FOR 1900 AND 1910 AND WHAT THEY SHOW.

  1. GROWTH OF THE CHURCHES IN THE PAST TWENTY YEARS..... lxxi
  2. THE LARGEST ABSOLUTE INCREASES....................... lxxi
  3. GROWTH OF THE ROMAN CATHOLIC CHURCH................ lxxi
  4. RELIGIOUS POPULATION IN 1910........................... lxxii
  5. CHANGES OF TWENTY YEARS............................ lxxiii
  6. ORDER ACCORDING TO DENOMINATIONAL FAMILIES OR GROUPS. lxxv

PART IV.—DOMINANT RELIGIOUS ELEMENTS.

  1. THE CHARACTERISTICS OF AMERICAN CHRISTIANITY.......... lxxvii
  2. EVANGELICAL CHRISTIANITY DOMINANT.................... lxxx
  3. EVANGELICAL CHRISTIANITY SYSTEMATICALLY ORGANIZED..... lxxxi
  4. EVANGELICAL CHRISTIANITY EVANGELISTIC................. lxxxiii
  5. CO-OPERATION, FEDERATION AND UNION................... lxxxiv
  6. HOW THE CHURCH AFFECTS SOCIETY....................... lxxxvi

CHAPTER   PAGE
   I. THE ADVENTISTS... 1
  II. THE BAPTISTS.. 16
 III. THE RIVER BRETHREN..................................... 55
 IV. THE PLYMOUTH BRETHREN............................... 59
  V. THE CATHOLICS... 66
 VI. THE CATHOLIC APOSTOLIC CHURCH....................... 84
VII. CHINESE TEMPLES....................................... 86
VIII. THE CHRISTADELPHIANS................................... 89

CONTENTS.

CHAPTER		PAGE
IX.	THE CHRISTIANS	91
X.	THE CHRISTIAN MISSIONARY ASSOCIATION	95
XI.	THE CHRISTIAN SCIENTISTS	96
XII.	THE CHRISTIAN UNION CHURCHES	99
XIII.	THE CHURCH OF GOD	102
XIV.	THE CHURCH TRIUMPHANT (SCHWEINFURTH)	105
XV.	CHURCH OF THE NEW JERUSALEM	107
XVI.	COMMUNISTIC SOCIETIES	111
XVII.	THE CONGREGATIONAL CHURCHES	119
XVIII.	THE DISCIPLES OF CHRIST	125
XIX.	THE DUNKARDS	129
XX.	THE EVANGELICAL ASSOCIATION	139
XXI.	THE FRIENDS	143
XXII.	FRIENDS OF THE TEMPLE	153
XXIII.	THE GERMAN EVANGELICAL PROTESTANT CHURCH	155
XXIV.	THE GERMAN EVANGELICAL SYNOD	156
XXV.	THE JEWS	159
XXVI.	THE LATTER-DAY SAINTS	165
XXVII.	THE EVANGELICAL LUTHERANS	175
XXVIII.	THE MENNONITES	206
XXIX.	THE METHODISTS	221
XXX.	THE MORAVIANS	272
XXXI.	THE PRESBYTERIANS	277
XXXII.	PROTESTANT EPISCOPAL BODIES	317
XXXIII.	THE REFORMED BODIES	329
XXXIV.	THE SALVATION ARMY	340
XXXV.	THE SCHWENKFELDIANS	344
XXXVI.	THE SOCIAL BRETHREN CHURCH	346
XXXVII.	THE SOCIETY FOR ETHICAL CULTURE	348
XXXVIII.	THE SPIRITUALISTS	350

CONTENTS.

CHAPTER		PAGE
XXXIX.	THE THEOSOPHICAL SOCIETY	353
XL.	THE UNITED BRETHREN	355
XLI.	THE UNITARIANS	365
XLII.	THE UNIVERSALISTS	369
XLIII.	INDEPENDENT CONGREGATIONS	376

GENERAL STATISTICAL SUMMARIES.

TABLE		PAGE
I.	SUMMARY BY STATES OF ALL DENOMINATIONS	378
II.	SUMMARY OF INDIVIDUAL DENOMINATIONS	380
III.	SUMMARY OF DENOMINATIONAL FAMILIES	392
IV.	SUMMARY OF DENOMINATIONS ACCORDING TO NUMBER OF COMMUNICANTS	394
V.	DENOMINATIONAL FAMILIES ACCORDING TO NUMBER OF COMMUNICANTS	397
VI.	DENOMINATIONS CLASSIFIED ACCORDING TO POLITY	398
VII.	SUMMARY OF COLORED ORGANIZATIONS	400
VIII.	CHURCHES IN CITIES	404
	STATISTICAL SUMMARY BY STATES ACCORDING TO THE CENSUS OF 1906	417
	STATISTICAL TABLES FOR 1900 AND 1910	463
	INDEX	479

CONDITION AND CHARACTERISTICS
OF CHRISTIANITY IN THE UNITED STATES

IN FOUR PARTS

PART I.—RESULTS OF THE CENSUS OF 1890.

The purpose of this volume is to describe and classify all denominations, with statistical exhibits, so as to give a clear idea of the character and strength of the religious forces of the United States, as represented by ecclesiastical organizations.

1. THE SOURCES OF INFORMATION AND THE PLAN.—The body of this volume is occupied by the results of the United States Census of Religious Denominations taken in 1890. Some results of the government census of 1906 are also furnished, and statistical summaries for 1900 and 1910, gathered by the author from denominational sources, official and unofficial, published and unpublished, and so arranged as to show the gains and the losses for each decade and changes in the list of denominations by union or division, by dissolution or creation.

The government report for 1890 is very voluminous. It makes the county the civil unit and the classis, conference, diocese, presbytery, synod, etc., the ecclesiastical unit. That is, the statistics of each denomination are given by counties and States and by dioceses, presbyteries, conferences, etc., and denominations. In this volume it is deemed sufficient to give summaries by States and Territories and by conferences, dioceses, etc., advising those who want more minute details to consult the census volumes. The descriptive accounts are, in the main, those prepared for the census of 1890. Their object is to show the general characteristics of denominational families, or groups; to give the date, place, and circumstances of the origin of each denomination, together with its peculiarities in doctrine, polity, and usage; to state the cause of every division, and to indicate the differences which separate branches bearing the same family name.

The order of the alphabet is followed in presenting the denominations. The first chapter is given to the Adventists, the second to the Baptists, and so on through the list. A different rule is observed, however, in the arrangement of the branches of denominational families or groups. The stem, or oldest body, is given the first place, and the others appear in chronological order, according to the date of their origin, except in cases where there has been one or more divisions in a branch. To illustrate, let us take the Adventist family. The Evangelical branch is generally conceded to be the oldest. The Advent Christians are second in the order of time, and the Seventh-Day body third. The Life and Advent Union would be fourth, were it not that the Church of God, which is more recent, is a division of or secession from the Seventh-Day branch. The Church of God therefore occupies the fourth place, next to its parent body. The same rule applies to the arrangement of Methodist and other branches. The historical order has been observed because it is the more logical and convenient. The alphabetical order would inevitably lead to confusion and frequent and unnecessary repetition in the descriptive accounts; and arrangement according to numerical strength would be open to the same objection. The method chosen allows the reader to follow the historical development of every denominational group and study the causes of each successive division in the order in which it occurred. The historical rule is not strictly followed in all cases. For example, the Unitarian Churches, though historically an outgrowth of the Congregational denomination, are separately presented, because they have long been a distinct body, differing widely in doctrine from the parent body and resembling it chiefly in ecclesiastical form.

2. THE SCOPE AND METHOD OF THE CENSUS OF 1900.— The census of 1890 was the first successful effort of the government in this direction. In 1850, 1860, and 1870 religious statistics were gathered by United States marshals or their agents. In the censuses of 1850 and 1860 three items only were given, viz., churches, church accommodations, and value of church property. In 1870 a distinction was made between churches or church societies and church edifices, thus making an additional item. In 1880 large preparations were made for a census which should not only be thorough, but exhaustive in the number of its inquiries. A vast mass of detailed information was obtained; but the appropriations were exhausted before it was tabulated, and the results were wholly lost. Having been appointed in 1889 by the Hon. Robert P. Porter, superintendent of the eleventh census, to the charge of this division of the census office, the author of this volume determined to make the scope of the inquiry broad enough to embrace the necessary items of information, and narrow enough to insure success in collecting, tabulating, and publishing them, and to devise a method of collecting the statistics which would serve the ends of accuracy, completeness, and promptness. It was in some sense to be a pioneer effort, and the plan and methods adopted were designed to bring success within the range of possibility. The scope of the inquiry of 1880 was therefore greatly reduced. Many questions which, if fully answered, would yield desirable information were omitted from the census of 1890, which covers these points: (1)

organizations or congregations; (2) church edifices; (3) seating capacity; (4) other places of worship, with (5) their seating capacity; (6) value of church property; (7) communicants or members. The number of ministers is also given in the totals for denominations.

Great diversity, as every ecclesiastical student knows, exists in the statistical schemes of the various denominations. Some embrace many, others few, items; some give congregations or societies, but not edifices; others edifices but not societies; some report value of church property, while others do not; most give members or communicants, while one, the chiefest of all,[1] gives only population. There are also as many varieties of the statistical year as there are months. Moreover, quite a number of denominations have never made any returns whatever. These considerations suggest the great difficulty of securing anything like uniformity in the returns; but uniformity was kept steadily in view, and it was attained. All denominations thus appear in the census of 1890 on the same statistical basis. For the first time the Roman Catholic Church was represented by communicants, and not by population.

The method of gathering the statistics was to make the presbytery, the classis, the association, the synod, the diocese, the conference, etc., the unit in the division of the work, and to ask the clerk or moderator or statistical secretary of each to obtain the desired information from the churches belonging to his presbytery, association, or diocese, as the case might be. This officer received full instructions how to proceed, and sufficient supplies of circulars, schedules, etc., to communicate with each church. This method proved to be quite practicable, and very satisfactory. Several thousand agents thus gave information which they were best qualified to secure, and the results

---

[1] Roman Catholic.

were found, when tests were applied, to be full and accurate. I may mention that, having a large force of clerks with ample supplies, a vast correspondence was conducted. For example, desiring to obtain a complete list of Lutheran congregations unattached to synods, a letter of inquiry was addressed to every Lutheran minister asking him to report any such congregations in his neighborhood. In this way, much information, otherwise unattainable, was received.

It should be understood that the census enumerators, who take the population by domiciliary visitation, are not allowed to ask individuals as to their religious connections. In the first place, they have but a brief time in which to complete their work; in the second place, their schedules are already overburdened with inquiries; and in the third place, the constitutional provision of the First Amendment, restraining Congress from making any "Law respecting an establishment of religion, or prohibiting the free exercise thereof," is interpreted as forbidding it. Many persons would, under this constitutional guarantee, refuse to answer questions as to their religious faith, and it is doubtful whether the courts would not uphold them in their refusal. The census authorities believed that it would add greatly to the difficulties of a successful enumeration if some questions were mandatory and some not. This is the reason we cannot have in this country what the census reports of Canada, Australia, and certain other countries include— statistics of religious populations.

3. VARIETY IN RELIGION.—The first impression one gets in studying the results of the census is that there is an infinite variety of religions in the United States. There are Churches small and Churches great, Churches white and Churches black, Churches high and low, orthodox and heterodox, Christian and pagan, Catholic and Protestant, Liberal and Conservative, Calvinistic and Arminian, native and

foreign, Trinitarian and Unitarian. All phases of thought are represented by them, all possible theologies, all varieties of polity, ritual, usage, forms of worship. In our economical policy as a nation we have emphasized the importance of variety in industry. We like the idea of manufacturing or producing just as many articles of merchandise as possible. We have invented more curious and useful things than any other nation. In matters of religion we have not been less liberal and enterprising. We seem to have about every variety known to other countries, with not a few peculiar to ourselves. Our native genius for invention has exerted itself in this direction also, and worked out some curious results. The American patent covers no less than two original Bibles—the Mormon and Oahspe—and more brands of religion, so to speak, than are to be found, I believe, in any other country. This we speak of as "the land of the free." No man has a property in any other man, or a right to dictate his religious principles or denominational attachment. No Church has a claim on the State, and the State has no claim on any Church. We scarcely appreciate our advantages. Our citizens are free to choose a residence in any one of fifty States and Territories, and to move from one to another as often as they have a mind to. There is even a wider range for choice and change in religion. One may be a pagan, a Jew, or a Christian, or each in turn. If he is a pagan, he may worship in one of the numerous temples devoted to Buddha; if a Jew, he may be of the Orthodox or Reformed variety; if a Christian, he may select any one of 125 or 130 different kinds, or join every one of them in turn. He may be six kinds of an Adventist, seven kinds of a Catholic, twelve kinds of a Mennonite or Presbyterian, thirteen kinds of a Baptist, sixteen kinds of a Lutheran, or seventeen kinds of a Methodist. He may be a member of any one of 143 denominations, or of all in succession. If subdivisions into which Protestantism has fallen since? We no longer classify these divisions as units, but as families of units. The Presbyterians are not simply one of these divisions, but a whole family. The Methodists, who were a sort of *ecclesiola in ecclesia* in Wesley's day in England, are now an *ecclesia ecclesiarum* the world over. According to the scientists, no atom is so small that it may not be conceived of as consisting of halves. It may be divided into halves, and these halves may in turn be divided, and so on *ad infinitum*. No denomination has thus far proved to be too small for division. Denominations appear in the list given in this volume with as few as twenty-five members. I was reluctantly compelled to exclude from the census one with twenty-one members. The reason was, that while they insisted that they were a separate body and did not worship with other Churches, they had no organized church of their own. Twelve of them were in Pennsylvania, divided between Philadelphia and Pittsburg, six in Illinois, and three in Missouri. They were so widely scattered they could not maintain public worship.

It is not easy to define clearly and to apply discriminatingly the term "Evangelical." It comes, of course, from the Greek word "evangel," for which our Anglo-Saxon "gospel," or good news, is the close equivalent. In a general way, we mean, I suppose, when we say certain denominations are Evangelical, that they hold earnestly to the doctrines of the gospel of Christ as found in the New Testament. Evangelical and non-Evangelical are terms used generally to designate classes of Churches in the Protestant division. The Evangelical Churches are those which hold to the inspiration, authority, and sufficiency of the Scriptures; the Trinity, the deity of Christ, justification by faith alone, and the work of the Holy Ghost in the conversion and sanctification of the sinner. The non-Evangelical Churches are those which take a rationalistic view of the deity of Christ and the doctrines of grace, of which the Unitarians may be taken as an example. There are some denominations which have the word "Evangelical" in their title, and yet are thoroughly rationalistic and therefore non-Evangelical. Practically, we may distinguish as Evangelical all those bodies which are members of the general organization known as the Evangelical Alliance, or in harmony with its articles of faith; and as non-Evangelical all other Protestant bodies.

5. DENOMINATIONAL TITLES.—The numerous divisions make modern ecclesiastical history an interesting study. It is interesting because it necessarily deals with so many distinct phases of religious thought, so many diverse denominational movements, and so many divergencies, great and small, in usage, discipline, and polity. But it is a peculiarly difficult study, because of the multiplicity of denominational divisions and the labyrinth of details which must be mastered. No worse puzzle was ever invented than that which the names of the various denominations present.

We have, for example, the "Presbyterian Church in the United States" and the "Presbyterian Church in the United States of America"; the "Reformed Church in the United States" and the "Reformed Church in America." Which is which? There are doubtless many members of these bodies who could not tell. The only apparent distinction in each of these cases is geographical. But what is the difference between the "United States" and the "United States of America"? How is anybody to distinguish between the "Presbyterian Church in the United States" and the "Presbyterian Church in the United States of America"?

There are, no doubt, theological distinctions between the

"Reformed Church in the United States" and the "Reformed Church in America." But what precisely are these distinctions? They cannot be of fundamental importance, because both Churches accept the same symbol, the Heidelberg Catechism. We might reasonably expect the theologians of the two Churches to know; but what about the body of ministers? Many may have known once, but might find it difficult to recall the exact shades of difference. As to the laymen, few of them have probably ever heard the difference described. The way we learn to distinguish between the two Churches is by identifying the Reformed Church in America as the "Dutch" body, and the Reformed Church in the United States as the "German" body; and so when we want to use these titles intelligently we bracket the words "Dutch" and "German" in connection with them.

Among the Presbyterians there are four bodies of the Reformed variety. I have always had great difficulty in distinguishing between them. One is called the Reformed Presbyterian Church in the United States of America; another, the Reformed Presbyterian Church in North America. One has a synod and the other a general synod. But it is not always easy to remember which has the synod and which the general synod. I used to find in their monthly organs a more sure method of distinction. One of these organs had a blue cover and the other a pink cover. The blue-cover organ represented the general synod, and the general synod represents the Reformed Presbyterian Church in North America; the pink-cover organ represented the synod, and the synod represents the Reformed Presbyterian Church in the United States of America.

About a century ago a number of ministers and churches seceded from the Kirk in Scotland and organized the

Secession Church. Soon after, half of this Secession Church seceded from the other half, and in process of time the halves were quartered. Then, as a matter of course, there was a dispute among them as to who were the first seceders. Those who thought their claim best prefixed the word "Original" to their title and became Original Seceders. Then there was a union of Seceders and Original Seceders, and the result was the United Original Secession Church, or, more properly, the Church of the United Original Seceders. This is probably the only instance in which the ideas of division and union are both incorporated in one title. This title being neither ecclesiastical nor doctrinal, and not even geographical, we may properly term it mathematical, and think of the Church as the Original and Only Addition-Division Church in the Presbyterian family.

There are twelve bodies of Presbyterians to be distinguished, and eighteen bodies of Methodists; and Methodist titles are scarcely more helpful than Presbyterian. We have the Methodist Episcopal, which we recognize as the parent body, and which we sometimes distinguish as the Northern Church, though it covers the South as well as the North. We have the Methodist Episcopal, South, which resulted from the division in 1844 and which has churches in some of the Northern States. We have the African Methodist Episcopal, the African Methodist Episcopal Zion, the Colored Methodist Episcopal, the Union American Methodist Episcopal, the African Union Methodist Protestant, the Zion Union Apostolic, and the Evangelist Missionary—all colored bodies. We have also three bodies of Congregational Methodists, none of which are Congregational in fact, with Free, Independent, Protestant, Primitive, and other varieties of Methodists, the why of which must forever remain an inscrutable mystery to the mass of mankind. The word "Protestant" in the title of the Methodist Protestant Church does not, at least historically, mean Evangelical or anti-Catholic, but really anti-Episcopal. The Methodist reformers of 1830 protested against the episcopacy of the parent body as a barrier to the reforms they advocated. "Methodist Protestant" does not, therefore, indicate that there is a Methodist Catholic Church from which this is distinguished, but that there is a Methodist Episcopal Church from which this is distinguished as a Methodist anti-Episcopal Church. In the title Free Methodist Church the word "Free" does not mean free from State control or patronage, as it means in Presbyterian parlance in Scotland, but free from the pew system, free from worldliness, free from instrumental and choir music, and free from unsound preaching. This we ascertain from the history of the body, not from its title. The Primitive Methodist Church does not, of course, claim to belong to the age of Primitive Christianity, nor to be the original Methodist Church. It dates from 1810, and sprang from a revival of the early Methodist practice of field-preaching.

Of Baptist bodies we count thirteen, including the Regular, North, South, and Colored; the Freewill in two varieties; the General, Separate, United, Six-Principle, Seventh-Day, Primitive, white and colored, Old Two-Seed-in-the-Spirit Predestinarian; also the Baptist Church of Christ, which claims to have descended direct from the apostles. Beginning with the three principal bodies, called "Regular," we might, following the old classification of verbs, describe the Baptists as "Regular, Irregular, Redundant, and Defective." The most curious of all Baptist bodies is the Old Two-Seed-in-the-Spirit Predestinarian. Here we have a title that is definitive. It describes and distinguishes. These Baptists are Predestinarian. They believe that every action, whether good or bad, of every person and every event was predestinated from the beginning; not only the initial sin of Eve and the amiable compliance of Adam and the consequent fall of man, but the apostasy of Satan. They are thoroughly Predestinarian; and not only Predestinarian, but they are Old Two-Seed-in-the-Spirit Predestinarians. The two seeds are good and evil; and one or the other of them will spring up into eternal life or eternal death, according to the nature of the predestination decreed in each particular case.

There are four bodies of Brethren who object to any other designation. They are popularly known as (Plymouth) Brethren. By putting the word Plymouth in parenthesis we can distinguish them from other bodies of Brethren; but how shall we distinguish each of these four bodies of (Plymouth) Brethren from the other three? The device I was led to adopt for the census was that of Roman numerals, thus:

(Plymouth) Brethren I.,
(Plymouth) Brethren II.,
(Plymouth) Brethren III.,
(Plymouth) Brethren IV.,

the word "Plymouth" being in parenthesis in each case.

Much confusion often arises from the similarity of titles. There are, it will be noticed, several bodies called the Church of God, with only a slight variation in two instances. There are the Church of God and Churches of God in Christ Jesus, both Adventist; the Churches of God, otherwise distinguished as the denomination founded by Elder Winebrenner, and the Church of God in Christ. The large body, which appears in the list given in this volume as Disciples of Christ, since become two bodies, also often calls itself simply "The Christians." There is another denomination, with similar tenets and two branches, which uses the same designation, and is otherwise known as the Christian Connection. The authorities of the census in 1870 declared that in the results it was impossible to draw a line of separation between these denominations. A few years ago the Disciples were popularly distinguished as the body to which President Garfield belonged, and they are probably better known as Campbellites, a term which is offensive to them, than by either of their accepted titles.

Since we have divisions, and so many of them, we need good definitive titles. But•how shall we get them? Lord Beaconsfield waged a war to acquire a "scientific frontier" in India. Almost any means would be justifiable that would secure for us a scientific nomenclature. But there is this great difficulty: a definitive title cannot be given where there is no distinction to define. Baptist, Presbyterian, Congregational, Episcopal, are definitive titles; but between many of the Baptist and Presbyterian branches there is no difference which a title could be framed to designate. The only remedy I can suggest in such cases is reunion; and why such reunion has not taken place in scores of instances I cannot explain, except by the prevalence of the doctrine of the perseverance of the saints. It must be that the saints of the sects think they ought to persevere in sectarian division.

6. THE CAUSES OF DIVISION.—What is it that has caused so many divisions in our Christianity? The question is one of profound interest, whether considered as a matter of history, as indicating the course of controversy, or as affecting the influence, spirit, and power of organized religion. The differences in some cases between branches bearing the same generic name are important; in others they are not. How shall we explain the fact that there are six kinds of Advent-

ists, fifteen kinds of Baptists, seventeen kinds of Methodists, etc? The natural presumption is that the six branches
of Adventists are six kinds of Adventists, the fifteen branches
of Baptists fifteen kinds of Baptists, and so on. As a matter of fact, this is not so. Different titles and separate
existence, while logically implying distinct varieties, are in
some cases simply the result of differences which have long
ceased to exist. It would be a mistake, therefore, to say
that every one of the 143 distinct titles of denominations
represents a difference, either in doctrine or polity or form
of worship.

One of the most numerous of the denominational families is the Methodist. Methodism has had a marvelous
growth in the United States, and yet we find it broken
into eighteen divisions. There are no doctrinal differences
to account for them. They are all Arminian in theology,
agreeing in their opposition to the Calvinistic decrees; em-
phasizing the points of doctrine which Wesley made distinctive; and manifesting substantial oneness in the minor
matters of usage. They are one in spirit, and each has the
family resemblance in many characteristics. They differ,
first, in church government. Some are episcopal; others
presbyterian, with presidents of conferences instead of bishops; and one is independent. The oldest of the existing
divisions, the Methodist Protestant, became separated from
the parent body about 1830 in a controversy over the admission of laymen into the governing body of the Church.
Those who espoused this reform believed that bishops and
presiding elders were autocratic, and when they formed a
system of their own they brought the laymen to the front
and sent bishops and presiding elders to the rear. This
was a division on principles of government. Eight of the
branches became such because of color or race difference.
Nearly all of these separated from a white body. Two

other divisions, the American Wesleyan and the Methodist Episcopal, South, were due to the slavery question, which has been one of the most prolific causes, in the history of the last century, of ecclesiastical controversy and secessions. Another body, the Free Methodists, was the result of too little forbearance and too harsh exercise of discipline, on the one side, and to extravagances of preaching and behavior on the other. In other words, there was a misunderstanding, a quarrel, and a separation. The two Congregational Methodist branches (formerly three) are not really congregational in form of government. They were caused by disciplinary troubles. The Primitive branch comes to us, not by division, but from England through Canada.

To summarize, ten of the seventeen divisions were due to the race or the slavery question, and six to controversies over practical questions. Of course differences were increased, in some instances, by the natural process of development. The itinerancy, for example, has been modified in the Methodist Episcopal and in the Methodist Protestant Church, and the probationary system abolished in the Church, South. Leaving out the Independent and the four Congregational branches, which are very small, I doubt whether there is any difference between the various episcopal bodies that would be harder to overcome in any effort to unite them than that of race and section. There are five non-episcopal bodies which are not widely separated in practice or spirit.

Of the twelve Presbyterian bodies all are consistently Calvinistic but two, the Cumberland and the Cumberland Colored, which hold to a modified Calvinism. All use the Presbyterian system of government, with little variation. What, then, is it that divides them? Slavery divided the Northern and Southern, the race question the two Cumberland bodies; one branch is Welsh, and the rest are kept apart by minute variations. They have close points of agreement, but they differ on questions that seem to others utterly insignificant.

We may sum up the causes of division under four heads: (1) controversies over doctrine; (2) controversies over administration or discipline; (3) controversies over moral questions; (4) controversies of a personal character.

We are a nation made up of diverse race-elements. All varieties of speech, habits of thought, mental, moral, and religious training are represented among us by the older and the newer, the European and the Asiatic immigration. Here there is the utmost freedom for all forms of religion, with no exclusive favors to any. We must expect, from such a commingling, currents, counter-currents, and eddies of religious thought. Different systems of doctrine, different forms of worship, and different principles of discipline are brought into contact, and each has its influence upon the others. Calvinism affects Arminianism, and Arminianism Calvinism. The Teutonic element modifies the English and is modified by it in turn. Catholicism has been most profoundly affected by Protestantism, and some elements of Protestantism by Catholicism. Thus there are various forces acting upon religion in the United States, and producing phenomena in our religious life which the future historian will study with great interest.

Without attempting to consider with any degree of thoroughness the tendencies manifested in the history of religion in the United States, I must refer to that toward liberal views. Most denominations have become much more liberal in spirit than they used to be. It was the growth of this liberal spirit which caused many of the divisions of the past eighty or ninety years. Let me give a single illustration of the tendency. A band of Dunkards came across the sea from Germany to Pennsylvania in 1719.

They were a very simple people, interpreting the Bible literally, fashioning their outward as well as their spiritual lives by it, and believing they were called by God to be a peculiar and exclusive people. More unworldly men and women never inhabited cloister. They were in the world but not a part of the world. They thought it a virtue to resist its customs and ignore its fashions. In the character and cut of their garments, in the manner of wearing their hair, in the way they ordered their homes and their daily life, they were separate and peculiar. They adopted stringent rules of discipline to prevent the trimming of the beard, the wearing of hats instead of bonnets, the laying of carpets, the use of pianos, and similar acts, in order to keep themselves pure and unspotted from the world and maintain their simplicity of life and faith. For many years the influences of the world seemed to have no effect upon them; but gradually innovations crept into their habits, their discipline was insensibly relaxed, and the questions sent up to their annual meeting grew more numerous and perplexing, and differences of opinion became quite common. One year this question was presented, among others: "How is it considered for Brethren to establish or patronize a high-school?" After canvassing the Bible carefully for light, the following answer was returned: "Considered that Brethren should mind not *high* things, but condescend to men of low estate." Nevertheless the high-school was established and has since developed into a college. The Dunkards between 1880 and 1890 split into three bodies. Association with others inevitably changed the view and habits of a number of them, and led to innovation. These innovations were resisted by the more conservative, and division, where full toleration was not possible, was the inevitable result. Consequently, the body that had persisted for a century and a half as an unworldly, harmonious, and united communion was divided into three branches, a Progressive, a Conservative, and an Old Order branch.

Conservative and liberal tendencies appear in all organizations with which men have to do. They are manifested in all Churches. When circumstances accentuate them, only broad toleration and strong interests in common can prevent division.

7. ANALYSIS OF RELIGIOUS FORCES OF THE UNITED STATES.—The statistical results given in the census of 1890 more thoroughly and exhaustively than ever before show that the religious forces of the United States are almost entirely Christian. The number of organizations and members belonging to other than Christian bodies is a very small fraction of the whole, over one, but less than two, per cent. Among the non-Christian denominations we count the Orthodox and Reformed Jews, the Society for Ethical Culture, the Buddhists, and the Theosophists. (The pagan Indians are not included in the census, and no account is made of them here.) Those bodies are all insignificant, except the Jews, and are hardly sufficient in number to constitute a class. Including the Jews, there were in 1890 626 organizations and 132,301 members who are non-Christian. I assume that the Latter-Day Saints and the Spiritualists, whatever may be thought of certain features of their systems of religion, are as bodies properly classed as Christian. The Latter-Day Saints make much of the *name* of Christ, at least, embracing it in the title of both of their branches. The non-Christian bodies which, excepting the Jewish, are not growing, but rather decreasing, need not further engage our special consideration.

The aggregates by which the forces of religion were represented in 1890 were very large. There were, in the first place, 111,036 ministers. This number represents chiefly those in the active service as preachers, pastors, and missionaries. The percentage of those who, though retaining their ecclesiastical standing as ministers, have ceased to perform its duties cannot be large. On the other hand, it should be observed that the very numerous body of men known to Methodism as local preachers, some of whom are ordained, are not counted; nor are any returns given for those who exercise the functions of the ministry in bodies like the Plymouth Brethren, the Christadelphians, the Shakers, and similar societies. The ministry is not an order or an office among the Plymouth Brethren; but any believer who feels called to preach is given the opportunity to manifest his gifts. They have, therefore, no roll of ministers to be reported. The vast majority of the 111,036 ministers give their whole time to their ministerial work, and are supported by the churches they serve.

The number of organizations, or church societies, or congregations was 165,297. This covers not only all self-supporting churches, charges, or parishes, but also missions, chapels, and stations where public worship is maintained once a month, or oftener. Many of these places are supported by home mission societies or neighboring churches. It appears that upward of 23,000 organizations own no church edifices, but meet in halls, schoolhouses, or private houses.

It would be interesting to know how many meetings are held by all denominations in the course of a year. In some Catholic parishes five or six services of the mass, in a few cases even more, are provided every Sunday. In most Protestant churches there are two services on Sunday, besides the week-night prayer-meeting and special evangelistic gatherings. In sparsely settled sections of the South and West bi-monthly or monthly services are the rule. Besides the rented places, there are more than 142,000 Christian church edifices opened periodically to the general public. If monthly meetings only were held in these churches, there would be a grand total of 1,711,200 every year. But as a rule three services are held weekly, not including the Sunday-school. Probably the actual number of Sunday and week-night services, to say nothing about Sunday-school sessions, is between 15,000,000 and 20,000,-000 a year, with 10,000,000 sermons. Those who would get some idea of the activity of the Churches in publishing the good tidings and propagating the principles of religion must consider the tremendous significance of this conservative estimate.

The accommodations afforded to Christian worshipers by the 142,000 church edifices aggregate 43,000,000 and upward. That is, more than 43,000,000 people could find sittings at one time in the churches, to say nothing of other places where divine service is held. The question has been raised whether, if everybody wanted to go to church once a week, the churches could contain them. It is to be said, in the first place, that not all the inhabitants of any community could attend service at any particular hour or on any particular day. Infants, the infirm, the sick, and those who wait upon them must remain at home, and it is doubtful, under the most favorable circumstances, whether more than two-thirds of the population of any community of a thousand or more could be free to attend any one service. The churches alone, it appears, furnish accommodations for over two-thirds of the population, while the halls, schoolhouses, and other places where sermons are preached have room for nearly two and a quarter millions more. As most churches have at least two services every Sunday, and as many persons attend only one, it seems a very reasonable inference that if the entire population should so desire, and sickness and other controlling conditions did not intervene, they could attend divine worship once a week. In particular communities where the population is very sparse, the services may be too infrequent; in crowded centres the church accommodations may not in all cases be in adequate proportion to the numbers; but on the whole, taking all circumstances into consideration, it cannot be said that the spiritual interests of the millions are neglected, so far as privileges to worship are concerned.

It is an enormous aggregate of value (nearly $670,000,-000) which has been freely invested for the public use and the public good in church property. This aggregate represents not all that Christian men and women have consecrated to religious objects, but only what they have contributed to buy the ground and erect and furnish the buildings devoted to worship. The cost has in some cases run up into the hundred thousands; in many others it is covered by hundreds; in the vast majority of instances it is measured by thousands. Every community has one or more churches, according to the number, character, and needs of its population. In crowded cities, where real estate is quoted at high rates, and where churches generally occupy the best positions, the average value of the edifices rises to astonishing figures. This is especially true of the older cities, like New York, Philadelphia, Baltimore, Boston, and of the older denominations, such as the Episcopal, the Reformed Dutch, and the Friends. The average value of the churches, taking the whole country and all Christian bodies into account, is $4707. Of course in some denominations the average is much greater, in others much smaller. For example, among the Original Freewill Baptists of the Carolinas it is only $455; while in the Reformed (Dutch) Church it reaches $19,227; in the Unitarian, $24,725; and in the Reformed Jewish, $38,839, which is the highest for any denomination. The high average among the Jews is chiefly due to the fact that most of their communicants (nearly 88 per cent.) are to be found in the cities. Of Unitarian and Episcopal communicants, 48 per cent. are in cities of 25,000 population and upward. Denominations which, like the Disciples of Christ, the Methodist Episcopal Church, South, and the United Brethren, have a constituency made up chiefly of rural inhabitants, report a lower average of value. The figures for the Disciples of Christ are $2292, for the United Brethren, $1513, and for the Methodist Episcopal Church, South, $1480. It is to be noted that the average is much smaller in the Southern than in the Northern and New England States. As a matter of fact, at least 20 per cent. of the entire value of church property is returned by the State of New York alone; and New York, Pennsylvania, Massachusetts, Ohio, and Illinois together have more than 50 per cent. of it. No account is made in the census report of church debts, and the statistical plan of none of the denominations, with one or two exceptions, is designed to collect information on this point. The Methodist Episcopal Church, however, provides for it in its systematic yearly inquiries. In that body it appears that the debts on the churches constitute about 11 per cent. of their value. Whether this proportion holds good in other denominations it is impossible to say. In some, doubtless, it is less; in others, more. In the Protestant Episcopal Church no edifice can be canonically consecrated until it is fully paid for.

Among the mightiest of the religious forces of this country are to be reckoned the members or communicants of the Christian Churches. Allowing for those members who are dark beacons and either help not at all or help to lead astray, we have still an army of millions of men and women who, by lives devoted to the service of God and their own race, manifest the power of the gospel to reach and regenerate the human heart and satisfy its highest aspirations.

These are active forces, constant in purpose, with an influence all-pervading and all-persuasive, touching the hearts of the young and shaping their tender thoughts for eternity, helping the older to make choice while opportunity offers, and encouraging the weak and stumbling believer to persevere. There were in 1890 nearly twenty and a half millions of Christian believers, of all creeds and denominations. A considerable number are members of bodies only nominally Christian, and we should naturally exclude Spiritualists, Latter-Day Saints, and certain other denominations. With these omissions we would still have twenty millions of members, Protestant and Catholic, which is nearly one third of the entire population of the United States. When it is remembered that several millions of our population are children too young to be communicants, the showing for the Churches cannot be regarded as unfavorable, by any means. Nearly one person in every three of all ages is a Christian communicant.

8. THE RELIGIOUS POPULATION.—What is our religious population? While no enumeration has been made to ascertain the religious preferences of the people of the United States, it is quite possible to form an estimate upon the basis of the communicants reported, which will be sufficiently accurate for all purposes. The usual way of computing religious population is by multiplying the number of communicants of any Protestant denomination by $3\frac{1}{2}$. This is on the supposition that for every communicant there are $2\frac{1}{2}$ adherents, including, of course, young children. A careful examination has satisfied me that this supposition rests on good grounds. I find support for it in a comparison between the census returns of the religious populations of various communions in Canada with those which the denominations give themselves of communicants. It will be

convenient to arrange the returns for population and communicants in tabular form.

DENOMINATIONS.	Religious Population.	Communicants.
Methodists.....................	847,469	241,376
Presbyterians..................	755,199	169,152
Episcopalians.................	644,106	114,931
Baptists.......................	303,749	78,059

This table indicates that there are 2.5 Methodist, 3.5 Presbyterian, 4.6 Episcopalian, and 2.9 Baptist adherents to every communicant. The average is 3.2. This is higher than I feel warranted in applying to all denominations in the United States. The proportion varies with the denominations, and is probably much lower when the smaller and more obscure denominations are brought into consideration. Certainly, the results justify us in assuming that there are at least 2.5 adherents in the United States to each Protestant communicant, taking all the denominations together. In round numbers we may take 14,180,000 as representing the Protestant communicants. This leaves out not only the Catholics, but the Jews, the Theosophists, the Ethical Culturists, and the Spiritualists. It seems best to omit the Latter-Day Saints also. Multiplying this number by $3\frac{1}{2}$, we have 49,630,000, which represents the aggregate of Protestant communicants and adherents, or Protestant population. To this we must add the Catholic population, in order to get the entire Christian population. There are 6,257,871 Catholic communicants of all branches. Catholic communicants, according to Catholic estimates, constitute 85 per cent. of the Catholic population. There must, therefore, be a Catholic population of 7,362,000; adding this to the Protestant population, we have 56,992,000. This stands for the Christian population of the United States in 1890. As the population, according to the census, is 62,622,-250, it would appear that there are 5,630,000 people who are neither Christian communicants nor Christian adherents.

Making liberal allowance for the Jews and other religious bodies not embraced in the Christian population, there are 5,000,000 belonging to the non-religious and anti-religious classes, including free-thinkers, secularists, and infidels. We have, of course, no warrant for believing that the majority of these 5,000,000 who are outside the religious populations are atheists, or avowed unbelievers. There are but few real atheists; few who do not have some belief concerning a supreme being and a future. But most of the 5,000,000 are probably opposed to the Churches for various reasons. And we must not forget that in the fifty-seven millions counted as the Christian population are many who are indifferent to the claims of religion, and seldom or never go to a house of worship. Adding these, and the large number of members on whose lives religion exercises practically no power, to the 5,000,000, we have a problem of sufficient magnitude to engage the mind, heart, and hand of the Church for a generation. One out of every twelve persons is either an active or passive opponent of religion; two out of every three are not members of any Church.

9. THE GROWTH OF THE CHURCHES.—The normal condition of the Christian Church is a growing condition. In no other way can it manifest the spirit and power of the gospel; on no other consideration can it retain that spirit and power. It has received salvation that it might press it upon those who have it not; the power of the Spirit, that it might speak in His name; the world as its parish, that it might convert it. It must be aggressive or cease to be prosperous; it must diligently propagate or begin to decline. In the very nature of things this must be so. Death decimates yearly the list of communicants. The losses from this and other causes must be made good by accessions before actual growth is made apparent. There must be a measure of increase to prevent decline. All increase beyond that which repairs the losses we count as net increase. Our Churches,

almost without exception, manifest the conditions of prosperity and growth. Year by year they add to their numbers. In some cases the percentage of growth is large; in others, small; but growth is the rule and decline the rare exception. We ascertain this, of course, by comparison of one year's returns with those of another, as furnished by the denominations themselves, or most of them. It should be said, however, that denominational statistics are not of uniform completeness and excellence, and it is difficult in many instances to obtain them at all for a series of years. This makes it hard to secure anything like a fair comparison. The returns of the census of 1890 may be regarded as exhaustive and accurate as possible; but there is nothing in previous censuses with which to compare them. The published results of the seventh, eighth, and ninth censuses do not include communicants at all, and we cannot be sure from the way they were conducted that they were sufficiently accurate and complete for purposes of comparison. Results obtained in this way must be taken simply as indications of increase, not as accurate representations of it. No distinction was made in 1850 and 1860 between church organizations and church edifices. Two items only appeared in those three censuses in such form as to admit of fair comparison, viz., church accommodations or sittings, and value of church property. It appears that the gain in sittings in the ten years ending in 1860 was 34 per cent., and in value of church property over 100; in the ten years ending in 1870 it was only a little more than 13 per cent. in sittings, but about 100 per cent. in value. Since 1870 the gain in sittings has been about 101 per cent., and in value of church property, 92. These figures must not, however, be taken without allowance for the more or less imperfect returns of 1870. A more satisfactory comparison may be made for the larger denominations between the census returns of 1890 and returns of 1880 gathered from denominational year-books. The figures represent communicants.

DENOMINATIONS.	1880.	1890.	Increase
Baptist, Regular (3 bodies).......	2,296,327	3,429,080	1,132,753
Baptist, Freewill................	78,012	87,898	9,886
Congregational..................	384,332	512,771	128,439
Disciples of Christ..............	350,000	641,051	291,051
Dunkards.......................	60,000	73,795	13,795
Episcopal, Protestant............	343,158	532,054	188,896
Episcopal, Reformed.............	5,000	8,455	3,455
Evangelical Association..........	99,794	133,313	33,519
Friends........................	100,000	107,208	7,208
Lutheran (all bodies)............	693,418	1,231,072	537,654
Methodist Episcopal.............	1,707,413	2,240,354	532,941
Methodist Episcopal (South).....	830,000	1,209,976	379,976
Methodist (other)..............	987,278	1,138,954	151,676
Moravian.......................	9,212	11,781	2,569
Presbyterian (North)............	573,599	788,224	214,625
Presbyterian (South)............	121,915	179,721	57,806
Presbyterian, Cumberland.......	113,933	164,940	51,007
Presbyterian (other)............	122,078	145,447	23,369
Reformed (Dutch)...............	79,269	92,970	13,701
Reformed (German).............	151,761	204,018	52,257
United Brethren................	156,735	225,281	68,546
Total....................	9,263,234	13,158,363	3,895,129

The increase indicated is large, amounting to over 42 per cent. In the same period, ten years, the population increased at the rate of 24.86. These churches, which embrace all Protestant communicants except about a million, grew faster than the population by 17.19 per cent. That surely is encouraging. It is a large net gain, and means that Protestant Christianity, notwithstanding the large Catholic immigration of the decade, is advancing at a rapid pace.

The growth of the Roman Catholic Church for the same period must have been large. It was fed by a tremendous stream of immigrants from Catholic Europe and the Catholic section of Canada; and the natural increase of a population of six or seven millions must be considerable. How large it was, however, statistics cannot certainly show.   The Catholic year-books do not give exact returns of Catholic population, only estimates, based upon diocesan reports of births and deaths.   It is true that the census of 1890 makes returns for Catholic communicants; but what is there with which to compare them?   Sadlier's "Directory" of 1881 estimated the Catholic population of 1880 at 6,367,330; and in 1891 at 8,277,039 for 1890—an increase of 1,909,709, or about 30 per cent.   In view of all the circumstances this rate of growth does not appear to be too high.   If it may be taken as applying to the increase of Catholic communicants in the decade ending in 1890, it would appear that the Catholic Church must suffer very heavy losses, for its net increase is far below that of the Protestant Churches represented in the above table.   How otherwise can its moderate rate of increase be reconciled with the enormous accessions it must have received by an immigration which helped the Lutherans and a few other Protestant bodies to a far more limited degree?

10.   How the Religious Forces Are Distributed.— While the religious forces are established in every State and Territory of the Union and bear more than a hundred and forty different denominational titles, they are massed in a few denominations and in a comparatively few States. The five largest denominations comprise 60 per cent. of the entire number of communicants; and the ten largest, 75 per cent.   The Roman Catholic Church is first, with 6,231,000; the Methodist Episcopal second, with 2,240,-000; the Regular Baptists, Colored, third, with 1,349,000; the Regular Baptists, South, fourth, with 1,280,000; and the Methodist Episcopal, South, fifth, with 1,210,000.   The Catholic figures are truly of magnificent proportions.   They exceed by more than 150,000 the sum of those representing the four next largest denominations.   Every tenth person in the United States is a Catholic communicant.   It is only

fair, however, to remind those interested in this statement that while a communicant is a communicant considered statistically, whether he be a Catholic or a Protestant, there is a difference between the Protestant and the Catholic basis of membership which ought to be kept constantly in view when comparison is undertaken. The Catholic authorities count as communicants all who have been confirmed and admitted to the communion, and these virtually constitute the Catholic population, *less all baptized persons below the age of nine or eleven.* The Catholic discipline does not contemplate excommunication for violations of the moral code, only for lapses from the faith and refusal to obey the ecclesiastical commandments. There are many who go to make up the Protestant population who have been expelled from membership for offenses which the Catholic Church treats by a very different method. In other words, while the Catholic Church reckons that 85 per cent. of its population are communicants, among Protestants the proportion is estimated to be under, rather than over, 30 per cent. The Protestant basis of membership is belief and conduct; the Catholic, belief and obedience. In any given thousand of Catholic population there are 850 communicants and 150 adherents; while a thousand of Protestant population yields only about 300 communicants, the remaining 700 being adherents. Thus, while the 6,231,000 Catholic communicants represent a Catholic population of about 7,330,000, the 2,240,000 communicants of the Methodist Episcopal Church, alone, indicate a Methodist population of 7,840,000.

The Roman Catholic Church is first also in value of church property, of which it returns, in round numbers, $118,000,000. The Methodist Episcopal is second ($97,-000,000); the Protestant Episcopal third ($81,000,000); the Northern Presbyterian fourth ($74,000,000); and the Northern Baptists fifth ($49,000,000). Two of these denominations, the Episcopal and the Presbyterian, are not among the five which return the largest number of communicants. They stand third and fourth respectively in the table of church property, showing that they are much more wealthy in proportion to communicants than any of the five larger denominations.

In number of organizations, or congregations, the Methodist Episcopal Church comes first, with 25,861, and the Roman Catholic last, with 10,231. The Southern Baptists are second, with 16,238; the Southern Methodists third, with 15,017; and the Colored Baptists fourth, with 12,533. The reason the Catholic congregations number only two-fifths as many as the Methodist Episcopal is because their parishes are so much larger and more populous. Some Catholic parishes embrace from 12,000 to 16,000 communicants, all using the same edifice. It is a common thing in the cities for Catholic churches to have five and six different congregations every Sunday.

To recapitulate: The Roman Catholic Church is first in the number of communicants and value of church property, and fifth in number of organizations and houses of worship; the Methodist Episcopal is first in the number of organizations and houses of worship, and second in the number of communicants and value of church property.

Let us now see how the five leading denominational families or groups stand. The Catholics, embracing seven branches, come first as to communicants, with 6,258,000; the Methodists, embracing seventeen branches, come second, with 4,598,000; the Baptists, thirteen branches, are third, with 3,718,000; the Presbyterians, twelve branches, are fourth, with 1,278,000; and the Lutherans, sixteen branches, are fifth, with 1,231,000. It will be observed that the combined Methodist branches have about 1,600,000 fewer communicants than the combined Catholic branches.

As to the value of church property, the Methodist family is first, the figures being $132,000,000. The Catholic family is second, $118,000,000; the Presbyterian third, $95,000,000; Episcopalian fourth, $82,835,000; the Baptist fifth, $82,390,000. Thus, among denominational families the Catholics are first in the number of communicants, second in value of church property, and fourth in the number of organizations and houses of worship. The Methodists are first in the number of organizations and houses of worship and value of church property.

Naturally we should expect to find the greatest number of communicants in the States having the greatest population. New York has nearly 6,000,000 population, and returns 2,171,822 communicants. Pennsylvania, second in population, is also second in communicants, reporting 1,726,640. Illinois is third in population, but fourth in communicants; Ohio, fourth in population, but third in communicants; Missouri, fifth in population, but sixth in communicants; Massachusetts, sixth in population, but fifth in communicants. This shows that the percentage of communicants to population varies even in the older States. In New York it is 36.21; in Pennsylvania, 32.84; in Ohio, 33.13; in Illinois, 31.43; and in Massachusetts, 42.11. The highest in any State is 44.17, in South Carolina; the lowest, 12.84, in Nevada. The highest percentage is not found in any State, but in a Territory. New Mexico's population are communicants to the extent of 68.85 per cent.; and, strange to say, Utah is second, its percentage being 61.62. New Mexico is predominantly Catholic. This explains its high percentage of communicants. Utah is the stronghold of the Mormons, and, like the Catholics, they report a large membership in proportion to their population. The Catholics are numerically the strongest in thirty-three States and Territories, including the New England, the Pacific, the newer Northwestern, and various Western and Southern States; the Methodists in South Carolina, Tennessee, West

Virginia, Delaware, Florida, Indiana, Indian Territory, Kansas, and Oklahoma; the Baptists in Alabama, Arkansas, Georgia, Kentucky, Mississippi, North Carolina, Texas, and Virginia; and the Latter-Day Saints in Utah.

It is interesting to note that Pennsylvania is the stronghold of the Lutherans, the Presbyterians, the Moravians, the Mennonites, and the Reformed (German); North Carolina of the Methodists; New York of the Catholics, the Jews, the Episcopalians, the Universalists, and the Reformed (Dutch); Massachusetts of the Congregationalists, Unitarians, Swedenborgians, Spiritualists; Georgia of the Baptists; Missouri of the Disciples of Christ; Indiana of the Friends; Ohio of the United Brethren.

While New York is first among the States in number of communicants and also in value of church property, it does not occupy this position as respects number of organizations and of church edifices. Pennsylvania leads in both these particulars, having more organizations and church edifices than any other State. Ohio occupies the second place and New York the third as to edifices and the fifth as to organizations. The following table shows how the positions of the leading States vary in the different columns. In each list the States are arranged in the order of numerical precedence.

Communicants.	Value of Church Property.	Church Edifices.	Organizations.
1. New York.	1. New York.	1. Pennsylvania.	1. Pennsylvania.
2. Pennsylvania.	2. Pennsylvania.	2. Ohio.	2. Ohio.
3. Ohio.	3. Massachusetts.	3. New York.	3. Texas.
4. Illinois.	4. Ohio.	4. Illinois.	4. Illinois.
5. Massachusetts.	5. Illinois.	5. Georgia.	5. New York.
6. Missouri.	6. New Jersey.	6. North Carolina.	6. Missouri.
7. Indiana.	7. Missouri.	7. Missouri.	7. Georgia.
8. North Carolina.	8. Michigan.	8. Alabama.	8. North Carolina.
9. Georgia.	9. Indiana.	9. Indiana.	9. Indiana.
10. Texas.	10. Connecticut.	10. Tennessee.	10. Alabama.

Only six States appear in all these tables, viz., New York, Pennsylvania, Ohio, Illinois, Missouri, and Indiana. Texas.

which is tenth in the list arranged according to number of communicants, and does not appear at all in those for value of church property and number of church edifices, stands third in that for number of organizations. This indicates that the average number of communicants to each organization is much smaller in Texas than in the other States mentioned. Texas has a smaller percentage of urban population than the other States, excepting North Carolina, Alabama, and Georgia; it has an immense area, and it is therefore natural that its organizations should be small and numerous.

II. THE EVANGELICAL AND NON-EVANGELICAL ELEMENTS.—These terms are commonly applied to Protestants. The sense in which they are used has already been defined; but it is easier to define the terms than to classify denominations under them. In which class, for example, should Universalists be put? They have not been admitted to the Evangelical Alliance, chiefly because of their views respecting the nature and duration of future punishment; but on the main points of New Testament Christianity they are generally evangelical. On the single question of the future of the wicked dead some of the branches of the Adventist family and other bodies would be excluded from the evangelical list; but, on the whole, would it be quite fair to class as non-evangelical those who believe in the divinity of Christ, in the necessity and sufficiency of his atonement, and in salvation by faith alone? By some the Christians or Christian Connection have been classified with the Unitarians; but they have become, in late years, quite orthodox, and are undoubtedly evangelical. In most evangelical denominations persons are to be found who are non-evangelical; and in some of the non-evangelical denominations there are members who are thoroughly evangelical. Yet we cannot draw the line through denominations; we must draw it between them. The classification must therefore be more or less arbitrary, and due allowance should be made for this fact.

There are a few bodies which manifestly ought not to be classified as either evangelical or liberal. These may properly be put in a separate list.

EVANGELICAL DENOMINATIONS.

DENOMINATIONS.	Organizations.	Communicants.
Adventists	1,757	60,491
Baptists	43,029	3,717,969
Brethren (River)	111	3,427
Brethren (Plymouth)	314	6,661
Catholic Apostolic	10	1,394
Christadelphians	63	1,277
Christians	1,424	103,722
Christian Missionary Association	13	754
Christian Union	294	18,214
Church of God	479	22,511
Congregationalists	4,868	512,771
Disciples of Christ	7,246	641,051
Dunkards	989	73,795
Evangelical Association	2,310	133,313
Friends (3 bodies)	855	85,216
Friends of the Temple	4	340
German Evangelical Synod	870	187,432
Lutherans	8,595	1,231,072
Mennonites	550	41,541
Methodists	51,489	4,589,284
Moravians	94	11,781
Presbyterians	13,476	1,278,332
Protestant Episcopal (2 bodies)	5,102	540,509
Reformed	2,181	309,458
Salvation Army	329	8,742
Schwenkfeldians	4	306
Social Brethren	20	913
United Brethren	4,526	225,281
Independent Congregations	156	14,126
Total	151,158	13,821,683

CATHOLIC.

Catholic bodies	10,276	6,257,871

Non-Orthodox.

	Organizations.	Communicants.
Christian Scientists	221	8,724
Church of the New Jerusalem	154	7,095
Church Triumphant (Schweinfurth)	12	384
Communistic Societies	32	4,049
Friends (Hicksite)	201	21,992
German Evangelical Protestant	52	36,156
Latter-Day Saints	856	166,125
Spiritualists	334	45,030
Unitarians	421	67,749
Universalists	956	49,194
Total	3,239	406,498

Non-Christian.

Chinese Temples	47	......
Ethical Culturists	4	1,064
Jews	533	130,496
Theosophists	40	695
Total	624	132,255

Recapitulation.

Evangelical	151,158	13,821,683
Catholic	10,276	6,257,871
Non-Orthodox	3,239	406,498
Non-Christian	624	132,255
Total	165,297	20,618,307

From this it appears that the non-evangelical, non-orthodox, and non-Christian bodies count a little more than half a million, or about 2.6 per cent. of the aggregate. The evangelical communicants are to the non-evangelical as 76 to 1, and constitute more than 67 per cent. of all communicants, Christian and non-Christian.

It further appears that the evangelical organizations outnumber all other organizations nearly 11 to 1, and form more than 91 per cent. of the aggregate.

12. CLASSIFICATION ACCORDING TO POLITY.—The extended tables given at the end of this book are not, perhaps, very attractive. But they will repay careful study. There are many significant facts to be obtained from an examination of the summaries of colored organizations, of denominations arranged according to polity, and of churches in the cities. The last is a new feature in church statistics.

Of the classification according to polity a word of explanation is necessary. It is difficult in some cases to know how to classify. It is clear enough that Baptists, Congregationalists, and Disciples of Christ are congregational; but it is not so clear where the vast body of Lutherans belongs. They are not, I am persuaded, purely presbyterian, nor purely congregational, and certainly not purely episcopal. My own inclination was to classify them as presbyterian, and I wrote to representative men among them for their opinion, and it will be interesting to quote from some of the responses.

President Henry E. Jacobs, of the body known as the General Council, says:

I am not surprised at your perplexity concerning the classification of Lutherans with respect to church polity. As the form of government is regarded as unessential, and to be determined according to circumstances, there is a lack of uniformity. The Synodical Conference gives to synods only advisory power, and requires the ratification of all synodical resolutions, and even the election of professors of theology, by the congregations. Nevertheless, they agree with the Presbyterians in maintaining a distinction between the lay and preaching elders, as one resting upon Scriptural foundations. Muhlenberg's scheme of church government clearly belongs to a generic presbyterianism; and this has been propagated in General Council, General Synod, United Synod of South, and most of the independent synods. The General Council rejects, however, lay elders, as not warranted in Scripture; although in most of its older congregations the constitutions have not been changed and a lay eldership is retained simply as a useful but not a Scriptural or necessary church institution.

However you may classify us, you will, therefore, not escape criticism—and that, too, with some basis of truth; but taking everything into consideration, I believe that you are right in classifying us as presbyterian.

The Rev. J. Nicum, of the same branch, says the Lutheran Church is not strictly presbyterian, though usually so classified, nor is it congregational.

Everywhere in the Lutheran Church there are conferences, synods, consistories, etc., to whom questions of ordination, discipline, appeals from decisions of vestries or congregations are taken.

If you now ask me for a positive opinion as to what the polity of the Lutheran Church really is, I say it is episcopal, or at least more nearly so than anything else. Our presidents of conferences and of synods are really bishops. They are everywhere charged with the supervision of the churches, their visitation, the ordination of pastors, and the recommendation of suitable men to vacant parishes. They also lay the cornerstones to new church buildings, dedicate them, install ministers, or appoint suitable persons to attend to these matters for them. This practice is universally followed in the Synodical Conference, in the General Council, and in almost all the independent synods. *Jure divino*, every pastor is bishop of his flock, but the institution of diocesan bishops is a matter of human expediency. This is the Lutheran view.

Professor M. Günther, of the Synodical Conference, writes:

You may be right in supposing "that it is, rather, presbyterian," if you have in view Eastern bodies. But for them (General Council and General Synod) I would not speak.

As to the Synodical Conference, its polity is not strictly congregational, but near to it—in reference to the main principle of congregationalism, that every congregation is independent and self-governing. We differ in regard to the mode in which Congregational churches assist each other, etc.

Our congregations have freely entered into a synodical union for mutual assistance and oversight, for the purpose of more effectually securing unity and purity of doctrine, and of more successfully advancing the general interests of the church (institutions, missions, etc.). They are represented by their pastors and lay delegates, who act in their name, in some cases being instructed by them. (Pastors whose congregations have not as yet joined synod have no vote.) Synod with us has only advisory power, no legislative or judicial power.

Our synodical organization differs quite from that of other bodies, even Lutheran. In our body congregations govern themselves—decide matters in congregational meetings. In others, congregations are governed by church councils. Synods are regarded as legislative and judicial bodies, deposing pastors, etc., giving pastors whose congregations do not belong to synod a vote, etc.

The polity of the Synodical Conference is, therefore, neither strictly congregational nor presbyterian. It is based on the so-called "Collegial System" (in contradistinction to episcopalism and territorialism), formed according to the liberty which the church enjoys in this free country.

Professor George H. Schodde, of the Independent Synod of Ohio, says:

In theory, and in practice too, among the most thorough-going representatives of historic Lutheranism, the congregational principle is maintained and lived up to; in reality, and by common consent, so much power has been delegated the synods that the polity almost seems presbyterian. There is no disagreement in *principle* among us as to the congregational character of our polity; but in practice synods are generally a good deal more than advisory bodies. When, however, it comes to a clash, I have never heard of a synod of any prominence that has claimed a right to control the affairs of any congregation. The latter is the highest court of appeal. "Synod is merely an advisory body" is in theory the fundamental basis of our polity. The struggle between the Ohio Synod and the General Council some fifteen years ago was only on the practical application of this principle, not on the principle itself. I think our leading men would with one voice say that our polity is congregational, and the church to be classified as such.

I give a single other opinion, from a letter by Professor E. J. Wolf, of the General Synod. He says:

Theoretically, our polity is congregational. Practically, it has varied according to environment, especially so because Lutherans have never claimed any polity to be divine right. The Missourians carry out strictly the congregational idea. Their churches are republics, their ministers are presidents, though when in office they are almost absolute monarchs. In the other divisions we have synods corresponding to the presbyteries of Calvinism, and general bodies made up of deputies from the synods; but when it comes "to the powers and functions of the synod," they can hardly be said to conflict seriously "with the idea of pure congregationalism." These powers are almost wholly "advisory." The exceptions to this rule are that the Augsburg Confession is the acknowledged or implied basis of every Lutheran church, and the General Synod reserves the exclusive right of publishing hymn-books, liturgies, and catechisms. Should, however, any congregation decline to use such manuals as the General Synod provides, it cannot be disciplined, although cases may arise where the synod will forbid one of its members to officiate in a recalcitrant congregation. The congregation itself cannot be dissolved, and if it sees fit to withdraw from the synod, it does not lose its character as a Lutheran society, though the synod would not allow one of its menbers to serve such a congregation.

In other words, the synod has control over the ministers, which it can depose as well as ordain, although again theoretically, in both cases, only at the instance of a congregation. But the congregation does not stand or fall through any action of synod. And just here is the pivotal point where congregationalism and presbyterianism both come into our polity. A minister once a member of a synod is subject to its requirements—he must submit to the body he has joined. A congregation can defy a synod's action; but the only prejudice it suffers is to lose its connection with the synod. It resumes an independent relation, or it may join a synod connected with another general body.

Amid such conflicting opinions, I have deemed it proper to make a sort of compromise, and classify the Synodical Conference and the Ohio Synod, which all agree are less presbyterian than other Lutheran bodies, as congregational, and all the rest, except the independent congregations who also go into the congregational list, as presbyterian.

13. THE CHURCHES IN CITIES.—The tables devoted to the statistics of the Churches in the cities are quite exhaustive, including all municipalities having a population of 25,000 and upward. The cities are divided, for the sake of convenience, into three classes: first, those having 500,-000 population and upward; second, those having a population of 100,000 to 500,000; and third, those having a population of 25,000 to 100,000.

The results are, in brief, that there are 5,302,018 communicants in these cities, or more than a fourth of the aggregate for the whole country; 10,241 organizations, which is less than a sixteenth of the whole number; 9722 church edifices, which is a little larger proportion; and church property valued at $313,537,247, or more than 46 per cent. of the grand total. The large figures representing church property do not need an explanation. The high values of city property account for them. The cities have an aggregate population of 13,988,938. Of this population it appears that one for every 2.64 persons is a communicant. This is a higher average than obtains in the country generally, where it takes more than three persons to yield one communicant. In the United States there are 337+ communicants in every thousand population; in the cities, nearly 379 in every thousand. Much of this difference may be explained by the fact that the Roman Catholic strength is chiefly in the cities, and it has a larger proportion of communicants to its religious population than any other denomination. The fact that the average of communicants to population is so large in the cities must be an encouragement to those who fear that the church is losing its grip on the masses crowded into our cities.

In the matter of church edifices a little calculation will make it appear that the cities of the second and third classes have more in proportion to population than those of the first class. The latter have one to 2147 of the population; those of the second class, one to 1468; and those of the third class, one to 1052.

Of the denominations, 37 are not represented in any of the cities. Only three—the Roman Catholic, Methodist Episcopal, and Protestant Episcopal—are represented in all of them. Of the Jews (Orthodox), nearly 92 per cent. are in the cities; of the Jews (Reformed), more than 84 per cent.; of the Unitarians and Episcopalians, upward of 48; of the Roman Catholics, more than 42; of the Presbyterians (North), nearly 29; of the Methodists (Episcopal), nearly 15; and of the Southern Baptists and Southern Methodists, only about 4.

14. THE NEGRO IN HIS RELATIONS TO THE CHURCH.— The negro is a religious being wherever you find him and under whatever conditions. In his own continent, where civilizing influences have hardly begun to lift him above the state of savage degradation in which he has so long remained, his religious instincts are dominant. They find expression often in superstitious, idolatrous, and cruel rites and observances; but he has, nevertheless, conceptions of beings of exalted power who affect the destiny of men.

The negro of the United States has no religion but the Christian religion. He is not a heathen, like our native Indian. He worships but one God, who is a just and merciful God, desiring that all men should be free from sin, and should come to a knowledge of the way of life through Jesus Christ. He is still more or less superstitious; he still has some faith in the power of charms; there is still some trace of heathenish practices in him; but our own race has not altogether outgrown childish thoughts about unlucky days and the way to avoid the evil they bring, and how mascots procure success. We cannot condemn the negro for his superstition without taking blame upon ourselves for the tenacity with which we cling to belief in signs and times and things, lucky and unlucky.

The negro of the United States is a Christian, not an atheist or a doubter. He gives no countenance to secularist or free-thinking organizations; nor does he prefer abnormal types of religion, such as Mormonism and spiritualism. Moreover, he is not a rationalist, or a theosophist, or an ethical culturist. He does not turn aside to adopt the erratic ideas of little coteries of religionists. Neither does he show a preference for the Roman form of Christianity. The splendid ceremonies of Catholic worship might be supposed to have a strong attraction for him, but it is not so. The actual membership of separate negro Catholic churches does not exceed fifteen thousand, and yet the Catholic Church is not weak in Louisiana or Maryland or the District of Columbia. Thirty-one represents the total of separate Catholic negro churches, not including, of course, the negro communicants in mixed churches.

The negro is not only a Christian, he is an evangelical Christian. He is a devout Baptist and an enthusiastic Methodist. He loves these denominations, and seems to find in them an atmosphere more congenial to his warm, sunny nature, and fuller scope for his religious activity, than in other communions. Perhaps this is due to his long association with them and his training. There is no reason to believe that he might not have been as intense a Presbyterian as he is a Baptist, or as true a Congregationalist as he is a Methodist, if these denominations had been able to come as near to him in the days of his slavery as did the Baptist and Methodist churches. It was fortunate for him that, while he was the slave of the white master, that master was a Christian and instructed him in the Christian faith. The school was practically closed to him; but the church was open, and thus he came into personal freedom and into the rights of citizenship an illiterate man, but a Christian, with that measure of culture in things spiritual and moral that the Christian faith, voluntarily accepted, necessarily involves.

According to the census of 1890, there are 7,470,000 negroes in this country. This includes all who have any computable fraction of negro blood in their veins. Of these all except 581,000 are in the old slave territory, now embraced in sixteen States and the District of Columbia. In other words, notwithstanding the migration of negroes to the North and West, 91 per cent. of them are still in the South, on the soil where the Emancipation Proclamation of 1862 reached them, and made them forever free from involuntary bondage. The negro churches of the South, therefore, form a large and important factor in the Christianity of that section. In ten of those States the number of negro communicants ranges between 106,000 and 341,000, and in four of them it exceeds the total of white communicants. Thus in Alabama, Georgia, Mississippi, and South Carolina there are more colored than white communicants, although in Mississippi and South Carolina only does the negro population exceed the white. This shows that in point of church-membership the negro is quite as devoted as his white brother. Indeed, the proportion of colored people who are connected with the church throughout the United States is larger than that which obtains among the white people. About one in every three whites is a church-member. On this basis there should be 2,410,000 colored members. The actual number is 2,674,000, or an excess of 264,000 beyond the proportion that obtains among the whites.

The aggregate of colored communicants in the United States, so far as it could be ascertained by the careful methods of the census, is, in round numbers, 2,674,000. This includes all colored denominations, and all colored congregations in mixed denominations, so far as they could be ascertained; but it does not take account of colored communicants in mixed congregations. The number omitted, however, cannot be very large. The States in which the negro communicants are most numerous are as follows:

Georgia	341,433	Texas	186,038
South Carolina	317,020	Tennessee	131,015
Alabama	297,161	Louisiana	108,872
North Carolina	290,755	Arkansas	106,445
Virginia	238,617	Kentucky	92,768
Mississippi	224,404	Florida	64,337

In these twelve States are found 2,398,865 communicants, leaving about 275,000 to the rest of the States and Territories of the Union.

As to denominational connection, the negro is predominantly Baptist. More than half of all negro communicants are of this faith, the exact number being 1,403,559. Most of these are Regular Baptists, there being less than 20,000 in the Freewill, Primitive, and Two-Seed-in-the-Spirit branches. It is significant that the negro prefers the progressive and missionary type of the Baptist faith, and does not believe in the Hard-shell, Old School, or anti-missionary wing. Not less Calvinistic than the most Calvinistic of the Regular Baptists, he is also strict in his practice and thoroughly denominational in his spirit, and takes no little satisfaction in winning negro members of other bodies to the Baptist faith.

The number of negro Methodists is 1,190,638, or about 213,000 less than the aggregate of colored Baptists. The Methodists are divided into more branches than the Baptists, those having the episcopal system embracing the great majority of church-members. The Presbyterians have about 30,000, the Disciples of Christ 18,578, and the Protestant Episcopal and Reformed Episcopal bodies somewhat less than 5,000. The Baptists are organized into associations, and have State conventions; the Methodists and Presbyterians into annual conferences and presbyteries. A large measure of superintendence is characteristic of the Methodist bodies, the system of episcopal and sub-episcopal supervision resulting apparently in more intelligent endeavor, greater concert of action, and better discipline.

The increase in the number of colored communicants since emancipation has been marvelous. How many of the slaves were church-members is not and cannot be known certainly. Such statistics as we have must be regarded as imperfect, particularly of the colored Baptists. There were of colored Methodists at the outbreak of the war about 275,000, as nearly as I can ascertain. According to this, there has been an increase in thirty years of over 900,000 negro Methodists. This is truly enormous. In the Methodist Episcopal Church alone are more colored communicants, mainly in the South, than the Methodist Episcopal Church, South, reported in 1865, and the two leading African branches have had a marvelous growth. The number of colored Baptists in 1860 did not, probably, exceed 250,000. We do not know, of course, how many colored communicants there were who were not organized into churches and reported in denominational statistics. But according to the figures we have, there was an increase in thirty years of more than 1,150,000 colored communicants. I know of no parallel to this development in the history of the Christian church, when all the circumstances are considered.

The negro, considering the little wealth he had when slavery ceased, has achieved wonders in the accumulation of church property. The value of the churches he owns is $26,626,000, the number of edifices being 23,770. Making due allowance for the generous help which the whites have given, it still appears that the negro has not been unwilling to make large sacrifices for the sake of religion, and that his industry, thrift, and business capacity have been made to contribute to his successful endeavors to provide himself with suitable accommodations and to encourage men of his own race to fit themselves to serve him as ministers in the expectation of a reasonable support.

The foregoing pages apply entirely to conditions as shown by the census of 1890.

PART II.—THE GOVERNMENT CENSUS OF 1906.

It is to be regretted that the second complete census of religious denominations was not taken for the decennial year 1900. While the census law forbade the doing of any work for the first two years of the period except that of gathering and compiling the statistics of populations and manufactures, it might have been possible, beginning in 1902, to have obtained the statistical facts for 1900. For purpose of comparison the decennial period is quite as desirable and necessary for religious growth as for growth of population; indeed the one is associated with the other. Nevertheless a government census of religious denominations is of particular value, whenever taken, for the resources of the Census Office are not limited as to money, clerical and expert help, and facilities of communication. The mails are free for correspondence, and experts can be sent to any part of the country for personal inquiry where letters fail. The intelligence, perseverance, and skill brought to bear in securing the results of 1906 are to be highly commended, and the wide range of the inquiry brought together numerous items of information which the census of 1890 did not try to obtain. If in some particulars the census of 1906 seems unsatisfactory or doubtful, at most points it is complete and accurate. I do not adopt its summaries among the tables given in this volume, except of States, chiefly because they do not conform to the decennial period, but I use its figures for those denominations, mostly small and obscure, which make no returns and give no estimates, and of which little can be ascertained except by personal visitation and inquiry. I give herewith some of the special statistics afforded by the census of 1906.

The table, given further on, compiled from the census of 1906, shows the division by sex of communicants, something new in religious statistics, only a very few denominations ever having given it; value of church property (not including parsonages) not reported annually by a large number of denominations; and number of Sunday-school scholars, in which particular not all denominational statistics have been complete. It should be noted that the statistics include returns of sex of members for 193,229 organizations, or church societies, 19,001 not reporting; of value of church property for 186,132 organizations, 26,098 not reporting, and of Sunday-school scholars for 167,574 organizations, 44,656 organizations not reporting.

1. SEX IN MEMBERSHIP.—The highest percentage of female membership is reported for the Church of Christ, Scientist, 72.4; the Congregationalists, 65.9; the Seventh-Day Adventists, 65.2; the Protestant Episcopalians, 64.5; the Northern Presbyterians, 63.5; and the Methodist Episcopal Church, 62.6. The average for all denominations is 56.9. The Roman Catholics report nearly an even division, 50.7 per cent. female and 49.3 male. Of the Latter-Day Saints, 47.6 per cent. are males and 52.4 per cent. females. Immigration is undoubtedly an important factor in the percentages. There are naturally many more males among the newly arrived foreigners than females. This it is that makes the percentage of females in the Greek Orthodox Church only 6.1, and in the Hungarian Reformed Church 31.3. Of the 1,285,349 immigrants admitted to the United States in the year ending June 30, 1907, 929,976, or 72.4 per cent., were male, and 355,373, or 27.6 per cent., female. Nearly all those coming from Greece and Turkey, and other

countries of Eastern Europe, from East India, Korea, and Japan, were males. The census report calls attention to the fact that the percentage of males is generally higher in the South than the North.

TABLE OF SPECIAL STATISTICS.

	Members. Male.	Female.	Value Church Property.	Sunday-school Scholars.
Adventists (6 bodies)....	32,088	55,221	$2,425,209	69,110
Baptists (16 bodies).....	2,055,558	3,289,327	139,842,656	2,898,914
Brethren (Dunkards) (4 bodies)..............	39,928	53,676	2,802,532	78,575
Brethren (Plymouth) (4 bodies)..............	4,390	6,161	[1] 18,200	8,911
Brethren (River) (3 bodies).................	1,823	2,746	165,850	2,812
Buddhists (2 bodies)....	2,387	778	88,000	913
Catholic Apostolic (2 bodies).................	1,914	3,013	161,500	420
Catholics (Eastern Orthodox) (5 bodies).......	89,904	17,827	1,002,791	849
Catholics (Western) (3 bodies).................	5,194,279	5,332,544	293,193,487	1,482,824
Christadelphians........	626	786	3,245	480
Christians.............	40,740	60,022	2,740,322	72,963
Christian Catholic (Dowie).............	2,330	3,535	....	....
Christian Scientists.....	22,736	59,596	8,806,441	16,116
Christian Union........	5,626	7,406	299,250	9,234
Church of God (Winnebrennerian)..........	9,198	14,012	1,050,706	29,487
Churches of the Living God (Colored) (3 bodies).................	1,686	2,590	58,575	1,760
Church of the New Jerusalem (2 bodies)......	2,579	4,489	1,791,041	3,544
Communistic Societies (2 bodies)..............	966	1,306	31,190	103
Congregationalists......	236,968	457,615	63,240,305	638,089
Disciples of Christ (2 bodies).................	432,682	650,139	29,995,316	634,504
Evangelical (2 bodies)...	67,448	100,972	8,999,979	214,998
Faith Associations (14 bodies)..............	4,397	5,790	532,185	7,615
Free Christian Church...	740	1,095	5,975	340

[1] Only 9 congregations have church property.

	Members.		Value Church Property.	Sunday-school Scholars.
	Male.	Female.		
Friends (4 bodies)......	51,708	60,224	$3,857,451	53,761
Friends of the Temple...	158	218	11,000	168
German Evangelical Protestant..............	12,830	17,724	2,556,550	11,362
German Evangelical Synod...............	111,681	138,434	9,376,402	116,106
Jewish Congregations...	......	......	23,198,925	49,514
Latter-Day Saints (2 bodies)...........	117,026	128,776	3,168,548	130,085
Lutherans (24 bodies)...	853,339	998,009	74,826,389	782,786
Swedish Evangelical (2 bodies)..............	11,977	14,821	1,638,675	32,504
Mennonites (15 bodies)..	25,053	29,745	1,237,134	44,922
Methodists (15 bodies)..	2,042,713	3,268,664	229,450,996	4,472,930
Moravians (2 bodies)....	6,532	9,189	936,650	12,998
Non-Sectarian Bible Faith Churches............	3,368	3,028	25,910	1,976
Pentecostal Church.....	1,968	3,289	383,990	5,039
Presbyterians (12 bodies)	633,598	1,037,197	150,189,446	1,511,175
Protestant Episcopal (2 bodies)..............	255,165	462,851	126,510,285	474,215
Reformed (4 bodies).....	181,619	241,542	30,648,247	261,548
Salvationists (2 bodies)..	11,977	11,360	3,184,854	17,521
Schwenkfelders.........	318	407	38,700	991
Social Brethren.........	487	775	13,800	180
Society for Ethical Culture................	1,303	737	....	466
Spiritualists............	15,135	19,552	958,048	2,699
Theosophical Societies...	953	1,583	52,300	78
Unitarians.............	21,817	35,866	14,263,277	24,005
United Brethren (2 bodies)................	107,369	160,623	9,073,791	301,320
Universalists...........	18,279	33,346	10,575,656	42,201
Independent Congregations...............	26,895	38,012	3,934,267	57,680
Total.............	12,767,466	16,849,505	$1,257,575,867	14,685,997

2. VALUE OF CHURCH PROPERTY.—The total valuation
of church property, not including parsonages, of all denominations, was $1,257,575,867, showing an increase in the
16 years since the census of 1890 of $578,149,378, or 85.1
per cent. The increase, in the same period, of communicants,
was 60.4 per cent., exclusive of Jewish congregations.   The
increase in value is not accompanied by a corresponding in-

crease in the number of church edifices and in their seating capacity. The gain in church edifices was 50,308 in a total of 192,705, or a percentage of 35.3; and in seating capacity of 14,976,767 in a total of 58,536,830, or 34.4 per cent. The conclusion, therefore, is that more costly edifices have been erected, and that there has been a large natural increase in values, with increase in cost of living.

The gains in value of church property were very unequally distributed. The Roman Catholic Church, the largest of all denominations, reported $292,638,787, a gain of 147.7 per cent. The Methodist bodies standing next, with $229,450,996, gained only 73.6. The Presbyterian bodies, coming third, with $150,189,446, gained considerably less, 58.3; the Baptist bodies, with $139,842,656, gained nearly 70 per cent., and the Protestant Episcopal Church, with $125,040,498, gained 54 per cent. The Lutheran bodies more than doubled their church valuation, reporting in 1906 $74,826,389, an increase of $39,766,035, or 113.4 per cent. The Disciples of Christ advanced from $12,206,038 to $29,995,316, or 145.7 per cent.

The average value of church edifices has a wide variance. The Unitarians having their congregations mostly in cities report the highest average value—$35,141; the Jewish congregations, under similar conditions, come second, with $31,056; the Roman Catholics, whose vast strength is also largely in populous centres, is third, with $28,431; the Christian Scientists, fourth, with $21,961; the Protestant Episcopal Church, fifth, with $20,644. On the other hand, the Methodist and Baptist bodies being widely distributed, and each having a vast number of edifices, report average valuations of $3,884 and $2,834 respectively. As compared with the Roman Catholics, the Methodist bodies have more than five times as many edifices and the Baptist bodies more than four times as many.

3. AVERAGE OF MEMBERS TO CHURCH EDIFICES.—The Roman Catholic Church has only 11,881 church edifices for its 12,079,142 communicants, indicating an average of 1,017 communicants to each edifice. The Lutherans have one church edifice to 188 communicants, the Presbyterians one to 119, the Baptists one to 113, the Episcopalians one to 102, and the Methodists one to 96. As between Roman Catholic and Protestant denominations, the difference in average is very marked. It is due, of course, to the fact that Roman Catholic services Sunday mornings include from one to eight or nine masses, attended generally by different congregations, while in Protestant churches one service Sunday morning is the rule. Some Catholic parishes report a population of 10,000 or more. The entire seating capacity of Catholic churches is only 4,494,377, as against 17,053,392 of Methodist churches and 15,702,377 of Baptist churches. In other words, the seating capacity of Catholic churches is only sufficient to accommodate a little over one-third of the Catholic communicants at any one hour, while that of the Methodist churches would accommodate nearly three times as many persons as they have communicants.

4. TENDENCY OF POPULATION TO THE CITIES.—The marked tendency of the population to the cities is abundantly established by the last two or three decennial censuses; in none has it been so great as in that of 1910. The total of population in cities (50 in number) having over 100,000 was in 1890, 11,470,364; in 1900 it was 15,199,375; in 1910 it was 20,303,047, indicating an increase of 3,729,001 in the first of the two decades, and of 5,103,672 in the second; or, in percentage, of 32.5 for the first and 33.6 for the second decade. The percentages of increase in particular cities in the last decade were phenomenal—in Birmingham, Ala., over 245; in Los Angeles, Cal., over 211; in Seattle, Wash.,

194; in Spokane, Wash., over 183; in Portland, Ore., more than 129; and in Oakland, Cal., more than 124. Allowance must be made, in some cases, for annexation of suburban territory; most of the increase, however, is the result of the sweep of population to the cities.

Taking cities having 25,000 to 100,000 population in 1910, 179 in number, we find they have an aggregate of 8,204,960 population, against 5,878,814 in 1900, indicating an increase of 2,326,146, or 39.6 per cent., as compared with 34.3 per cent. in the previous decade.

The cities having 25,000 population and upward in 1910 number 229. The total of population they report is 28,-543,816, an increase for the decade of 7,465,627, or over 35 per cent. In round numbers, the total population of the United States, not including Alaska, Porto Rico, and Hawaii, is 92,000,000, and the gain of the decade about 16,000,000. It would appear, therefore, that while the population of the cities is 31 per cent. of the total population of the country, the absolute increase reported by them is more than 46 per cent. of the increase for the whole country. In other words, the increase for the whole country, including the cities, is 21, while the increase for the cities is over 35 per cent. Much more striking is the fact that the increase of the population, 54,900,000 in round numbers in 1900, and 63,498,450 in 1910, outside the cities was only 8,528,450, or between 15 and 16 per cent., while the increase in the 229 cities was 7,465,627, or over 35 per cent.

5. COMMUNICANTS IN THE CITIES.—The drift of population to the cities must, of course, affect the churches as profoundly as it affects the municipalities. The business area must increase, involving changes in the residence sections. Hence the down-town problem, congested areas, foreign-speaking sections, new residence areas, etc., requiring quick and extensive adjustments by the churches.

The following table, compiled from the United States Census of Religious Bodies for 1906, shows the relative strength of the various religious bodies in the cities, 160 in number, having, according to the census of 1900, 25,000 and more in population outside the cities:

COMMUNICANTS IN THE CITIES.

	Cities 25,000 and over.	Outside the cities.	Per cent. in the cities.	Per cent. outside the cities.
Baptist bodies.........	686,784	4,975,450	12.1	87.9
Christian Scientists.....	70,772	14,945	82.6	17.4
Congregationalists......	217,507	482,973	31.1	68.9
Disciples of Christ.....	130,755	1,011,604	11.4	88.6
Friends..............	13,129	100,643	11.5	88.5
Jewish Congregations...	89,947	11,510	88.7	11.3
Lutheran bodies........	521,494	1,591,000	24.7	75.3
Mennonite bodies......	1,176	53,622	2.1	97.9
Methodist bodies......	812,099	4,937,739	14.1	85.9
Presbyterian bodies.....	503,775	1,326,780	27.5	72.5
Protestant Episcopal...	453,966	432,976	51.2	48.8
Reformed bodies.......	137,937	311,577	30.7	69.3
Roman Catholic.......	6,307,529	5,776,613	52.2	47.8
Unitarians...........	32,840	37,702	46.6	53.4
All other bodies........	531,468	1,365,133	38.9	61.1
Total............	10,511,178	22,425,267	31.9	68.1

The percentage of church-members in the cities, 31.9, is, on the whole, a fair showing for the churches. Assuming that the change in population percentages since 1906 have not been very great, it would appear that the percentage of church-members in the cities, 31.9 in 1906, is only a few points behind that of the population, 33.6 in 1910.

6. VALUE OF CHURCH PROPERTY IN THE CITIES.—The following table, gathered from the United States Census of

1906, shows the value of church property in cities of the various classes:

AVERAGE VALUE OF CHURCH PROPERTY IN THE CITIES IN 1906.

CITIES.	No.	Church Edifices.	Value.	Average Value.
300,000 and over.........	11	5,770	$340,430,592	$59,000
100,000 to 300,000........	27	3,903	110,357,931	28,275
50,000 to 100,000........	40	3,075	82,271,671	26,755
25,000 to 50,000........	82	3,769	79,773,121	21,166
Total................	[1] 160	16,517	$612,833,315	$37,103
Outside the cities........		176,278	644,742,552	3,657
Grand Total..........		192,795	$1,257,575,867	$6,523

It will be observed that nearly half the total value of church property in the United States is reported in the 160 cities; the 16,517 churches in the cities returning a total valuation of $612,833,315, while 176,278 churches outside the cities returned a valuation of $644,742,552. That is to say, nearly eleven times as many churches outside the cities returned a valuation only $32,000,000 greater than the churches in the cities. This is not at all surprising, as not only is property vastly more valuable in the crowded centres, but there the churches command wealth, and buildings are much larger and more sumptuous. The average value of city edifices, including, of course, site and furniture, is $37,103, while the average value of churches outside the cities is $6,523.

7. GROWTH BY STATES IN COMMUNICANTS.—The changes in sixteen years shown in the column of communicants by States are quite remarkable. The increase in communicants for the United States, not including its colonial possessions and Alaska from 1890 to 1906, reached 12,332,990, or nearly 60 per cent. for the sixteen years. The increases in

[1] According to census of 1900 ; the number in 1910 was 229.

the various States would naturally be affected by the tides of migration—the flow from foreign immigration and the flow or ebb of population from or to other States; also by the prevalence of the Roman Catholic and Eastern Orthodox Churches, which report a much higher percentage of their "populations" as communicants than do other bodies. The States least affected by foreign immigration are naturally those of the South and the far West; but those of the far West have increased immensely by the migration of population from States east of the Rocky Mountains. The older South has contributed to the currents setting to the Pacific Coast, but more heavily to those which have filled up Texas, Oklahoma, and Arizona and crossed the border to the Canadian Northwest.

8. THE RATE OF GROWTH IN THE SOUTH.—The increase of communicants in the body of the South has naturally fallen below the percentage which obtains in the whole country. Virginia, to begin south of the Potomac, the Carolinas, Georgia, Alabama, Mississippi, Florida (despite the migration from the North), Arkansas, Kentucky, Tennessee, all fall below the general percentage of growth, North Carolina showing a gain of only 20 per cent. Louisiana constitutes a notable exception in the rate of increase, having almost doubled its number of communicants, which is far beyond the increase of population. The explanation is to be found in the growth of the Roman Catholic Church. It had in 1890 a little less than 20 per cent. of the population; in 1906 it had 31 per cent. In the same period the population increased nearly 38 per cent. Taking the States of the South, except Florida, Louisiana, and Texas, which had an unusual growth in the period under consideration, it will be found that in every State, save North Carolina alone, the net increase in communicants was large, considerably larger than the net increase of population, showing that the

Churches in that section of the country, whatever may be
said of other sections, enjoyed a high measure of prosperity.
The following table of increases will make this clear:

STATES.	Percentage of increase in population, 1890–1906.	Percentage of increase in communicants, 1890–1906.
Alabama	33	47
Arkansas	26	44
Florida	161	56
Georgia	33	52
Kentucky	25	42
Louisiana	48	95
Maryland	22	25
Mississippi	32	53
Missouri	26	63
North Carolina	27	20
South Carolina	26	79
Tennessee	23	26
Texas	54	81
Virginia	13	38

It is very remarkable that Virginia, gaining only 13 per
cent. in population, should have gained 38 per cent. in communicants; and simply amazing that Missouri and South
Carolina should show such immense advances in Church
growth beyond the growth in population. Oklahoma,
though properly a Southern State, is not included in the
above comparison, because its growth has been abnormal,
and has been gathered from many sources.

Putting the matter in another way, the Churches have
made, in most of the Southern States, a marked gain upon
what may be roughly called the unchurched population;
that is, those who are not communicants. For example,
in Missouri, in 1890, 72.5 per cent. of the population were not
church-members; in 1906 the percentage was 64.3; in Virginia, whose increase in population was only 13 per cent., the
number of persons in every 100 not church-members was
reduced from 65.6 in 1890 to 59.8 in 1906; in Louisiana,
from 64.2 in 1890 to 49.4 in 1906.

9. THE LARGEST ABSOLUTE INCREASES.—Turning now to the other States of the Union we find that the largest absolute increases in communicants were as follows:

New York	1,420,152	Wisconsin	444,420
Pennsylvania	1,250,382	Michigan	412,975
Illinois	874,609	Louisiana	378,909
Massachusetts	619,870	Georgia	349,986
Texas	549,745	New Jersey	349,197
Ohio	526,407	California	330,845
Missouri	463,400	Minnesota	301,852

In most of these States the chief factor in the gains is the Roman Catholic Church. In New York and New Jersey the Protestant percentage of the population was less in 1906 than in 1890, while the Catholic was greater. In Pennsylvania, the Protestant gain was 2.8, the Catholic 7.1; in Massachusetts, the Protestant gain was .6; the Catholic 8. In Texas the Protestants have 25.8 of the population, a gain of one-tenth of 1 per cent., while the Catholics advanced from 4.5 to 8.7. Ohio is still a strong Protestant State; Missouri likewise, but in the latter the Catholics are gaining faster than the Protestants. In Michigan and Wisconsin the rate of Catholic growth is large, the Catholic percentage of population in the latter having in the period under review passed the Protestant. Louisiana is, of course, strongly Catholic. Georgia is a Baptist State, and there the Catholic growth is inappreciable. California shows a gain in the Protestant percentage of population of 4.9 and of Catholic 8.6. The latter now have 21.5 in every 100 and the former 14.3. In Minnesota, which is a Lutheran State, the Protestant percentage has advanced from 19.7 to 22.2, while the Catholic percentage has fallen from 20.7 to 18.7. This is one of ten States which show an increase in the Protestant percentage and a decrease in the Catholic, namely Maryland, Florida, Minnesota, North

Dakota, Tennessee, Wyoming, New Mexico, Arizona, Utah, Oregon. The same is also true of the District of Columbia.

The growth by percentage brings into view a different list of States, as follows:

Oklahoma	652	South Dakota	89
Washington	227	New Hampshire	85
Idaho	210	Texas	81
Montana	202	Wisconsin	80
North Dakota	167	Rhode Island	79
Nevada	154	Nebraska	78
Colorado	137	Illinois	73
California	118	Michigan	73
Wyoming	105	Pennsylvania	72
Louisiana	95	Oregon	70

10. EFFECT OF MIGRATION.—In this group of States the large percentages are not specially significant, except as showing how migration into the newer States is affecting church growth. In seven of the States they are large because the numbers were so small in 1890; they were not remarkably large in 1906. Colorado and California have both grown by the flow of migration into their borders, but the gains of the Churches have been greater than those of population. New Hampshire has lost in Protestant and gained in Catholic percentage, due chiefly to immigration. The large Texas percentage is due chiefly to the enormous increase in population. Wisconsin, Rhode Island, Illinois, and Michigan owe their notable percentages largely to Catholic growth, to which immigrants have no doubt greatly contributed. Nebraska was nearly stationary in population; but the Churches, both Protestant and Catholic, appear to have been exceedingly active, and very successful in adding to their membership. Pennsylvania shows a much larger percentage of communicants of all faiths in 1906 than in 1890.

PART III.—THE RETURNS FOR 1900 AND 1910 AND WHAT THEY SHOW.

As already stated the Government census of religious bodies was not repeated in 1900 and 1910; but was taken in great elaboration of detail in 1906. As some of the denominations do not attempt to gather and publish annual statistics of their own numbers, it is necessary either to take the census returns for them or to prevail upon their leading ministers to furnish more or less approximate estimates. As the census agents do particularly effective work in reaching these denominations it is manifestly the part of wisdom to adopt the census figures in such cases. Therefore in the general tables of 1900, the census of 1890 has been followed in particular cases, and in those of 1910, that of 1906.

1. GROWTH OF THE CHURCHES IN THE PAST TWENTY YEARS.—A study of the denominational summaries for 1900 and 1910 will give much encouragement to those desirous that the Churches shall prosper and prevail. The growth in these periods, considering the increasing complexity of the population, the multiplication of languages, the immense tide of foreign immigration from Eastern, Southern, and Northern Europe, and other countries; the crowding of the cities with a heterogeneous population, and the creation of problems of congested foreign quarters, "down-town" churches, etc.; the draining of rural districts and the question of abandoned country churches; sudden migrations from older to newer States—considering the immense

difficulties the Churches have had to encounter, the growth of the last twenty years has been most remarkable.   There never was, it is safe to say, a more active double decade in the history of the country.   The problem of finance alone, which has been carried to a successful solution, would have brought a paralysis of discouragement upon a previous generation.   The building of new churches for new communities and in newer sections of older communities; of costly cathedrals and churches of modern character and equipment in cities and towns; of large and expensive structures to replace old and outgrown edifices; the increased expense of elaborate church adornments and furnishings; the constantly growing budget of current expenses for ministerial salaries, for music, maintenance, etc.; the call for home and foreign missions, schools, colleges, hospitals, and other necessary church institutions—these and similar demands have tested the loyalty and resources of church-members.

Church-members must have realized that though they may occasionally sing "Salvation's free," it costs enormously to maintain it, and yet they have multiplied in a remarkable degree.   The net gain in the first ten years was six and two-third millions and in the second seven and two-third millions—more than sixteen and a half millions in the two decades—1890–1910.   It must not be forgotten that before any net increase can be reported the losses due to death, removal, withdrawal, excommunication, etc., must be made good out of new accessions.   The 16,626,989 of net increase in the twenty years represent a growth of nearly 81 per cent.   In other words, at this rate of increase the aggregate of communicants in 1890—20,618,307—would be doubled in less than twenty-five years.   With all conceivable allowances for a large immigration, etc., this rate of advance is truly most remarkable.

2.   THE LARGEST ABSOLUTE INCREASES.—The denominations showing the largest absolute increase in communicants during the twenty years are: the Roman Catholic, 6,183,-680, or 99 per cent.; the Southern Baptist, 1,003,000, or 78 per cent.; the Methodist Episcopal, 946,508, or 42 per cent.; the Disciples of Christ (the older branch), 667,065, or 104 per cent.; the Methodist Episcopal Church, South, 641,173, or 53 per cent.; the Presbyterian (Northern), 540,490, or 69 per cent.; the Colored Baptist, 441,176, or 33 per cent.; the Northern Baptist, 410,263, or 51 per cent.; the Lutheran Synodical Conference, 409,128, or 115 per cent.; the Protestant Episcopal, 396,726, or 75 per cent.; and the Congregational, 222,629, or 43 per cent.

By denominational families or groups the chief gains were:

Catholic, chiefly Roman	6,199,588
Methodist	2,025,768
Baptist	1,885,168
Lutheran	1,012,414
Disciples of Christ	823,723
Presbyterian	642,433

3.   GROWTH OF THE ROMAN CATHOLIC CHURCH.—The miracle of growth is, of course, the Roman Catholic. It has been three times as great as that of the Methodist group and six times as great as that of the Lutheran group. Its natural increase, supposing that it holds most of those born of Catholic parents, would be very large; but Europe and French Canada have poured an immense stream into its pale and given it predominance wherever the foreign element is considerable. It is, indeed, a polyglott Church, holding more nationalities in its communion, doubtless, than any other Church; all assimilated in an effective domination by a hierarchy largely of the Irish race. Its cardinals, archbishops, bishops bear, at least the great majority of them do, unmistakable Celtic names. It is one

of the most remarkable facts of history that Ireland, so long deprived of home rule in the British Union, has made so great an impress upon not only the political history of the United States, but also upon its religious life, through both the Catholic and Protestant Churches.

4. RELIGIOUS POPULATION IN 1910.—Dividing the denominations into groups, we have:

	Communicants.
1. Evangelical Protestant	21,471,747
2. Roman Catholic and Eastern Orthodox	12,826,420
3. Unorthodox Protestant	795,414
4. Jewish	143,000
5. Miscellaneous, Buddhist, Theosophist, etc.	8,715
Total	35,245,296

It is quite probable that the ratio of 2½ adherents to each communicant, applied to the Protestant group in 1890, would be too large in 1910. The proportion of children who are church-members is unquestionably larger than it was twenty years ago. All Churches receive children into that relation much earlier in life than formerly and there are other factors tending to reduce the ratio of adherents to communicants, particularly the relaxation of discipline and the retention of some who formerly would have been dropped, expelled, or excommunicated. At any rate we cannot apply the ratio 3½. It would use up so much of the population that, with the other groups added, we should have more religious than actual population. Reducing the ratio to three for the Evangelical Protestant group; taking the Roman Catholic population as reported and estimating that of the Eastern Orthodox Churches on the same basis; putting down from denominational sources the Jewish population at 1,900,000; and giving liberal estimates for the populations of the remaining groups, we have the following result:

1. Protestant population............................ 64,415,241
2. Roman Catholic and Eastern Orthodox population.. 15,089,906
3. Jewish population................................. 1,900,000
4. Unorthodox Protestant population................. 1,000,000
5. Miscellaneous population......................... 12,000

Total religious population in United States....... 82,417,147

The population of the United States in 1910 was 91,972,-266. The religious population in the same year was 82,-417,147, leaving 9,555,119 persons presumed to be without any religious preference. Among this number are included the pagan Indians. Twenty years ago the total religious population was estimated at 59,992,000, and those without denominational preference at 5,630,000. It would appear that in the twenty years there has been a gain of 22,425,147 in the religious population, or 37 per cent., and of 3,925,119 in the non-religious population, or nearly 70 per cent. These figures, however, must be taken as approximate only. They are estimates which have no very sure basis and are given simply for what they are worth.

5. CHANGES OF TWENTY YEARS.—It will be seen that the list of denominations in 1910 is not shorter, but rather longer, than it was in 1890. The process of creating new denominations by division of existing ones has gone on with little or no interruption. The Salvation Army now exists as two bodies, the American Salvation Army being the newer branch; the Disciples of Christ has suffered a division and there is an organization known as Churches of Christ; the colored Primitive Baptists are now reported separately from the white Primitive Baptists; there is a second New Jerusalem Church and a second Catholic Apostolic Church; the Theosophists are divided, and the

United Evangelical Church and the Polish National Church represent separations, the former from the Evangelical Association, the latter from the Roman Catholic Church. The Scandinavian Evangelical bodies, three in number, take the place of one Swedish Evangelical body, which was in existence in 1890, but was not included in the census. Immigration has brought to the United States several Eastern Orthodox Churches not represented here in 1890—the Servian, the Syrian, the Roumanian, and the Bulgarian; also the Union of Bohemian and Moravian Brethren, the Hungarian Reformed Church, and the Japanese Buddhists. On the other hand, a number of denominations, all quite small, have disappeared, including six communistic societies, the Old Catholic Church, and other insignificant bodies. Union has practically done nothing to reduce the total of denominations. In 1906 a union was in part consummated of the Cumberland Presbyterian with the Northern Presbyterian Church, but the Cumberland organization is still maintained and it claims a majority of members reported in 1906. A union for co-operation in general denominational work, missionary, educational, etc., has been arranged between the Northern and Free Baptists, and it may lead to a consolidation of churches and associations. Denominations represented in 1890 as consisting of two branches, the Jews and the Christians, are now classed as one, with no better reason for doing so, however, than obtained twenty years ago.

The total of denominations may be set down at 170 in 1910, counting the Faith Associations separately, which is perhaps questionable, and consolidating certain evangelistic churches with independent congregations. This aggregate indicates an increase of 27 in the twenty years, the number returned in 1890 being 143. What is said of the religious bodies of 1890 can be said just as truly of those of 1910;

many of them are small and unimportant. A full half of the 170 bodies report less than 10,000 communicants each, and 70 have less than 5,000 each. To put the matter in another way, the great mass of communicants are found in the first 37 denominations in Table III, embracing all denominations having 100,000 and upward. These 37 bodies contain more than 95 per cent. of all communicants, or 33,580,000, leaving only 1,665,000 for all the remaining 133 bodies. From all which it appears that the division of religious bodies is more a matter of name than of fact.

6. ORDER ACCORDING TO DENOMINATIONAL FAMILIES OR GROUPS.—In the order of number of communicants the several denominational groups stand as follows in 1910:

1.	Roman Catholic (3 bodies)	12,443,520
2.	Methodist (16 bodies)	6,615,052
3.	Baptist (15 bodies)	5,603,137
4.	Lutheran (23 bodies)	2,243,486
5.	Presbyterian (12 bodies)	1,920,765
6.	Disciples of Christ (2 bodies)	1,464,774
7.	Episcopalian (2 bodies)	938,390
8.	Reformed (4 bodies)	448,190
9.	Latter-Day Saints (2 bodies)	400,650
10.	Eastern Orthodox (7 bodies)	385,000
11.	United Brethren (2 bodies)	303,319
12.	Evangelical (2 bodies)	182,065
13.	Friends (4 bodies)	123,718
14.	Brethren (Dunkards) (4 bodies)	122,847
15.	Adventist (6 bodies)	95,646
16.	Scandinavian Evangelical (3 bodies)	62,000
17.	Mennonite (11 bodies)	54,798
18.	Salvationist (2 bodies)	26,275

The Catholics, Methodists, and Baptists maintain the order of 1890. The chief changes in the twenty years have been as follows: the Lutherans take fourth place from the Presbyterians, and the latter fall back to fifth place; the Disciples (one body in 1890) take sixth place and the

Episcopalians fall back to seventh place; the Eastern Orthodox Churches come into view the first time and take tenth place, the United Brethren going down from the eighth to the eleventh place. The other changes are not significant.

7. INCREASE IN NEGRO COMMUNICANTS.—The negro population of the United States increased from 7,488,676 in 1890 to 9,828,294 in 1910. This indicates a net gain in the twenty years of 2,335,618, or 31 per cent. The table given among the summaries for 1900 and 1910 shows that the gain in the same period in negro communicants was 1,061,152. This is more than 40 per cent. It appears, therefore, that the Negro is gaining in church membership faster than he is gaining in population. He must also be growing in financial ability, for the increase in negro churches has been about 60 per cent.

PART IV—DOMINANT RELIGIOUS ELEMENTS.

1. CHARACTERISTICS OF CHRISTIANITY IN THE UNITED STATES.—The Christianity which prevails in the United States is Orthodox and Evangelical, using Orthodox as descriptive of the Churches, Roman Catholic and Oriental, which adhere to the Ecumenical Creeds, and Evangelical as applicable to such bodies as Baptists, Congregationalists, Methodists, Lutherans, Presbyterians, Reformed, and Episcopalians. Together these Orthodox and Evangelical bodies constitute the great bulk of the Christian forces which possess the country and determine and dominate its religious life.

Foremost numerically as a denomination is the Roman Catholic Church. Though it was the first to set up the Christian altar on this soil, and its missionaries were pioneers in exploration and settlement in the great West and far South, it was not a strong Church at the close of the colonial period. There were in 1784 hardly 30,000 Catholics, most of whom were in Maryland and Pennsylvania, the rest being widely scattered. Immigration from Ireland gave the Church its first considerable impulse of growth, and immigration—Irish, German, French, Italian, Polish, etc.—has made it the largest and most composite Church in the United States. The wonder is that the Church could receive and care for such masses of diverse nationalities. Its energies have been severely taxed, but it has managed to organize and equip its parishes as rapidly as necessity required, and in recent years to give more attention to its educational facilities, which had been neither excellent nor adequate. A church composed so largely of European elements, with an episcopate foreign in nativity or extraction, education, and ideas, under the immediate control of a foreign pope and his councilors, would hardly be expected to fall in at once with American ideas, particularly with that idea which distinguishes our system of popular education from that of all other countries. The Catholic hierarchy has been openly hostile to our public schools, denouncing them as either sectarian or godless, protesting against the injustice of being taxed for the support of institutions they could not patronize, and insisting that they be relieved of school rates or that the school moneys be divided and a fair share given to Catholic schools. The determined popular resistance to this demand increased Catholic hostility and made the struggle a somewhat bitter one. It is not strange that many Protestants should regard a foreign church, with foreign ideas and under foreign domination, as a menace to American institutions; but no candid observer will hesitate to admit that, whatever may be said concerning the attitude of the priesthood, the Catholics as a body are as American as the Lutherans. No impartial and intelligent person now believes that they want to subvert our liberties or destroy our government. We may justly accuse them of meddling too much at times in party politics; we may deprecate the favor they sometimes receive in municipal councils; but in all those fundamentals which make our government thoroughly and securely Republican, Catholics are at one with Protestants. Their sentiment toward the public schools is still antagonistic, and it would be too much to say that they are becoming reconciled to it. Their opposition, however, though perhaps not less firm, is less demonstrative. Apparently they are convinced that their demands concerning the public schools and public-school moneys cannot be obtained, and they are developing their system of parochial schools at heavy cost, thus seeking to provide, at much sacrifice, schools for their own children, particularly of primary and grammar grade, in which the tenets of their faith are freely and fully taught. Their attitude toward the public-school problem is represented by the American Federation of Catholic Societies in the following propositions:

"1. Let our schools remain as they are. 2. Let no compensation be made for religious instruction. 3. Let our children be examined by a State or municipal board," and, if the work done is satisfactory, let payment for the support of Catholic schools be made from the public funds. There were, in 1910, 4,972 parochial schools with an attendance of 1,270,131.

The Catholic Church in the United States, while thoroughly loyal to the central government at Rome and obedient to the decrees of the pope, is nevertheless an American institution. When, some years ago, the centenary of the first Catholic bishop in the United States was observed, the preacher, an archbishop, declared with emphasis that the Catholic Church in the United States must be definitely and thoroughly American. The ecclesiastical garment must not be of a foreign cut or have a foreign lining even. Perhaps the distinguished prelate would not so express himself to-day, for conservative rather than progressive churchmen seem to get recognition when cardinals' hats are bestowed; but nevertheless the American school of thought exists and makes its influence felt.

It is a curious fact that while Catholicism is numerically the leading denomination in considerably more than half of the States, actually outnumbering in old New England the Protestant communicants combined, it is in no State in the ascendant in influence. New England is still Protestant in its characteristics, and there are as yet no signs of a revolution in its distinctive institutions. The reason is not far to seek. The Roman Catholic force is in its masses; the Protestant power lies in generations of occupancy and training. Protestantism furnishes the ideas which have made New England what it is and which maintain it essentially unchanged. The Protestant leaven is more powerful and persistent than the Catholic leaven.

2. EVANGELICAL CHRISTIANITY DOMINANT.—Evangelical Christianity is the dominant religious force of the United States. In its various denominational forms it shapes the religious character of the American people. That it has been influenced in no degree by the non-evangelical or rationalistic churches, I would not venture to say. Doubtless its humanitarian impulses have been quickened and strengthened by the example of Unitarianism; but I should be at a loss to name the particular influence which the Church of Rome has exerted upon it. There has been an increase of what some call churchliness, and confessionalism has developed to a remarkable degree among the Lutherans; but these are limited movements, and do not give character to the Christianity of the day. The Catholic revival in the Protestant Episcopal Church is spending itself within the denomination, and High and Broad Church parties are now in control.

The great and absorbing purpose of Evangelical Christianity seems to me to be the spread of the gospel. There are those living who can remember when a far less exalted idea possessed the Church, when it seemed to think its sphere was not in the world, and its main duty not to the world, but to those within its own pale. Now it knows that it is in the world to save the world; that while God loves the saint, he also loves the sinner; that while he has "more graces for the good," he has messages of love for the bad.

It considers itself as commissioned to carry these messages to every heathen land, to every destitute community, to every godless home, and to every unconverted person. Evangelical Churches are like bustling camps of spiritual soldiers who are being told off to go to this country and that, to this destitute section and that, with the gospel of peace, to conquer the whole world for Christ. So thoroughly has this missionary spirit possessed the body of evangelical Christians, that the smallest and most obscure divisions feel constrained not only to evangelize home communities, but to have their representatives abroad.

3. EVANGELICAL CHRISTIANITY SYSTEMATICALLY ORGANIZED.—This dominant purpose has made agencies and organizations and financial methods necessary. The business of saving the world requires organization complete and extensive; it requires administrators, agents, means, machinery, enterprise. All these the Church has provided, and a great system has been worked out, rivaling in its universal operations and the volume of its transactions that of any commercial project of which we have knowledge. Any kingdom, country, province, island, settlement, with hardly an exception, can be reached directly and quickly through the numerous channels of communication established by gospel enterprise. If a devoted man or woman wants to enter a field of work abroad, the widest range of choice is presented. Any country between Greenland and New Zealand, in the western or eastern circuit of the globe, may be selected, and there is a gospel society to commission him and send and support him. If any one has a sum of money to be applied to the proclamation of the gospel, he may have it expended in any presidency in India, in any division in Japan, in any kingdom in Africa, or in any island of the sea. The machinery exists to place it wherever he wants it to go.

We have the same appliances for work at home. Here are Indians, Chinese, and negroes; ignorant and vicious populations; groups of foreigners; the frontiers of civilization and the centres of cities; the prairies and the slums; the jails, asylums, and workhouses. Here is book and Bible work, evangelistic work, reformatory work, educational work, missionary work, and many other forms of gospel benevolence, with abundance of machinery for all the exigencies of service. Places are ready for the men and women, and societies exist to commission and direct them, and to collect and administer the necessary funds.

Organization is, indeed, one of the characteristics of the Church of to-day. The idea of organization was in the first church ever formed. Where two or more believers are, there is a call for fellowship, for association, and for co-operation. The Church of the present is but working out more fully the central idea of Christian fellowship. This fellowship is now understood to be for mutual helpfulness and for service. We are saved to serve, and we can serve best if we serve according to some system. Hence we organize. Every church has come to have its committees for regular and special work. The women are organized for those parish duties which they can best perform; for missionary work for which they have special aptitude. They are given a much larger share of the Lord's business than our forefathers dreamed of allotting to them. We have organized our young people. This is one of the most remarkable movements of the century in religious work. This mighty development has come almost within a generation. The young people of both sexes have been banded together into Endeavor Societies, Epworth Leagues, Unions, and the like, and their members are numbered by the million. By organization for prayer, praise, and Christian work, and particularly training in public service, a great body of young believers have been made a positive, aggressive force in all our Churches. Who can measure the influence which these young people thus organized will exert in the immediate future? Not many years ago the cry was raised: "We are losing our hold on the young people. They are not coming into the Church. They are growing up indifferent to religion." To-day we have no more devoted and enthusiastic and helpful workers in the Church than the young people.

4. EVANGELICAL CHRISTIANITY EVANGELISTIC.—The evangelical Christianity of to-day is not polemic. It is intensely practical. It emphasizes more than it used to the importance of Christian character and of Christian work. It is less theological in its preaching, making more, indeed, of biblical exposition, but less of doctrinal forms and definitions. And yet it would be wrong to say that it makes little or no account of belief. All that it says, all that it does, is based upon profound and unshaken belief. It is the gospel it declares and is trying to work out in a practical way. The Church of to-day is a gospel Church. It has the fullest confidence in the power of the gospel, and believes it was given for all men, is adapted to all conditions, and is to become supreme in the world. Christ, the centre of this gospel, is the divine Lord and Master of the Church. Belief in Him as a human manifestation of the divine love and a divine manifestation of a perfect humanity was never more clear and strong. It is upon Him, as the corner-stone, His atonement, and His teachings that the evangelical Church builds its system of religion; and while this is the age of the higher biblical criticism, the most critical and careful study of the Bible has confirmed no conclusions which shake belief in its character as the Word of God, or in its authority, or in its moral and spiritual teachings. It would be misleading, however, to contend that no change has taken place

in the attitude of the evangelical Churches generally toward the Bible and toward doctrinal preaching. The Bible is still held in reverence; but the generation of to-day is much freer in its criticism and interpretation of it than the generation which is passing off the stage. The human side of the Book is recognized, and this recognition naturally means that the divine side is not held in such a way as to preclude error. The revival method has also been largely abandoned; that is, the method of Finney and Moody and Hammond. More emphasis appears to be placed in what has been called cultural or educational evangelism, and upon the Sunday-school as an efficient recruiting agency for the Church. Thorough indoctrination of the child in the principles of the faith is a cardinal doctrine of the Roman Catholic Church. Evangelical Churches seem to be appropriating it or adapting it to Protestant children. It may be truthfully said that revival sermons, such as were formerly preached in revival campaigns and at camp-meetings, are becoming somewhat rare in this day. The sharp lines that used to be drawn between the Church and the world, between the saint and the sinner, between the state of grace and the lost condition, between the joys of heaven and the woes of hell, are blurred and indistinct in most modern preaching, and the Church in general seems to have less interest in the prodigals or less zeal in reaching them, and to give more attention to the prevention of prodigals.

5. CO-OPERATION, FEDERATION, AND UNION.—No development of the past quarter of a century has been more noteworthy than the tendency to co-operation and union among the evangelical Churches. This spirit of oneness has had its most remarkable manifestation in the conduct of foreign missions. All the societies in the United States and Canada conducting missions in foreign lands have

united in a conference, held annually in January, in which questions of common interest are discussed, and under the authority of which an *ad interim* Committee of Reference and Counsel acts for the societies in appeals to governments and in other matters affecting the affairs of all. Out of this have grown co-operative agencies at home, such as the Missionary Education Movement, which aims specially at the creation of missionary literature for mission study classes and the Student Volunteer Movement, which seeks to enlist an army of trained young men and women for service as missionaries. In the mission field itself, co-operation and union have been going forward in a way simply astonishing. The mission churches of various societies are uniting to form large and comprehensive native Churches, as, for example, the Methodist Mission Churches of Japan, which have organized a Methodist Church of Japan; the Presbyterian Mission Churches of China, which have formed with other Presbyterian and Reformed Churches a united native Church. The same thing has taken place in India. Moreover, union in educational, publication, and hospital work is the order of the day, and comity is everywhere recognized and intrusion into fields already occupied is discouraged.

Not much in the way of organic union has been accomplished in the United States. Negotiations between bodies of similar belief and practice are in progress; but no immediate results are probable. The Free Baptists have resolved to use the missionary and other general agencies of the Northern Baptists, and this measure of consolidation may be followed in time by a merging of the two denominations. The most influential movement among the evangelical Churches is doubtless that known as the Federal Council of Churches of Christ. In this body thirty-two of the leading evangelical Churches are federated for the purpose of fellowship and action. It is founded on the basis of unity in Christ, and in purpose and aim it seeks to establish comity and co-operation and prevent rivalry and waste in effort and means.

There are also such general bodies as the Alliance of Reformed Churches, the Ecumenical Methodist Conference, the World Baptist Congress, which seek to draw into closer relations bodies belonging to the same denominational group or family. Religious controversy over questions of doctrine and practice is a thing of the past. The denominations are not now divided into separate camps of a more or less hostile character, but are coming into closer sympathy and fellowship, making less and less of denominational differences and more and more of the points of agreement.

6. How the Church Affects Society.—It is to be remembered that all the houses of worship have been built by voluntary contributions. They have been provided by private gifts, but are offered to the public for free use. The government has not given a dollar to provide them, nor does it appropriate a dollar for their support. And yet the church is the mightiest, most pervasive, most persistent, and most beneficent force in our civilization. It affects, directly or indirectly, all human activities and interests.

It is a large property-holder, and influences the market for real estate.

It is a corporation, and administers large trusts.

It is a public institution, and is therefore the subject of protective legislation.

It is a capitalist, and gathers and distributes large wealth.

It is an employer, and furnishes means of support to ministers, organists, singers, janitors, and others.

It is a relief organization, feeding the hungry, clothing the naked, and assisting the destitute.

It is a university, training children and instructing old

and young, by public lectures on religion, morals, industry, thrift, and the duties of citizenship.

It is a reformatory influence, recovering the vicious, immoral, and dangerous elements of society and making them exemplary citizens.

It is a philanthropic association, sending missionaries to the remotest countries to Christianize savage and degraded races.

It is organized beneficence, founding hospitals for the sick, asylums for orphans, refuges for the homeless, and schools, colleges, and universities for the ignorant.

It prepares the way for commerce, and creates and stimulates industries. Architects, carpenters, painters, and other artisans are called to build its houses of worship; mines, quarries, and forests are worked to provide the materials, and railroads and ships are employed in transporting them. It requires tapestries and furnishings, and the looms that weave them are busy day and night. It buys millions of Bibles, prayer-books, hymn-books, and papers, and the presses which supply them never stop.

Who that considers these moral and material aspects of the Church can deny that it is beneficent in its aims, unselfish in its plans, and impartial in the distribution of its blessings? It is devoted to the temporal and eternal interests of mankind.

Every corner-stone it lays, it lays for humanity; every temple it opens, it opens to the world; every altar it establishes, it establishes for the salvation of souls. Its spires are fingers pointing heavenward; its ministers are messengers of good tidings, ambassadors of hope, and angels of mercy.

What is there among men to compare with the Church in its power to educate, elevate, and civilize mankind?

EXPLANATIONS OF THE TERMS USED.

1. By "organizations" is meant church societies, or congregations. The returns under this head include chapels, missions, stations, etc., when they are separate from churches and have separate services.

2. Under the title "church edifices" are given all buildings erected for divine worship. Chapels under separate roofs are counted as distinct buildings. The fractions which appear in this column indicate joint ownership. A large number of church edifices are owned and occupied by two or more denominations, and the proportion which each owns is expressed by the fractions ¼, ½, ⅔, etc. The tables do not show how many churches are thus owned. Many fractions have disappeared in the process of addition. If there were, for example, twenty churches in a State or conference or diocese or presbytery, in which a particular denomination had a fractional interest of ½ each in eighteen, ⅓ in another, and ¼ in another, the eighteen halves would be converted into nine integers in the footing, and the sum of ⅓ and ¼, or $\frac{7}{12}$, would be the only fraction that would appear.

3. "Seating capacity" indicates the number of persons a church edifice is arranged to seat. The accommodations of halls and schoolhouses are given separately, and those of private houses are not counted at all.

4. "Value of church property" covers only the estimated value of church edifices with their chapels, the ground on which they stand, and their furnishings. It does not embrace parsonages, cemeteries, or colleges, or convents, only the chapels belonging thereto. No deductions are made for church debts.

5. "Communicants" embraces all who have the privilege of partaking of the sacrament of the Lord's Supper, and of members in denominations like the Friends, Unitarians, etc. The Jewish returns are mostly for heads of families who are pewholders. Those for Unitarians are larger, in proportion, than those for the Universalists, because the terms of Unitarian membership are less restrictive.

6. The statistics given in this volume are for the United States only. No returns are included for missions or churches in other lands.

RELIGIOUS FORCES OF THE UNITED STATES.

Statistics 1890

CHAPTER I.

THE ADVENTISTS.

THE movement out of which the various Adventist bodies have come began about the year 1831 with a series of lectures on the personal coming of Christ, delivered by William Miller.   Mr. Miller, a native of Massachusetts, was converted and joined the Baptist Church at Low Hampton, N. Y., in 1816.   He had been a Deist, according to his own statement.   A diligent study of the Bible inclined him to the belief in 1818 that the millennium was to begin not before but after the end of the world, and that the second advent of Christ was near at hand.   Further examination of the Scriptures fully convinced him of the correctness of this view, and in August, 1831, he began to lecture on the subject.   His study of the Apocalypse and the Gospels satisfied him that the " only millennium " to be expected " is the thousand years which are to intervene between the first resurrection and that of the rest of the dead "; that the second coming of Christ is to be a personal coming; that the millennium " must necessarily fol-

1

low the personal coming of Christ and the regeneration of the earth"; that the prophecies show that "only four universal monarchies are to precede the setting up of God's everlasting kingdom," of which three had passed away—the Babylonian, the Medo-Persian, and the Grecian—and the fourth, that of Rome, was in the last stage; that the periods spoken of in the Book of Daniel of "2300 days," of the "seven times of Gentile supremacy," and of "1335 days," were prophetic periods, and, applied chronologically, led to a termination in 1843, when Christ would personally descend to the earth and reign with the saints in a new earth a thousand years.   In 1833 he published a pamphlet entitled "Evidences from Scripture and History of the Second Coming of Christ, about the Year 1843, and of His Personal Reign of One Thousand Years."

He made many converts to his views, both among ministers and laymen of the Baptist, Christian, Methodist, and other denominations, and the new doctrine was widely proclaimed.   In 1840 a general gathering of friends of the cause was held in Boston, and an address issued which stated that while those who participated in the conference were not in accord in fixing the year of the second advent, they were unanimously of the opinion that it was "specially nigh at hand."   A number of papers, one of which was a daily, appeared, bearing such titles as *The Midnight Cry, The Signs of the Times, The Trumpet of Alarm*, etc., and helped greatly to spread Mr. Miller's views.   When the year in which the advent was fully expected had passed, Mr. Miller wrote a letter confessing his "error" and acknowledging his "disappointment," but expressing his belief that "the day of the Lord is near, even at the door."   He also attended a conference of Adventists held in Boston late in May, 1844, and made a similar statement, admitting that he had been in error in fixing a definite time. Subsequently he became convinced that the end would come on or about the 22d of October, 1844, and said if Christ did not then appear he should "feel twice the disappointment" that he had already felt. Some of those who had joined the movement left it after the time for the end of the world had passed without a fulfillment of their expectations; but many still believed that the great event was near at hand, and urged men to live in a constant state of readiness for it.

Various views were developed among the Adventists, after the second date had passed without result, respecting the resurrection of the body, the immortality of the soul, and the state of the dead, and these differences resulted in course of time in different organizations.

At a general conference of Adventists held in Albany, N. Y., April 29, 1845, a report was adopted holding to the visible, personal coming of Christ at an early but indefinite time, to the resurrection of the dead, both the just and the unjust, and to the beginning of the millennium after the resurrection of the saints, denying that there is any promise of the world's conversion, or that the saints enter upon their inheritance, or receive their crowns, at death.

Small companies of Adventists at various times after the failures of 1843 and 1844 set new dates for the second advent, and there were gatherings in expectation of the great event; but the "time brethren," as they are often called, have at no time since 1844 formed a large proportion of the Adventists.

Ministers are ordained to the office of elder by the laying on of hands, upon the recommendation of the churches of which they are members, and after approval by a committee of elders. Baptism is administered by immersion. The Adventists are Congregational in polity, excepting the Seventh-Day branch, which has a government of a presbyterial character. Camp-meetings form prominent and popular annual gatherings among the Adventists. On these occasions some of their societies hold business sessions.

The following is a complete list of Adventist bodies, excepting the Adonai Shomo, which is a small communistic body, and is given elsewhere in that group:

1. Evangelical Adventists,   4. Church of God,
2. Advent Christians,   5. Life and Advent Union,
3. Seventh-Day Adventists,   6. Churches of God in Christ Jesus.

I.—THE EVANGELICAL ADVENTISTS.

Those who could not accept the views of the Advent Christians as to the mortality of the soul began in 1855 to hold separate meetings, and to be known as Evangelical Adventists. They believe that the soul is immortal; that all the dead will be raised, the saints first and the wicked last; that the former will enter upon the millennial reign with Christ and after the judgment receive as their reward an eternity of bliss; that the wicked, who will rise at the end of the millennial reign, will be sent away into everlasting punishment. They also hold, contrary to the belief of the Advent Christians, that the dead do not always sleep, but are in a conscious state. In other respects their doctrinal views do not differ from those of the second branch.

They have two annual conferences, besides five congregations, unattached, and are found in Vermont, Massachusetts, Rhode Island, and Pennsylvania. Besides the church edifices reported, this denomination occupies as places of worship 5 halls, etc., with a seating capacity of 775.

SUMMARY BY STATES.

STATES.	Organizations.	Church Edifices.	Seating Capacity.	Value of Church Property.	Communicants.
Massachusetts	3	2	250	$4,500	150
Pennsylvania	21	16	3,805	18,500	509
Rhode Island......	2	2	1,100	33,000	325
Vermont..........	4	3	700	5,400	163
Total.........	30	23	5,855	61,400	1,147

SUMMARY BY CONFERENCES.

CONFERENCES.					
Northern Vermont .	4	3	700	$5,400	163
Pennsylvania	21	16	3,805	18,500	509
Unorganized	5	4	1,350	37,500	475
Total.........	30	23	5,855	61,400	1,147

2.—THE ADVENT CHRISTIANS.

A difference of opinion on the question of the immortality of the soul led to a division in 1855. Those who believe that man, both body and soul, is wholly mortal, and that eternal life is to be had only through personal faith in Christ as the gift of God, constitute the branch known as the Advent Christian Church. They hold to the proximate personal coming of Christ, and that after he comes the millennium will begin; they deny the inherent immortality of the soul, insisting that those only shall put on immortality at Christ's coming who are his true disciples; they believe that all the dead are in an unconscious state;

that all shall rise therefrom—the just first, to receive the gift of immortality and to reign with Christ; the unjust last, to receive sentence of banishment and to be punished by annihilation.

The Advent Christians have twenty conferences, with which three fifths of them are connected. The rest are in congregations which are not associated. The congregations are somewhat loosely organized, there being no general set of rules or particular form of government provided for them. They occupy as places of worship 281 halls, schoolhouses, and private houses, with an aggregate seating capacity of 34,705 for the two former. The seating capacity of private houses is not given in any of the tables in this volume.

SUMMARY BY STATES.

STATES.	Organizations.	Church Edifices.	Seating Capacity.	Value of Church Property.	Communicants.
Alabama..........	15	13¼	3,825	$3,055	688
Arkansas	22	6	1,750	2,900	671
California	14	8	1,525	13,700	558
Connecticut	26	21	4,825	54,300	1,358
Florida	4	1	200	100	60
Georgia...........	15	5	2,000	2,850	873
Illinois............	21	14	3,775	32,800	1,019
Indiana...........	10	7	2,490	9,400	455
Iowa	32	14	3,305	17,300	1,272
Kansas	30	3	725	3,200	990
Louisiana	2	1	250	500	51
Maine	65	28¼	7,520	38,100	2,317
Massachusetts	39	21	5,605	70,500	2,611
Michigan..........	14	7	2,025	9,800	591
Minnesota	14	9	2,375	28,150	710
Mississippi	1	..	....	......	30
Missouri	7	¼	400	300	230
Nebraska	7	..	....	......	98
New Hampshire ...	43	26	6,500	36,500	1,978
New York	17	10	2,500	25,500	1,048
North Carolina	18	15	4,750	8,075	1,549

SUMMARY BY STATES.—*Continued.*

STATES.	Organi- zations.	Church Edifices.	Seating Ca- pacity.	Value of Church Property.	Com- muni- cants.
Ohio.............	23	17	5,650	$20,500	953
Oregon...........	8	1½	450	1,000	132
Pennsylvania......	16	8½	2,426	9,800	469
Rhode Island......	12	10	2,650	27,450	950
South Carolina	10	6½	2,350	2,300	811
South Dakota	6	1	300	1,000	163
Tennessee	7	3	1,100	1,900	185
Texas	9	1	300	2,000	321
Utah	1	..	....	......	8
Vermont..........	28	14$\frac{9}{12}$	3,485	26,000	1,079
Virginia	2	2	350	2,200	165
Washington.......	7	1	200	700	129
West Virginia	15	6	2,100	2,200	681
Wisconsin.........	20	12	2,580	11,525	613
Total.........	580	294	80,286	$465,605	25,816

SUMMARY BY CONFERENCES.

	Organi- zations.	Church Edifices.	Seating Ca- pacity.	Value of Church Property.	Com- muni- cants.
Alabama..........	15	13¼	3,825	$3,055	688
Arkansas	22	6	1,750	2,900	671
California	14	8	1,525	13,700	558
Connecticut	26	21	4,825	54,300	1,358
Dakota	6	1	300	1,000	163
Georgia...........	15	5	2,000	2,850	873
Illinois............	21	14	3,775	32,800	1,019
Indiana...........	10	7	2,490	9,400	455
Iowa	32	14	3,305	17,300	1,272
Kansas	30	3	725	3,200	990
Maine	65	28¼	7,520	38,100	2,317
Michigan	14	7	2,025	9,800	591
Minnesota	14	9	2,375	28,150	710
Missouri	7	¼	400	300	230
Nebraska	7	..	....	......	98
New Hampshire ...	43	26	6,500	36,560	1,978
Ohio	23	17	5,650	20,500	953
Oregon and Wash- ington	15	2½	650	1,700	261
Tennessee	7	3	1,100	1,900	185
Texas	9	1	300	2,000	321
Unorganized	185	107$\frac{9}{12}$	29,246	186,150	10,125
Total.........	580	294	80,286	$465,605	25,816

3.—THE SEVENTH-DAY ADVENTISTS.

These form a branch of the general movement of 1840–44. They differ from other Adventists in observing the seventh day of the week as the Sabbath, in interpretation of the prophetic periods, and in form of organization. They believe that the prophetic period of 2300 days referred to in the Book of Daniel closed in 1844; but that the coming of Christ was not to be looked for then, but is to occur in the indefinite future. They hold that Christ, in 1844, at the termination of the 2300 days, entered as priest upon the work of cleansing the heavenly sanctuary, or temple, from " the presence of our sins." This period, which is to be brief, is to close with the second coming, the time of which cannot be forecast. The observance of the seventh day began with a congregation of Adventists in New Hampshire in 1844. The doctrine respecting the " cleansing of the sanctuary " has helped to establish and confirm this observance. They believe that the second advent is to precede, not follow, the millennium, that the state of the dead is one of unconsciousness, and that immersion is the proper form of baptism. They practice the ceremony of feet-washing when the Lord's Supper is administered.

Their congregations are organized into conferences, of which there are twenty-six, besides five missions. There is also a general conference, which meets annually, composed of delegates from the various conferences. Ordained ministers are not pastors, but traveling evangelists. The local churches are served by local officers who need not be ordained ministers. Members are expected to contribute a tenth of their income to the church.

There are 995 organizations with 418 edifices, valued at $644,675, and 28,891 communicants. The average seating capacity of the edifices is 225, and their average value $1542. The headquarters of the Seventh-Day Adventists are at Battle Creek, Michigan, and about a sixth of their communicants are in that State. Their congregations, however, are found in nearly all the States and Territories. They occupy as places of worship 555 halls, etc., with a seating capacity of 27,865.

SUMMARY BY STATES AND TERRITORIES.

STATES.	Organi- zations.	Church Edifices.	Seating Ca- pacity.	Value of Church Property.	Com- muni- cants.
Arizona	1	..	......	......	12
Arkansas	15	3	850	$1,000	363
California	34	24	8,328	157,150	2,226
Colorado	13	2	650	4,650	414
Connecticut	3	1	150	2,000	91
Delaware	2	1	150	800	26
District of Columbia	1	..	......	......	96
Florida	6	..	......	......	119
Georgia	4	..	......	40	81
Idaho	5	2	400	4,000	148
Illinois	24	16	3,550	52,400	871
Indiana	55	34$\frac{1}{2}$	7,900	32,010	1,193
Iowa	85	48	11,249	58,925	2,197
Kansas	67	21	4,165	15,950	1,990
Kentucky	6	1½	400	800	80
Louisiana	5	3	650	200	116
Maine	25	4⅔	1,550	7,400	459
Maryland	1	..	......	......	23
Massachusetts	15	2	600	5,900	490
Michigan	134	63	15,875	104,075	4,715
Minnesota	71	31	5,215	27,550	2,313
Missouri	24	7	1,500	6,350	815
Montana	2	1	200	1,250	49
Nebraska	38	9	1,025	12,500	829
Nevada	4	2	300	2,025	56
New Hampshire	4	1	200	500	112
New Jersey	5	3	425	1,000	85
New York	42	13	3,000	23,300	1,176
North Carolina	5	3	400	500	83

SUMMARY BY STATES AND TERRITORIES.—*Continued.*

STATES.	Organizations.	Church Edifices.	Seating Capacity.	Value of Church Property.	Communicants.
North Dakota	4	..	......	......	95
Ohio	55	21½	5,575	$25,450	1,189
Oregon	26	8	1,800	11,300	683
Pennsylvania	36	10½	2,350	16,300	884
Rhode Island......	6	4	500	1,025	108
South Dakota	30	9	2,350	7,400	884
Tennessee	10	5¼	1,350	2,425	211
Texas	15	1	800	800	452
Utah	1	..	......	......	29
Vermont...........	26	4	1,150	4,500	526
Virginia	6	2	600	1,800	114
Washington	21	10	1,925	20,050	560
West Virginia	5	3	450	2,500	136
Wisconsin.........	58	43	7,045	28,850	1,892
Total.........	995	418	94,627	$644,675	28,991

SUMMARY BY CONFERENCES AND MISSIONS.

Arkansas..........	15	3	850	$1,000	363
Atlantic	10	4	575	1,800	309
California	40	26	8,628	159,175	2,323
Colorado..........	13	2	650	4,650	414
Illinois............	24	16	3,550	52,400	871
Indiana	55	34¹⁄₂	7,900	32,010	1,193
Iowa	85	48	11,249	58,925	2,197
Kansas	67	21	4,165	15,950	1,990
Maine	25	4⅔	1,550	7,400	459
Michigan	134	63	15,875	104,075	4,715
Minnesota	75	31	5,215	27,550	2,408
Missouri	24	7	1,500	6,350	815
Nebraska	38	9	1,025	12,500	829
New England	28	8	1,450	9,425	801
New York	31	10	2,400	22,800	883
North Pacific......	35	12	2,425	20,300	879
Ohio	55	21½	5,575	25,450	1,189
Pennsylvania	46	13½	2,950	16,800	1,098
South Dakota	30	9	2,350	7,400	884
Tennessee River ...	11	5¾	1,550	2,425	220
Texas	15	1	800	800	452
Upper Columbia...	17	8	1,700	15,050	512
Vermont...........	26	4	1,150	4,500	526
Virginia	6	2	600	1,800	114
West Virginia	5	3	450	2,500	136
Wisconsin.........	58	43	7,045	28,850	1,892

SUMMARY BY CONFERENCES AND MISSIONS.—*Continued.*

STATES. MISSIONS.	Organizations.	Church Edifices.	Seating Capacity.	Value of Church Property.	Communicants.
Cumberland.......	5	1	200	$800	71
Louisiana	5	3	650	200	116
Montana..........	2	1	200	1,250	49
North Carolina	5	3	400	500	83
South Atlantic.....	10	..	......	40	200
Total.........	995	418	94,627	$644,675	28,991

4.—THE CHURCH OF GOD.

The Church of God is a branch of the Seventh-Day Adventists. A division occurred among the latter in the years 1864–66. This division resulted in the organization of the Church of God. The chief cause of the division was, it is stated, the claim of the Seventh-Day Adventists that Mrs. Ellen G. White was inspired and that her visions should be accepted as inspired. There are differences between the two bodies on the subject of health-reform—which is made prominent by the parent body—abstinence from swine's flesh, tea, and coffee—which the latter recommends—and with relation to prophecy.

The Church of God has three annual conferences, also a general conference representing the whole denomination. The number of members is 647. There are 23 halls, etc., with a seating capacity of 1445.

SUMMARY BY STATES.

STATES.	Organizations.	Church Edifices.	Seating Capacity.	Value of Church Property.	Communicants.
Indiana...........	2	..	....	......	20
Kansas	1	..	....	......	20
Michigan	15	..	....	$600	248
Missouri	11	1	200	800	359
Total.........	29	1	200	$1,400	647

SUMMARY BY CONFERENCES.

STATES.	Organizations.	Church Edifices.	Seating Capacity.	Value of Church Property.	Communicants.
Kansas & Nebraska	1	..	....	......	20
Michigan	17	..	....	$600	268
Missouri	11	1	200	800	359
Total........	29	1	200	$1,400	647

5.—THE LIFE AND ADVENT UNION.

This branch differs from the Evangelical and Advent Christian bodies respecting the doctrine of the resurrection of the wicked dead.   Both the latter believe that the wicked dead will rise at the end of the millennial reign and be sentenced to everlasting punishment which, according to the Evangelical Adventists, will be everlasting suffering, and according to the Advent Christians, everlasting destruction.   The Life and Advent Union holds that they will not rise at all; that when they die they die never to wake, but are doomed to sleep eternal.   This belief had adherents as early as 1844.   The branch, however, dates from 1864.   It was organized in Wilbraham, Mass.

It has 28 organizations, fourteen of which are in New England.   It has about 1000 members.   There are 19 halls, etc., with a seating capacity of 1830.

SUMMARY BY STATES.

STATES.	Organizations.	Church Edifices.	Seating Capacity.	Value of Church Property.	Communicants.
Connecticut	6	1	100	$3,040	243
Delaware	1	..	......	......	75
Iowa	1	..	......	......	20
Maine	7	3	1,200	1,250	188
Massachusetts	5	2	500	2,000	177
New Jersey........	1	1	150	900	56
New York.........	2	1	300	9,500	140
Rhode Island......	1	..	......	100	75
Virginia	4	..	......	......	44
Total	28	8	2,250	$16,790	1,018

6.—THE CHURCHES OF GOD IN CHRIST JESUS.

The members of this branch are popularly known as Age-to-Come Adventists. They believe that God is pledged, through the mouth of the prophets, to the final restitution of all things, and expect to see the kingdom of God established on earth, with Christ as King of kings, the saints being associated with him in the government of the world. They believe that Israel will be restored to rule in Jerusalem; that the dead will have a literal resurrection, the righteous to receive the blessings of immortality and the wicked to be destroyed; and that eternal life comes only through Christ. They hold that acceptance of the gospel, repentance, immersion in the name of Christ for the remission of sins, are conditions of forgiveness of sins, and that a holy life is essential to salvation.

They have churches in twenty-three States. They are associated in district conferences, and there is also a general conference. There are 61 halls, etc., with a seating capacity of 4825.

SUMMARY BY STATES.

STATES.	Organizations.	Church Edifices.	Seating Capacity.	Value of Church Property.	Communicants.
Arkansas	3	3	400	$500	59
California	3	..	......	......	38
Delaware	1	..	......	......	16
Florida	1	..	......	......	10
Illinois............	10	4	700	2,700	541
Indiana...........	19	9	3,050	9,900	621
Iowa	4	1	200	2,000	121
Kansas	9	1	200	400	205
Louisiana	1	..	......	......	10
Maryland	2	1	180	275	47
Michigan	7	2	375	3,800	170
Mississippi	1	½	200	100	9
Missouri	3	..	......	......	49
Nebraska	9	1	200	500	205
New Jersey........	2	..	......	......	31
New York	1	..	......	400	48

SUMMARY BY STATES.—*Continued.*

STATES.	Organi-zations.	Church Edifices.	Seating Ca-pacity.	Value of Church Property.	Com-muni-cants.
Ohio	5	5	1,175	$21,500	319
Oregon	6	1 ½	550	1,000	89
Pennsylvania	1	1	300	3,000	90
South Dakota	2	..	......	......	29
Washington	3	..	......	......	99
West Virginia	1	..	......	......	30
Wisconsin	1	..	......	......	36
Total	95	30	7,530	$46,075	2,872

The following table represents the six branches of Adventists:

SUMMARY OF ALL ADVENTISTS.

STATES.	Organi-zations.	Church Edifices.	Seating Ca-pacity.	Value of Church Property.	Com-muni-cants.
Alabama	15	13	3,825	$3,055	688
Arizona	1	..	......	......	12
Arkansas	40	12	3,000	4,400	1,093
California	51	32	9,853	170,850	2,822
Colorado	13	2	650	4,650	414
Connecticut	35	23	5,075	59,340	1,692
Delaware	4	1	150	800	117
District of Columbia	1	..	......	......	96
Florida	11	1	200	100	189
Georgia	19	5	2,000	2,890	954
Idaho	5	2	400	4,000	148
Illinois	55	34	8,025	87,900	2,431
Indiana	86	51	13,440	51,310	2,289
Iowa	122	63	14,754	78,425	3,610
Kansas	107	25	5,090	19,550	3,205
Kentucky	6	1	400	800	80
Louisiana	8	4	900	700	177
Maine	97	36	10,270	46,750	2,964
Maryland	3	1	180	275	70
Massachusetts	62	27	6,955	82,900	3,428
Michigan	170	72	18,275	118,275	5,724
Minnesota	85	40	7,590	55,700	3,023
Mississippi	2	½	200	100	39
Missouri	45	8	2,100	7,450	1,453
Montana	2	1	200	1,250	49
Nebraska	54	10	1,225	13,000	1,132

SUMMARY OF ALL ADVENTISTS.—*Continued.*

STATES.	Organi-zations.	Church Edifices.	Seating Ca-pacity.	Value of Church Property.	Com-muni-cants.
Nevada	4	2	300	$2,025	56
New Hampshire ...	47	27	6,700	37,000	2,090
New Jersey	8	4	575	1,900	172
New York.........	62	24	5,800	58,700	2,412
North Carolina.....	23	18	5,150	8,575	1,632
North Dakota	4	..	......	......	95
Ohio	83	44	12,400	67,450	2,461
Oregon	40	11	2,800	13,300	904
Pennsylvania	74	36	8,881	47,800	1,952
Rhode Island......	21	16	4,250	61,575	1,458
South Carolina	10	7	2,350	2,300	811
South Dakota	38	10	2,650	8,400	1,076
Tennessee	17	8	2,450	4,325	396
Texas	24	2	1,100	2,800	773
Utah	2	..	......	......	37
Vermont..........	58	22	5,335	35,900	1,768
Virginia	12	4	950	4,000	323
Washington.......	31	11	2,125	20,750	788
West Virginia	21	9	2,550	4,700	847
Wisconsin.........	79	55	9,625	40,375	2,541
Total.........	1,757	774	190,748	$1,236,345	60,491

CHAPTER II.

THE BAPTISTS.

THERE are numerous bodies of Christians who are called Baptists. While they differ on other points they all agree on these: that (1) the only proper subjects of Christian baptism are those who have been converted and profess personal faith in Christ; and that (2) the only Scriptural baptism is immersion. They therefore reject infant baptism as invalid, and sprinkling or pouring as unscriptural. There are certain denominations which accept these principles in whole or in part—the Disciples of Christ, the Christians, the Mennonites, and others—but they are not Baptists in name, and are not counted as such in any strict classification. The Disciples of Christ accept the two principles above stated, but also hold that it is only through baptism that " divine assurance of remission of sins and acceptance with God " is received. The Christians generally believe in immersion for believers, but do not refuse to tolerate pouring or sprinkling; while the Mennonites baptize usually by pouring.

The Baptists appear in history as early as the first quarter of the sixteenth century. Beginning in Switzerland in 1523, they soon took root in Germany, Holland, and other countries on the Continent, whence they found their way to England, driven thence by the persecution which their rejection of infant baptism occasioned. Persons who had been baptized in infancy, on professing conversion and applying for admission to Baptist churches were baptized again. Hence the persecuted people were often called Anabaptists. The first Baptist churches in England were organized before the middle of the seventeenth century. The American Baptists did not spring historically from the English Baptists. They trace their origin to Roger Williams, a minister of the Church of England, who came over to Massachusetts, whence he was driven because he did not conform to Congregationalism, which was the established religion of that province. He became the founder of the colony of Rhode Island, which, by the charter secured by him in 1644, was declared free to all forms of religion. Five years previously Mr. Williams had become a convert to Baptist principles, and had been immersed by one of the members of his Church, Ezekiel Holliman, whom he in turn immersed, with ten others. Of these he organized a Baptist church in Providence. Of course there were Baptists among the immigrants who came across the sea in the seventeenth century and later, and Baptist churches became numerous in New England, New York, Pennsylvania, Virginia, Georgia, and other States before the close of the eighteenth century.

The Baptists are variously divided. The Regular Baptists, who constitute the great majority in this country, exist in three bodies, Northern, Southern, and Colored. They are Calvinistic in doctrine. The Freewill Baptists, existing in two bodies, together with the General Baptists and others, are Arminian in doctrine. The Primitive or Old-School Baptists, of which there are two or three branches, are strongly Calvinistic. They also oppose Sunday-schools, missionary societies, and other "human institutions."

Baptist churches are defined as "bodies of baptized believers, with pastors and deacons, covenanted together for religious worship and religious work." All Baptist denominations are Congregational in polity, with, perhaps, the exception of the Original Freewill Baptists. Each church manages its own affairs. There are associations and similar organizations, composed of ministers and representatives of the churches, but they have no ecclesiastical power. There are also State conventions, variously constituted of representatives of associations, of other organizations, and of churches. Associations and conventions are chiefly concerned with the general interests of the churches, such as missions, Sunday-schools, education, etc. Men are ordained to the pastorate by councils consisting of ministers and representatives of neighboring churches. Councils also "recognize" new churches, and advise churches whenever requested so to do in cases of difficulty. Deacons are officers of the church, charged with the care of the poor, the visitation of the sick, and similar duties.

The following is a complete list of the various Baptist bodies:

1. Regular (North),
2. Regular (South),
3. Regular (Colored),
4. Six Principle,
5. Seventh-Day,
6. Freewill,
7. Original Freewill,
8. General,
9. Separate,
10. United,
11. Baptist Church of Christ,
12. Primitive,
13. Old Two-Seed-in-the-Spirit Predestinarian.

THE REGULAR BAPTISTS.

There are three bodies of Regular Baptists, the Northern, Southern, and Colored. They are not separate by virtue of doctrinal or ecclesiastical differences; but each, nevertheless, has its own associations, State conventions, and general missionary and other organizations.

The question of slavery was the cause of the separation between the Baptists of the Northern and the Baptists of the Southern States. In 1844 the controversy, which had been going on for some time, entered upon the decisive stage. The Alabama State convention, representing the Baptists of that State, adopted in that year a series of resolutions demanding " from the proper authorities in all these bodies to whose funds we have contributed . . . the distinct, explicit avowal that slaveholders are eligible and entitled equally with non-slaveholders to all the privileges and immunities of their several unions, and especially to receive any agency or mission or other appointment which may run with the scope of their operations or duties." The Board of Foreign Missions, which had its headquarters in Boston, and received contributions from the whole denomination, made answer to the demand of the Alabama convention, saying: " If any one should offer himself as a missionary, having slaves and insisting on retaining them as his property, we could not appoint him. One thing is certain, we can never be a party to any arrangement which would imply approbation of slavery." The board of the Home Mission Society made a similar declaration of policy, and division took place in 1845.

The Regular Baptists accept the Bible as the only rule of faith and practice. To its authority all appeals are made. There are, however, two general confessions of faith, which have weight among them as expressions of their belief. The older one, known as the Philadelphia Confession, first appeared in London in the seventeenth century; the other, called the New Hampshire Confession, was adopted by the New Hampshire State convention in 1833. The Philadelphia Confession follows closely the Westminster (Presbyterian) Confession of Faith, with such changes and additions as were required to set forth the Baptist views as to the proper subjects and mode of baptism and related questions, and as to church government. The New Hampshire Confession was formulated to express the views of the Calvinistic Baptists in their controversy with the Freewill Baptists, who were of the Arminian type of theology. It is regarded as fairly representing the doctrinal opinions of Northern Baptists, while the Philadelphia Confession is more acceptable, perhaps, to Southern Baptists. It is the common practice of Southern associations to print articles of faith in their annual minutes. In a few instances the whole New Hampshire Confession thus appears; in other cases it is shortened by the omission of two or more articles. The following articles taken from it express the views of all Regular Baptists:

"We believe that a visible church of Christ is a Congregation of baptized believers associated by covenant in the faith and fellowship of the gospel, observing the ordinances of Christ, governed by his laws, and exercising the gifts, rights, and privileges invested in them by his word; that its only scriptural officers are bishops or pastors and deacons, whose qualifications, claims, and duties are defined in the epistles to Timothy and Titus.

"We believe that Christian baptism is immersion in water of a believer, into the name of the Father and Son and Holy Ghost, to show forth, in a solemn and beautiful emblem, our faith in the crucified, buried, and risen Saviour, with its effect in our death to sin and resurrection to a new life; that it is prerequisite to the privileges of a church relation and to the Lord's Supper, in which the members of the church, by the sacred use of bread and wine, are to commemorate together the dying love of Christ, preceded always by solemn self-examination."

The Southern associations generally set forth brief articles of faith, varying somewhat in phraseology, but declaring the same doctrines. One of these compendiums consists of twelve articles. It appears more often than any other form in the minutes of the various associations, sometimes with two or more articles omitted, sometimes with a distinct one added. Articles 1 and 2 state the doctrine of the Trinity, and accept the Scriptures of the Old and New Testament as the word of God and only "rule of faith and practice"; Article 3 declares that "God chose his people in Christ Jesus before the foundation of the world" and "predestinated them unto the adoption of children"; Article 4, that man is a sinner and consequently in a lost condition; Article 5, that he has no power of his own free will and ability to recover himself from his fallen state; Article 6, that sinners are "justified in the sight of God only by the righteousness of Jesus Christ"; Article 7, that the elect are "called, regenerated, and sanctified by the Holy Spirit through the Gospel"; Article 8, that nothing can separate true believers from the love of God, "and that they shall be kept by the power of God through faith unto salvation"; Article 9, that baptism and the Lord's Supper are ordinances of Christ, and that believers are the only subjects of them, and immersion is the only baptism; Article 10, that the dead shall rise, and there shall be a final judgment; Article 11, that the "punishment of the wicked will be everlasting and the joys of the righteous eternal"; Article 12, that no minister has the right to administer the ordinances unless he is called of God, has " come under the imposition of hands by a presbytery," and is " in fellowship with the church of which he is a member." This summary fairly represents the various forms of confession in use. Some of the colored associations insert as an additional article the doctrine that " pedobaptism by immersion is not valid even when the administrator himself has been immersed." One colored association in Louisiana has an abstract of faith which declares that the " blessings of salvation are free to all "; that election by God is consistent with man's free agency; and that only such as are real believers persevere to the end. These are modified statements of the doctrines of election, free agency, and final perseverance as usually held by Baptist associations in the South. A few associations enjoin the washing of the saints' feet as a religious rite.

I.—THE REGULAR BAPTISTS (NORTH).

The Baptist churches in the Northern States, after the division of 1845, continued to support, on an antislavery basis, the Home Mission Society and the Baptist Union, the latter taking the place of the Board of Foreign Missions. In 1879 the question of the organic union of Northern and Southern Baptists came up, but nothing was accomplished. The Southern Baptist convention of that year, in appointing five delegates to the anniversaries of the Northern Baptist societies, expressed its fraternal regard; but insisted on " the wisdom and policy of preserving our separate organizations." On the part of the Northern Baptists a leading denominational journal said they were generally agreed that it would be " wholly unadvisable to try to bring about organic union between the Baptists of the North and South.''

The Northern Baptists have churches in all the States north of the Virginias, Kentucky, Missouri, and Texas, including the District of Columbia. Some churches on the border divide their contributions for the general benevolences between the Northern and Southern Baptist bodies, and one educational society represents both.

There are 414 associations of Northern Baptists, who are strongest in the States of New York (129,711), Illinois (95,237), and Pennsylvania (83,122). In three other States they have over 50,000 communicants each: Massachusetts, 59,830; Ohio, 57,685; and Indiana, 54,080. There are in all 800,450 communicants, belonging to 7907 organizations, with 7070 edifices, valued at $49,530,504. The average value of the edifices is $7006, and the average seating capacity 308; 1165 halls, etc., with a seating capacity of 109,350, are also occupied.

There is a considerable number of German Baptist churches, most of which are in the Northern and Western States. The earliest of them were organized in Pennsylvania in 1840 and 1841. These German Baptists are not to be confounded with the Dunkards, who are often called German Baptists. Their churches are reported in connection with the various associations within whose bounds they are situated, but they also have conferences of their own. There are five of these conferences, the Eastern, Central, Southwestern, Northwestern, and Texas, and they meet annually. There is also a general conference in which they are all represented. This conference meets once in three years. There are in all upward of 200 German churches with about 17,000 members. There are also some 200 Swedish churches with more than 12,000 members, a few Danish churches, and a number of Welsh churches.

SUMMARY BY STATES.

STATES.	Organizations.	Church Edifices.	Seating Capacity.	Value of Church Property.	Communicants.
Arizona...........	6	4	875	$11,200	197
California.........	163	121	34,025	744,360	11,204
Colorado..........	54	40	10,935	440,000	4,944
Connecticut.......	135	138	47,280	1,650,050	22,372
Delaware.........	13	16	4,782	165,300	1,823
District of Columbia	2	2	1,900	65,000	3,000
Idaho.............	20	10	2,180	26,100	656
Illinois............	996	911	282,463	3,495,010	95,237
Indiana...........	552	515	164,055	1,313,422	54,080
Iowa	417	340	89,231	1,162,640	30,901
Kansas	545	339	87,015	893,233	32,172
Maine	237	223	61,669	921,550	18,917
Massachusetts	318	346	142,589	6,107,830	59,830
Michigan	395	353	101,535	1,858,419	34,145
Minnesota	194	161	40,575	1,107,839	14,698
Montana..........	14	11	2,950	89,000	683
Nebraska	230	164	36,590	514,710	11,917
Nevada...........	1	1	500	7,000	63
New Hampshire ...	85	97	28,310	585,050	8,768
New Jersey........	224	252	94,575	2,957,628	38,757
New Mexico.......	15	4	1,250	22,000	355
New York	875	898	309,581	12,938,913	129,711
North Dakota	54	33	7,675	90,300	2,298
Ohio	616	585	168,835	2,543,888	57,685
Oregon	108	69	17,740	317,325	5,306
Pennsylvania	634	642	219,589	5,984,322	83,122
Rhode Island......	68	73	28,693	1,151,960	12,055
South Dakota......	83	54	11,311	227,175	3,856
Utah	4	3	700	65,000	327
Vermont..........	100	103	28,124	584,500	8,933
Washington.......	90	55	12,540	241,760	3,870
West Virginia	458	324	94,045	381,200	34,154
Wisconsin.........	192	180	46,131	838,945	14,152
Wyoming.........	9	3	525	27,875	262
Total........	7,907	7,070	2,180,773	$49,530,504	800,450

2.—THE REGULAR BAPTISTS (SOUTH).

This is the more numerous branch of white Baptists. After the division of 1845 the Southern churches organized the Southern Baptist convention, which meets annually, to consider, promote, and direct the general interests of the denomination, such as home and foreign missions and Sunday-schools. It is composed of delegates from associations and other organizations, and from churches. It has no ecclesiastical authority whatever. It represents churches in sixteen States, including Kansas, which has a few churches belonging to an association in Missouri, the District of Columbia, the Indian Territory, and Oklahoma.

The oldest Baptist churches and associations are in the North. Of the seventy-seven churches reported for 1770 only seven were in the South; these were in Delaware, the Carolinas, and Virginia. In the next decade churches rose in Georgia, Tennessee, and Kentucky. There were none, however, in Missouri, Mississippi, and Louisiana until after the present century opened, and none in Arkansas until a considerably later date. The first association in the South was that of South Carolina, organized in 1751; those of Sandy Creek and Kehukee, in North Carolina, were organized in 1758 and 1765 respectively; the Ketocton, in Virginia, in 1766; and the Holston, in Tennessee, in 1786. Virginia was in 1784 the Baptist stronghold, having more than forty-two per cent. of all the members. It maintained the lead for nearly half a century, then lost it, and regained it from New York in 1850, and held it until Georgia took it some fifteen or twenty years later.

Kentucky, North Carolina, Georgia, Texas, Missouri, and

Tennessee are the great Baptist States of the South. They contain nearly two thirds of the total of members. Kentucky has 153,668; North Carolina, 153,648; Georgia, 137,-860; Texas, 129,734; Missouri, 121,985; and Tennessee, 106,632—making a total of 803,527 in these six States. Alabama reports 98,185; Virginia, 92,693; Mississippi, 82,315; and South Carolina, 76,216. In all, the Southern Baptists number 1,280,066. These members are divided among 16,238 organizations, which report 13,502 edifices, with a seating capacity of 4,349,407, and an aggregate value of $18,196,637. Besides the edifices, 2641 halls, etc., with a seating capacity of 326,000, are used as places of worship.

Southern Baptists seem to be very thoroughly distributed over the States they occupy. They have organizations in all the counties in the State of Alabama (66). In the State of Arkansas they have organizations in 74 counties out of 75; in South Carolina, in 34 out of 35; in Florida, in 44 out of 45; in Georgia, in 135 out of 137; in Kentucky, in 111 out of 119; in Louisiana, in 38 out of 59; in Mississippi, in 74 out of 75; in Missouri, in 114 out of 115; in North Carolina, in 95 out of 96; in Tennessee, in 92 out of 96; in Texas, in 185 out of 244; in Virginia, in 96 out of 100.

There are 658 associations, the largest of which is the Dover, of Virginia, having 11,711 members. The associations are given alphabetically under each State, but are not footed by States, because many of them cross State lines.

The average seating capacity of edifices is 322, and the average value $1348.

SUMMARY BY STATES.

STATES.	Organi- zations.	Church Edifices.	Seating Ca- pacity.	Value of Church Property.	Com- muni- cants.
Alabama........	1,495	1,373	407,119	$1,170,219	98,185
Arkansas	1,107	732	220,390	408,885	58,364
Dist. of Columbia	16	16	6,000	466,000	3,621
Florida	403	334	73,435	208,933	18,747
Georgia........	1,647	1,602	519,050	1,848,675	137,860
Indian Territory	181	110	18,485	35,765	9,147
Kansas	6	4	700	2,100	273
Kentucky	1,441	1,277	426,720	2,364,238	153,668
Louisiana	482	438	108,730	333,977	27,736
Maryland	47	48	21,420	651,050	8,017
Mississippi	1,125	1,071	319,370	689,451	82,315
Missouri	1,636	1,265	390,775	2,386,898	121,985
North Carolina .	1,480	1,472	603,938	1,662,405	153,648
Oklahoma	8	....	......	....	216
South Carolina .	759	748	234,080	894,724	76,216
Tennessee	1,287	1,159	396,715	1,802,015	106,632
Texas	2,318	1,081	332,348	1,384,035	129,734
Virginia	787	762	266,982	1,859,292	92,693
West Virginia ..	13	10	3,150	27,975	1,009
Total......	16,238	13,502	4,349,407	$18,196,637	1,280,066

3.—THE REGULAR BAPTISTS (COLORED).

The Colored Baptists of the South constitute the most numerous body of Regular Baptists. Not all Colored Baptists are embraced in this division; only those who have separate churches, associations, and State conventions. There are many Colored Baptists in Northern States, who are mostly counted as members of churches belonging to white associations. None of them are included in the following tables.

The first State convention of Colored Baptists was organized in North Carolina in 1866; the second in Alabama and the third in Virginia in 1867; the fourth in Arkansas in 1868; and the fifth in Kentucky in 1869. There are colored conventions in fifteen States.

In addition to these organizations the Colored Baptists of the United States have others more general in character: the American National Convention, the purpose of which is " to consider the moral, intellectual, and religious growth of the denomination," to deliberate upon questions of general concern, and to devise methods to bring the churches and members of the race closer together; the Consolidated American Missionary Convention; the General Association of the Western States and Territories; the Foreign Mission Convention of the United States, and the New England Missionary Convention. All except the first are missionary in their purpose.

The American National Convention, in its annual session in 1890, adopted a resolution recommending that the practice of receiving into membership persons immersed in Pedobaptist churches be discontinued, on the ground that Pedobaptist organizations are not churches, and therefore have no power to administer baptism. The exchange of pulpits with Pedobaptists was also condemned as " inconsistent and erroneous."

It was extremely difficult to obtain returns of a third or more of the Colored Baptist associations in the South. No response was made, in many instances, to repeated requests to clerks or moderators for statistics. Some of their State missionaries, professors, and others were induced to undertake the work of gathering the returns of such associations for the eleventh census, and after more than a year and a half of earnest endeavor, all possible resources being exhausted in the effort, full reports were secured from all.

Several correspondents reported to the Census Office that radical changes in colored associations are frequent. A few discontented churches often withdraw and form a new association, which continues for a year or two, and then is absorbed by another association. The boundaries of these bodies change frequently, and sometimes they are also quite irregular, embracing not contiguous territory, but counties or portions of counties widely separated.

The Colored Baptists are represented in fifteen States, all in the South, or on the border, and in the District of Columbia. In Virginia and Georgia they are very numerous, having in the latter 200,516, and in the former 199,871 communicants. In Alabama they have 142,437; in North Carolina, 134,445; in Mississippi, 136,647; in South Carolina, 125,572; and in Texas, 111,138 members. The aggregate is 1,348,989 members, who are embraced in 12,533 organizations, with 11,987 church edifices, valued at $9,038,549. There are 416 associations, of which 66 are in Alabama, 63 in Georgia, 49 in Mississippi, 40 in North Carolina, and 23 in Virginia. As associations generally conform to county lines, the excess of associations in Georgia and Alabama over Virginia is probably chiefly due to the greater number of counties.

The average seating capacity of the church edifices is 287, and their average value $754. There are 663 halls, etc., with a seating capacity of 45,520.

While some of the Colored Baptist churches are very large, particularly in the cities, there are many weak congregations in the rural districts which, as is the case among the smaller white churches, do not have regular Sunday services oftener than once or twice a month.

SUMMARY BY STATES.

STATES.	Organi- zations.	Church Edifices.	Seating Ca- pacity.	Value of Church Property.	Com- muni- cants.
Alabama........	1,374	1,341	376,839	$795,384	142,437
Arkansas	923	870	243,395	585,947	63,786
Dist. of Columbia	43	33	18,600	383,150	12,717
Florida	329	295	61,588	137,578	20,828
Georgia........	1,818	1,800	544,546	1,045,310	200,516
Kentucky	378	359	109,030	406,949	50,245
Louisiana	865	861	191,041	609,890	68,008
Maryland	38	34	12,389	150,475	7,750
Mississippi	1,385	1,333	371,115	682,541	136,647
Missouri	234	212	60,015	400,518	18,613
North Carolina .	1,173	1,164	362,946	705,512	134,445
South Carolina .	860	836	275,529	699,961	125,572
Tennessee......	569	534	159,140	519,923	52,183
Texas	1,464	1,288	282,590	664,286	111,138
Virginia	1,001	977	358,032	1,192,035	199,871
West Virginia ..	79	50	14,175	59,090	4,233
Total......	12,533	11,987	3,440,970	$9,038,549	1,348,989

4.—GENERAL SIX-PRINCIPLE BAPTISTS.

This small body of less than 1000 members is represented only in three States. Its first church was organized in 1670 in Rhode Island. The creed is formed from the first and second verses of Chapter VI. of the Epistle to the Hebrews, and consists of six principles: 1. Repentance from dead works; 2. Faith toward God; 3. The doctrine of baptism; 4. The laying on of hands; 5. Resurrection of the dead; 6. Eternal judgment. Hence they derive their name.

They have two yearly meetings: one in Pennsylvania, and one in Rhode Island and Massachusetts. There are 18 organizations, 12 of which are in Rhode Island. They occupy 4 halls, with a seating capacity of 400.

SUMMARY BY STATES.

STATES.	Organizations.	Church Edifices.	Seating Capacity.	Value of Church Property.	Communicants.
Massachusetts	1	..	.....	......	4
Pennsylvania	5	3	1,300	$3,800	218
Rhode Island......	12	11	2,300	15,700	715
Total.........	18	14	3,600	$19,500	937

5.—THE SEVENTH-DAY BAPTISTS.

Baptists who observed the seventh day of the week as the Sabbath appeared in England as early as the latter part of the sixteenth century, and were known as Sabbatarian Baptists, until the general conference of the body in the United States changed the name in 1818. The first Seventh-Day Baptist church in this country was organized in Newport, R. I., in 1671, by Stephen Mumford, an English Sabbatarian Baptist. From this Rhode Island church the denomination has gradually developed in the United States. As early as 1700 Philadelphia became a second center of Seventh-Day Baptists, and soon after Piscataway, N. J., a third.

In doctrine the Seventh-Day Baptists differ from other Baptist bodies only concerning the observance of the seventh day. They believe that the seventh day is the Sabbath of the Lord, that it was instituted in Eden, promulgated at Sinai, made binding upon all men at all times, and is in the nature of its relation to God and to man irrepealable. They hold that any attempt to connect the Sabbath law and obligation with any other day of the week is illogical and tends to destroy the institution.

The Seventh-Day Baptists have two collegiate institutions, one at Milton, Wis., the other at Albert Center, N. Y. Both sexes are admitted on equal terms to these colleges. Albert Center is also the headquarters of its publishing interests.

The denomination is represented in twenty-four States, having 106 organizations, 78 church edifices, valued at $265,260, and 9143 communicants. The average seating capacity of the edifices is 285; average value, $3401. Eighteen halls, etc., with a seating capacity of 1125, are also occupied.

SUMMARY BY STATES.

STATES.	Organizations.	Church Edifices.	Seating Capacity.	Value of Church Property.	Communicants.
Alabama...........	1	..	.....	......	11
Arkansas..........	2	1	240	$900	60
Connecticut	2	2	600	4,500	103
Florida	1	1	200	1,500	14
Idaho	1	1	200	400	28
Illinois	9	6	1,650	8,825	350
Iowa	3	2	500	4,300	169
Kansas	3	1	300	3,500	229
Kentucky	1	..	.....	......	6
Louisiana	1	..	.....	......	36
Minnesota	5	2	500	2,500	246
Mississippi	1	..	....	......	33
Missouri	1	1	200	500	13
Nebraska	4	2	400	3,900	267
New Jersey........	4	5	1,400	55,285	745
New York	28	24	7,015	71,025	3,274
North Carolina	1	..	.....	......	10
Ohio	1	1	350	3,000	131
Pennsylvania	5	4	1,300	5,800	224
Rhode Island......	7	7	2,162	55,700	1,271
South Dakota	2	1	225	1,000	28
Texas	4	..	.....	......	50
West Virginia	9	8	1,800	15,900	767
Wisconsin.........	10	9	2,425	26,725	1,078
Total.........	106	78	21,467	$265,260	9,143

6.—THE FREEWILL BAPTISTS.

The first church of this denomination was organized by Benjamin Randall in New Durham, N. H., in 1780. He was at first a Congregationalist. Changing his views on the subject of baptism, he became a Baptist; but he did not adhere to the Calvinistic doctrines of predestination, election, limited atonement, and final perseverance of the saints, as generally held at that time in that denomination. He was therefore adjudged unsound, and fellowship was withdrawn from him by the Baptists. This was in 1779. In 1780 he was ordained by two Baptist ministers who sympathized with his doctrinal views, and in the same year the first Freewill Baptist church was organized, as already stated. This church and others of like faith which sprung up in New England were simply called Baptist churches. At the close of the century the distinctive word "Freewill" was adopted, members having been popularly designated "Freewillers," in allusion to the doctrine held concerning the freedom of the will. The churches multiplied. At the end of the first year there were 5, at the close of the first decade 18, and at the close of the first half-century 450, with 21,000 members. The denomination was gradually extended beyond the bounds of New England into the West. Its strong antislavery sentiment prevented its advance into the South. In 1835 the general conference, speaking for the whole body, took a pronounced position against slavery. In 1841 the Free-Communion Baptists of New York united with the Freewill Baptists, adding 55 churches and 2500 members. The body lost several thousand members, however, by the Adventist movement and by local divisions. It had 60,000 in 1845, but in 1857 this

number had been reduced to less than 49,000. Its numbers also declined during the war, many of its ministers
and members going into the army. By 1870 it had recov-
ered from all its losses, reporting 60,000 members as returned in 1845. A fact deserving mention is that women
began to labor as preachers among the churches as early as
1791. They are not debarred from ordination.

The principles of doctrine and practice held by the Freewill Baptists are embodied in a " Treatise" ordered by the
general conference in 1832 and published in 1834 and since
revised. The doctrinal chapters, twenty-one in number,
declare (to give their more distinctive statements) that
though man cannot in his fallen state become the child of
God by natural goodness and works of his own, redemption and regeneration are freely provided for him. The
" call of the gospel is coextensive with the atonement to
all men," so that salvation is " equally possible to all."
The " truly regenerate " are " through infirmity and mani-
fold temptations " in " danger of falling," and " ought
therefore to watch and pray, lest they make shipwreck of
faith." Christian baptism is immersion, and participation
in the Lord's Supper is the " privilege and duty of all who
have spiritual union with Christ," and " no man has a right
to forbid these tokens to the least of his disciples." The
denomination has always advocated open communion, as
expressed in the foregoing sentence, in opposition to close
communion, which is the rule among the Regular Baptists.
In the brief articles of faith provided for churches the
" human will " is declared to be " free and self-determined,
having power to yield to gracious influences and live, or
resist them and perish," and the doctrine of election is described, not as an " unconditional decree " fixing the future

state of man, but simply as God's determination " from the beginning to save all who should comply with the conditions of salvation."

The Freewill Baptists have quarterly and yearly conferences, and a general conference meeting once in two years. The quarterly conference consists of delegates representing a number of churches. It inquires into the condition of the churches, and is empowered to advise, admonish, or withdraw fellowship from them. It may not, however, " deprive a church of its inependent form of government nor its right to discipline its members, nor labor with individual members of churches as such "; it may only deal with the churches as churches. The yearly meeting is composed of delegates elected by quarterly meetings. It occupies the same relation to quarterly meetings as quarterly meetings do to the churches. The general conference, which is charged with the care of the general interests of the denomination, is composed of delegates from the yearly meetings. It may discipline yearly meetings, but not quarterly meetings or churches. It is expressly forbidden to reverse or change the decisions of any of the subordinate bodies. Those desiring to become ministers are licensed for a year by the quarterly meeting and ordained by a council of the meeting. Each church, besides its pastor, clerk, and treasurer, has a board of deacons, who assist at baptism and the Lord's Supper, which is observed monthly, have the care of the poor, and conduct religious meetings in the absence of the pastor.

The denomination has 51 yearly meetings (some are called associations), with 1586 organizations, 1225 edifices, valued at $3,115,642, and 87,898 communicants. It also occupies 349 halls, etc., having a seating capacity of 37,260.

It is represented in thirty-three States, chiefly Northern and Western. It is strongest in New England, where it originated. In Maine there are 16,294 members. This is the banner State of the denomination.

The average seating capacity of the churches is 285, and the average value $2543.

SUMMARY BY STATES.

STATES.	Organi- zations.	Church Edifices.	Seating Ca- pacity.	Value of Church Property.	Com- muni- cants.
Alabama	15	13	3,100	$1,245	847
Arkansas	1	1	500	250	40
California	2	2	900	19,500	179
Connecticut	2	2	400	2,200	125
Florida	3	....	......	......	22
Illinois	115	83	19,320	71,500	6,096
Indiana	31	28	8,075	39,000	1,926
Iowa	45	36	9,740	65,800	2,029
Kansas	36	11	4,900	12,425	1,361
Kentucky	21	17	4,450	7,980	1,641
Louisiana	40	25	4,830	24,245	1,000
Maine	280	232	67,930	584,750	16,294
Maryland	3	3	525	1,800	98
Massachusetts	20	17	6,265	188,200	3,122
Michigan	128	113	29,145	277,275	5,435
Minnesota	30	24	5,385	94,550	1,497
Mississippi	25	20	7,880	7,540	1,339
Missouri	108	56	15,720	59,825	4,752
Nebraska	43	19	4,990	29,600	1,185
New Hampshire	94	89	33,325	379,000	8,004
New York	134	128	36,727	529,050	8,636
North Carolina	1	....	200	100	11
Ohio	128	103	30,645	149,350	6,982
Oklahoma	1	....	......	......	100
Pennsylvania	56	40	9,695	76,300	2,478
Rhode Island	26	26	7,845	226,757	3,252
South Dakota	5	4	700	11,500	168
Tennessee	53	35	10,895	22,825	2,864
Texas	8	6	887	3,300	261
Vermont	43	34	9,110	94,375	2,325
Virginia	9	6	1,725	7,000	478
West Virginia	32	10	3,350	34,000	1,668
Wisconsin	48	42	10,150	94,400	1,683
Total	1,586	1,225	349,309	$3,115,642	87,898

7.—THE ORIGINAL FREEWILL BAPTISTS.

In the first half of the eighteenth century a number of
General Baptist churches were organized in North Carolina.
These, with some which had been formed in Virginia a
little earlier, constituted an association in 1729. Thirty
years later many of these General had become Calvinistic
or Regular Baptist churches. Those who did not unite
with the Calvinistic associations were popularly called
" Freewillers," because they held to the doctrine of the
freedom of the will. Accepting that term, they became
known eventually as Original Freewill Baptists, the word
" original " probably referring to their early history.

Their doctrines are set forth in a confession of faith consisting of eighteen articles. It declares that Christ " freely
gave himself a ransom for all, tasting death for every
man "; that God wants all to come to repentance; that
" all men, at one time or another, are found in such capacity as that through the grace of God they may be eternally
saved "; that those " ordained to condemnation " are the
ungodly who refuse to repent and believe the gospel;
that children dying in infancy are not subject to the
second death; that God has not " decreed any person
to everlasting death or everlasting life out of respect or
mere choice," except in appointing the " godly unto life
and the ungodly who die in sin unto death "; that only
believers should be baptized, and the only baptism is immersion. They believe in washing the saints' feet and in
anointing the sick with oil.

The churches hold for business purposes quarterly conferences, in which all members may participate; they have
a clerk, a treasurer, deacons who prepare for the communion service and care for the poor, and ruling elders to settle

controversies between brethren. Communion and feet-washing are as a rule held quarterly. Members of churches are forbidden to frequent the " race-track, the card-table, shooting-matches, or any other place of disorder." In church trials it is provided that " no person of color within the pale of the church shall give testimony against any person" except one " of color." Only male members shall occupy the offices of the church. Annual conferences, composed of all the elders (pastors), ministers (ordained), and preachers (licentiates) in good standing, and of delegates from the churches, have power to " silence " preachers, try and disown or discontinue elders, receive new churches, and settle difficulties in churches.

There are three conferences, with churches in the two Carolinas. The number of organizations is 167, with 125 church edifices, valued at $57,005, and 11,864 communicants. The average seating capacity of the edifices is 331, and their average value $455. Forty-three halls, etc., afford seating capacity for 4650 persons.

SUMMARY BY STATES.

STATES.	Organizations.	Church Edifices.	Seating Capacity.	Value of Church Property.	Communicants.
North Carolina	133	99	35,750	$52,355	10,224
South Carolina	34	26	5,650	4,650	1,640
Total	167	125	41,400	$57,005	11,864

8.—THE GENERAL BAPTISTS.

The General Baptists are thus distinguished because originally they differed from the Particular or Regular Baptists in holding that the atonement of Christ was general, not particular; that is, for the whole race, and not simply for those effectually called. There were General Baptists in England early in the seventeenth century. Indeed, some of their historians claim that they appeared both in England and America before the Particular or Regular Baptists.

General Baptists in New England associated themselves in a yearly meeting at the beginning of the eighteenth century. Churches of the same faith and order were also organized in the first half of that century in Maryland, Virginia, and the Carolinas. Most of these early churches, it appears, subsequently became Regular or Calvinistic churches.

The first association of General Baptists in the West, where the denomination now has its entire strength, was the Liberty, of Kentucky, organized in 1824. In 1830 it adopted the practice of open communion, and about 1845 changed one of its articles of belief, which had been formulated at its organization, so as to embrace " infants and idiots " in the covenants of God's grace, and another so as to say that " he that shall endure to the end, the same shall be saved," instead of declaring that " the saints will finally persevere through grace to glory." These changes indicated the desire to eliminate such elements of Calvinism as had been introduced when the articles were adopted a few years before.

In 1870 the General Baptists formed a general association, in which all General Baptist associations are represented. The purpose of the general association was to bring " into more intimate and fraternal relation and effective coöperation various bodies of liberal Baptists." The denomination has received accessions of Freewill churches, but some of its churches have in turn joined Freewill and other Baptist bodies. It has increased in membership quite rapidly. In 1870 it had 8000 members; in 1880, 12,367; and in 1890, 21,362. It is represented in the States of Indiana, Illinois, Kentucky, Tennessee, Missouri, Arkansas, and Nebraska.

The confession of faith adopted by the general association declares that the Bible is the only rule of faith and practice; that there is one God, the Father, the Son, and the Holy Ghost; that man is "fallen and depraved" and has no ability in himself to salvation; that he that endures to the end shall be saved; that rewards and punishment are eternal; that the only proper mode of baptism is immersion; that the only proper subjects of baptism are believers; that none save infants and idiots can partake of the benefits of the atonement, which was made for all, except by repentance and faith. They are in substantial agreement with the Freewill Baptists.

The General Baptists have 22 associations, 399 organizations, 209 edifices, valued at $201,140, and 21,362 communicants. The average seating capacity of the edifices is 344, and their average value $964. There are 180 halls, etc., with a seating capacity of 28,201.

SUMMARY BY STATES.

STATES.	Organizations.	Church Edifices.	Seating Capacity.	Value of Church Property.	Communicants.
Arkansas	33	4	2,000	$1,565	1,217
Illinois............	41	30	8,400	12,125	2,605
Indiana	64	59	22,800	135,425	5,351
Kentucky	68	27	10,125	20,950	4,455
Missouri	166	70	21,025	22,675	6,654
Nebraska	5	..	......	......	72
Tennessee	22	19	7,500	8,400	1,008
Total	399	209	71,850	$201,140	21,362

9.—THE SEPARATE BAPTISTS.

The Separate Baptists of the last century were those who favored the great Whitefield revival movement. They separated from those Baptists who, for various reasons, opposed the revival. They had considerable accessions from the Congregational churches, and became numerous in New England, Virginia, and elsewhere. Most of these Separate Baptists formed a union with the Regular Baptists a century or more ago, but a few still maintain separate organizations. Two associations which retain the word "Separate" in their title are counted as Regular Baptists.

Separate Baptists are generally in doctrinal agreement with the Freewill Baptists, holding to a general atonement and rejecting the doctrine of election and reprobation.

There is one association, with 24 organizations, 19 church edifices, valued at $9200, and 1599 communicants. The average seating capacity of the edifices is 297, and their average value $484. There are 5 halls, etc., with a seating capacity of 525.

SUMMARY.

STATE.	Organizations.	Church Edifices.	Seating Capacity.	Value of Church Property.	Communicants.
Indiana	24	19	5,650	$9,200	1,599

10.—THE UNITED BAPTISTS.

There being in Congregational and Baptist churches in New England some opposition to the great revival movement of the eighteenth century led by George Whitefield, a separation occurred in many instances, and there were

" Separates" both among the Congregationalists and Baptists.   The latter were called Separate Baptists, and those
from whom they separated were called, by way of distinction, Regular Baptists, a name which they still retain.   The
Separate Baptists became quite numerous in New England
(where many of those who separated from the Congregational churches united with them) and elsewhere.   But in
the last quarter of the eighteenth century and the beginning of the present, Separate and Regular Baptists came
together in Virginia, Kentucky, and elsewhere, and called
themselves United Baptists.   The great body of these are
now known as Regular or Missionary Baptists.

There are still a few United Baptists who retain the old
title and an independent existence.   These are tabulated
herewith separately.   A few associations in full fellowship
with the Regular Baptists still use the word " United."
The doctrinal basis on which the union of Separate and
Regular Baptists was accomplished in Kentucky in 1801
was not distinctly Calvinistic.   While it did declare the
final perseverance of the saints, it did not set forth election
or reprobation, and it stipulated that the holding of the
doctrine that " Christ tasted death for every man" (general atonement) should be " no bar to communion."   The
United Baptists, according to the articles of faith set forth
by most of their associations, are now moderately Calvinistic.   These articles declare that Christ " suffered and died
to make atonement for sin," not indicating whether this
atonement was general or particular; that though the gospel is to be preached to all nations, and sinners are to be
called upon to repent, such is their opposition to the gospel
that they freely choose a state of sin; that God in his
" mere good pleasure" elected or chose in Christ a great

multitude among all nations; that through the influences of the Holy Spirit he "effectually calls them," and they "freely choose Christ for their Saviour"; that those who are united to God by a living faith are forgiven and justified "solely on account of the merits of Christ"; that those who are justified and regenerated will persevere to the end; that baptism should be administered only to believers and by immersion; that the Lord's Supper should be "observed by those who have been regenerated, regularly baptized, and become members of a gospel church"; that feet-washing ought to be practiced by all baptized believers.

There are 12 associations of United Baptists, with 204 organizations, 179 church edifices, valued at $80,150, and 13,209 communicants. The average seating capacity of the churches is 336, and their average value $448. Halls, etc., 23, with a seating capacity of 3650.

SUMMARY BY STATES.

STATES.	Organizations.	Church Edifices.	Seating Capacity.	Value of Church Property.	Communicants.
Alabama..........	15	15	4,900	$5,900	702
Arkansas	3	3	1,000	925	146
Kentucky	81	78	29,850	39,750	6,443
Missouri	45	32	11,920	15,975	2,738
Tennessee	60	51	12,550	17,600	3,180
Total.........	204	179	60,220	$80,150	13,209

II.—THE BAPTIST CHURCH OF CHRIST.

This body holds a separate position among Baptists. Its oldest associations, the Elk River and Duck River, were organized in 1808 in Tennessee, where more than half of the communicants reported are to be found. Its articles of faith set forth a mild form of Calvinism, with a general atonement. They declare that Christ " tasted death for every man " and made it possible for God to have mercy upon all who come unto him on gospel terms; that sinners are justified by faith; that the saints will persevere; that true believers are the only proper subjects of baptism; that immersion is the only proper baptism; and that baptism, the Lord's Supper, and feet-washing are ordinances of the gospel to be continued until Christ's second coming. This body claims to be the oldest body of Baptists, and that there were no others in Tennessee until 1825, when the Two-Seed churches came into existence as the result of what is known as the Antinomian Controversy.

There are 152 organizations, 135 church edifices, valued at $56,755, and 8254 communicants. Of the latter, 5065 are in Tennessee; the rest are divided between Alabama, Arkansas, Mississippi, Missouri, North Carolina, and Texas. The average seating capacity of the edifices is 304, and their average value $422. Seventeen halls, etc., are occupied as places of worship. They have a seating capacity of 1275.

SUMMARY BY STATES.

STATES.	Organizations.	Church Edifices.	Seating Capacity.	Value of Church Property.	Communicants.
Alabama..........	18	18	4,800	$5,200	782
Arkansas..........	27	18	4,700	7,800	887
Mississippi	8	8	2,400	4,950	368
Missouri	4	2	435	900	185
North Carolina	16	16	4,600	5,400	659
Tennessee.........	69	69	22,950	31,355	5,065
Texas	10	3	1,000	1,150	308
Total.........	152	135	40,885	$56,755	8,254

12.—THE PRIMITIVE BAPTISTS.

Those who are variously known as "Primitive," "Old School," "Regular," and "Anti-Mission" Baptists are so called because of their opposition, begun more than fifty years ago, to the establishment of Sunday-schools, mission, Bible, and other societies, which they regard as modern and human institutions unwarranted by the Scriptures and unnecessary.

Opposition among Baptists to the missionary and other church societies was manifested some years before the division began. In 1835 the Chemung Association, having churches in New York and Pennsylvania, adopted a resolution declaring that as a number of associations with which it had been in correspondence had "departed from the simplicity of the doctrine and practice of the gospel of Christ," "uniting themselves with the world and what are falsely called benevolent societies founded upon a monied basis," and preaching a gospel "differing from the gospel of Christ," it would not continue in fellowship with them. It urged all Baptists who could not approve the new ideas to come out and be separate from those holding them. The Baltimore (Md.) Association made a similar declaration in 1836, and a gradual separation was the result. The Warwick Association of New York issued a circular letter in 1840, which shows that a warm controversy was then in progress. This letter, which was written in behalf of the "new ideas," charged the Primitive brethren with holding hyper-Calvinistic doctrines, and insisted that their predestinarianism was such as practically to deny any responsibility in man for his conduct or condition. It attributed to them statements to the effect that God carries on his work " without the least instrumentality whatever," and that " all the preaching from John the Baptist until now, if made to bear on one unregenerated sinner," could not " quicken his poor dead soul." The Primitive Baptists do not oppose the preaching of the gospel, but believe that God will convert the world in his own way and own good time without the aid of missionary societies.

Primitive Baptist associations generally print in their annual minutes articles of faith, a form of constitution, and rules of order. The articles of faith, while practically the same in doctrinal view, vary in length and phraseology. Some of them have eleven articles, some less, some more. They declare that by Adam's fall or transgression " all his posterity became sinners in the sight of God"; that the " corruption of human nature " is such that man cannot by his own free will and ability " reinstate himself in the favor of God"; that " God elected, or chose, his people in Christ before the foundation of the world"; that sinners are justified " only by the righteousness of Christ, imputed to them "; that the saints will finally persevere and " not one of them will ever be finally lost"; that " baptism, the Lord's Supper, and washing the saints' feet are ordinances of the gospel and should be continued until Christ's second coming"; that " the institutions of the day [church societies] are the works of man"; that it is therefore " wrong to join them," and that no fellowship should be had with them. An article of the constitution declines " fellowship with any church or churches " which support any " missionary, Bible, tract, or Sunday-school union society or advocates State conventions or theological schools," or " any other society " formed " under the pretense of circulating the gospel of Christ." The Primitive Baptists have no State conventions or theological seminaries. They acknowledge no other mode of baptism than immersion, and insist that only believers are proper subjects of it, that it is a prerequisite to the Lord's Supper, and that no minister has a right to administer the ordinances unless he has been " called of God," " come under the imposition of hands by a presbytery," and is " in fellowship with the church of which he is a member."

The denomination is represented in twenty-eight States and the District of Columbia. Its strongholds are: Georgia, 18,535; Alabama, 14,903; Tennessee, 13,972; North Carolina, 11,740; and Kentucky, 10,665. It has little strength in any Northern State except Indiana and Illinois. The total of members is 121,347. There are 3222 organizations which have 2849 edifices, with a seating capacity of 899,273 and a value of $1,649,851. The average seating capacity is 312 and the average value $580.

According to the Baptist Almanac of 1844, there were in that year 184 Primitive Baptist associations, with 1622 churches, 900 ordained ministers, and 61,162 members. If these returns were correct they have gained since that date 1600 churches and about 60,000 members. While their associations usually print annual minutes, which give statistics of membership and number of churches, no general returns for the denomination are published. For many years its membership has been estimated at 45,000 by statisticians of other churches. The census tables show that this estimate was wide of the mark. There are 279 associations, of which 15 are colored. Colored members are not numerous.

SUMMARY BY STATES.

STATES.	Organizations.	Church Edifices.	Seating Capacity.	Value of Church Property.	Communicants.
Alabama..........	360	325	105,076	$125,364	14,903
Arkansas	121	93	21,708	29,032	2,994
Delaware	6	7	1,550	19,000	183
District of Columbia	2	..	......	......	34
Florida	67	65	15,820	27,525	1,997
Georgia...........	483	475	168,935	210,455	18,535
Illinois............	160	132	40,100	93,100	5,301
Indiana...........	144	128	50,024	123,550	7,078
Iowa	34	15	5,300	9,950	853
Kansas	19	7	2,300	10,100	468
Kentucky	225	208	60,580	151,425	10,665
Louisiana	43	42	14,775	18,955	1,602
Maine	3	3	625	3,300	137
Maryland	16	15	3,325	27,950	373
Massachusetts	1	1	150	5,500	10
Mississippi	109	104	26,620	38,600	3,259
Missouri	129	93	28,250	83,975	3,763
Nebraska	2	1	300	800	40
New Jersey........	4	4	1,400	8,000	258
New York.........	31	26	8,700	84,700	1,019
North Carolina	311	294	89,800	129,695	11,740
Ohio	139	138	40,285	123,190	4,262
Pennsylvania	15	10	3,420	14,100	314
South Carolina	23	23	5,750	7,050	531
Tennessee.........	316	290	97,165	147,455	13,972
Texas	156	91	27,220	34,675	4,201
Virginia	234	191	62,195	93,205	9,950
West Virginia	65	64	16,700	24,700	2,777
Wisconsin.........	4	4	1,200	4,500	128
Total	3,222	2,849	899,273	$1,649,851	121,347

13.—THE OLD TWO-SEED-IN-THE-SPIRIT PREDESTINARIAN BAPTISTS.

These are very conservative Baptists, who are not in fellowship with the Regular or Missionary, nor with the Primitive or any other body of Baptists. They are strongly Calvinistic, holding firmly to the doctrine of predestination, as their name indicates. The phrase " Two Seed " is understood to indicate their belief that there are two seeds —one of evil and one of good. This doctrine is generally accredited to Elder Daniel Parker, a native of Virginia, who was ordained in Tennessee in 1806, and labored in that State till 1817, in Illinois till 1836, and then in Texas, where he died. He published in 1826 a pamphlet which set forth the two-seed doctrine, and in 1829 another, entitled " Second Dose of the Doctrine of Two Seeds." The following explanation of the doctrine has been given by a writer who had access to the pamphlets and other writings relating to it :

" The essence of good is God ; the essence of evil is the devil. Good angels are emanations from or particles of God; evil angels are particles of the devil. When God created Adam and Eve they were endowed with an emanation from himself, or particles of God were included in their constitution. They were wholly good. Satan, however, infused into them particles of his essence, by which they were corrupted. In the beginning God had appointed that Eve should bring forth only a certain number of offspring ; the same provision applied to each of her daughters. But when the particles of evil essence had been infused by Satan, the conception of Eve and of her daughters was increased. They were now required to bear the original number, who were styled the seed of God, and an additional number, who were called the seed of the serpent.

" The seed of God constituted a part of the body of Christ. For them the atonement was absolute; they would all be saved. The seed of the serpent did not partake of the benefits of the atonement, and would all be lost. All the manifestations of good or evil in men are but displays of the essence that has been infused into them. The Christian warfare is a conflict between these essences."

Not all the associations accept the peculiar title given above. Some call themselves simply "Regular," others, "Regular Predestinarian," and still others, "Regular Two-Seed Predestinarian Primitive Baptists." Their articles of faith also vary in phraseology. One set is quite brief, having only ten articles; another is more extended and embraces twelve articles. The latter declares that God is the Creator of all things and governs all things in righteousness; that man was created holy, but by sin fell into a depraved state, from which he is utterly unable to extricate himself; that God's elect were chosen in Christ before the world began, and "appointed to faith and obedience in love" by the Spirit of God because of the "righteousness, life, death, resurrection, and ascension" of Christ; that God's elect will in due time be effectually called and regenerated, the righteousness of God being imputed to them; that they will never finally fall away; that good works are the fruits of faith and grace in the heart and follow after regeneration; that ministers should receive "legal authority" through the imposition of the hands of a presbytery acting for a gospel church, and should be subject to the discipline of the church; that the "eternal work of the Holy Spirit" is manifested externally as well as internally, in experimental religion and the call to the ministry, and the true church should distinguish itself from all "false sects," and have no fellowship with them; that the church is a spiritual kingdom which men in a state of nature cannot see, and it should therefore receive as members only those who have hope in Christ and an experimental knowledge of salvation; that the ceremony of feet-washing ought to be observed, and that the joys of the righteous and the punishment of the wicked will be endless.

Two-Seed Predestinarian Baptists differ from Primitive Baptists concerning the doctrine of Predestination. The former hold, according to the statements of one of their prominent elders, that God predestined all his children to eternal life, and the devil and all his spiritual children to the eternal kingdom of darkness; that he foreordained all events whatever, from the creation to the consummation of all things, not suffering, in his infinite wisdom and perfect knowledge, anything to occur to change his plans. The Primitive Baptists hold, as explained by the same authority, that while God predestined some to eternal life, his predestination did not extend absolutely to all things, for this doctrine would, they insist, blasphemously impute to the Almighty the existence of evil, and do away with sin and human accountability. Some of the Old Two-Seed Baptists claim Peter Waldo, John Calvin, Wyclif, Knox, and Bunyan as " elders " who held the true faith as to the two seeds, and say that Arminius was the great corrupter of sound doctrine on this subject.

Many of the Two-Seed Baptists are strongly opposed to a paid ministry. They hold that the calling of the ministry is "to comfort Zion, feed the flock, and contend earnestly for the faith once delivered to the saints." They are antinomians, and do not believe that the help of a minister is needed by the Saviour to reach and save sinners. He is a full and complete Saviour and carries on the work of salvation without the help of men. " Modern institutions," such as Sunday-schools, theological seminaries, Bible and missionary societies, are regarded with marked disfavor, as among the Primitive Baptists.

There are 50 associations, with 473 organizations, 397 church edifices, valued at $172,230, and 12,851 communicants. Though the communicants are scattered over twenty-four States, they are most numerous in Texas, Tennessee, Kentucky, Mississippi, and Arkansas. The average seating capacity of the edifices is 339, and the average value $434. There are 75 halls, etc., with a seating capacity of 5285.

SUMMARY BY STATES.

STATES.	Organizations.	Church Edifices.	Seating Capacity.	Value of Church Property.	Communicants.
Alabama..........	24	24	4,900	$7,050	538
Arkansas.	62	58	24,880	30,800	1,230
Florida	4	4	800	400	39
Georgia...........	18	18	4,900	4,950	330
Idaho.............	2	2	550	700	61
Illinois............	3	1	200	800	51
Indiana...........	14	14	5,000	6,700	346
Iowa	1	..	.....	.....	10
Kansas	8	2	500	600	162
Kentucky	58	58	21,700	29,450	2,401
Louisiana	10	10	2,050	1,900	170
Maine	3	3	1,000	1,400	115
Mississippi	26	26	6,800	10,250	840
Missouri	32	23	7,900	9,050	668
New York.........	3	3	1,300	1,900	96
North Carolina	9	3	850	680	183
Ohio	1	1	300	400	33
Oregon	15	2	1,400	1,800	194
Pennsylvania	5	5	4,900	4,000	264
Tennessee	37	36	13,900	16,800	1,270
Texas	101	82	23,075	31,650	2,831
Virginia	7	2	675	1,050	142
Washington	5	1	150	400	71
West Virginia	25	19	7,000	9,500	806
Total	473	397	134,730	$172,230	12,851

The following table gives a summary of all Baptist bodies. The returns in one or two cases are somewhat fuller than those of the census.

SUMMARY BY STATES OF ALL BAPTIST BODIES.

STATES.	Organizations.	Church Edifices.	Seating Capacity.	Value of Church Property.	Communicants.
Alabama........	3,302	3,109	906,734	$2,110,362	258,405
Arizona........	6	4	875	11,200	197
Arkansas	2,279	1,780	518,813	1,066,104	128,724
California	165	123	34,925	763,860	11,383
Colorado.......	54	40	10,935	440,000	4,944
Connecticut	139	142	48,280	1,656,750	22,600
Delaware	19	23	6,332	184,300	2,006
District of Columbia.......	63	51	26,500	914,150	19,372
Florida	807	699	151,843	375,936	41,647
Georgia........	3,966	3,895	1,237,431	3,109,390	357,241
Idaho..........	23	13	2,930	27,200	745
Illinois.........	1,324	1,163	352,133	3,681,360	109,640
Indiana........	829	763	255,604	1,627,297	70,380
Indian Territory	181	110	18,485	35,765	9,147
Iowa...........	500	393	104,771	1,242,690	33,962
Kansas	617	364	95,715	921,958	34,665
Kentucky	2,273	2,024	662,455	3,020,742	229,524
Louisiana	1,441	1,376	321,426	988,967	98,552
Maine	523	461	131,224	1,511,000	35,463
Maryland.......	104	100	37,659	831,275	16,238
Massachusetts ..	340	364	149,004	6,301,530	62,966
Michigan	523	466	130,680	2,135,694	39,580
Minnesota	229	187	46,460	1,204,889	16,441
Mississippi	2,679	2,562	734,185	1,433,332	224,801
Missouri	2,355	1,755	536,240	2,980,316	159,371
Montana.......	14	11	2,950	89,000	683
Nebraska	284	186	42,280	549,010	13,481
Nevada	9	1	500	7,000	63
New Hampshire	179	186	61,635	964,050	16,772
New Jersey.....	232	261	97,375	3,020,913	39,760
New Mexico....	15	4	1,250	22,000	355
New York......	1,071	1,079	363,323	13,625,588	142,736
North Carolina .	3,124	3,048	1,098,084	2,556,147	310,920
North Dakota ..	54	33	7,665	90,300	2,298
Ohio	885	828	240,415	2,819,828	69,093
Oklahoma......	1	....	....	....	316

SUMMARY BY STATES OF ALL BAPTIST BODIES.—*Continued.*

STATES.	Organi- zations.	Church Edifices.	Seating Ca- pacity.	Value of Church Property.	Com- muni- cants.
Oregon	123	71	19,140	$319,125	5,500
Pennsylvania ...	720	704	240,204	6,088,322	86,620
Rhode Island...	113	117	41,000	1,450,117	17,293
South Carolina..	1,676	1,633	521,009	1,606,385	203,959
South Dakota ..	90	59	12,236	239,675	4,052
Tennessee......	2,413	2,193	720,815	2,566,373	186,174
Texas	4,061	2,551	667,120	2,119,096	248,523
Utah	4	3	700	65,000	327
Vermont.......	143	137	37,234	678,875	11,258
Virginia	2,038	1,938	689,609	3,152,582	303,134
Washington....	95	56	12,690	242,160	3,941
West Virginia ..	681	485	140,220	552,365	45,414
Wisconsin......	254	235	59,906	964,570	17,041
Wyoming......	9	3	525	27,875	262
Total	43,029	37,789	11,599,534	$82,392,423	3,717,969

CHAPTER III.

THE RIVER BRETHREN.

THOSE who first constituted the body popularly known as River Brethren came to this country from Switzerland in 1750 and settled near the Susquehanna River in eastern Pennsylvania. They have no history to which the inquirer can refer, and they are able to give few particulars of the early life of the denomination. They were, it is supposed, Mennonites. As the result of a revival movement, beginning in 1770, many of these people who had been formal in their worship became zealous believers, and organized separate congregations. The first members were baptized, it is believed, in the Susquehanna River, and the denomination thus came to be known as River Brethren. Jacob Engle was their first minister.

In their belief they hold to trine immersion, the washing of feet, nonresistance, and nonconformity to the world. In many points in belief and practice they are like the Mennonites.

I.—THE BRETHREN IN CHRIST.

This is by far the largest and best organized branch of the River Brethren. Its churches, of which there are 78, are associated in district conferences, and there is also a general conference, representing the whole body. There are twenty of the district conferences. The total of communicants is 2688. The average seating capacity of the churches is 422, and their average value $1623. There are 27 halls, etc., with a seating capacity of 1080.

SUMMARY BY STATES.

STATES.	Organi-zations.	Church Edifices.	Seating Ca-pacity.	Value of Church Property.	Com-muni-cants.
Illinois................	12	6	2,300	$13,700	181
Indiana................	7	2	700	1,800	130
Iowa	2	..	.....	.....	40
Kansas	9	5	2,150	9,500	588
Maryland	1	1	600	3,000	36
Michigan	7	2	250	550	52
New York.............	1	1	400	1,800	32
Ohio	13	9	3,900	14,100	410
Pennsylvania	26	19	8,705	28,600	1,219
Total.............	78	45	19,005	$73,050	2,688

SUMMARY BY DISTRICTS.

DISTRICTS.					
Ashland, Ohio........	3	2	500	$1,500	56
Center, Pa.............	3	..	.....	......	23
Clarence Center, N. Y...	1	1	400	1,800	32
Cumberland, Pa........	2	2	800	3,000	130
Dayton, Ohio and Ind...	6	4	1,900	8,400	235
Donegal, Pa.	2	2	1,200	4,500	222
Indiana, Ind.	6	1¾	700	1,800	120
Iowa, Iowa	2	..	.....	......	40
Lykins Valley, Pa.	5	4	1,105	4,000	216
Morrison's Cove, Pa.....	4	4	1,900	3,600	137
New Guilford, Pa. & Md.	2	2	1,000	4,200	72
North Dickinson, Kan...	5	5	2,150	9,500	289
North Franklin, Pa.	6	3	1,700	4,600	234
Pine Creek, Ill.	2	1	500	1,200	43
Port Huron, Mich.	7	2	250	550	52
Rapho, Pa.............	3	3	1,600	7,700	221
Shannon, Ill.	6	4	1,500	11,300	91
South Dickinson, Kan...	4	..	.....	......	299
Wayne, Ohio..........	5	3¼	1,500	4,200	129
Whiteside, Ill.	4	1	300	1,200	47
Total.............	78	45	19,005	$73,050	2,688

2.—THE OLD ORDER OF YORKER BRETHREN.

This branch is generally called "Yorker" Brethren, because when the River Brethren were divided in 1862 the churches in York County were not affected by the division. It is an extremely small body, holding to the original doctrines and practices of the River Brethren.

SUMMARY BY STATES.

STATES.	Organizations.	Church Edifices.	Seating Capacity.	Value of Church Property.	Communicants.
Indiana...............	1	..	..	..	12
Iowa	1	..	..	..	15
Ohio	2	..	..	..	38
Pennsylvania..........	4	..	..	..	149
Total.............	8	..	..	..	214

3.—THE UNITED ZION'S CHILDREN.

This branch is the result of a division which occurred in Dauphin County, Pa., in 1853. It has the same confession of faith as the River Brethren, and differs from them only in unimportant particulars. In observing the ceremony of feet-washing one person both washes and dries; among the River Brethren one person does the washing and another the drying. Services are held in the churches alternately every six weeks. Communion is celebrated once or twice a year.

The 25 organizations are all in Pennsylvania. They own that number of houses of worship, valued at $8300. The number of members is 525.

SUMMARY.

STATE.	Organi-zations.	Church Edifices.	Seating Capacity.	Value of Church Property.	Communicants.
Pennsylvania	25	25	3,100	$8,300	525

SUMMARY BY STATES OF ALL RIVER BRETHREN.

STATE.	Organi-zations.	Church Edifices.	Seating Capacity.	Value of Church Property.	Communicants.
Illinois............	12	6	2,300	$13,700	181
Indiana	8	2	700	1,800	142
Iowa	3	..	.....	......	55
Kansas	9	5	2,150	9,500	588
Maryland	1	1	600	3,000	36
Michigan	7	2	250	550	52
New York	1	1	400	1,800	32
Ohio	15	9	3,900	14,100	448
Pennsylvania	55	44	11,805	36,900	1,893
Total.........	111	70	22,105	$81,350	3,427

CHAPTER IV.

THE PLYMOUTH BRETHREN.

THIS body of Christians originated in several separate and spontaneous movements in 1827–30. The first public meeting held by them was in Dublin, Ireland. A large company of them was gathered in Plymouth, England, whence they are popularly called " Plymouth " Brethren, a title they do not accept. They speak of themselves as believers, Christians, saints, or Brethren. Division soon came among them, and they now exist in England in several branches. From England they came to Canada and the United States.

The Brethren accept the Scriptures as their only guide, acknowledging no creeds, rituals, or anything " which savors of reason or mere expediency." They do not allow that ordination is necessary to the ministry. They hold that gift is sufficient authorization for the exercise of the privilege of the priesthood of all believers, the Holy Spirit being the guide. Hence they have no presiding officers in their public meetings. Woman's sphere is considered as private.

They accept the evangelical doctrines of the Trinity, of the sinless humanity and absolute divinity of Christ, and of Christ's atonement by his sacrificial death, and hold that the Holy Spirit is present in the believer and in the church, and that believers are eternally secure. They look for the personal premillennial coming of Christ, and believe that the punishment of the wicked will be eternal.

Their view of the church is that it is one and indivisible. Christ is the head of it, the Holy Spirit the bond of union, and every believer a member.   It was begun at Pentecost and will be completed at the second advent.

They regard the various denominations as based upon creeds, an ordained ministry, and separate organizations, and do not therefore fellowship them.   They meet every Sunday to " break bread," which is the term they use to designate the sacrament of the Lord's Supper.   Other meetings are held for Bible study and prayer, and, when-ever occasion offers, for the unconverted.   They own no church edifices, but meet in halls and private houses.

The divisions in England are partly reproduced in the United States.   The last division in this country, by which the third and fourth branches were created out of the third, was due to a question of belief.   The following are the branches, the Roman numerals being introduced for the sake of distinction:

Plymouth Brethren I.
Plymouth Brethren II.
Plymouth Brethren III.
Plymouth Brethren IV.

I.—THE PLYMOUTH BRETHREN I.

This is the main body of Brethren.   They are regarded as more conservative than the second branch, but less so than the third and fourth branches.   They have 109 assemblies or organizations, with 2279 members, who are divided among twenty-seven States and the District of

Columbia. As the Plymouth Brethren have no houses of worship, and consequently no church property, those columns are omitted, and the table is arranged to show the number of halls occupied and their seating capacity.

SUMMARY BY STATES.

STATES, ETC.	Organi-zations.	Halls, etc.	Seating Ca-pacity.	Com-muni-cants.
California	4	4	105	49
Colorado	1	1	90	14
Delaware	3	3	320	44
District of Columbia	1	1	25	8
Florida	1	1	150	75
Georgia	2	2	60	17
Illinois	5	5	550	158
Indiana	1	1	100	14
Iowa	9	9	490	163
Kansas	1	1	16	6
Kentucky	1	1	25	5
Maine	1	1	20	5
Maryland	1	1	30	24
Massachusetts	7	7	316	119
Michigan	9	9	637	192
Minnesota	11	11	850	243
Missouri	2	2	350	151
Nebraska	1	1	25	9
New Hampshire	1	1	80	15
New Jersey	9	9	770	213
New York	19	18	1,600	494
North Carolina	1	1	25	3
Ohio	2	2	37	5
Pennsylvania	11	11	572	164
Texas	1	1	20	6
Vermont	1	1	20	4
Washington	2	2	40	19
Wisconsin	1	1	120	70
Total	109	108	7,423	2,289

2.—THE PLYMOUTH BRETHREN II.

Those constituting this branch are often called the "Open Brethren," because they are regarded as less strict in discipline than either of the other three branches. They also hold a somewhat different view of the ministry, a view approaching that common among the denominations which have regular pastors. The column headed " church prop-erty " represents furniture.

They have 88 organizations and 2419 members, and are represented in twenty-three States, their chief strength being in Illinois.

SUMMARY BY STATES.

STATES.	Organi-zations.	Halls, etc.	Seating Ca-pacity.	Value of Church Property.	Com-muni-cants.
Arkansas	1	1	....	....	3
California	4	4	515	$90	115
Colorado	1	1	100	....	13
Illinois	13	13	1,350	250	410
Indiana	5	5	450	150	79
Iowa	2	2	250	....	48
Kansas	6	6	800	....	115
Louisiana	1	1	100	....	20
Massachusetts	6	6	750	650	274
Michigan	6	6	700	....	170
Minnesota	4	4	400	25	95
Missouri	2	2	200	....	60
Nebraska	4	4	....	....	47
New Jersey	4	4	700	....	85
New York	8	8	975	100	353
North Dakota	1	1	....	....	6
Ohio	3	3	175	....	72
Oregon	1	1	....	....	10
Pennsylvania	5	5	600	....	214
Rhode Island	3	3	200	....	55
Texas	4	4	300	....	105
Virginia	3	3	260	....	50
Washington	1	1	100	....	20
Total	88	88	8,925	$1,265	2,419

3.—THE PLYMOUTH BRETHREN III.

These are the strictest division of the Brethren. Their separation from the Brethren of the first and largest division some years ago was the result of a controversy on a point of doctrine and a matter of discipline. They claim that such divine power is vested in the church, that all the Brethren are under moral obligation to submit to a decision rendered by the church, even though the decision were regarded as unjust.

They have 86 organizations and 1235 members. Most of them are to be found in the State of Illinois.

SUMMARY BY STATES.

STATES.	Organizations.	Halls, etc.	Seating Capacity.	Value of Church Property.	Communicants.
California	4	4	100	....	40
Colorado	1	1	200	....	35
Connecticut	3	3	....	....	16
Florida	4	4	100	....	33
Georgia	4	4	100	....	32
Illinois	9	9	380	....	234
Iowa	6	6	800	....	166
Kansas	6	6	150	....	79
Louisiana	1	1	....	....	2
Maryland	1	1	....	....	12
Massachusetts	4	4	100	....	59
Michigan	4	4	80	$200	47
Minnesota	1	1	....	....	12
Missouri	2	2	....	....	18
Nebraska	6	6	....	....	50
New Hampshire	1	1	....	....	4
New Jersey	5	5	270	....	83
New York	4	4	75	....	76
North Dakota	3	3	....	....	29
Ohio	3	3	100	....	89
Oregon	1	1	....	....	12
Pennsylvania	4	4	180	....	57
Rhode Island	1	1	....	....	11
Tennessee	1	1	....	....	8
Vermont	1	1	....	....	2
Virginia	2	2	....	....	13
Washington	3	3	....	....	12
Wisconsin	1	1	85	....	4
Total	86	86	2,720	$200	1,235

4.—THE PLYMOUTH BRETHREN IV.

This branch is due to a difference arising quite recently among those formerly constituting the third division. Some held that a second impartation of divine power must be received before a believer could be said to be in full possession of eternal life. This view gave rise to various complications respecting the person of Christ and the condition of the Old Testament saints. Those who refused to accept this teaching formed new assemblies or congregations, and constitute the fourth division.

They have 31 organizations, with 718 members. They are found in fifteen States, principally in California, Ohio, and Massachusetts.

SUMMARY BY STATES.

STATES.	Organizations.	Halls, etc.	Seating Capacity.	Communicants.
California	6	6	850	137
Colorado..............	1	1	...	8
Georgia..............	1	1	...	6
Illinois..............	2	2	...	28
Indiana..............	1	1	150	35
Kansas	1	1	...	12
Maryland	2	2	300	67
Massachusetts	1	1	200	100
Michigan	2	2	200	57
Minnesota	2	2	75	37
Nebraska	2	2	...	30
New Jersey............	5	5	120	58
Ohio	3	3	100	110
Pennsylvania	1	1	100	25
South Carolina	1	1	...	8
Total.............	31	31	2,095	718

Summary by States of All Plymouth Brethren.

STATES, ETC.	Organizations.	Halls, etc.	Seating Capacity.	Value of Church Property.	Communicants.
Arkansas	I	I	,....	$90	3
California	18	18	1,570	....	341
Colorado...........	4	4	390	....	70
Connecticut	3	3	.....	....	16
Delaware...........	3	3	320	....	44
District of Columbia	I	I	25	....	8
Florida	5	5	250	....	108
Georgia.............	7	7	160	....	55
Illinois.............	29	29	2,280	250	830
Indiana	7	7	700	150	128
Iowa...............	17	17	1,540	....	377
Kansas	14	14	966	....	212
Kentucky	I	I	25	....	5
Louisiana	2	2	100	....	22
Maine	I	I	20	....	5
Maryland	4	4	330	....	103
Massachusetts	18	18	1,366	650	552
Michigan	21	21	1,617	200	466
Minnesota..........	18	18	1,325	25	387
Missouri	6	6	550	....	229
Nebraska	13	13	25	....	136
New Hampshire ...	2	2	80	....	19
New Jersey.........	23	23	1,860	100	439
New York..........	31	30	2,650	....	923
North Carolina	I	I	25	....	3
South Dakota	4	4	.....	....	35
Ohio	11	11	412	....	276
Oregon	2	2	.....	....	22
Pennsylvania	21	21	1,452	....	460
Rhode Island	4	4	200	....	66
South Carolina	I	I	.....	....	8
Tennessee	I	I	.....	....	8
Texas	5	5	320	....	111
Vermont...........	2	2	20	....	6
Virginia	5	5	260	....	63
Washington........	6	6	140	....	51
Wisconsin..........	2	2	205	....	74
Total.........	314	308	21,163	$1,465	6,661

CHAPTER V.

THE CATHOLICS.

As this term is commonly used, it applies to the Church of Rome, to the Eastern or Orthodox Churches, and to the Old and Reformed Catholic bodies, which have lately arisen. As the result of a controversy beginning in the ninth century the Christian Church was divided into the Roman and Greek Churches. The Church of Rome, which is the more numerous division, is officially called the " Holy, Catholic, Apostolic, and Roman Church," and claims to be the only church founded by Christ. It has a hierarchy, including a pope, who is supreme pontiff, a college of cardinals, and numerous archbishops and bishops. Its doctrine is expressed in the œcumenical creeds—the Apostles', the Nicene (with the *Filioque*), and the Athanasian—and in the decrees of twenty œcumenical councils, the latest of which was that of the Vatican, in 1870. The Greek Church, whose full title is " Holy, Orthodox, Catholic, Apostolic, Oriental Church," includes the Church of Russia, the Church of Greece, the Armenians, and various other divisions. The Orthodox or Eastern Church holds to the decrees and canons of the first seven œcumenical councils, accepting the Nicene Creed without the Latin *Filioque*. This creed is its chief doctrinal expression. Its highest officials are patriarchs. It has besides, metropolitans or archbishops, and bishops. The Uniates are Greek Christians who have acknowledged the supremacy of the

pope.   The Old and Reformed Catholics are bodies origi-
nating in this country in withdrawals from the Roman
Church.

I.—THE ROMAN CATHOLIC CHURCH.

The first Christian congregations organized in the territory now constituting the United States were those of the
Roman Catholic faith.   The oldest was established in St.
Augustine, Fla., shortly after that settlement was founded
in 1565.   But Catholic services were held on Florida soil
long before that date.   Missionaries accompanied the Spanish expeditions of discovery and settlement in the first half-
century after Columbus made his first voyage to America,
and these raised the cross and conducted divine worship.
John Juarez, who had been appointed by the pope Bishop
of Florida, landed with the expedition of Narvaez in 1528,
but is supposed to have been slain or to have perished from
hunger the same year.   After St. Augustine was established many companies of missionaries went out into Florida, Alabama, Georgia, and Carolina to labor among the
Indians.   The second oldest town, Santa Fé, was founded
by Spaniards in 1582.   Missionaries in connection with
Coronado's exploring expedition preached among the Indians of New Mexico forty years earlier, but they soon perished.   After the founding of Santa Fé missionary work
was more successful, and many tribes of Indians accepted
the Catholic faith.   Franciscans established missions in
California in 1601, and French priests held worship on
Neutral Island, on the coast of Maine, in 1609, and three
years later on Mount Desert Island.   Jesuit missions, begun on the upper Kennebec in 1646, were more successful

and permanent, many Indian converts being among their fruits. In 1665 Catholics sought to convert the Onondagas and other tribes in New York. Similar attempts among the Great Lakes were made as early as 1641.

The history of the Catholic Church among the English colonists began with the immigration of English and Irish Catholics to Maryland in 1634. They founded the town of St. Mary's the first year. Ten years later, as the result of a conflict with Protestant colonists, their privileges of worship were curtailed, but restored in 1646. A toleration act was passed by the legislature of Maryland in 1649, but it was repealed in 1654. The Catholics received their rights again in 1660, to be restricted once more in 1704, and these restrictions were not entirely removed until the period of the War of Independence. In Virginia, the Carolinas, Georgia, and New England severe laws were enforced against Catholics for many years. In New York, which is now the stronghold of Catholicism, there were, it is said, no more than seven Catholic families in 1696, and the few Catholics found on Manhattan Island eighty years later had to go to Philadelphia to receive the sacraments.

In 1784, at the close of the Revolutionary War, the pope appointed the Rev. John Carroll prefect apostolic. Before this date the Catholics in this country had been under the jurisdiction of the vicar apostolic of London, England. Six years later Dr. Carroll was consecrated bishop in London, and Baltimore became the first Catholic diocese. The new bishop estimated the number of Catholics in the United States at that time at about 30,000, of whom 16,000 were in Maryland, and 7000 in Pennsylvania. The rest were scattered over a broad territory stretching into the west as far as Michigan, Indiana, and Illinois. The church

was gradually extended to Kentucky (1787), South Carolina (1789), Ohio, and other parts of the country. It grew
rapidly when immigration set in from Ireland and Europe.
This has been the chief cause of the rapid increase of the
church in the last half-century. In 1807 there were about
80 churches, and a Catholic population of 150,000. In
1820 this population had doubled; in 1830 it had doubled
again. In the next decade it increased from 500,000 to
1,500,000; in 1850 it had become 3,500,000; in 1860,
4,500,000; and in 1876, 6,500,000. These figures were
given by the late Prof. A. J. Schem, who was regarded as
good authority in church statistics.

An immense territory was covered until 1808 by the
single diocese of Baltimore. In that year Baltimore became
a metropolitan see, with four suffragan bishoprics—New
York, Philadelphia, Boston, and Bardstown. The purchase
of Louisiana in 1803 had added the diocese of New Orleans,
which had been erected in 1803. In 1846 Oregon City
became a metropolitan see; in 1847 the same dignity was
conferred on St. Louis, and in 1850 Cincinnati, New York,
and New Orleans were erected into provinces. There are
now 13 provinces, the metropolitan sees being those of
Baltimore, Oregon, St. Louis, New Orleans, Cincinnati,
New York, San Francisco, Santa Fé, Philadelphia, Milwaukee, Boston, Chicago, and St. Paul. Connected with
these provinces are 66 dioceses, 5 vicariates apostolic, and
1 prefecture apostolic.

The doctrinal system of the Roman Catholic Church is
embodied in the Apostles', Nicene, and Athanasian creeds,
and the dogmatic decisions of the œcumenical councils
from 325 to 1870. The doctrine of the church is that it
consists of all who hold the true faith, receive the true sacra-

ments, and acknowledge the rule of the pope of Rome as head of the church. While the Bible, including the books commonly called apocryphal, is accepted as the Word of God, the authority of ecclesiastical tradition is honored. The church is held to be infallible; the Virgin Mary, the saints, their pictures and relics are venerated; seven sacraments—baptism, the eucharist, confirmation, penance, extreme unction, ordination, and matrimony—are administered; justification is held to be by faith and works conjoined; transubstantiation and the adoration of the elements, baptismal salvation, priestly absolution, the sacrifice of the mass, prayers for the dead, the immaculate conception of the Virgin Mary, a temporary place between heaven and hell for departed spirits, are also features of Catholic belief. The worship of the church is conducted in the Latin language according to an established ritual, the mass occupying the central place in the services.

The government of the church is hierarchical. At its head is the pope with a college of cardinals. Next in order are archbishops, who are set over provinces; bishops, who preside over dioceses; and various other ecclesiastical dignitaries, besides the heads of orders, monasteries, etc. In the ministering priesthood there are two orders—those of priest and deacon. The governing authority of each diocese is its bishop, who receives his ecclesiastical power from the pope. The government of the church in the United States is conducted through the Propaganda at Rome, the United States being regarded for this purpose as missionary territory.

In the specially difficult task of gathering the statistics of the churches, chapels, missions, and stations of the various dioceses and vicariates, the archbishops, bishops, and other ecclesiastical officers gave cordial coöperation. At the earnest request of the special agent of the Census Office they nominated to him suitable persons to do the work at his appointment and under his instruction, urged those in charge of congregations to give the information required, and most of them inspected and approved the final returns before they were certified and reported to the Census Office for acceptance.

As the Roman Catholic Church always gives in its published annual statistics the number of baptized members or population instead of communicants, the census appointee in each diocese was requested to comply with the requirements of the census schedules and furnish the number of communicants, in order that the statistics of all the denominations might be uniform. This was done in every case. According to information received from bishops, it is the custom of the church for baptized persons to make their first communion between the ages of nine and eleven years. Baptized persons below the age of nine years are not included, therefore, in the census returns. Some ecclesiastical authorities estimate that members of this class constitute about fifteen per cent. of the population of the church, which, of course, embraces both baptized members and communicants.

In order that proper significance may be given to the figures representing the seating capacity of churches, chapels, etc., it will be necessary to take into consideration the fact that in populous places from three to four and sometimes as many as six or seven services, or even more, are held in the same church on Sunday. In most Protestant churches there are two services only, and in some but one service. Separate services of the mass in Catholic churches are usually attended by different audiences. It may help to a better understanding of the matter to quote a few sentences from letters written by heads of dioceses.

Archbishop Elder, of Cincinnati, says:

"The most of our churches have at least two, often three, and as many as six masses every Sunday, and each is attended by a different body of worshipers."

Archbishop Janssens, of New Orleans, speaks of from "two, three, to six masses," and refers to the fact that many persons stand during service. In the archdiocese of Baltimore, according to the secretary of Cardinal Gibbons, there are usually four different congregations on Sunday in a single edifice. In the archdiocese of Boston there are five services in the cathedral, which has a communicant membership of 12,000, and reports 2600 seating capacity. Archbishop Corrigan, of New York, says the "same space is used over and over again by different worshipers at different hours." An examination of the returns for that see shows that of 77 churches in the city of New York, 1 has one service of the mass, 6 have two services, 4 have three, 12 have four, 17 have five, 22 have six, 10 have seven, 3 have eight, 1 has nine, and 1 has ten every Sunday. Of an equal number of churches in the rural part of the archdiocese, 26 have one mass, 24 have two masses, 11 have three, 4 have six, and 1 has five every Sunday; 4 have mass twice a month, and 5 have it once a month. Bishop McGovern, of Harrisburg, says:

"It is true there are many services in our churches, but each service is not always attended by persons who were not at another service. Some persons attend all the services. Then, again, in some of the churches many stand up for want of seats."

Bishop Phelan, of Pittsburg, writes:

" We have in this diocese about 140 churches. In some there is one, in many two, in some three, and in a couple even four morning services (masses) every Sunday. The afternoon or evening services should not count, as these worshipers are, or ought to be, the same who were present in the forenoon."

The use made of the accommodations for worshipers is also indicated by the number of communicants belonging to a parish. In many cases from 8000 to 15,000 communicants are reported for a single parish. In one diocese there is a parish, consisting entirely of Poles, which has 17,490 communicants, who are accommodated in a single church with a seating capacity of 1900. Here the proportion of communicants to seating capacity is almost as nine to one. But this is an extreme case. In Baltimore, Boston, and Chicago it is less than three to one; in New York, more than three to one; in New Orleans, nearly four to one; in Oregon, Philadelphia, St. Paul, and San Francisco, upward of two to one; in Cincinnati and Milwaukee, less than two; while in Santa Fé it is less than one. The average in the thirteen metropolitan sees is about two and a quarter to one.

The total number of communicants is 6,231,417, who are attached to 10,231 organizations (churches, chapels, and stations), making an average of 609 communicants to each congregation. Of the 10,231 organizations, 1469, or about 14.4 per cent., worship in halls, schoolhouses, or private houses, which, exclusive of private houses, represent a seating capacity of 69,159, while the 8776 edifices owned by the church have a seating capacity of 3,365,754, making a total of 3,435,913 for the whole church, which is somewhat more than half the number of communicants. Some of the parishes which have no church edifices, but use temporarily such accommodations as private houses can afford, are very large. One of these parishes reports no fewer than 14,000 communicants. In eleven of the eighty-five sees, including the archdioceses of New Orleans, Philadelphia, and San Francisco, every organization has its own church edifice.

The total value of church property, including edifices, the ground on which they stand, furniture, bells, etc., is $118,069,746. The average value of each edifice is therefore about $13,454. The metropolitan see of New York, with its 472,806 communicants, has church property valued at nearly $9,000,000; that of Chicago comes second, with property worth $6,457,064; and that of Boston third, with a total of $6,379,078. The diocese of Brooklyn comes fourth, with a valuation of $5,751,907, and Newark fifth, with $4,297,482. These five sees have more than one fourth of the entire valuation of the church.

In the distribution of communicants, the archdiocese of New York comes first, with 472,806; Boston second, with 419,660; Chicago third, with 326,640; Philadelphia fourth, with 251,162; Brooklyn (diocese) fifth, with 228,785; St. Paul sixth, with 203,484; and Baltimore seventh, with 176,578. There are twenty-two sees which contain upward of 100,000 communicants each.

In the tabulation by States the following facts appear: there are 959 organizations, with 1,153,130 communicants, in the State of New York (seven dioceses), and the value of church property is $25,769,478; in the State of Massachusetts (two dioceses) there are 614,627 communicants, belonging to 381 organizations, with church property valued at $9,816,003; in the State of Pennsylvania (five dioceses), 551,577 communicants, 654 organizations, and $10,068,770 of church property; in the State of Illinois (four dioceses), 473,324 communicants, 688 organizations, and church property valued at $9,946,819; in the State of Ohio (three dioceses), 336,114 communicants, 586 organizations, and $7,395,640 of church property. In these five States there are 3,128,772 communicants, or a little more than one half of the total for the whole church, and there is church property of the value of $62,996,710, which is considerably more than half of the total valuation.

The church is represented in every State and Territory in the country, including Alaska and the District of Columbia. It has organizations in every county but one in the six New England States; also in every county in New York, New Jersey, Wisconsin, and other States and Territories. In the six New England States there are 1,005,-120 Catholic communicants. This exceeds the total of Protestant communicants by more than 240,000. Catholic communicants exceed Protestant communicants in Massachusetts and Rhode Island, Boston and Providence being great Catholic centers; but in the other four States Protestant communicants predominate.

Embracing immigrants from nearly all the countries of Europe, the Roman Catholic is a polyglot church. Confessions are heard, among other languages, in German, Polish, Lithuanian, Hungarian, Bohemian, French, Spanish, and Italian. In the diocese of Scranton there are seven Polish, seven German, four Hungarian, one Lithuanian, one Polish and Lithuanian, and Italian, besides English congregations.

The average seating capacity of the church edifices is 384, and the average value $13,453.

SUMMARY BY STATES.

STATES.	Organizations.	Church Edifices.	Seating Capacity.	Value of Church Property.	Communicants.
Alabama........	70	42	10,520	$602,750	13,230
Alaska..........	6	5	500	9,700	559
Arizona.........	52	22	6,490	124,500	19,000
Arkansas	47	47	8,580	219,100	3,845
California	249	243	83,740	2,627,950	156,846
Colorado........	110	94	23,378	843,637	47,111
Connecticut	148	133	79,444	3,093,750	152,945
Delaware	19	16	8,780	201,500	11,776
District of Columbia	17	17	12,800	1,015,800	37,593
Florida	44	33	8,140	225,100	16,867
Georgia.........	64	44	10,746	485,123	11,228
Idaho...........	52	22	4,265	70,050	4,809
Illinois..........	688	666	235,784	9,946,819	473,324
Indiana.........	311	303	106,202	3,534,691	119,100
Indian Territory .	17	8	1,680	5,850	1,240
Iowa	445	455	138,452	3,872,400	164,522
Kansas	367	271	55,730	625,561	67,562
Kentucky	222	180	62,806	1,800,550	92,504
Louisiana	206	184	57,885	1,568,200	211,763
Maine	88	70	29,941	597,550	57,548
Maryland	180	169	60,860	2,108,670	141,410
Massachusetts ...	381	324	242,267	9,816,003	614,627
Michigan	406	360	131,641	3,671,350	222,261
Minnesota	465	404	149,085	3,514,325	271,319
Mississippi	67	60	13,448	321,525	11,348
Missouri	442	402	138,943	4,070,370	162,864
Montana........	94	40	8,668	184,100	25,149
Nebraska	213	179	38,396	1,179,160	51,503
Nevada	20	12	3,500	88,500	3,955
New Hampshire .	68	52	23,825	205,600	39,920
New Jersey......	219	191	99,290	6,050,682	222,274
New Mexico.....	317	306	93,770	296,755	100,576
New York.......	959	877	480,974	25,769,478	1,153,130
North Carolina ..	60	24	4,935	90,262	2,640
North Dakota....	115	60	13,615	171,550	26,427
Ohio	586	515	197,813	7,395,640	336,114
Oklahoma	13	6	1,300	4,300	1,270
Oregon	95	48	11,462	290,090	30,231
Pennsylvania	654	610	305,014	10,068,770	551,577
Rhode Island....	51	52	40,625	2,295,700	96,755
South Carolina ..	66	23	7,425	384,500	5,360

SUMMARY BY STATES.—*Continued.*

STATES.	Organizations.	Church Edifices.	Seating Capacity.	Value of Church Property.	Communicants.
South Dakota ...	177	100	19,218	$246,030	25,729
Tennessee	60	36	11,105	434,200	17,950
Texas	263	189	55,925	1,018,800	99,691
Utah	28	12	2,210	68,000	5,958
Vermont........	79	77	31,101	866,400	42,810
Virginia	69	44	14,811	458,800	12,356
Washington.....	86	58	11,345	156,050	20,848
West Virginia ...	67	62	16,229	340,155	15,653
Wisconsin	646	620	189,831	4,859,950	249,164
Wyoming.......	67	9	1,260	173,450	7,185
Total.......	10,231	8,776	3,365,754	$118,069,746	6,231,417

SUMMARY BY DIOCESES.

ARCHDIOCESES, DIOCESES, ETC.	Organizations.	Church Edifices.	Seating Capacity.	Value of Church Property.	Communicants.
ARCHDIOCESES.					
Baltimore	174	170	69,995	$3,078,020	176,578
Boston..........	204	166	142,209	6,379,078	419,660
Chicago	278	271	115,065	6,457,064	326,640
Cincinnati.......	172	164	68,200	3,269,970	132,220
Milwaukee	264	262	93,011	3,074,230	119,271
New Orleans	148	148	50,415	1,535,900	181,964
New York.......	275	234	328,303	8,907,525	472,806
Oregon	95	48	11,462	290,090	30,231
Philadelphia.....	153	157	107,667	3,388,000	251,162
Saint Louis......	297	267	102,025	2,778,545	123,230
Saint Paul	231	201	91,180	2,474,435	203,484
San Francisco ...	124	123	49,805	2,021,260	112,180
Santa Fé........	290	289	80,370	272,055	89,261
DIOCESES.					
Albany	153	124	64,647	3,164,700	130,660
Alton...........	141	138	40,168	1,216,480	57,285
Belleville........	95	93	25,994	916,400	25,900
Brooklyn........	109	113	73,133	5,751,907	228,785
Buffalo.........	156	150	72,639	3,403,900	134,518
Burlington	79	77	31,101	866,400	42,810
Charleston	66	23	7,425	384,500	5,360
Cheyenne.......	67	9	1,260	173,450	7,185
Cleveland.......	297	250	92,062	2,805,200	155,351

SUMMARY BY DIOCESES.—*Continued.*

ARCHDIOCESES, DIOCESES, ETC.	Organizations.	Church Edifices.	Seating Capacity.	Value of Church Property.	Communicants.
DIOCESES.					
Columbus........	117	101	37,551	$1,320,470	48,543
Concordia.......	80	46	9,700	108,011	11,500
Covington	98	62	18,606	380,200	25,793
Davenport	138	136	38,536	1,008,165	47,910
Denver	110	94	23,378	843,637	47,111
Detroit	185	182	68,139	2,260,000	102,551
Dubuque........	303	319	99,916	2,864,235	116,612
Duluth	63	41	9,086	119,375	13,589
Erie.............	120	103	36,988	873,300	51,017
Fort Wayne.....	148	135	42,311	1,376,000	45,229
Galveston	106	81	21,325	601,000	36,013
Grand Rapids ...	161	115	39,652	890,250	72,830
Green Bay	187	181	54,329	991,010	70,665
Harrisburg......	61	55	23,673	877,860	26,262
Hartford	148	133	79,444	3,093,750	152,945
Helena	94	40	8,668	184,100	25,149
Jamestown	113	60	13,615	171,550	26,227
Kansas City	79	77	21,809	828,025	23,626
La Crosse	195	177	42,491	794,710	59,228
Leavenworth	208	176	38,945	392,800	48,906
Lincoln	96	76	18,774	264,200	22,131
Little Rock......	47	46½	8,580	219,100	3,845
Louisville	125	119	44,260	1,420,850	66,801
Manchester	68	52	23,825	205,600	39,920
Marquette.......	60	63	23,850	521,100	46,880
Mobile..........	82	48	11,820	647,550	16,109
Monterey and Los Angeles	73	68	19,470	233,690	32,881
Nashville	59	35	11,045	433,700	17,860
Natchez.........	68	61	13,598	322,525	11,427
Natchitoches	57	35	7,320	31,300	29,720
Nesqually.......	86	58	11,345	156,050	20,848
Newark.........	116	108½	63,462	4,297,482	162,802
Ogdensburg.....	86	83	34,694	836,246	60,579
Omaha	117	103	19,622	914,960	29,372
Peoria	174	164	54,557	1,356,875	63,499
Pittsburg........	198	185	78,986	3,307,025	134,976
Portland	88	70	29,941	597,550	57,548
Providence	86	87	61,265	3,374,500	156,850
Richmond	58	46	15,475	477,500	13,261
Rochester	91	91	45,775	1,907,300	65,670
Sacramento	56	56	15,865	421,000	13,805

SUMMARY BY DIOCESES.—*Continued.*

ARCHDIOCESES, DIOCESES, ETC. DIOCESES.	Organizations.	Church Edifices.	Seating Capacity.	Value of Church Property.	Communicants.
Saint Augustine..	32	27	6,840	$180,300	13,988
Saint Cloud	73	70	19,408	402,765	19,998
Saint Joseph.....	66	58	15,109	463,800	16,008
San Antonio.....	116	68	26,700	326,500	30,870
Savannah	64	44	10,746	485,123	11,228
Scranton........	122	110	57,700	1,622,585	88,160
Sioux Falls......	179	100	19,218	246,030	25,920
Springfield	142	123	79,418	2,358,125	134,872
Syracuse........	89	82	41,783	1,712,900	60,112
Trenton	103	83	35,828	1,753,200	59,472
Vancouver Island	6	5	40	9,700	559
Vincennes	163	168	80	2,158,691	73,871
Wheeling.......	77	59	175	309,455	14,698
Wichita.........	79	49	.....	124,750	7,156
Wilmington	43	33	125	259,950	14,251
Winona.........	98	92	692	517,750	34,248
VICARIATES APOSTOLIC.					
Arizona.........	85	44	980	164,300	36,905
Brownsville......	35	35	.....	76,200	26,218
Idaho..........	52	22	980	70,050	4,809
North Carolina ..	60	24	225	90,262	2,640
Utah	44	20	1,355	108,500	7,893
PREFECTURE.					
Indian Territory.	30	14	200	10,150	2,510
Total.......	10,231	8,776	3,365,754	$118,069,746	6,231,417

2.—THE GREEK CATHOLIC CHURCH (UNIATES).

The Greek Catholic Church, commonly called Uniates, represents a body quite numerous in Austria, Hungary, and other eastern countries in Europe. This body is in communion with the Church of Rome, holding, contrary to the other Greek churches of the East, to the procession of the Holy Spirit from the Son as well as from the Father, in accordance with the belief of the Latin Church, but maintaining otherwise its ancient discipline, allowing the lower clergy to marry, administering the communion in both kinds (bread and wine) to the laity, and using the Greek language in its ritual. The congregations, whose statistics are given herewith, are not in full ecclesiastical connection with the dioceses of the Roman Catholic Church, and are therefore given separately.

SUMMARY BY STATES.

STATES.	Organizations.	Church Edifices.	Seating Capacity.	Value of Church Property.	Communicants.
Illinois.............	1	..	.....	......	2,000
Minnesota.........	1	1	600	$3,000	450
New Jersey........	2	2	740	11,400	1,000
Pennsylvania	10	10	3,888	48,900	7,400
Total	14	13	5,228	$63,300	10,850

3.—THE RUSSIAN ORTHODOX CHURCH.

The full title of this body is the " Holy, Orthodox, Catholic, Apostolic, Oriental Church." It arose in the middle ages from the Filioque controversy, there being a difference of doctrine between the eastern and western Christians of Europe concerning the procession of the Holy Spirit. The Western Church maintains that the Holy Spirit proceeds from the Father and the Son; the Eastern that the procession is from the Father alone. The chief governing body of the Russian branch of the Greek Church is the holy synod at St. Petersburg. The churches of this faith in California and Alaska are under the ecclesiastical oversight of Bishop Vladimir, of San Francisco, and many of them are supported financially by the imperial government of Russia.

SUMMARY.

STATE AND TERRITORY.	Organizations.	Church Edifices.	Seating Capacity.	Value of Church Property.	Communicants.
Alaska............	11	22	2,900	$180,000	13,004
California	1	1	250	40,000	500
Total	12	23	3,150	$220,000	13,504

4.—THE GREEK ORTHODOX CHURCH (GREECE).

This is the national church of the kingdom of Greece. It is the same in faith as the Orthodox Church of Russia. It has one chapel in this country, in connection with the consulate of Greece in New Orleans. This chapel is under the care of Archimandrite Misael.

SUMMARY.

STATE.	Organizations.	Church Edifices.	Seating Capacity.	Value of Church Property.	Communicants.
Louisiana	1	1	75	$5,000	100

5.—THE ARMENIAN CHURCH.

The Armenian Church of Turkey is separate from both the Latin and Greek Catholic churches. As many Armenians have come to this country, congregations of them have been gathered during the past ten years in New York, Massachusetts, and Rhode Island. They have no churches of their own, but meet for worship in chapels owned by the Protestant Episcopal Church. Their services are held in the Armenian language.

SUMMARY BY STATES.

STATES.	Organizations.	Communicants.
Massachusetts.............	3	195
New York	1	70
Rhode Island	2	70
Total	6	335

6.—THE OLD CATHOLIC CHURCH.

The Old Catholic churches in this country are due to the Old Catholic movement in Europe, with which they are in sympathy in doctrine and polity. They have a bishop or archbishop—Vilatte—consecrated May 1, 1892, by a prelate of the Jacobite Church in India. Archbishop Vilatte received orders in Switzerland as deacon and priest in 1885 at the hands of the Old Catholic bishop of Berne, in that city. The Old Catholics hold that the pope is a bishop simply, but is entitled to the primacy of honor. They agree with the Greek Church in rejecting *filioque* in the Creed, acknowledge seven sacraments, revere the monastic life, and venerate saints, angels, and sacred icons.

SUMMARY.

STATE.	Organizations.	Church Edifices.	Seating Capacity.	Value of Church Property.	Communicants.
Wisconsin.........	4	3	700	$13,320	665

7.—THE REFORMED CATHOLIC CHURCH.

This body is Catholic only in name and origin. It is the result of a movement begun in New York City ten or twelve years ago. Priests of the Roman Catholic Church who had renounced that communion adopted Protestant doctrines, and entered upon an evangelical work, chiefly among Roman Catholics. There are congregations in connection with the movement in New York, Massachusetts, Pennsylvania, and Illinois. It has no church edifices.

SUMMARY BY STATES.

STATES.	Organizations.	Halls, etc.	Seating Capacity.	Communicants.
Illinois	1	1	400	150
Massachusetts.........	2	2	1,100	250
New York	4	4	1,500	450
Pennsylvania	1	1	600	150
Total	8	8	3,600	1,000

As the Roman is the chief Catholic body, the other six branches having in all only 45 organizations, it seems unnecessary to give a table of all Catholic bodies by States. The totals are as follows: organizations, 10,276; church edifices, 8816; seating capacity, 3,374,907; value of church property, $118,371,366; communicants, 6,257,871.

CHAPTER VI.

THE CATHOLIC APOSTOLIC CHURCH.

In 1830 and 1831 several Presbyterians in Scotland and London prayed for a restoration of the "gifts of the Spirit." Members of the Episcopal Church were at the same time looking for such manifestations. In response, gifts of "tongues and prophesyings" came, it is said, upon a number of people, some of whom were connected with a Presbyterian church in London, of which the Rev. Edward Irving was pastor. Mr. Irving was identified with the movement, and has often been spoken of as the founder of the Catholic Apostolic Church. But its representatives, while cordially recognizing his services, do not so regard him. The spiritual manifestations were "accompanied by many works of divine power, such as the healing of the sick"; and in 1832, after the "reality of the prophetic gift had been fully established by the experience of almost three years," the office of apostle was revived, a layman of the Church of England being the first person designated by the Holy Ghost to fill it. Others were designated from time to time until the number was completed and there were twelve. Several congregations were organized, and in time the movement extended to other countries.

The first church in the United States was constituted in Potsdam, N. Y., and the second in New York City in 1851.

The Catholic Apostolic Church accepts the three œcumenical creeds—the Apostles', Nicene, and Athanasian—

holds to the plenary inspiration of the Scriptures, and also to the traditions of the church as sources whence the doctrine of Christ is to be derived. It regards baptism as an ordinance for the conveyance of the new or resurrection life, and the Lord's Supper as a sacrament for the nourishing and strengthening of that life. It believes that the gift of the Spirit is conveyed by the laying on of apostles' hands. The doctrine of predestination is accepted, although it is denied that God's mercies are limited to the elect.

In its system of worship the Eucharist has the central place. It is celebrated every Sunday. There is also a daily service, morning and evening. A full ritual is used in public worship.

Apostles, prophets, evangelists, and angels or chief pastors are recognized as constituting a fourfold ministry. Angels are pastors of local churches, in which there are also elders, deacons, and deaconesses. Each church is regarded as complete in itself.

The Catholic Apostolic Church has 10 organizations and 1394 members. The average seating capacity of its church edifices is 250, and their average value $22,017. There are 7 halls, with a seating capacity of 350.

SUMMARY BY STATES.

STATES.	Organizations.	Church Edifices.	Seating Capacity.	Value of Church Property.	Communicants.
California	1	..	....	$800	88
Connecticut	3	1	300	3,250	186
Illinois............	1	..	....	6,500	155
Massachusetts	1	..	....	500	70
New York.........	3	2	450	55,000	822
Pennsylvania	1	..	....	......	73
Total	10	3	750	$66,050	1,394

CHAPTER VII.

CHINESE TEMPLES.

EVERY Chinese temple is a house of prayer or worship, but no sermon is preached, no priest installed, no religious instruction given, and no seating accommodations provided. There is always at least one shrine, the more frequented temples having several, so that a number of persons can perform the usual ceremony, each for himself, without being obliged to take turns. The worshipers do not meet in a body, nor is any particular time set for devotions. When about to enter upon a new enterprise or to take a journey, or when in doubt concerning any particular course of action, the Chinese are careful to consult their gods and patron saints. Every worshiper provides himself with incense sticks, candles, and sacrificial papers, which are generally to be had of attendants at small cost. Offerings of wine and meat are added on special occasions. The candles and incense sticks are lighted and placed in their proper receptacles. If wine is used, it is put in minute cups scarcely larger than thimbles, and these are ranged in a row before the shrine. The meat offerings may be roast chicken, roast pig, or any other table luxury. When everything is properly placed the genuflexions begin and the request is presented. If the answer required is a simple affirmative or negative, the worshiper drops a pair of lenticular pieces of wood on the floor a number of times and calculates the answer from the frequency with which each face turns up. Another method of obtaining responses, particularly when fuller responses are desired, is by shaking a box filled with numbered slips of bamboo, one of which will fall out, and then consulting a book containing numbered answers in Chinese verse.

The interior of Chinese temples is often highly decorated. The walls and ceilings are hung with tablets having inscriptions in the Chinese character, and there are often rows of lanterns and embroidered silk umbrellas. Fine wood carving is also to be seen. The decorations are the gifts of worshipers.

Most Chinese temples are free to all. No register is kept of members. Of the four temples in New York City one, Chung-wa-kung-saw, claims 7000 worshipers; Chap-sing-tong, 700; Hok-san-kung-saw, 1000; Lung-kong-kung-saw, 1000. Chung-wa-kung-saw is an organization in which every Chinaman in New York is supposed to be interested. Chap-sing-tong admits laundrymen only, and the other temples are supported by those who come from Hok-san and Lung-kong respectively. A laundryman from the district of Hok-san may therefore be a member of three of the temples. For this reason no statistics of members can be given.

Chinese temples are usually well supported. The revenues are derived largely from the privilege, sold at auction to the highest bidder, of selling the articles of worship, which every worshiper must have. Thus the privilege of selling for the Lung-kong-kung-saw of San Francisco brought in 1890 $12,365.50, and that for the How-wang-mew in the same city $3961.60.

According to the returns of population there are 107,475 Chinese in the United States, of whom 72,472 are in California, 9540 in Oregon, 3260 in Washington, and 2935, the next largest number, in New York. In view of the fact that one of the four temples in New York City claims 7000 worshipers, while the whole State has a Chinese population of less than 3000, there would seem to be a large discrepancy. If that one temple has 7000 worshipers, the number of visitors must be greater than the resident Chinese population. Doubtless 7000 is the number that worship in the temple in the course of a year. In other words, the same individual is counted many times. A considerable number of the Chinese are members of Christian churches.

SUMMARY BY STATES.

STATES.	Organizations.	Temples.	Shrines.	Value of Church Property.	Communicants.
California	40	41	178	$37,000	....
Idaho.............	2	2	...	......	....
New York.........	4	3	4	25,000	....
Oregon	1	1	...	......	....
Total	47	47	182	$62,000	....

CHAPTER VIII.

THE CHRISTADELPHIANS.

JOHN THOMAS, M.D., an Englishman, came to this country in 1844, and identified himself with the Disciples of Christ. Soon after, his views changed and he became convinced by a study of the Bible that the cardinal doctrine of the existing churches correspond with those of the apostate church predicted in Scripture. He began to publish his views, and organized a number of societies in this country, Canada, and Great Britain. No name was adopted for these societies until the Civil War broke out. The members applied to the government to be relieved from military duty in consequence of conscientious scruples, and finding it necessary to have a distinctive name, that of Christadelphians, or Brothers of Christ, was adopted.

The Christadelphians do not accept the doctrine of the Trinity. They hold that Christ was Son of God and Son of man, manifesting divine power, wisdom, and goodness in working out man's salvation and attaining unto power and glory by his resurrection. He is the only medium of salvation. The Holy Spirit is an effluence of divine power. They believe in the natural mortality of the soul, and that eternal life is only given by God to the righteous; that the devil is the evil principle of human nature; that Christ will shortly come personally to the earth and set up the kingdom of God in place of human governments; that this

kingdom will be established in Canaan, where the twelve
tribes of Israel will be gathered; and that at the end of a
thousand years judgment will be pronounced upon all, the
just receiving eternal life, the unjust eternal death.

The Christadelphians practice immersion. They have
no ordained ministers. Those who speak and conduct
services are called "lecturing" or "serving" brethren.
Their meetings are all held, with four exceptions, in public
halls or private houses. They have in all 63 organizations,
with 1277 members, who are scattered over twenty States.
There are 59 halls, with a seating capacity of 6085.

SUMMARY BY STATES.

STATES.	Organi-zations.	Church Edifices.	Seating Ca-pacity.	Value of Church Property.	Com-muni-cants.
Arkansas............	5	..	...	.....	74
California	2	..	...	.....	30
Colorado..........	2	..	...	.....	16
Illinois.............	8	1	100	$500	117
Iowa	5	..	...	.....	67
Kansas............	4	..	...	.....	39
Kentucky	2	1	400	500	89
Maryland	1	..	...	.....	40
Massachusetts	9	..	...	.....	245
Michigan..........	1	..	...	.....	4
Missouri	2	..	...	.....	20
New Jersey........	1	..	...	.....	90
New York.........	7	..	...	.....	92
Ohio..............	1	..	...	.....	10
Oregon............	1	..	...	.....	25
Pennsylvania	3	1	200	700	60
Texas.............	3	..	...	.....	100
Virginia...........	4	1	250	1,000	137
West Virginia	1	..	...	.....	7
Wisconsin.........	1	..	...	.....	15
Total	63	4	950	$2,700	1,277

CHAPTER IX.

I.—THE CHRISTIANS.

THIS body, which is commonly known as the Christian Connection, but owns only the simple designation "The Christians," had its beginning in the early part of the present century in the union of three distinct movements: one in which Rev. James O'Kelley, of Virginia, a Methodist, was prominent; another in which Abner Jones, M.D., of Vermont, a Baptist, was first; and a third in which Barton W. Stone, and other Presbyterian ministers in Kentucky and Ohio, coöperated. These three movements, each independent and unknown to the leaders of the others until 1806, were alike in taking the Bible as the only rule of faith, and in rejecting Calvinism. Mr. Stone and many ministers and congregations subsequently united with the Disciples of Christ, with which this denomination is often confounded. They are much alike in many respects; they have no creeds, taking the Bible simply as their rule of faith and practice; they emphasize the importance of the union of all believers in Christ; they believe that immersion is the only true form of baptism (a few ministers among the Christians also believe that sprinkling is baptism), and that believers only are its proper subjects, rejecting infant baptism.

The Christians make difference of theological views no bar to membership. Holding to the inspiration and divine authority of the Bible, they allow every one to interpret it for himself. They believe in the divinity of Christ and in his preëxistence, and that he made atonement for the sins of all men. They admit to the communion table believers of other denominations, and also receive into membership persons who do not believe in immersion.

In church government the Connection is Congregational. It has, however, annual conferences, composed of ministers and lay delegates from the churches. These conferences receive and ordain pastors, but they can pass no regulations binding on the churches. There is a general convention which meets once every four years, called the American Christian Convention, which cares for the missionary, educational, and other general interests of the Church.

At the General Convention held in Cincinnati in 1854, in consequence of the adoption of resolutions declaring against slavery, representatives of the Southern churches withdrew, the result of which was the organization of the Christian Church, South. The two bodies have agreed upon a form of union, by which each retains its general conference.

There are 75 annual conferences, covering, in whole or in part, twenty-four States. The strongholds of the denomination are Ohio, where it has nearly 26,000 members, and Indiana, where it has somewhat less than 20,000. In all there are 90,718 members, divided among 1281 organizations or congregations. These organizations have 963 church edifices, which are worth $1,637,202. The average value is $1700, and the average seating capacity 313. Halls to the number of 218, with a seating capacity of 24,725, are occupied as places of worship.

Summary by States.

STATES.	Organi-zations.	Church Edifices.	Seating Capacity.	Value of Church Property.	Com-muni-cants.
Arkansas........	6	2	650	$1,600	181
Connecticut	3	3	540	2,800	105
Illinois..........	104	64	20,239	63,135	5,745
Indiana.........	214	186	64,660	230,925	19,832
Iowa............	54	32	9,460	32,775	2,555
Kansas	49	8	1,665	8,250	1,676
Kentucky	41	15	5,650	5,605	2,146
Maine	60	28	7,690	76,380	3,451
Massachusetts ...	28	29	8,325	160,300	2,722
Michigan........	40	29	7,975	62,200	1,834
Missouri	35	12	4,000	12,791	1,627
Nebraska	4	2	475	1,000	148
New Hampshire..	23	22	6,178	62,950	1,522
New Jersey......	15	15	4,400	66,700	1,489
New York.......	120	109	28,710	257,850	7,520
North Carolina ..	65	57	17,710	23,055	4,896
Ohio............	273	247	83,105	392,500	25,952
Pennsylvania	69	54	17,060	98,500	3,219
Rhode Island	8	8	2,525	48,800	972
Texas	6	..	.....	.....	118
Vermont........	5	3	900	9,800	335
Virginia	23	16	4,550	8,875	1,390
West Virginia...	11	8	1,775	4,456	704
Wisconsin.......	25	16	3,450	5,955	579
Total	1,281	963	301,692	$1,637,202	90,718

2.—THE CHRISTIAN CHURCH, SOUTH.

In consequence of the adoption by the General Convention of Christians, held at Cincinnati in 1854, of resolutions opposed to slavery, and denouncing it as an evil, the churches of the South withdrew and formed a separate organization. The Christian Church, South, is in general agreement in doctrine and practice with the Northern churches, and it is claimed by some that the two bodies are now practically one.

The Southern Church is strongest in North Carolina and Virginia. It has five annual conferences, with 143 organizations, 135 church edifices, valued at $138,000 and 13,004 communicants. The average seating capacity of the edifices is 341, and the average value $1022. Eight halls, with a seating capacity of 750, are occupied.

SUMMARY BY STATES.

STATES.	Organizations.	Church Edifices.	Seating Capacity.	Value of Church Property.	Communicants.
Alabama	10	9	4,100	$5,625	687
Georgia	2	1	400	500	97
North Carolina	93	89	30,555	74,650	7,840
Virginia	38	36	10,950	57,225	4,380
Total	143	135	46,005	$138,000	13,004

The two bodies have a total of 1424 organizations, 1098 church edifices, with a seating capacity of 347,697 and a value of $1,775,202, and 103,722 communicants. Both are represented in only two States, viz., North Carolina and Virginia.

CHAPTER X.

THE CHRISTIAN MISSIONARY ASSOCIATION.

THIS association represents, in Christian work in Kentucky, a number of churches, without name, without creed, and without any ecclesiastical system. Each church is entirely independent. The churches claim to be unsectarian. The first was organized in Berea by Mr. John G. Fee. The doctrines preached are those common to evangelical Christianity. Immersion is held to be the proper form of baptism, but is not insisted upon. One hall, with a seating capacity of 100, is occupied.

SUMMARY.

STATE.	Organi-zations.	Church Edifices.	Seating Ca-pacity.	Value of Church Property.	Com-muni-cants.
Kentucky	13	11	3,300	$3,900	754

CHAPTER XI.

THE CHRISTIAN SCIENTISTS.

CHRISTIAN SCIENTISTS are those who believe that all ills of body and all evils of whatever nature are subject to the healing power of mind or spirit.

Mrs. Mary Baker G. Eddy, of Boston, Mass., claims to have discovered in 1866 and introduced in 1867 the "first purely metaphysical system of healing since the apostolic days." She began in that year to impart information as to the principles of the system. Out of this beginning was developed the Massachusetts Metaphysical College, which was chartered in 1881. Mrs. Eddy, with six of her students, constituted the first Christian Scientist association in 1876. Three years later a Christian Scientist Church was organized in Boston with 26 members. Mrs. Eddy was called to be its pastor the same year, and accepted the position. In 1881 she was ordained. Other churches and associations sprang up in different parts of the country, and in 1886 a National Christian Scientist Association was formed, the first meeting being held in New York City. There are regular churches, with pastors, in thirty-three States, and Sunday services are held in numerous places where churches have not been organized. There are also thirty or more Christian Science dispensaries. The organ of the denomination, *The Christian Science Journal* (monthly), publishes many columns of cards of practitioners of the science of mind healing.

The principles of Christian Science have been set forth authoritatively by Mrs. Eddy. According to her statements, all consciousness is mind, and mind is God. There is but one mind, and that is the divine mind. This is infinite good, which supplies all mind by reflection instead of subdivision. God is reflected, not divided. Soul is spirit, and spirit is God. There is but one soul, and that is God. The flesh is evil, not the soul. Soul is "substance in truth"; matter is "substance in error." Soul, spirit, or mind is not evil, nor is it mortal. Life is eternal. It implies God. Whatever errs is mortal, and is a departure from God. Evil is simply the absence of good. Evil is unreal; good only is real. The divine mind is one and indivisible, and therefore never out of harmony. Man is immortal, being coeternal with God. The divine power is able to bring all into harmony with itself. Hence Christian Science says to all manner of disease: "Know that God is all-power and all-presence, and there is nothing beside him, and the sick are healed." "Sickness is a belief, a latent fear, made manifest in the body in different forms of fear or disease. This fear is formed unconsciously in the silent thought." It is to be dissipated by actual consciousness of the "truth of science" that man's harmony is no more to be invaded than the rhythm of the universe. Suffering exists only in the "mortal mind"; "matter has no sensation, and cannot suffer." "If you rule out every sense of disease and suffering from mortal mind, it cannot be found in the body." All drugs are to be avoided. The only means of cure proposed by Christian Science is spiritual. Sin, like sickness and death, is unreal. In order to cure it the sinner's belief in its reality must be overthrown.

The denomination has only 7 church edifices. Meetings are held in 213 halls, which have a seating capacity of 19,690.

SUMMARY BY STATES.

STATES.	Organizations.	Church Edifices.	Seating Capacity.	Value of Church Property.	Communicants.
California	8	..	....	......	814
Colorado	4	..	....	......	147
Connecticut	4	..	....	......	75
Delaware...........	1	..	....	......	3
District of Columbia	1	..	....	......	15
Florida	2	..	....	......	33
Georgia.............	2	..	....	......	40
Illinois.............	13	1	300	$2,126	1,271
Indiana	5	..	....	900	134
Iowa...............	22	1	300	5,200	640
Kansas	15	..	....	300	424
Maine	2	..	....	......	60
Massachusetts	10	..	....	15,000	499
Michigan	6	..	....	150	125
Minnesota..........	10	..	....	200	264
Missouri	9	..	....	300	374
Nebraska	20	1	100	365	650
New Hampshire	3	..	....	......	54
New Jersey.........	2	..	....	100	35
New York..........	28	..	....	......	1,268
North Dakota.......	1	..	....	......	75
Ohio	14	3	650	14,000	564
Oklahoma..........	1	..	....	......	16
Oregon	3	..	....	......	62
Pennsylvania	5	..	....	......	155
Rhode Island	1	..	....	......	75
South Dakota.......	2	..	....	......	33
Tennessee..........	1	..	....	......	3
Texas..............	5	..	....	......	112
Utah	1	..	....	......	100
Vermont	2	..	....	......	40
Washington	2	..	....	......	90
Wisconsin..........	16	1	150	2,025	474
Total	221	7	1,500	$40,666	8,724

CHAPTER XII.

THE CHRISTIAN UNION CHRUCHES.

THIS body, which is now called the Independent Churches of Christ in Christian Union, was organized in Ohio during the first years of the Civil War. Elder J. V. B. Flack was one of the most prominent leaders of the movement, which was outspoken in opposition to the war. They believed that it had been " produced by an unwarrantable meddling both North and South, and great injustice and insane haste on the part of extreme leaders in both sections." They were opposed to the introduction of politics into the pulpit, and withdrew from existing denominations because they could not tolerate what they regarded as political preaching. Elder Flack declared that he was persecuted by the ministers and members of the Methodist Episcopal Church, in which he was a pastor. Writing of the matter some years later, he said :

"We refused to vote in the conference for resolutions of war. We refused to pray for the success of war. We refused to bring politics into our pulpit. We refused to join in the ranks that marched on the streets at war meetings. We refused to make certain war speeches. We refused to prefer charges against members of the church whom the fanatics accuse of being disloyal. We refused to preside at forced trials of good men who were tried for political opinions."

He claimed that on account of taking this attitude he was severely persecuted, and led to withdraw from the Methodist Episcopal Church in 1863. He preached to various companies of men and women after his withdrawal from the Methodist Episcopal Church; but the first church of the new denomination was organized by the Rev. Ira Norris, at Lacon, Ill., late in 1863 or early in 1864. At a convention held in Columbus, O., in February, 1864, persons representing five different denominations being present, the foundation of the new denomination was laid. The principles of the Christian Union are in brief as follows:

1. The oneness of the Church of Christ.
2. Christ the only head.
3. The Bible the rule of faith and practice.
4. Good fruits the only condition of membership.
5. Christian union without controversy.
6. Each local church self-governing.
7. Partisan preaching discountenanced.

The church claims to be non-partisan, non-sectarian, and non-denominational. It aims to furnish a basis for the union of all true believers by making its organization as simple as possible and by eliminating from its system controversial questions in doctrine and polity. It has 294 congregations, 183 church edifices valued at $234,500, and 18,214 communicants; 105 halls, with a seating capacity of 14,705, are occupied as meeting-places. For many years prior to the census of 1890 its membership was estimated at over 100,000 by Elder Flack and others.

SUMMARY BY STATES.

STATES.	Organizations.	Church Edifices.	Seating Capacity.	Value of Church Property.	Communicants.
Arkansas.............	4	...	......	....	101
Colorado............	12	...	......	....	571
Florida	1	...	......	....	50
Illinois..............	6	4	1,450	$3,850	206
Indiana	26	21	7,600	25,700	1,599
Indian Territory	3	...	......	....	130
Iowa................	31	20	6,850	21,500	1,258
Kansas	16	4	1,250	4,600	495
Kentucky	5	1	300	1,000	443
Maryland	1	1	350	1,000	15
Michigan	8	3	1,650	12,000	436
Missouri	56	31	13,500	39,050	3,926
New Hampshire	2	1	400	4,000	102
Ohio	103	94	33,250	114,350	8,002
Rhode Island	1	1	300	3,500	50
Tennessee..........	8	2	800	1,400	376
Texas..............	6	...	......	....	190
Vermont...........	5	1	300	2,500	264
Total	294	184	68,000	$234,450	18,214

CHAPTER XIII.

THE CHURCH OF GOD.

JOHN WINEBRENNER, the founder of this denomination, which in doctrine, polity, and usage resembles both the Baptist and Methodist Churches, became a member of the first Reformed German Church, Philadelphia, in 1817, and three years later pastor of a church of the same denomination in Harrisburg. There were four congregations under his care. Under his plain and pungent preaching a revival of religion began, the progress of which was opposed. The opposition continued five years or more, resulting in a separation from the church. The revival extended into various parts of Pennsylvania and even into Maryland, and hundreds of persons were converted. These persons were organized into separate churches. Meanwhile, Elder Winebrenner, after a careful study of the Bible, had changed his views respecting points of doctrine and polity. In 1830 he, with Andrew Miller, John Eliot, John Walborn, David Maxwell, and James Richards, who were recognized as teaching elders, met in conference and agreed upon a basis of church organization. The following are the leading principles:

1. That the believers in any given locality according to the divine order are to constitute one body. The division of believers into sects and parties under human names and creeds is contrary to the spirit and letter of the New

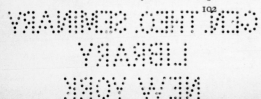

Testament, and constitutes the most powerful barrier to the success of Christianity.

2. That the believers of any community organized into one body constitute God's household or family, and should be known by the name of the Church of God.

3. That the Scriptures without note or comment constitute a sufficient rule of faith and practice. Creeds and confessions tend to divisions and sects.

4. That there are three ordinances binding upon all believers; namely, immersion in water in the name of the Trinity, the washing of the saints' feet, and the partaking of bread and wine in commemoration of the sufferings and death of Christ.

Upon the basis of these principles the denomination was organized, the first conference being held in 1831.

The conferences of the Church of God, of which there are several, are held annually, and are called elderships. There is a general conference or general eldership which meets triennially. This is the chief legislative and judicial body. The presiding officer of an annual eldership, or of the general eldership, is called the Speaker. There are itinerant and local ministers and exhorters, as in Methodism, and the weaker congregations are organized into circuits. The itinerant ministers are appointed to pastorates by stationing committees of the annual elderships.

The Church of God is represented in fourteen States and the Indian Territory. Its chief strength, however, lies in the State of Pennsylvania, where it originated. Fully one half of its total communicants are to be found in Pennsylvania, Ohio, and Indiana. It has sixteen annual elderships. There are 479 organizations in all, with 338 church edifices, having an average seating capacity of 342 and an average value of $1902. There are 129 halls, with a seating capacity of 13,840.

SUMMARY BY STATES.

STATES.	Organizations.	Church Edifices.	Seating Capacity.	Value of Church Property.	Communicants.
Arkansas...........	19	1	200	$500	577
Illinois..............	36	33	10,725	41,850	1,495
Indiana	44	32	10,915	53,500	2,575
Indian Territory	16	11	1,285	1,200	811
Iowa................	18	10	3,275	13,400	683
Kansas	26	6	1,750	7,300	956
Maine	3	...	....	....	75
Maryland	21	20	5,800	25,700	816
Massachusetts	1	...	....	....	20
Michigan	16	10	3,425	8,300	373
Missouri	7	4	1,300	4,100	221
Nebraska	9	2	400	1,900	332
Ohio................	75	66	24,575	99,550	3,352
Pennsylvania	162	135	48,580	375,185	9,344
West Virginia	26	8	3,300	10,700	881
Total	479	338	115,530	$643,185	22,511

CHAPTER XIV.

THE CHURCH TRIUMPHANT (SCHWEINFURTH).

THE founder and head of this body is George Jacob Schweinfurth, who was born in Marion County, O., in 1853. He entered the ministry of the Methodist Episcopal Church in Michigan, but soon left it and became a disciple of Mrs. Beekman, who, before her death, which occurred in 1883, declared herself the " spiritual mother of Christ in the second coming," and pronounced Schweinfurth the " Messiah of the New Dispensation." He accordingly became the acknowledged head of her followers, and removed the headquarters of the sect from Byron, nine miles from Rockford, Ill., to the Weldon farm, six miles from Rockford, changing the name of the body to the Church Triumphant. A large frame house, called " Mount Zion " or " Heaven," is occupied by Schweinfurth and a number of his disciples. There are also other companies, each of which is presided over by an " apostle," who reads weekly the sermons previously delivered by Schweinfurth at Mount Zion. There are no rites, ceremonies, or forms of worship. The single condition of membership is recognition of Schweinfurth as the " Christ of the Second Coming " and discipleship.

The Church Triumphant accepts the Bible as the Word of God, but denies the essential divinity of Christ. He was a mere man, but passed through an experience in which he was freed from the power and curse of sin, after which he received the Spirit of God and became divine. Schweinfurth does not claim to be Jesus of Nazareth, but to have received the same Spirit and to be equal to him. He claims to be sinless, to perform miracles, and to be able to bestow the Spirit on whomsoever he chooses. He also declares his power over sin, not only to save from its curse but to save from its commission.

There are in all 12 organizations and 384 members. All the services are held in private houses with one exception, Mount Zion being returned as a hall.

SUMMARY BY STATES.

STATES.	Organizations.	Halls, etc.	Seating Capacity.	Value of Church Property.	Communicants.
Colorado...........	1	1	...	....	12
Illinois.............	5	5	...	$15,000	190
Kentucky	1	1	...	....	25
Michigan	2	2	...	....	37
Minnesota..........	2	2	100	....	100
Missouri	1	1	...	....	20
Total	12	12	100	$15,000	384

CHAPTER XV.

THE theological writings of Emanuel Swedenborg, born in Stockholm, Sweden, in 1688, died in London, England, in 1772, led to the organization of the New Jerusalem Church. Its members are often spoken of as Swedenborgians. He was called, according to his own words, "to a holy office by the Lord himself, who most mercifully appeared before me, his servant, in the year 1743, when he opened my sight into the spiritual world, and enabled me to converse with spirits and angels." From that time he began to "publish the various arcana" or sacred truths, seen by or revealed to him, "concerning heaven and hell, the state of man after death, the true worship of God, the spiritual sense of the Word, and many other important matters conducive to salvation and wisdom." His voluminous religious works contain the body of doctrine to which his followers adhere. The greater portion of them consist of the exposition of the spiritual meaning of the Scriptures.

The first meeting for organization was held in London in 1783, eleven years after his death. The next year his teachings were set forth in Boston and Philadelphia, and a congregation was established in Baltimore in 1792. This was the beginning of the church in this country. It was gradually established in other cities and towns, and is represented now in twenty-nine States, besides the District of Columbia. It has 154 organizations, and 7095 members or communicants, more than a fourth of whom are to be found in Massachusetts.

The doctrines of the New Jerusalem Church declare that God is one in essence, person, and nature, manifesting himself as Father, Son, and Holy Spirit—the Father being the infinite divine essence, the Son the human organization with which the Father clothed himself to accomplish the redemption of mankind when immersed in sin, and the Spirit being the divine power flowing forth into act; that the Lord accomplished this redemption by fighting against and overcoming the infernal hosts which had long enslaved mankind, and restoring man to spiritual freedom; that life is not created, only the forms which receive it, man's mind and body being organic forms for the reception of life, which is maintained by the constant conjunction of man and God; that man has a spiritual body which is fitted to receive and manifest the divine forces, and the mind or spirit constitutes this spiritual body; that the material body is only the husk, so to speak, and its death is caused by man's resurrection from it; that the spiritual world is a substantial world, the realm of causes, and exists in three divisions—heaven, the world of spirits, and hell; that the world of spirits, which all enter immediately after death, is the place of preparation for heaven or for hell, according to the character brought into it; that the life in this intermediate state is similar to the one in this world, except that it is not a life of probation, but a life devoted to bringing discordant elements in man's nature into harmony, and to receiving instruction; that gradually the scene changes and men rise to heaven or sink to hell, drawn by the irresistible affinities of their true character; that hell is not a place or state of constant punishment, but its inhabitants have all the enjoyments of which their perverted nature is capable, living under restraint of penalties which follow every violation of law; that heaven is a place of useful activity, in which each finds his appropriate sphere of action and happiness, and becomes subject to the process of perfectibility which goes on forever; that in the Scriptures there is a spiritual principle or fact corresponding to every natural act and object they record, a spiritual meaning distinct from, yet harmonizing with and based upon, the natural meaning of every word and sentence; that while the books of the Bible were written through various authors, each in his own natural style, it is nevertheless, by virtue of the infinite store of truth within it, a divine book, the Lord himself being its author. This view of the Bible is one of the chief distinctions of Swedenborgian belief.

The organization of the New Jerusalem Church is a modified Episcopacy, each society being, however, free to manage its own affairs. There are associations of societies, generally conforming to State lines, and a general convention composed of representatives of the associations, and also of a number of societies which have no associational connection. The service is generally liturgical. A variety of liturgies are in use in the different congregations or societies; the greater number, however, use the "Book of Worship," published by the General Convention. Three orders are recognized in the ministry. In connection with each association there is a general pastor, who bears the same relation to the association that a pastor does to a society. There are also pastors of societies, and preachers not yet in full orders.

The average seating capacity of the church edifices is 236, and their average value $15,755; 70 halls, with a seating capacity of 7165, are used as meeting-places.

SUMMARY BY STATES.

STATES.	Organizations.	Church Edifices.	Seating Capacity.	Value of Church Property.	Communicants.
Arkansas	1	1	400	$55	3
California	12	3	750	41,500	347
Colorado...........	2	1	40	2,500	41
Connecticut	1	..	.....	....	28
Delaware	1	1	200	12,000	50
District of Columbia.	1	..	.....	....	93
Florida	3	..	.....	....	30
Georgia............	2	1	180	9,000	48
Illinois............	14	10	1,895	163,700	641
Indiana............	4	4	950	16,500	104
Iowa	6	3	495	6,200	138
Kansas	3	1	75	5,000	62
Kentucky	1	..	.....	....	61
Maine	4	3	1,125	33,000	289
Maryland	9	4	1,215	44,600	244
Massachusetts	22	18	5,025	368,500	1,684
Michigan	5	4	975	34,600	163
Minnesota..........	2	2	250	29,000	80
Missouri	5	4	800	24,600	309
New Hampshire	1	..	.....	....	42
New Jersey.........	6	4	800	24,500	323
New York..........	11	5	1,350	192,900	560
Ohio...............	13	8	1,625	103,500	657
Oregon	2	1	100	300	45
Pennsylvania	13	4	1,600	230,500	774
Rhode Island.......	3	3	610	39,000	130
Tennessee..........	3	1	75	500	64
Texas..............	1	1	200	4,000	40
Virginia	1	1	75	500	2
Wisconsin..........	2	..	.....	....	43
Total	154	88	20,810	$1,386,455	7,095

CHAPTER XVI.

COMMUNISTIC SOCIETIES.

ALL societies observing the communal life, whether founded on a religious or secular basis, are embraced in these returns. Two of the societies are not religious, the Icarian and the Altruist, but it was deemed best not to omit them, on the technical ground that they are not organized to practice a faith, but to apply a social principle.

There are nine societies which properly come under this head. One of these, the Bruederhoef Mennonite, is omitted in this chapter because it is given in that on the Mennonites. The other societies are these:

1. Shakers,	5. New Icaria,
2. Amana,	6. Altruists,
3. Harmony,	7. Adonai Shomo,
4. Separatists,	8. Church Triumphant
	(Koreshan Ecclesia).

I.—THE SOCIETY OF SHAKERS.

The oldest of all existing communities in the United States is that of the Shakers, or, more accurately, "The Millennial Church, or United Society of Believers." Their first community was organized at Mount Lebanon, N. Y., in 1792.

They count themselves as followers of Ann Lee, an English woman, who was born in 1736 in Manchester and died in 1784 in this country. They revere " Mother Ann," as she was called, as the second appearance of Christ on earth. She was a member of the Society of Quakers, and in a persecution which arose against them was cast into prison. While in prison she saw Christ and had a special divine revelation, which showed her that the only way mankind could be restored to the proper relation to God was by leading a celibate life. She came to this country in 1774 and settled at Watervliet, N. Y., in 1775, and died there. The popular designation " Shakers " was first used in England. Those Quakers who joined " Mother Ann " were noted for " unusual and violent manifestations of religious fervor," and were therefore spoken of as " Shaking Quakers." Hence the term " Shakers."

The Shakers are strict celibates, have a uniform style of dress, and use the words " yea " and " nay," but not " thee " or " thou." They are spiritualists, holding that there is a " most intricate connection and the most constant communion between themselves and the inhabitants of the world of spirits." They believe, as already stated, that the second coming of Christ is past, and that they constitute the true Church, and that " revelation, spiritualism, celibacy, oral confession, community, non-resistance, peace, the gift of healing, miracles, physical health, and separation from the world are the foundations of the new heavens." They reject the trinitarian conception of God, holding that he is a dual person, male and female, and that the distinction of sex inheres in the soul and is eternal. Christ, they believe, first appeared in Jesus as a male and then in Ann Lee as a female. They worship only God.

Both sexes are represented in the ministry. Religious services, held on Sunday, consist of exhortation, singing, and marching and dancing to music. There is little audible prayer.

There are 15 communities of Shakers—3 each in Ohio and Massachusetts, 2 each in Kentucky, Maine, New Hampshire, and New York, and 1 in Connecticut. They have 16 church edifices, with a seating capacity of 5650, or an average of 353, and a valuation of $36,800, or an average of $2300. The number of members is 1728. In 1875, according to Nordhoff's "Communistic Societies," they had 18 communities and 2415 members. This indicates that they are decreasing.

SUMMARY BY STATES.

STATES.	Organi- zations.	Church Edifices.	Seating Ca- pacity.	Value of Church Property.	Com- muni- cants.
Connecticut	1	1	400	$5,000	100
Kentucky	2	2	700	1,900	371
Maine	2	2	1,000	5,000	100
Massachusetts	3	4	1,000	5,800	129
New Hampshire ...	2	2	700	1,500	250
New York	2	2	1,100	12,000	575
Ohio	3	3	750	5,600	203
Total	15	16	5,650	$36,800	1,728

2.—THE AMANA SOCIETY.

This society calls its organizations, of which there are seven, "True Inspiration Congregations." The community is confined to Iowa County, Ia., where its members exist in seven towns. They came from Germany in 1842 and settled near Buffalo, N. Y., whence they removed thirteen years later to their present location in Iowa. They are a religious rather than an industrial community, and are devoted Bible readers, believing that all parts of the Book are inspired. They hold to the Trinity, to justification by faith, to the resurrection of the dead, but not to eternal punishment. The wicked are to be purified in fire. They do not observe the sacrament of baptism, but make much of that of the Lord's Supper, which, however, is celebrated not oftener than once in two years. They believe that an era of inspiration began at the opening of the eighteenth century, the Holy Ghost revealing the secrets of the heart and conscience to messengers or new prophets. The elders or ministers are guided by the spirit of inspiration, and the community has at its head some one (at one time it was a woman) who is under the direct inspiration of God. There are three orders of members: the highest, the middle, and the lowest or children's order. They hold religious services every evening, and also on Sunday, Wednesday, and Saturday mornings. The general meeting is held Saturday morning; the other meetings are mostly for prayer.

SUMMARY.

STATE.	Organizations.	Church Edifices.	Seating Capacity.	Value of Church Property.	Communicants.
Iowa	7	22	2,800	$15,000	1,600

3.—THE HARMONY SOCIETY.

The founder of this society was George Rapp, who was born in Germany in 1757 and died in Economy, Pa., in 1847. His followers are celibates, having adopted this rule early in the present century, and follow the example of patriarchal rule set in the Old Testament and hold to a community of property. They are literalists in interpreting the Scriptures, and they believe that the millennium is near at hand and that all mankind will ultimately be saved, those who marry being classified with the number who will have to undergo a probation of purification. They do not believe in spiritualism. They observe as holy days Christmas, Good Friday, Easter, and Pentecost. They celebrate the Lord's Supper annually in October. The town of Economy is described by Nordhoff as a " trim, well-kept village." The society has one organization, one church edifice, valued at $10,000, and 250 members.

SUMMARY.

STATE.	Organizations.	Church Edifices.	Seating Capacity.	Value of Church Property.	Communicants.
Pennsylvania	I	I	500	$10,000	250

4.—THE SOCIETY OF SEPARATISTS.

The Separatists originated in Germany. They settled at Zoar, O., in 1817 and adopted communal life in 1819. They were called Separatists in Germany because they separated from the State church, in the belief that they could thus enjoy a more spiritual faith. They reject religious ceremonies. Marriages are allowed but not favored. They are entered upon by a civil compact, there being no religious celebration. Their Sunday services do not include public prayer.

SUMMARY.

STATE.	Organizations.	Church Edifices.	Seating Capacity.	Value of Church Property.	Communicants.
Ohio	I	I	500	$3,000	200

5.—THE NEW ICARIA SOCIETY.

The New Icaria Society was organized in 1879. It has no creed but "rationalism founded on observation," and opposes all "anti-scientific revelations." Marriage is approved. The system of rule is democratic. The society has disbanded since the census.

SUMMARY.

STATE.	Organizations.	Church Edifices.	Seating Capacity.	Value of Church Property.	Communicants.
Iowa	1	..	....	......	21

6.—THE SOCIETY OF ALTRUISTS.

The Altruists, like the New Icarians, are non-sectarian. The principles of the community are thus expressed:

"It holds the property of all its members in common, and all work according to their ability and are supplied according to their wants, and live together in a common home for their mutual assistance and support and to secure their greatest wealth, comfort, and enjoyment. It allows equal rights and privileges to all its members, both men and women, in all its business affairs, which are conducted in accordance with their majority vote by its officers who are thereby elected; and it makes no interference with the marriage or family affairs of its members, nor with their religious, political, or other opinions."

SUMMARY.

STATE.	Organizations.	Church Edifices.	Seating Capacity.	Value of Church Property.	Communicants.
Missouri	1	..	....	......	25

7.—THE ADONAI SHOMO.

This community was organized and legally established as a corporation in 1876 in Petersham, Mass. At its organization it had 11 members. It came out of the Adventist movement. Its leading principles are faith in Christ as the Son of God, and a community of goods. All members, male and female, have an equal voice in matters of government and property. There is a common treasury, whence individual needs are supplied. All labor for the common maintenance, agriculture being the chief industry.

SUMMARY.

STATE.	Organizations.	Church Edifices.	Seating Capacity.	Value of Church Property.	Communicants.
Massachusetts	1	..	....	$6,000	20

8.—THE CHURCH TRIUMPHANT (KORESHAN ECCLESIA).

The founder of this body is Cyrus Teed. Cyrus in Hebrew is Koresh; hence the terms Koreshan Ecclesia, or the Koreshan Church, and Koreshanity, the system of Koresh. The foundation principle of the movement is the " reëstablishment of church and state upon a basis of divine fellowship," the law of which is love to neighbor. It has three departments: the ecclesia, or church; the college of life, or educational department; and the society Archtriumphant. As the aims of Koreshanity cannot be secured where the spirit of competition operates, the life of the disciples is communal. Celibacy is a fundamental doctrine. It is held as desirable in order to conserve the forces of life, and necessary to the attainment of that purity of life which issues in immortality.   The disciples hope to pass out of the world as did Enoch, Elijah, and Christ.   They have no churches, but occupy 6 private houses.   The property in Chicago, though returned as private, is held for denominational purposes.

SUMMARY BY STATES.

STATES.	Organizations.	Church Edifices.	Seating Capacity.	Value of Church Property.	Communicants.
California	1	..	....	......	15
Illinois	2	..	....	$36,000	160
Massachusetts	1	..	....	......	15
Oregon	1	..	....	......	15
Total.........	5	..	....	$36,000	205

SUMMARY BY STATES OF ALL COMMUNISTIC SOCIETIES.

California	1	..	.....	......	15
Connecticut	1	1	400	$5,000	100
Illinois............	2	..	.....	36,000	160
Iowa	8	22	2,800	15,000	1,621
Kentucky	2	2	700	1,900	371
Maine	2	2	1,000	5,000	100
Massachusetts	5	4	1,000	11,800	164
Missouri	1	..	.....	......	25
New Hampshire ...	2	2	700	1,500	250
New York.........	2	2	1,100	12,000	575
Ohio	4	4	1,250	8,600	403
Oregon	1	..	.....	......	15
Pennsylvania	1	1	500	10,000	250
South Dakota......	5	5	600	4,500	352
Total.........	37	45	10,050	$111,300	4,401

South Dakota is added to give the Bruederhoef Mennonite community.

CHAPTER XVII.

THE CONGREGATIONAL CHURCHES.

THE first church of the Congregational faith and order in the United States came over the sea to Plymouth, Mass., in the " Mayflower," in 1620. Before the close of the first half of that century there were in New England 51 Congregational churches, besides two or three on Long Island and one in Virginia.

Congregationalism developed great strength in New England, spreading but slowly over other sections of the country. In 1801 a plan of union was entered into with the Presbyterian Church concerning the formation of churches in new settlements, and under it Congregationalists going west from New England generally entered Presbyterian churches. This plan continued in force until 1852, when it was formally abrogated by a convention of Congregationalists at Albany, on the ground that it practically excluded Congregationalism from the country west of New England. It is noticeable that in the older States where there are many Congregationalists there are comparatively few Presbyterians, and *vice versâ*. Since the abrogation of the plan of union the growth of Congregational churches in the West, particularly in Illinois and the yet newer States of the Northwest, has been quite rapid. Their antislavery record entirely shut them out of the States of the South until after the Civil War. Their numbers in that section are still limited and include a good proportion of colored members, to whose education they have been much devoted.

The Pilgrims and Puritans, who constituted the early Congregational churches, were not averse to Presbyterianism on doctrinal grounds. Congregationalists and Presbyterians were in substantial agreement, the Westminster Confession serving acceptably as the doctrinal symbol of both for many years. It was adopted by the Congregationalists at a general synod at Cambridge, Mass., in 1646–48. The Savoy Confession of Faith, which is similar to that of Westminster, was adopted by local synods in 1680 and in 1708, and a national council held in 1865, in Boston, Mass., expressed its adherence to the faith "substantially embodied" in these two confessions, and adopted a declaration, known as the "Burial Hill Declaration," affirming the general unity of the church of Christ in all the world, and setting forth the "fundamental truths in which all Christians should agree," as a basis of general coöperation and fellowship. In 1871 a National Triennial Council was held in Oberlin, O. The following was adopted as a part of the constitution of the council:

"They [the Congregational churches] agree in belief that the Holy Scriptures are the sufficient and only infallible rule of faith and practice; their interpretation thereof being in substantial accordance with the great doctrines of the Christian faith, commonly called Evangelical, held in our churches from the early times, and sufficiently set forth by former general councils."

Dr. William Ives Budington, the moderator of the council, afterward gave the following interpretation of this paragraph:

"Any churches recognizing the independency of the

local church, and professing the historic faith of Christ's church, are actually and intentionally embraced within the fellowship of the national council. The distinctions of Old School and New School were ignored, and just as much Arminianism and Calvinism."

According to this, Congregationalism welcomes Arminians as well as Calvinists to its churches. In 1883 a commission appointed by the national council formulated a confession, consisting of twelve articles. It is of a general evangelical character.

The polity of the Congregational churches is based on the principle of the complete autonomy of each local church. Connected with this principle is that of the fellowship of the churches. The Cambridge platform, adopted in the middle of the seventeenth century, declares that "although churches be distinct and therefore may not be confounded with one another, and equal and therefore have not dominion one over another, yet all churches ought to preserve church communion one with another, because they are all united unto Christ, not only as a mystical, but as a political, head, whence is derived a communion suitable thereunto." The fountain of ecclesiastical power is in the local church, and not in any association or council of churches. Each church manages its own affairs. When differences arise between churches, or between members of the same church, or between a church and its pastor, they may be referred to a council specially summoned, composed of pastors and representatives of neighboring churches of the same faith and order. The decisions of councils are, however, not mandatory, but simply advisory. Councils have to do chiefly with questions of denominational fellowship. They examine, ordain, and install pastors, and recognize churches.   There are local associations purely ministerial, meeting for fellowship, and which in some sections assume the duty of examining candidates for license to preach, the license being in the nature of a certification to the churches of the fitness of the licentiate.   There are also local and State associations or conferences of churches and ministers which hold regular meetings for consultation concerning the benevolent and missionary work of the churches within their bounds.   The Triennial National Council embraces representatives of all the local associations and conferences; but equally with the local bodies it has no other province than that of giving counsel to the churches and benevolent societies.

The Congregational idea of the minister is that he is a teacher who is *primus inter pares.*   He is a member of the church which he serves, and is subject to its discipline like any other member.   The officers of a church consist of one or more pastors, also called bishops or elders; and of deacons, who are laymen charged with the administration of the sacraments and of the charitable interests.   Connected with most churches is a religious society embracing all members and supporters of the church.   The church calls a pastor, and the society approves the call and fixes the salary.

In New England for many years Congregationalism was the established religion.   In the colonies of New Haven and Massachusetts membership in a Congregational church was a condition of the exercise of the political franchise, and the churches in most of New England were supported by monies raised in the tax levies.   In course of time this system was modified so as to allow persons to contribute to whatever church they preferred.

It was formally abolished in Connecticut in 1816, and in Massachusetts in 1833.

There are Congregational churches in all the States except Delaware, and in all the Territories except Alaska. The total of members in this country, not including several thousand converts in connection with missions of the American Board in foreign lands, is more than half a million. Massachusetts, where Congregationalists were the first colonists, has a larger proportion of the total than any other State, 101,890; Connecticut comes second, with 59,154; New York third, with 45,686; Illinois fourth, with 35,830; and Ohio fifth, with 32,281. Of the total valuation of church property, $43,335,437, Massachusetts has more than a fourth, or $11,030,890; Connecticut, $5,366,201; New York, $5,175,262; and Illinois, $2,975,-812. There are only 15 places in Massachusetts used by Congregationalists as places of worship which they do not own. There are 62 such places in South Dakota, 50 in Iowa, and 47 in Michigan. In all, 456 halls, with a seating capacity of 42,646, are used by congregations. The 4868 organizations own 4736 edifices, with an aggregate seating capacity of 1,553,080, indicating an average of 328 to each house. The average value of each edifice is $9150.

SUMMARY BY STATES.

STATES.	Organi-zations.	Church Edifices.	Seating Ca-pacity.	Value of Church Property.	Com-muni-cants.
Alabama	28	22	5,505	$91,755	1,683
Arizona	3	3	550	9,500	162
Arkansas	7	5	1,600	26,000	669
California	182	149½	37,773	1,014,975	11,907
Colorado	49	38½	11,010	377,090	3,217
Connecticut	306	383	147,688	5,366,201	59,154
District of Columbia	6	6	3,370	339,000	1,399
Florida	39	29	7,600	73,775	1,184

SUMMARY BY STATES.—*Continued.*

STATES.	Organizations.	Church Edifices.	Seating Capacity.	Value of Church Property.	Communicants.
Georgia............	73	58	15,500	$75,350	3,880
Idaho.............	5	3	420	6,400	105
Illinois...........	302	296	103,036	2,975,812	35,830
Indiana...........	55	42½	12,200	221,650	3,081
Indian Territory ...	6	....	....	....	127
Iowa	285	243½	68,081	1,231,886	23,733
Kansas	183	152	34,975	485,975	11,945
Kentucky	8	6	1,750	20,200	449
Louisiana	20	11	3,825	23,800	1,057
Maine	240	272½	85,591	1,512,030	21,523
Maryland	3	3	1,150	71,500	336
Massachusetts	559	671¾	298,910	11,030,890	101,890
Michigan	331	299½	82,458	1,533,055	24,582
Minnesota	175	152	37,403	1,114,800	13,624
Mississippi	7	5	1,150	6,975	210
Missouri	80	69	29,550	650,344	7,617
Montana..........	7	5	1,130	38,800	345
Nebraska	172	144	32,019	640,204	10,045
Nevada	1	1	200	1,000	50
New Hampshire ...	188	226	73,346	1,405,050	19,712
New Jersey........	33	36	14,050	655,300	4,912
New Mexico.......	4	4	625	17,800	175
New York.........	301	324½	128,179	5,175,262	45,686
North Carolina	20	16	3,705	14,200	1,002
North Dakota	65	38	5,955	81,800	1,616
Ohio	247	252½	83,029	2,044,525	32,281
Oklahoma.........	10	....	....	....	170
Oregon	35	27	7,500	160,200	2,037
Pennsylvania	108	100¼	34,605	672,588	9,818
Rhode Island	34	39	19,080	905,800	7,192
South Carolina	3	3	1,100	31,350	376
South Dakota......	138	80	14,967	200,665	5,164
Tennessee.........	26	20	4,570	106,000	1,429
Texas	15	12	3,250	55,300	846
Utah	14	2	600	76,000	460
Vermont..........	198	217	65,112	1,318,100	20,465
Virginia	2	2	550	7,500	156
Washington	104	62	13,698	316,230	3,154
West Virginia	2	2	750	18,500	136
Wisconsin.........	182	196	52,615	1,089,750	15,841
Wyoming..........	7	6	1,350	44,550	339
Total........	4,868	4,736	1,553,080	$43,335,437	512,771

CHAPTER XVIII.

THE DISCIPLES OF CHRIST.

THIS body, often called also Christians, was one of the results of the great revival movement which began in Tennessee and Kentucky in the early part of the present century. Rev. Barton W. Stone, a Presbyterian minister who was prominent in the revival movement, withdrew from the Presbyterian Church, and in 1804 organized a church with no other creed than the Bible and with no name but that of Christian. One of his objects was to find a basis for the union of all Christian believers. A little later Thomas and Alexander Campbell, father and son, who came from Ireland, where the former had been a Presbyterian minister, organized union societies in Pennsylvania. Changing their views as to baptism, they joined the Redstone Association of Baptists. Shortly after, when Alexander Campbell was charged with not being in harmony with the creed, he followed the Burch Run Church, of which he was pastor, into the Mahoning Baptist Association, which, leavened with his teachings, soon ceased to be known as a Baptist association. In 1827, after some correspondence with Rev. B. W. Stone and his followers of the Christian Connection, there was a union with a large number of congregations in Ohio, Kentucky, and Tennessee, and the organization variously known as " Disciples of Christ" and " Christians" is the result.

The leading principles of the Disciples of Christ are, to quote from one of their tracts: (1) "To restore the lost unity of believers and so of the Church of Christ by a return in doctrine, ordinance, and life to the religion definitely outlined" in the New Testament; (2) no human creed, but the Bible only as the rule of faith and practice; (3) baptism by immersion of believers only, in which "comes a divine assurance of remission of sins and acceptance with God"; (4) the celebration of the Lord's Supper as a "feast of love" every Sunday. The central doctrine of their teaching is that "Jesus is the Christ, the Son of God." They hold that "personal trust in a personal Redeemer" is the faith that is necessary to salvation.

In polity they are congregational. Their ministers are ordained, but are not, in denominational usage, addressed with the title "Rev." They have as church officers elders, also called bishops, pastors, or presbyters, deacons, and evangelists. The latter are itinerant missionaries. The churches are united in State and district associations for missionary work, and there is also a national convention for home and another organization for foreign missions, and a Woman's Board of Missions for both home and foreign missions.

The Disciples of Christ are represented in all the States but New Hampshire and Nevada, and in all the Territories except Alaska. In number of members Missouri leads the States, with 97,773; Indiana is second, with 78,942; Kentucky third, with 77,647; Illinois fourth, with 60,867; and Ohio fifth, with 54,425. They have an aggregate of 7246 organizations, 5324 church edifices, valued at $12,-206,038, and 641,051 members or communicants. The average seating capacity of the churches is 302, and the average value $2292; 1141 halls, with a seating capacity of 139,325, are occupied.

In many States no little difficulty was encountered in the attempt to gather full statistics for the census. The most competent person in each State was appointed to do the work, but it was not possible to get returns for all congregations known or believed to be in existence. This was particularly true of Tennessee, where estimates only, founded on various sources of information, were possible for several counties. A small percentage of members in a number of the States is not, therefore, embraced in the following tables, which are believed, however, to be the most complete of any ever before published:

SUMMARY BY STATES.

STATES.	Organi- zations.	Church Edifices.	Seating Ca- pacity.	Value of Church Property.	Com- muni- cants.
Alabama	201	128	30,818	$78,185	9,201
Arizona	3	1	150	3,000	78
Arkansas	265	123	34,785	106,360	14,385
California	89	62	17,675	291,250	7,433
Colorado	31	18	4,945	151,625	2,400
Connecticut	2	1	500	16,000	337
Delaware	4	3	450	4,800	95
District of Columbia	2	2	1,200	80,000	700
Florida	49	22	5,150	14,850	1,306
Georgia	64	60	20,805	197,925	4,676
Idaho	6	1	300	2,000	350
Illinois	641	550	155,505	1,145,275	60,867
Indiana	733	651	219,320	1,329,370	78,942
Indian Territory	82	9	2,805	3,350	1,977
Iowa	403	308	83,450	708,100	30,988
Kansas	352	197	55,045	468,975	25,200
Kentucky	632	530	169,635	1,321,510	77,647
Louisiana	4	4	1,000	22,300	202
Maine	9	3	700	6,100	293
Maryland	14	14	5,200	66,200	1,774
Massachusetts	4	3	1,700	67,200	777
Michigan	73	49	14,870	160,650	5,788

SUMMARY BY STATES.—*Continued.*

STATES.	Organizations.	Church Edifices.	Seating Capacity.	Value of Church Property.	Communicants.
Minnesota	37	29	5,070	$73,000	1,917
Mississippi	111	69	12,675	55,422	5,729
Missouri	1,120	830	263,280	1,632,531	97,773
Montana..........	13	9	1,789	58,800	785
Nebraska	100	83	22,660	269,375	7,715
New Jersey........	1	....	....	....	105
New Mexico.......	4	....	....	....	65
New York	41	36	11,810	363,650	4,316
North Carolina	186	136	38,520	71,157	12,437
North Dakota	1	....	....	....	20
Ohio	475	446	138,778	1,462,250	54,425
Oklahoma.........	9	2	300	500	265
Oregon	74	40	10,950	76,700	4,067
Pennsylvania	125	101	33,785	533,147	12,007
Rhode Island......	1	1	150	3,000	35
South Carolina	50	37	8,060	10,200	2,880
South Dakota......	15	6	1,350	10,800	490
Tennessee	322	245	80,510	410,660	41,125
Texas	536	267	78,370	467,900	41,859
Utah	2	....	....	....	270
Vermont..........	2	2	475	5,000	262
Virginia	161	148	45,228	240,929	14,100
Washington	86	29	7,150	93,400	5,816
West Virginia	85	51	16,709	92,292	5,807
Wisconsin.........	24	18	5,825	30,300	1,317
Wyoming..........	2	....	....	....	48
Total.........	7,246	5,324	1,609,452	$12,206,038	641,051

CHAPTER XIX.

THE DUNKARDS.

THE Dunkards, or German Baptists, or Brethren, are of German origin, and trace their beginning back to Alexander Mack, of Schwartzenau, Germany. Early in the eighteenth century Mack and several others formed a habit of meeting together for the study of the New Testament. They were convinced that its doctrines and principles of church order were not being faithfully followed, either by the Lutheran or the Reformed Church. They therefore resolved to form a society of their own. Alexander Mack was chosen as their pastor. Persecution soon arose, and they were scattered. In 1719 most of them got together and came to the United States, settling in Pennsylvania, where their first church was organized about 1723. Like the Mennonites, they chose Germantown, where Christian Saur, one of their number, edited and printed the first German Bible in America, the unbound sheets of which were used by the British soldiers to litter their horses after the battle of Germantown, in the Revolutionary War. Later a number of these sheets were gathered up and several volumes were made of them, some of which are still in existence.

The Dunkards were an earnest and devout people, endeavoring to shape their lives according to the teachings of the New Testament, and they increased quite rapidly, drawing their converts, of course, from the German element. One of their most important principles is nonconformity to the world. They have sought, while living in the midst of the world, to preserve a simple, unostentatious life, ignoring the fashions and the customs of society in dress, in household furnishing, and in general mode of life. Through a long course of years this subject occupied more or less attention at every Annual Meeting. Bishops and heads of families were exhorted to be careful that they and their households set a good example in rejecting the "high fashions" of the times. As early as 1822 it was decided that with those who should continue to disregard the rule of nonconformity after the third admonition the Brethren should not break bread. In 1840 complaint was heard at the Annual Meeting of the increase of the "evil" of conformity to the world. Some Brethren, it was said, conform too much to the world in "building, house-furniture, apparel, etc., and even in sleighing have bells upon their horses." Five years later a solemn warning was given against "fashionable dressing, building and ornamenting houses in the style of those high in the world," as an "alarming and dangerous evil." In 1846 the overseers of churches were instructed to see that members did not have paintings, carpets, fine furniture, or fine houses. Much attention was given at the various Annual Meetings to the fashions of women. In 1862 they were forbidden to wear "hoops" and bonnets, and enjoined never to be without the cap, or prayer-covering, in church worship. Among the queries sent up in later years was one asking whether it was lawful for Brethren to establish or patronize high-schools. The reply was that Brethren should not mind *high* things but condescend to men of low estate.

The Brethren, however, continued to maintain a high-school, and have even established colleges. Despite their utmost care, innovations crept in gradually among them; carpets, musical instruments, gold watches, and other forbidden articles found their way gradually into use, and the cut and character of their garments were changed. Their discipline became insensibly relaxed, and the differences between them and their neighbors of other denominations were less striking. The result was that the more conservative, rallying against these innovations and insisting upon adherence to the old rules of discipline, found themselves strongly opposed by the more progressive element, and a division occurred about ten years ago. As the outcome of this division there are three branches, known as the Conservative, the Progressive, and the Old Order Brethren. There is, besides, a fourth called the Seventh-Day Baptist, German. This was due to a secession from the Dunkards, led by Conrad Beissel, in 1728. Beissel and his disciples observed the seventh day of the week as the Sabbath, and adopted a communal life.

On the general doctrines of the evangelical faith the Brethren are in harmony with other Protestant churches. They interpret the Scriptures literally, and hold that unquestioning obedience should be given to both letter and spirit. They agree with the Baptists in holding that immersion is the only proper form of baptism, and that believers are the only proper subjects of the ordinance. They do not practice infant baptism. The ordinance is administered to candidates in a kneeling position. They are dipped thrice, once at the mention of each name of the Trinity in the baptismal formula. They are dipped forward instead of backward, contrary to the usual custom of immersion.

One reason given for dipping forward is that when Christ died upon the cross his head fell forward on his breast. Immediately after the third immersion the administrator lays his hands upon the candidate's head and offers prayer.

Endeavoring to follow all the customs as well as the commandments of the New Testament, the Dunkards hold communion in the evening. It is preceded by the feast of love, or the *agapæ* of the Greeks. After partaking of a full meal, which is served at tables, the bread and wine of the sacrament are administered. In connection with this they extend the right hand of fellowship to one another and exchange the kiss of charity. This part of the service is observed separately by the sexes. Before the supper is eaten the ceremony of washing one another's feet is performed, the brethren observing it among themselves and the sisters doing likewise.

The ministry consists of bishops or elders, ministers, and deacons, all of whom are elected by the congregations. Deacons are advanced to be ministers, ministers are advanced to the second degree, and bishops or elders are elected from the list of ministers of the second degree. Ministers are chosen from the body of the brethren. In most cases they receive nothing for their services.

The polity of the Dunkards is partly Congregational and partly Presbyterian. Their chief ecclesiastical body is the Annual Meeting or Conference, whose decisions are considered binding upon district conferences and churches. Questions in doctrine and usage are sent from the district conferences to the Annual Meeting, which returns replies, generally with a Scriptural quotation to indicate the authority on which the replies are based. Each district conference sends to the Annual Meeting one bishop and one delegate. The bishops compose the Standing Committee of the conference. This Standing Committee provides for the organization of the meeting by choosing officers and bringing the business before the meeting in the proper shape for action; and also appoints committees in cases of difficulty in local churches. After the division changes were made in the manner of holding the Annual Meeting in each branch except the Old Order.

The Brethren hold not only to the principle of nonconformity but also to that of nonresistance, and earnestly protest against secret societies. Their ministers are not trained men, but pursue their ordinary business avocations during the week, preaching on Sundays and other occasions, as required. There are four branches, as follows:

1. Conservative.
2. Progressive.
3. Old Order.
4. Seventh-Day, German.

I.—THE CONSERVATIVE BRETHREN.

The Conservatives constitute the largest branch of the Dunkards. The division occurred, as already stated, as the result of a disagreement concerning the enforcement of discipline in matters of conformity. The Conservatives found themselves between two fires. On the one hand, there were quite a number of Brethren who demanded more liberty in the matter of the wearing of dress, and in other customs which had hitherto been frowned upon. On the other hand, there was a body of Brethren who insisted upon a rigorous enforcement of the prohibitions against the adoption of modern dress and modern customs. It was the policy of the Conservatives to deal leniently with those who wanted more liberty, and to conciliate, if possible, those who wanted a more rigorous enforcement of the discipline. The Old Order Brethren, however, felt that the Progressive Brethren had already departed from the ancient order of the church. The principle of dress as held by the Conservatives was that plainness, modesty, and economy in dress is a gospel principle, and that to retain the form of plainness was to insure the retention of the principle of plainness. The Progressive Brethren believed in the principle of plainness, but declared that there was no merit in adhering to a particular form of plainness. The Progressives, therefore, became a distinct branch.

One of the points of disagreement between the Conservatives and the Old Order Brethren was that of the introduction of Sunday-schools. The Old Order Brethren stoutly opposed this as an innovation, while the Conservatives held that it was simply an application of the principle of the fathers that the children should be religiously educated. The Old Order Brethren were likewise opposed to educational institutions. The Conservatives say on this point that the fathers themselves, if they were now living, would be favorable to Sunday-schools and high-schools, and also to missionary work. This, then, is the position of the Conservative body. They are in favor of retaining the principle of nonconformity to the world, but of not enforcing it so rigorously as was done twenty-five or fifty years ago. They believe in Sabbath-schools and missionary work, and also in educating their own people. They are represented in twenty-eight States and two Territories, being strongest in Pennsylvania, Indiana, and Ohio, where more than one half of their communicants are found. There are 180 halls, with a seating capacity of 15,048. The average value of the houses of worship is $1313, and the average seating capacity 414.

SUMMARY BY STATES.

STATES.	Organizations.	Church Edifices.	Seating Capacity.	Value of Church Property.	Communicants.
Arkansas	4	1	400	$300	78
California	3	2	375	2,200	211
Colorado	1	1	300	1,200	110
Florida	1	1	200	600	41
Idaho	1	1	200	1,000	40
Illinois	55	59	22,850	96,860	3,701
Indiana	107	129	58,565	179,870	10,224
Indian Territory	1	...	......	......	27
Iowa	52	37¾	14,125	49,505	2,769
Kansas	62	34	13,150	53,425	3,228
Kentucky	1	...	......	......	10
Louisiana	1	...	......	......	17
Maryland	29	39⅔	15,825	60,200	2,446
Michigan	12	11	3,728	11,425	560
Minnesota	2	2	600	1,500	104
Missouri	32	26	9,670	23,025	1,845
Nebraska	28	10	3,650	14,500	998
New Jersey	3	3	950	5,000	191
North Carolina	9	5	1,625	2,000	510
Ohio	95	127½	50,620	153,365	8,490
Oklahoma	2	...	......	......	46
Oregon	6	4	1,600	4,400	250
Pennsylvania	101	224¹½	94,738	354,008	14,194
South Dakota	4	...	......	......	102
Tennessee	19	16	7,450	11,700	1,249
Texas	6	1	150	300	95
Virginia	42	87	40,635	73,523	6,659
Washington	3	...	......	......	26
West Virginia	33	32	12,180	21,635	2,710
Wisconsin	5	...	......	......	170
Total	720	854	353,586	$1,121,541	61,101

2.—THE PROGRESSIVE BRETHREN.

The reasons for the division which resulted in the formation of this branch of the Dunkards have already been given. They constitute the most advanced section of the body of Dunkards. Their rules respecting nonconformity to the world are far less strict than those of the Conservatives. They call themselves simply Brethren, or The Brethren, and do not wish to be known as Dunkards. The number of their communicants is but a little more than one eighth of that of the Conservatives. They occupy 37 halls, which have a seating capacity of 4455. The average value of their edifices is $1521, and the average seating capacity 342.

SUMMARY BY STATES.

STATES.	Organi-zations.	Church Edifices.	Seating Ca-pacity.	Value of Church Property.	Com-muni-cants.
California	2	¼	150	$250	72
Colorado..........	1	..	.....	.....	17
Illinois............	4	3½	1,200	7,500	193
Indiana...........	22	15¾	5,875	22,620	1,479
Iowa	7	4	1,425	6,850	601
Kansas	16	3	785	5,400	507
Maryland	1	5	1,400	2,600	200
Michigan	6	5	1,570	5,850	240
Missouri	3	1	200	....	90
Nebraska	5	4⅔	1,950	8,900	396
Ohio	27	17⅓	7,000	30,700	1,542
Oregon	1	1	200	200	20
Pennsylvania	23	28	8,335	50,400	2,008
Virginia	4	3	1,300	2,450	397
West Virginia	6	4½	1,350	2,050	327
Total.........	128	96	32,740	$145,770	8,089

3.—THE OLD ORDER BRETHREN.

This is the smallest of the three branches into which the Dunkards were divided about ten years ago. The Old Order Brethren aim to prohibit conformity to the fashions of the world as rigorously as did the fathers fifty years ago. They are opposed to Sunday-schools, missionary endeavor, and high-schools or colleges. The census authorities had much difficulty in getting returns from them. They were opposed to the numbering of their people for Scriptural reasons, and refused in many cases to give information, which was otherwise obtained. There are 62 halls, with a seating capacity of 2330, occupied as places of worship. The average value of the church edifices is $1279, average seating capacity 408.

SUMMARY BY STATES.

STATES.	Organi- zations.	Church Edifices.	Seating Ca- pacity.	Value of Church Property.	Com- muni- cants.
Arkansas	1	..	......	......	4
California	1	..	......	......	7
Illinois.............	12	3	725	$970	225
Indiana	21	11½	5,050	16,400	647
Iowa	9	1½	800	2,600	100
Kansas	13	3	1,200	2,800	332
Kentucky	1	..	......	......	3
Maryland	6	2	1,200	3,000	328
Michigan	3	1	150	200	44
Missouri	9	2	200	1,600	155
Nebraska	4	1	350	600	47
North Carolina	1	..	......	......	15
Ohio	31	28	10,825	44,000	1,766
Oregon	1	..	......	......	10
Pennsylvania	4	5	2,900	5,000	311
Virginia	4	3	1,400	2,500	188
West Virginia	12	2	950	1,100	179
Wisconsin	1	..	......	......	29
Wyoming	1	..	......	......	21
Total.........	135	63	25,750	$80,770	4,411

4.—THE SEVENTH-DAY BAPTISTS, GERMAN.

This is the oldest secession from the body of Dunkards. As already stated, Conrad Beissel founded it in 1728. Only a very few members are now reported. These observe the seventh day as the Sabbath, and some features of the communal life. They are found in Bedford, Franklin, Lancaster, and Somerset counties, Pa.

SUMMARY.

STATE.	Organizations.	Church Edifices.	Seating Capacity.	Value of Church Property.	Communicants.
Pennsylvania	6	3	1,960	$14,550	194

SUMMARY BY STATES OF ALL DUNKARDS.

STATES.					
Arkansas	5	1	400	$300	82
California	6	2	525	2,450	290
Colorado.........	2	1	300	1,200	127
Florida	1	1	200	600	41
Idaho	1	1	200	1,000	40
Illinois...........	71	65	24,775	105,330	4,119
Indiana...........	150	156	69,490	218,890	12,350
Indian Territory ...	1	..	......	....	27
Iowa	68	43	16,350	58,955	3,470
Kansas	91	40	15,135	61,625	4,067
Kentucky.........	2	...	......	....	13
Louisiana	1	...	......	....	17
Maryland	36	47	18,425	65,800	2,974
Michigan	21	17	5,448	17,475	844
Minnesota	2	2	600	1,500	104
Missouri	44	29	10,070	24,625	2,090
Nebraska	37	16	5,950	24,000	1,441
New Jersey........	3	3	950	5,000	191
North Carolina	10	5	1,625	2,000	525
Ohio	153	173	68,445	228,065	11,798
Oklahoma.........	2	...	......	....	46
Oregon	8	5	1,800	4,600	280
Pennsylvania	134	261	107,933	423,958	16,707
South Dakota	4	...	......	....	102
Tennessee	19	16	7,450	11,700	1,249
Texas	6	1	150	300	95
Virginia	50	93	43,335	78,473	7,244
Washington	3	...	......	....	26
West Virginia	51	38	14,480	24,785	3,216
Wisconsin.........	6	...	......	....	199
Wyoming.........	1	...	......	....	21
Total.........	989	1,016	414,036	$1,362,631	73,795

CHAPTER XX.

JACOB ALBRIGHT, originally a Lutheran, born in 1759, was the founder of the Evangelical Association. Near the close of the last century he became an earnest revival preacher. He labored among the German-speaking population, and in 1800 formed a society of converts in Pennsylvania for "social prayer and devotional exercises" every Sunday and every Wednesday night. This was the rise of the movement which resulted in the Evangelical Association. The first conference was held in 1807. This conference elected Jacob Albright a bishop. Two years later a church discipline very similar to that of the Methodist Episcopal Church was published. Some years after the death of Bishop Albright (1808) the name Evangelical Association of North America was adopted. Previously to this his followers had been known as "The Albright People," or "The Albrights."

In doctrine and polity the Evangelical Association is Methodist. It has annual conferences, a quadrennial general conference, which is the supreme legislative and judicial body, quarterly conferences, presiding elders, and an itinerant and a local ministry, exhorters, class leaders, etc. It also has bishops, who, however, are not elected for life, but for a term of four years. Its Articles of Faith, twenty-one in number, are the same in substance and almost the same in language as the twenty-five articles of the Methodist churches, with a few omissions. Formerly the constituency of the church was almost entirely German; now it is largely English.

The Evangelical Association has twenty-six annual conferences. Four of the conferences are in other lands: one in Canada, one in Germany, one in Switzerland, and one in Japan.

The church is in a divided state. In October, 1891, two bodies, each claiming to be the legal general conference, were held, one in Indianapolis, the other in Philadelphia, and each elected a different set of bishops and general church officers. The differences are of long standing. They were augmented in the application in 1890 and 1891 of disciplinary processes to the three bishops of the Association, all of whom were tried and suspended. The Philadelphia General Conference took order restoring Bishop Dubs to his functions. That of Indianapolis, representing the majority, declared the proceedings against Bishops Esher and Bowman void. The secular courts have been appealed to in various cases, and have decided generally in favor of the Indianapolis Conference. The church was divided into two bodies in 1894.

Summary by States.

STATES.	Organizations.	Church Edifices.	Seating Capacity.	Value of Church Property.	Communicants.
California	13	10	2,350	$72,100	472
Colorado..........	3	1	150	1,600	87
Florida	2	4	450	2,000	69
Illinois............	134	132	35,000	438,500	10,934
Indiana	124	104⅔	30,445	214,390	6,738
Iowa	188	147	30,910	299,235	9,761
Kansas	96	50	10,060	85,600	4,459
Kentucky	3	3	850	16,000	213
Maryland	14	14	5,800	123,900	1,743
Michigan	134	97	22,775	188,450	6,677
Minnesota.........	134	89	17,165	170,550	6,181
Missouri	26	20	6,750	39,700	1,102
Nebraska	81	47	8,935	86,100	3,458
New Jersey........	10	10	2,675	59,250	669
New York.........	86	80½	18,870	401,850	6,222
North Dakota	31	10	2,035	21,100	784
Ohio	216	215½	60,835	491,975	14,673
Oregon	25	24	3,300	63,900	1,199
Pennsylvania	662	627⅓	178,750	1,590,605	42,379
South Dakota	74	15	2,280	20,450	1,628
Texas	8	7	1,400	22,950	296
Washington.......	7	6	1,200	14,900	451
West Virginia	15	13	2,825	5,475	565
Wisconsin.........	224	172	33,525	355,100	12,553
Total.........	2,310	1,899	479,335	$4,785,680	133,313

Summary by Conferences.

CONFERENCES.					
Atlantic...........	30	30	9,625	$317,250	2,903
California	13	10	2,350	72,100	472
Cen'l Pennsylvania.	259	253⅓	76,900	487,315	15,616
Dakota	111	25	4,315	41,550	2,512
Des Moines	77	61	14,620	117,500	4,592
East Pennsylvania..	218	218½	59,790	778,265	17,899
Erie	49	47	12,775	211,400	3,996
Illinois............	106	105	30,200	397,250	9,570
Indiana	132	113⅙	33,470	228,265	7,140
Iowa	108	83	15,740	178,135	5,069
Kansas	115	71	16,860	124,900	5,533
Michigan	145	108	25,275	205,700	7,386

SUMMARY BY CONFERENCES.—*Continued.*

CONFERENCES.	Organizations.	Church Edifices.	Seating Capacity.	Value of Church Property.	Communicants.
Minnesota	128	89	17,165	$170,550	6,081
Nebraska	61	34	5,450	64,950	2,126
New York	71	66	15,370	262,250	5,295
Ohio	138	140	38,835	293,600	8,999
Oregon	32	30	4,500	78,800	1,650
Pittsburg	208	178	48,735	263,300	9,738
Platte River	30	13	3,585	23,150	1,447
South Indiana	44	44	8,800	89,300	2,341
Texas	8	7	1,400	22,950	296
Wisconsin.........	227	173	33,575	357,200	12,652
Total.........	2,310	1,899	479,335	$4,785,680	133,313

CHAPTER XXI.

THE FRIENDS.

THE Friends, or Quakers, as they are often called, own as their founder George Fox, an Englishman, born in Drayton, Leicestershire, in 1624. He began to preach experimental holiness of heart and life in 1647. He had large congregations, and in 1656 was assisted by sixty ministers. The first general meeting of Friends was held in London in 1668, the second in 1672. The Yearly Meeting was established in 1678. Encountering much opposition and severe persecution in England, many Friends emigrated to this country. A few arrived at Boston in 1656, whence they were subsequently scattered by persecution; many came to New Jersey and Pennsylvania after 1674.

The first Yearly Meeting in America is believed to have been held in Rhode Island in 1661. George Fox met with it in 1672, and in 1683 it was set off from the London Yearly Meeting. It was held regularly at Newport until 1878. Since that date it has alternated between Newport and Portland, Me. Yearly Meetings were organized in Maryland in 1672, in Pennsylvania and New Jersey in 1681, in North Carolina in 1708, and in Ohio in 1812.

The Friends have no creed, no liturgy, and no sacraments. They believe in a spiritual baptism and a spiritual communion, and hold that the outward rites are unnecessary. They accept the Old and New Testaments as a divine revelation, and in general the doctrine of the atonement by Christ and sanctification by the Holy Spirit. Belief in the "immediate influence of the Holy Spirit" is pronounced by President Chase, of Haverford College, the most distinctive feature of their faith. They believe in the guidance of the Holy Spirit in worship and all religious acts. Periods of silence occur in their meetings, when no one feels called upon to speak, and when each worshiper is engaged in communion with God and inward acts of devotion. The Friends believe that a direct call to the ministry comes to persons old or young or of either sex. Those who, after a sufficient probation, give evidence of a divine call are acknowledged as ministers, and allowed seats at the head of the meeting. Besides ministers, there are in the local meetings or congregations, elders of both sexes, who are appointed by Monthly Meetings, and who advise the ministers, and, if necessary, admonish them.

Their societies or congregations are usually called meetings, and their houses of worship meeting-houses. There are Monthly Meetings, embracing a number of local meetings. They deal with cases of discipline, accept or dissolve local meetings, and are subordinate to Quarterly Meetings, to which they send representatives. Quarterly Meetings hear appeals from Monthly Meetings, record certificates of ministers, and institute or dissolve Monthly Meetings. The highest body is the Yearly Meeting. No Quarterly Meeting can be set up without its consent. It receives and determines appeals from Quarterly Meetings, and issues advice or extends care to subordinate meetings.

The Friends are divided into four bodies, popularly distinguished as (1) Orthodox, (2) Hicksite, (3) Wilburite, and (4) Primitive.

I.—THE FRIENDS (ORTHODOX).

These constitute by far the most numerous branch. In 1887, at a General Conference held in Richmond, Ind., they adopted a "Declaration of Christian Doctrine," as an expression of "those fundamental doctrines of Christian truth that have always been professed by our branch of the Church of Christ." This declaration sets forth the evangelical view of the Trinity, the Scriptures, the fall of man, justification and regeneration, the resurrection and the final judgment, the issues of which are eternal. In the article on the Holy Spirit these sentences appear:

"We own no principle of spiritual light, life, or holiness, inherent by nature in the mind or heart of man. We believe in no principle of spiritual light, life, or holiness, but the influence of the Holy Spirit of God, bestowed on mankind, in various measures and degrees, through Jesus Christ our Lord."

The article on public worship recognizes "the value of silence, not as an end, but as a means toward the attainment of the end—a silence not of listlessness or of vacant musing, but of holy expectation before the Lord."

The discipline of the Western Yearly Meeting makes as "disownable offenses," for which members are disowned or excommunicated, denial of the divinity of Christ, the revelation of the Holy Spirit, the divine authenticity of the Scriptures; engaging in the liquor traffic, drunkenness, profanity, joining the army or encouraging war, betting, participating in lotteries, dishonesty, taking or administering oaths, etc.

Each Yearly Meeting has its own discipline, but fellowship is maintained between them by epistolary correspondence. There is also a general agreement between them on the fundamentals of doctrine and discipline. The Philadelphia Yearly Meeting, which is one of the oldest, has a discipline incorporating various decisions and advices adopted since its organization in 1681.

There are 10 Yearly Meetings, with 794 organizations, 725 church edifices, valued at $2,795,784, and 80,655 members. The average seating capacity of their edifices is 297, and their average value $3718. Halls to the number of 90, with a seating capacity of 7085, are occupied.

SUMMARY BY STATES.

STATES.	Organizations.	Church Edifices.	Seating Capacity.	Value of Church Property.	Communicants.
Arkansas..........	5	3	500	$1,950	338
California.........	11	7	1,785	14,100	1,009
Colorado..........	1	1	120	300	38
Delaware	1	1	260	11,000	122
Dist. of Columbia ..	1	...	.....	....	19
Florida	2	2	375	1,200	70
Illinois............	21	23	6,155	36,760	2,015
Indiana	188	172	54,775	325,577	25,915
Indian Territory ...	10	3	250	1,300	468
Iowa	74	73	19,795	102,632	8,146
Kansas	65	51	14,304	74,415	7,762
Louisiana	1	...	.....	....	66
Maine	23	21	5,653	35,975	1,430
Maryland	6	6	2,025	77,800	525
Massachusetts	28	28	6,370	117,700	1,560
Michigan	17	16	4,550	26,500	1,433
Minnesota	6	3	675	35,100	305
Missouri	5	5	950	10,800	615
Nebraska	13	8	1,354	4,800	782
New Hampshire ...	10	11	2,860	8,800	413
New Jersey........	20	21	6,655	84,200	982
New York	50	47	10,270	203,900	3,644
North Carolina	47	43	17,475	36,850	4,904
Ohio	95	94	31,930	202,250	10,884
Oklahoma	2	2	180	1,225	108
Oregon	7	6	2,125	10,550	766

SUMMARY BY STATES.—*Continued.*

STATES.	Organizations.	Church Edifices.	Seating Capacity.	Value of Church Property.	Communicants.
Pennsylvania	39	43	13,445	1,279,700	3,490
Rhode Island	11	11	3,720	58,800	617
South Dakota	4	2	475	1,000	266
Tennessee	15	8	2,975	9,400	1,001
Texas	1	..	. . . . .	. . . .	120
Vermont	4	4	575	4,800	251
Virginia	7	7	2,300	14,900	387
West Virginia	1	1	150	400	50
Wisconsin	3	2	400	1,100	154
Total	794	725	215,431	$2,795,784	80,655

SUMMARY BY YEARLY MEETINGS.

YEARLY MEETINGS.					
Baltimore	17	16	5,150	$101,500	1,012
Indiana	177	160	51,725	350,437	22,105
Iowa	117	100	26,429	168,532	11,391
Kansas	89	64	16,084	88,940	9,347
New England	72	71	18,603	221,275	4,020
New York	54	51	10,845	208,700	3,895
North Carolina	62	51	20,450	46,250	5,905
Ohio	47	48	15,475	90,950	4,733
Philadelphia	57	62	19,535	1,366,100	4,513
Western	102	102	31,135	153,100	13,734
Total	794	725	215,431	$2,795,784	80,655

2.—THE FRIENDS (HICKSITE).

This body of Friends is so named from Elias Hicks, a minister who was foremost in preaching doctrines which became a cause of separation. They object to being called Hicksites. Elias Hicks was born in 1748, and died in 1830. He emphasized the principle of "obedience to the light within," and so stated the doctrines of the preëxistence, deity, incarnation, and vicarious atonement of Christ, of the personality of Satan, and of eternal punishment, that he was charged with being more or less in sympathy with Unitarianism.

Those identified with this body of Friends insist that Mr. Hicks's views were "exactly those of Robert Barclay," an English Friend of the seventeenth century, whose "Apology for the True Christian Divinity " is still regarded as a fair exposition of the doctrinal views of Friends. They decline to make orthodox theology a test of membership.

The separation took place in the Philadelphia Yearly Meeting in 1827, and in New York, Baltimore, Ohio, and Indiana in 1828. There was no separation in New England or North Carolina. The Genesee, in western New York, and the Illinois Yearly Meetings were formed many years later.

They have 7 Yearly Meetings, with 201 organizations, 213 church edifices, valued at $1,661,850, and 21,992 members. The average seating capacity of their church edifices is 341, and their average value $7802. They occupy 4 halls, with a seating capacity of 325.

SUMMARY BY STATES.

STATES.	Organizations.	Church Edifices.	Seating Capacity.	Value of Church Property.	Communicants.
Delaware	6	6	1,440	$54,500	622
District of Columbia	1	1	300	50,000	40
Illinois	5	4	870	4,900	440
Indiana	8	8	2,550	47,100	1,376
Iowa	4	4	1,300	3,800	440
Maryland	17	18	5,410	133,050	1,547
Michigan	1	1	100	400	25
Nebraska	3	1	200	1,400	198
New Jersey	23	26	9,980	183,500	2,279
New York	45	45	13,575	561,850	3,331
Ohio	16	18	4,485	61,350	1,187
Pennsylvania	65	74	29,158	546,700	10,001
Virginia	7	7	3,200	13,300	506
Total	201	213	72,568	$1,661,850	21,992

Summary by Yearly Meetings.

YEARLY MEETINGS.	Organi-zations.	Church Edifices.	Seating Ca-pacity.	Value of Church Property.	Com-muni-cants.
Baltimore.........	29	30	10,490	$211,300	2,797
Genesee	13	13	3,900	14,500	751
Illinois...........	14	11	2,920	11,100	1,301
Indiana...........	12	14	3,885	97,100	1,743
New York.........	36	37	10,950	567,250	2,803
Ohio	9	9	2,500	8,850	568
Philadelphia.......	88	99	37,923	751,750	12,029
Total.........	201	213	72,568	$1,661,850	21,992

3.—THE FRIENDS (WILBURITE).

The Wilburite Friends are thus called because John Wilbur, of New England, was their principal leader in opposing Joseph J. Gurney and his teaching. They separated from the Orthodox body in the New England Yearly Meeting in 1845, in the Ohio in 1854, and in the western Iowa and Kansas in 1877. They are very conservative, and were unwilling to adopt the new methods devised as the church became aggressive in evangelistic and missionary work. They make much of the doctrine of the light within, holding that every man, by reason of the atonement, has an inward seed, or light, given him, which, as it is heeded, will lead him to salvation. They deny instantaneous conversion and the resurrection of the body. The controlling portion of the Philadelphia Yearly Meeting hold to the views of Wilbur, though they have not separated from the body of the church further than to decline epistolary correspondence with it. They are counted with the Orthodox branch.

The Wilburite Friends have 5 Yearly Meetings, with 52 organizations, 52 church edifices, valued at $67,000, and

4329 members. They are represented in the States of Indiana, Iowa, Kansas, Massachusetts, Ohio, Pennsylvania, and Rhode Island. The average seating capacity of their church edifices is 253, and the average value $1288. There are no halls. A single private house is occupied.

SUMMARY BY STATES.

STATES.	Organi-zations.	Church Edifices.	Seating Ca-pacity.	Value of Church Property.	Com-muni-cants.
Indiana...........	9	9	1,810	$8,200	489
Iowa	12	13	2,925	12,350	1,539
Kansas	5	5	2,030	10,400	495
Massachusetts	2	2	480	3,500	28
Ohio	20	20	5,534	24,900	1,676
Pennsylvania	1	1	140	650	30
Rhode Island......	3	2	250	7,000	72
Total.........	52	52	13,169	$67,000	4,329

SUMMARY BY YEARLY MEETINGS.

YEARLY MEETINGS.					
Iowa	7	7	1,500	$7,000	714
Kansas	5	5	2,030	10,400	495
New England......	5	4	730	10,500	100
Ohio	24	25	6,735	30,200	2,451
Western	11	11	2,174	8,900	569
Total.........	52	52	13,169	$67,000	4,329

4.—THE FRIENDS (PRIMITIVE).

The Primitive Friends are in faith and practice Wilburite. They separated from the Philadelphia Yearly Meeting because that body refused to correspond with the New England and Ohio (Wilbur) Yearly Meetings, and they do not affiliate with the latter because they recognize the Philadelphia meeting by ministerial visitations and by exchanging certificates of membership.

They have 9 organizations, 5 church edifices, valued at $16,700, and 232 members. They are found only in Massachusetts, New York, Pennsylvania, and Rhode Island. The average seating capacity of their church edifices is 210, and the average value $3340. One hall, with a seating capacity of 50, and 3 private houses are occupied.

SUMMARY BY STATES.

STATES.	Organizations.	Church Edifices.	Seating Capacity.	Value of Church Property.	Communicants.
Massachusetts	2	1	200	$1,000	14
New York.........	2	2	400	1,700	103
Pennsylvania......	3	2	450	14,000	106
Rhode Island......	2	..	...	......	9
Total	9	5	1,050	$16,700	232

SUMMARY BY STATES OF ALL FRIENDS.

Arkansas	5	3	500	$1,950	338
California	11	7	1,785	14,100	1,009
Colorado...........	1	1	120	300	38
Delaware	7	7	1,700	65,500	744
District of Columbia.	2	1	300	50,000	59
Florida	2	2	375	1,200	70
Illinois.............	26	27	7,025	41,660	2,455
Indiana	205	189	59,135	380,877	27,780
Indian Territory	10	3	250	1,300	468
Iowa	90	90	24,020	118,782	10,125
Kansas	70	56	16,334	84,815	8,257
Louisiana	1	...	......	......	66
Maine	23	21	5,653	35,975	1,430
Maryland	23	24	7,435	210,850	2,072
Massachusetts	32	31	7,050	122,200	1,602
Michigan	18	17	4,650	26,900	1,458
Minnesota..........	6	3	675	35,100	305
Missouri	5	5	950	10,800	615
Nebraska	16	9	1,554	6,200	980
New Hampshire	10	11	2,860	8,800	413
New Jersey.........	43	47	16,635	271,700	3,261
New York	97	94	24,245	767,450	7,078
North Carolina	47	43	17,475	36,850	4,904

SUMMARY BY STATES OF ALL FRIENDS.—*Continued.*

STATES.	Organizations.	Church edifices.	Seating Capacity.	Value of Church Property.	Communicants.
Ohio	131	132	41,949	$288,500	13,747
Oklahoma..........	2	2	180	1,225	108
Oregon	7	6	2,125	10,550	766
Pennsylvania	108	120	43,193	1,841,050	13,627
Rhode Island.......	16	13	3,970	65,800	698
South Dakota	4	2	475	1,000	266
Tennessee	15	8	2,975	9,400	1,001
Texas	1	...	......	....	120
Vermont...........	4	4	575	4,800	251
Virginia	14	14	5,500	28,200	893
West Virginia	1	1	150	400	50
Wisconsin..........	3	2	400	1,100	154
Total..........	1,056	995	302,218	$4,541,334	107,208

CHAPTER XXII.

FRIENDS OF THE TEMPLE.

THIS is a small body which had its origin in Würtemburg, Germany, upward of fifty years ago. It is variously called Temple Society, Friends of the Temple, "Hoffmannites." The Rev. Christopher Hoffmann, president of the Temple colonies in Palestine, and author of most of its standard literature, appears to be its chief leader.

The Friends of the Temple have for their great object the gathering of the people of God in Palestine. To this end they constitute Temples, i.e., spiritual communities, in various countries, and these assist in the construction of the Temple in the Holy Land, which is to become a center for regenerated humanity. They believe in the power of God which raised Christ from the dead, to build up a "spiritual house, a holy priesthood," and without formulating their doctrines declare their full acceptance of the Scriptures, of the law of Moses as well as the Gospel of Christ. They believe that all the prophecies will be fulfilled, and that as Christ came to work out the fulfillment, that should also be the mission of his followers. The chief task of the Temple Society is to secure the spiritual development of its members, who are under the oversight of presidents and other officers, and meet for worship on Sundays and on special occasions. No regulations have been adopted concerning baptism and the Lord's Supper, individual convictions being allowed full play.

In 1874 the Temple Society established four colonies in Palestine—at Joppa, Sharon, Haifa, and Jerusalem. The cost of these colonies has been met in large part by voluntary contributions.

SUMMARY BY STATES.

STATES.	Organizations.	Church Edifices.	Seating Capacity.	Value of Church Property.	Communicants.
Kansas	1	1	200	$800	55
New York..........	3	4	950	14,500	285
Total..........	4	5	1,150	$15,300	340

CHAPTER XXIII.

THE GERMAN EVANGELICAL PROTESTANT CHURCH.

THIS is a body of scattered congregations, with a center in Cincinnati. Some of its churches are a century old, and some are quite new. The German language is almost exclusively spoken. In theology it is very liberal, rationalistic views generally prevailing. It has no synodical organization, but there are non-ecclesiastical associations, or *vereine*, of ministers.

SUMMARY BY STATES.

STATES.	Organizations.	Church Edifices.	Seating Capacity.	Value of Church Property.	Communicants.
Illinois	2	2	800	$16,000	735
Indiana	8	7	3,270	54,150	1,886
Kentucky	3	2	2,100	51,000	1,250
Louisiana	1	1	1,000	40,000	3,500
Missouri	2	2	2,600	70,000	1,700
Nebraska	1	1	200	5,000	40
Ohio	22	23	15,850	438,800	11,793
Pennsylvania	9	10	6,655	439,000	12,287
Texas	2	2	1,000	10,500	1,050
West Virginia	2	2	1,700	63,000	1,915
Total	52	52	35,175	$1,187,450	36,156

CHAPTER XXIV.

THE GERMAN EVANGELICAL SYNOD.

THE German Evangelical Synod of North America represents in this country the State church of Prussia, which is a union of Lutheran and Reformed elements. The first ecclesiastical organization was formed October 15, 1840, at a meeting held at Gravois Settlement, in Missouri, by six evangelical ministers. Out of the principles then agreed upon the constitution of the Synod has been gradually developed. In 1850 the Society formed in Missouri and the German Evangelical Society of Ohio, formed in 1850, united. To this union there was a further addition in 1860, when the United Evangelical Society of the East was consolidated with it. In 1872 two other bodies—the Evangelical Synod of the Northwest and the United Evangelical Synod of the East—entered and completed the union. All were kindred bodies, holding the same doctrines and governed by the same ecclesiastical principles.

The Synod accepts the Bible as the only rule of faith and practice, holding to the Augsburg Confession, Luther's Catechism, and the Heidelberg Catechism, in so far as they agree with one another, as correct interpretations of it. Concerning those points on which these symbols do not agree the Synod stands upon the Scripture passages relating to them, and allows liberty of conscience.

The church is divided into districts, of which there are fifteen. They correspond as nearly as possible to synods in the Lutheran Church. A General Conference representing the whole church meets once every three years. It is composed of the presidents of the districts, and of delegates, clerical and lay, in the proportion of one for every nine ministers and one for every nine churches.

Since 1872, when the union of the various Evangelical Societies was completed, the church has grown rapidly. It had then 219 organizations and 8032 communicants. Now it has 870 organizations and 187,432 communicants —the organizations having been multiplied by 4 in this period of eighteen years, and the communicants by 23. It is represented in twenty-two States, being strongest in Illinois, 37,138; Ohio, 31,617; Missouri, 25,676; and New York, 17,409.

The average seating capacity of its church edifices is 313, and the average value $5878. It also holds meetings in 83 halls, which have a seating capacity of 5970.

SUMMARY BY STATES.

STATES.	Organizations.	Church Edifices.	Seating Capacity.	Value of Church Property.	Communicants.
California	4	4	618	$8,460	315
Colorado	2	1	250	18,000	135
Illinois	164	155	47,081	813,450	37,138
Indiana	75	75	22,635	337,660	15,274
Iowa	59	43	11,413	110,300	6,902
Kansas	28	19¾	3,794	37,750	2,053
Kentucky	11	10	5,525	137,400	4,912
Louisiana	3	3	1,550	26,450	1,250
Maryland	12	11	6,300	223,500	4,405
Michigan	50	43	14,710	242,450	10,926
Minnesota	53	40	9,072	97,900	5,567
Missouri	124	115¼	31,922	575,650	25,676
Nebraska	23	19	3,290	43,500	2,142

SUMMARY BY STATES.—*Continued.*

STATES.	Organizations.	Church Edifices.	Seating Capacity.	Value of Church Property.	Communicants.
New Jersey	3	2	1,190	39,000	1,890
New York	50	49	21,160	681,570	17,409
North Dakota	5	3	600	3,300	440
Ohio	107	106	41,019	836,200	31,617
Pennsylvania	12	12	5,670	132,150	5,293
Texas	19	14	2,380	36,300	1,864
Virginia	1	1	700	30,000	700
West Virginia	2	1	216	800	114
Wisconsin	63	58	14,686	182,700	11,410
Total	870	785	245,781	$4,614,490	187,432

SUMMARY BY DISTRICTS.

DISTRICTS.	Organizations.	Church Edifices.	Seating Capacity.	Value of Church Property.	Communicants.
Atlantic	26	23	11,490	$380,650	9,825
Indiana	80	79	31,890	724,600	25,444
Iowa	65	49	12,973	127,625	7,885
Kansas	32	22¾	4,254	57,250	2,248
Michigan	73	66	21,180	332,410	15,937
Minnesota	59	44	9,842	101,700	6,127
Missouri	93	87¼	25,030	424,650	21,566
Nebraska	21	17	3,080	42,000	2,082
New York	48	48	20,680	639,070	17,284
North Illinois	83	79	26,340	511,675	22,814
Ohio	95	93	33,645	582,000	23,875
South Illinois	81	76	21,671	318,900	15,216
Texas	19	14	2,380	36,300	1,864
West Missouri	33	30	6,810	153,460	3,975
Wisconsin	62	57	14,516	182,200	11,290
Total	870	785	245,781	$4,614,490	187,432

CHAPTER XXV.

THE JEWS.

THE first company of Jews in this country came from Brazil in 1654. The first synagogue was established in Mill Street, New York City, now known as Broad Street. It was called the Shearith Israel (Remnant of Israel), and the society is still in active existence, occupying a building on West Nineteenth Street. As according to custom ten males above the age of thirteen can form a Jewish congregation, it is quite probable that there was Jewish worship before the first synagogue was opened, although it was doubtless conducted with some secrecy, as a petition to the authorities of New Amsterdam in 1685 for the privilege of exercising the rites of the Jewish religion was denied. "No public worship," so ran the reply, "is tolerated by act of assembly but to those that profess faith in Christ." Later some of the Jews in New York removed to Newport, R. I., and there held regular services, securing in 1763 a synagogue, to which the chief contributors were sons of the minister of the congregation, the Rev. Isaac Touro. One of these sons, Abraham Touro, gave $10,000 for the completion of the Bunker Hill monument. Jewish congregations were organized in Savannah, Ga., in 1733; in Lancaster, Pa., in 1776; in Philadelphia in 1780 and 1782; and in Charleston, S. C., in 1791. Of these congregations those in the South and one of those in Philadelphia used the ritual of the Portuguese Jews, the others that of the German Jews.

The Jews of America have no religious head. Each congregation is autonomous, and responsible to its members only. It is said that an effort in New York to bring the Orthodox congregations under the care of a chief rabbi is not wholly satisfactory.

The statistics of Jewish congregations are not frequently or periodically gathered, as is the custom of most religious denominations; but twice at least in the last forty years efforts have been made to ascertain the number of Jewish congregations in the United States, once in 1854 and again in 1880. According to the earlier report there were in 1854 97 regularly organized congregations, of which 30 were in the State of New York. The latter count was made under the auspices of the Board of Delegates of American Israelites and the Union of Hebrew Congregations, and it required several years to complete the compilation. The results, which have been regarded as quite accurate, indicated the existence of 270 congregations, with 12,546 members, or about 50,000 communicants. The value of the real estate held by the congregations was returned at $4,706,700, with other property aggregating $1,497,878, or a total of $6,204,578, exclusive of burying-grounds.

The tables presented herewith show that there are 533 congregations of Orthodox and Reformed Jews, with 130,-496 communicants. It should be noted that in Jewish congregations the head of a family only is counted. The members of the family are represented by one person. The number given as communicants, therefore, does not indicate the number of members of a synagogue. Members of families may, on attaining their majority, rent a pew and be counted as a member of a synagogue or temple, but they seldom do so until they have a household of their own.

I.—THE ORTHODOX JEWS.

There are two branches or schools of thought in the Jewish religion, commonly designated the Orthodox and the Reformed. The attempt is here made to tabulate the statistics in accordance with this classification. It is difficult, however, in some cases to know how to draw the lines. Under the above heading those congregations are embraced which adhere to the ancient rites and ceremonies, observing the Bible as expounded and expanded by the prophets and rabbis. The Orthodox Jews accept the Schulchan Aruch as authoritative in all its requirements. It is a codification, made by Rabbi Joseph Karo in the middle of the sixteenth century, of the laws and ceremonies expounded by the rabbis of the Talmud and handed down from generation to generation by tradition. It provides for the minutest details of Jewish life, and those who accept it consider it as binding as the law of Moses itself. Halls to the number of 193, with a seating capacity of 24,847, are occupied as places of worship. The average seating capacity of the churches is 384, and the average value $22,967.

SUMMARY BY STATES.

STATES.	Organizations.	Church Edifices.	Seating Capacity.	Value of Church Property.	Communicants.
Alabama	1	..	.....	......	325
California	7	5	2,225	$93,000	2,344
Colorado	4	3	800	25,500	662
Connecticut	6	1	500	12,000	926

SUMMARY BY STATES.—*Continued.*

STATES.	Organizations.	Church Edifices.	Seating Capacity.	Value of Church Property.	Communicants.
District of Columbia	1	1	75	$2,000	40
Georgia...........	3	1	200	8,000	240
Illinois............	12	4	2,175	121,500	4,405
Indiana...........	8	3	650	6,500	1,299
Iowa.............	1	..	......	....	50
Kansas	4	1	260	12,000	403
Kentucky	2	1	175	1,500	200
Louisiana	8	2	575	20,000	629
Maryland	3	3	1,200	43,000	775
Massachusetts	7	4	1,775	110,500	1,201
Michigan	6	5	2,150	36,000	2,150
Minnesota	3	1	400	25,000	750
Missouri..........	8	2	1,100	58,000	1,432
Montana..........	1	..	......	....	140
Nebraska	4	1	100	5,500	550
New Jersey........	19	10	2,575	44,300	2,521
New York	152	44	21,245	1,919,500	29,064
North Carolina	1	1	180	6,500	73
North Dakota	1	..	......	....	30
Ohio	17	6	2,790	67,000	2,313
Oregon	2	1	350	16,000	475
Pennsylvania	17	13	2,862	116,250	2,447
Rhode Island......	3	1	200	20,000	685
Tennessee	4	3	1,450	8,500	425
Texas	1	..	......	....	65
Vermont..........	1	..	......	....	44
Virginia	4	3	675	17,000	493
Washington	1	..	......	....	150
Wisconsin.........	4	2	150	7,000	291
Total.........	316	122	46,837	$2,802,050	57,597

2.—THE REFORMED JEWS.

Under this classification are included all Jewish congregations which do not recognize as absolute the authority of the Schulchan Aruch. In some cases the departure from orthodoxy is slight, as in worshiping with the hat off, the mingling of the sexes in the synagogue or temple, and the introduction of the organ and female choir. There are 38 halls, with a seating capacity of 6360, occupied as places of worship. The average seating capacity of the edifices is 516, and their average value $38,839, which is unequaled.

SUMMARY BY STATES.

STATES.	Organizations.	Church Edifices.	Seating Capacity.	Value of Church Property.	Communicants.
Alabama	7	5	3,050	$103,500	2,843
Arkansas	5	5	1,450	44,000	744
California	8	7	3,150	303,000	3,835
Colorado	1	1	600	50,000	400
Connecticut	2	2	850	75,000	695
District of Columbia	1	1	900	40,000	936
Florida	2	2	318	13,500	147
Georgia	6	6	2,900	151,000	1,846
Illinois	12	11	6,645	465,000	5,766
Indiana	15	13	4,050	160,000	2,318
Iowa	5	4	1,160	58,000	487
Kansas	2	..	.....	....	83
Kentucky	5	4	850	16,000	755
Louisiana	5	4	2,875	255,000	2,745
Maryland	9	6	3,900	223,500	2,800
Massachusetts	2	2	2,440	135,000	1,300
Michigan	4	4	1,900	118,000	1,543
Minnesota	2	2	724	45,000	674
Mississippi	6	5	1,750	64,000	1,370
Missouri	9	6	3,033	183,800	3,018
Nebraska	2	1	500	15,000	512
New Jersey	5	4	3,420	124,000	1,755
New Mexico	1	..	.....	....	50
New York	27	25	18,927	2,395,700	16,743
North Carolina	3	1	400	30,000	313
Ohio	17	13	7,020	636,225	6,576
Oregon	1	1	850	80,000	690
Pennsylvania	18	15	7,980	552,500	5,582
Rhode Island	2	1	420	25,000	225
South Carolina	3	3	850	78,000	800
Tennessee	5	4	2,950	106,000	1,335
Texas	10	8	2,380	182,000	1,929
Utah	1	1	750	40,000	100
Virginia	7	6	1,875	70,500	694
West Virginia	3	2	650	9,000	350
Wisconsin	4	4	1,880	105,000	940
Total	217	179	92,397	$6,952,225	72,899

SUMMARY BY STATES OF ALL JEWS.

STATES.	Organizations.	Church Edifices.	Seating Capacity.	Value of Church Property.	Communicants.
Alabama	8	5	3,050	$103,500	3,168
Arkansas	5	5	1,450	44,000	744
California	15	12	5,375	396,000	6,179
Colorado	5	4	1,400	75,500	1,062
Connecticut	8	3	1,350	87,000	1,621
District of Columbia	2	2	975	42,000	976
Florida	2	2	318	13,500	147
Georgia	9	7	3,100	159,000	2,086
Illinois	24	15	8,820	586,500	10,171
Indiana	23	16	4,700	166,500	3,617
Iowa	6	4	1,160	58,000	537
Kansas	6	1	260	12,000	486
Kentucky	7	5	1,025	17,500	955
Louisiana	13	6	3,450	275,000	3,374
Maryland	12	9	5,100	266,500	3,575
Massachusetts	9	6	4,215	245,500	2,501
Michigan	10	9	4,050	154,000	3,693
Minnesota	5	3	1,124	70,000	1,424
Mississippi	6	5	1,750	64,000	1,370
Missouri	17	8	4,133	241,800	4,450
Montana	1	..	.....	....	140
Nebraska	6	2	600	20,500	1,062
New Jersey	24	14	4,995	168,300	4,276
New Mexico	1	..	.....	....	50
New York	179	69	40,172	4,315,200	45,807
North Carolina	4	2	580	36,500	386
North Dakota	1	..	.....	....	30
Ohio	34	19	9,810	703,225	8,889
Oregon	3	2	1,200	96,000	1,165
Pennsylvania	35	28	10,842	668,750	8,029
Rhode Island	5	2	620	45,000	910
South Carolina	3	3	850	78,000	800
Tennessee	9	7	4,400	114,500	1,760
Texas	11	8	2,380	182,000	1,994
Utah	1	1	750	40,000	100
Vermont	1	..	.....	....	44
Virginia	11	9	2,550	87,500	1,187
Washington	1	..	.....	....	150
West Virginia	3	2	650	9,000	350
Wisconsin	8	6	2,030	112,000	1,231
Total	533	301	139,234	$9,754,275	130,496

CHAPTER XXVI.

THE LATTER-DAY SAINTS.

THE Church of Jesus Christ of Latter-Day Saints is of American origin. It was founded in 1830 by Joseph Smith, its first Prophet. He was born in Sharon, Vt., in 1805, removing to Palmyra, N. Y., ten years later. Between the ages of fourteen and fifteen he began earnestly to inquire how he could with certainty save his soul, and how he might ascertain which one of the many denominations was the true Church of Christ. While thus seeking he had a vision of a great light, and two " glorious personages " appeared and informed him that his sins were forgiven, and instructed him in the doctrine of the one true religion, which was not, he was told, represented by any of the existing churches. Another vision was granted him in 1823, when an " angel of the Lord " appeared and told him that the preparatory work for the second coming of Christ was soon to begin, and that he was to be chosen to bring about some of the purposes of the coming dispensation. The vision was frequently renewed. By the directions received in one of them he was enabled to obtain the sacred records, which have since been known as the " Book of Mormon." These records were received, it is stated, in 1827. They were " engraved on plates which had the appearance of gold," and these plates were " filled on both sides " with words in reformed Egyptian characters.

Having become the subject of persecution on account of the visions, he fled to Pennsylvania, and translated, " by the gift and power of God," the records which had been miraculously delivered to him. The Book of Mormon claims to give a history of ancient America, from a settlement by a colony who came from the Tower of Babel, at the confusion of tongues.

An angel appeared in 1829, it is stated, to Joseph Smith and Oliver Cowdery and ordained them as priests of the order of Aaron and directed them to baptize each other. In 1830 a church was organized at Fayette, Seneca County, N. Y. The new gospel was preached, miracles were announced as an attestation of the new faith, and missionaries were sent out, among whom Brigham Young, Sidney Rigdon, and the Pratt brothers—Parley P. and Orson—were prominent. Churches were established in several States. In 1831 the headquarters of the denomination were removed west to Kirtland, O., and a colony was formed in Jackson County, Mo. After having been driven out of Missouri, a settlement was made at Nauvoo, Ill., where a large temple was erected and where the headquarters of the church were fixed. In 1843 Joseph Smith announced a revelation in favor of the celestial order of marriage including polygamy. In disturbances which subsequently arose he was shot and killed by a mob, June 27, 1844, at Carthage, Ill., and Brigham Young became his successor as Prophet. In 1846 and 1847 there was a general migration from Illinois to Salt Lake, the present headquarters of the church.

There are two divisions—the Church of Jesus Christ of Latter-Day Saints, and the Reorganized Church of Jesus Christ of Latter-Day Saints.

I.—THE CHURCH OF JESUS CHRIST OF LATTER-DAY SAINTS.

Those who migrated to Salt Lake devised a system for active propagation of the doctrines of the Book of Mormon and subsequent revelations, and their numbers increased steadily. The "celestial law of marriage" was openly practiced after 1852, when it was promulgated. After the death of Brigham Young, August, 1877, John Taylor succeeded as president of the church. In 1890 Wilford Woodruff, the successor of John Taylor as "seer, revelator, and first president," announced a revelation prohibiting the contracting of further polygamous marriages.

The chief points of the doctrinal belief of the Latter-Day Saints, as stated by President Wilford Woodruff, are in substance: God exists as a Trinity of Father, Son, and Holy Ghost; men are to be punished for actual sins, and not for the transgression of Adam; salvation is for all men, through the atonement of Christ, by obedience to the laws and ordinances of the gospel; these ordinances are faith, repentance, baptism by immersion for the remission of sins, and the laying on of hands for the gift of the Holy Ghost; men are called of God to the ministry by prophecy and the laying on of hands by those in authority; there is the gift of tongues, prophecy, revelation, visions, healing, and interpretation of tongues; the Bible is the Word of God, so far as it is translated correctly, also the Book of Mormon; God has revealed much and has much yet to reveal; there is to be a literal gathering of Israel and the restoration of the ten tribes; Zion is to be built on this continent; Christ will reign personally upon the earth, which is to be renewed.

The organization of the church includes features of both

the Jewish and Christian systems. There are two orders of the priesthood, the Melchizedek or higher, and the Aaronic or lesser. The first embraces apostles, patriarchs, high-priests, seventies, and elders, and has charge over all the spiritual interests of the church, preaching, baptizing, laying on of hands for confirmation and ordination, healing, blessing, administering the Lord's Supper, and officiating in all the ordinances. The Aaronic priesthood, including bishops, priests, teachers, and deacons, administers, under the direction of the Melchizedek priesthood, the outward ordinances and temporal affairs. In organization for church government the place of the ordinary parish is taken by the ward. Each ward has its meeting-house and bishop, and two counselors. A number of wards constitute a stake of Zion. At the head of each stake or district is a president and two counselors, who are high-priests, and a council of twelve high-priests who sit as a court in church matters. There is a general conference which meets in April and October of each year for the management of the general affairs of the church. The missionaries and preachers are organized into seventies. Each seventy has seven presidents, and is under the direction of the Twelve Apostles. The highest officers are those of the First Presidency, which has supreme authority, and are elected by the whole church.

The chief strength of the church is in Utah, but it also has organizations in twenty-two States and Territories. There are in all 425 organizations, 266 church edifices, valued at $825,506, and 144,352 communicants. The average seating capacity of the edifices is 346, and their average value $3103 ; 178 halls, etc., with a seating capacity of 28,310, are occupied.

Summary by States.

STATES.	Organizations.	Church Edifices.	Seating Capacity.	Value of Church Property.	Com. municants.
Alabama..........	2	..	......	......	166
Arizona..........	27	16	4,815	$26,400	6,500
Colorado..........	3	3	1,380	7,200	1,640
Georgia..........	1	..	......	......	175
Idaho	62	48	11,682	45,560	14,816
Indiana...........	1	..	......	......	14
Kansas	1	..	......	......	34
Kentucky.........	1	..	......	......	199
Maryland	1	..	......	......	58
Mississippi	1	..	......	......	123
Nevada...........	5	..	......	......	417
New Mexico.......	5	2	300	1,430	453
New York.........	2	..	......	......	56
North Carolina	1	..	......	......	108
Pennsylvania......	4	..	......	......	44
South Carolina	1	..	......	......	203
Tennessee.........	2	..	......	......	134
Utah	293	191	72,375	733,216	117,640
Virginia..........	1	..	......	......	137
West Virginia	2	..	......	......	81
Wisconsin	1	..	......	......	32
Wyoming.........	8	6	1,550	11,700	1,322
Total.........	425	266	92,102	$825,506	144,352

Summary by Stakes.

STAKES.					
Bannock..........	20	18	4,420	$9,720	4,343
Bear Lake	25	15	3,660	17,350	4,986
Beaver...........	6	5	1,395	25,100	1,342
Box Elder.........	14	6	1,750	20,750	3,993
Cache	23	21	7,920	87,000	6,962
Cassia	6	4	622	740	1,377
Davis.............	10	9	4,700	36,500	4,686
Emery............	9	1	125	11,475	1,968
Juab	6	5	1,800	19,661	3,190
Knab.............	8	1	300	1,400	2,161
Malad	9	9	2,050	7,850	2,317
Maricopa	5	..	....	4,800	1,785
Millard	8	3	1,325	11,000	2,815
Morgan...........	9	3	950	3,200	1,479
Oneida	15	10	2,940	21,600	4,445

SUMMARY BY STAKES.—*Continued.*

STAKES.	Organi-zations.	Church Edifices.	Seating Ca-pacity.	Value of Church Property.	Com-muni-cants.
Panguitch.........	8	8	1,750	$11,750	1,786
Parowan..........	5	5	1,950	17,700	2,251
Saint George......	24	8	1,650	4,150	3,086
Saint John's.......	7	4	625	1,980	1,413
Saint Joseph	9	7	2,540	9,050	2,067
Salt Lake	43	38	13,015	222,694	23,428
San Juan	7	5	1,080	6,000	829
San Luis..........	2	2	1,100	5,700	1,454
Sanpete...........	16	14½	7,760	56,980	12,713
Sevier	19	8½	2,850	19,665	5,226
Snowflake.........	8	6	1,800	11,000	1,478
Summit...........	15	10	5,200	28,350	2,611
Tooele............	7	6	1,575	13,266	1,974
Uinta.............	6	1	500	800	1,588
Utah	27	18	7,050	69,450	19,240
Wasatch	6	5	2,900	7,700	3,379
Weber............	21	10	4,800	61,125	10,351
MISSIONS.					
Northern States....	10	..	......	......	352
Southern States....	12	..	......	......	1,277
Total	425	266	92,102	$825,506	144,352

2.—THE REORGANIZED CHURCH OF JESUS CHRIST OF LATTER-DAY SAINTS.

Like the Mormons of Utah, the members of this organization, sometimes called Nonpolygamous Mormons, trace their origin back to the movement begun by Joseph Smith in 1830. They claim to represent this movement and to be true to the principles and doctrines proclaimed by him, and insist that those who followed Brigham Young were led away from the truth into error. They deny that the revelation concerning polygamy which was communicated to the church in Salt Lake City in 1852 by Brigham

Young was genuine, and declare that the true successor to Joseph Smith in the presidency of the church was not Brigham Young, but Joseph Smith's eldest son, Joseph. It is said that none of the members of the family of the first Prophet have united with the Utah branch, but all have become members of the Reorganized Church.

The first conference was held in 1852, and it was then that the leadership of Brigham Young, James J. Strang, Sidney Rigdon, and others was disowned and the society organized. Its headquarters are at Lamoni, Ia., where it has a large publishing-house.

The Reorganized Church accepts three books as of divine origin: first, the Bible; second, the Book of Mormon; third, the Book of Covenants. The latter consists of the revelations given to the church in the present century as a guide in church government. The Book of Mormon is accepted as a history of the ancient inhabitants of America and the revelation given them by God, beginning at a period two thousand years before Christ and continuing until four hundred years after Christ. In doctrine they adhere to the Trinity, to the atonement by Jesus Christ, to the resurrection of the dead, to the second coming of Christ, and to the eternal judgment, believing that each individual will receive reward or punishment in strict measure according to the good or evil deeds done in life. They hold that men are to be saved by faith in God and Christ, by forsaking sin, by immersion for the remission of sin, and by the laying on of hands. They believe that revelations of God are still given by the Holy Spirit for the guidance of the church, and that the gifts, blessings, and powers of the Holy Spirit in Bible times are continual. Their order of church government is such as they find authority for in the New Testament and such as they understand that the Apostolic Church observed. It includes the presidency, consisting, when full, of three persons, which has jurisdiction over the whole church as its chief presiding authority; twelve apostles, whose special duty is to take charge of all missionary work abroad; one or more quorums of seventy, who are set apart from the body of elders and assist the apostles; high-priests, who have charge over States and districts; priests or pastors, teachers and deacons, and bishops, of whom three are set at the head of the business affairs of the church. Other bishops and agents assist in collecting the tithes. As to marriage, they believe that it is ordained of God, and that there should be but one companion for man or woman in wedlock until the contract is broken by death or transgression. They characterize the doctrine of polygamy or plural wives as an abomination.

The Reorganized Church is represented in thirty-six States and three Territories, including that of Utah. It returns 21,773 members, of whom 5303 are in Iowa. The next largest number, 3189, is in Missouri; Illinois has 1909, Michigan 1540, and California 1396. Meetings are held in 254 halls, etc., with a seating capacity of 15,370. The value of the church property is $226,285, which indicates an average valuation of $1847. The average seating capacity is 251. The church is not fully organized into districts.

SUMMARY BY STATES.

STATES.	Organizations.	Church Edifices.	Seating Capacity.	Value of Church Property.	Communicants.
Alabama..........	12	2	300	$350	426
Arkansas	1	..	.....	......	60
California	28	7	1,700	14,400	1,396
Colorado	5	1	200	2,000	122
Connecticut	..	..	.....	......	8
Florida	9	..	.....	......	257
Idaho.............	7	..	.....	......	156
Illinois............	52	15	3,500	19,200	1,909
Indiana	13	2	900	1,800	366
Indian Territory ...	2	..	.....	......	46
Iowa	59	27	6,785	44,985	5,303
Kansas	25	4	800	3,300	1,072
Kentucky	1	1	200	1,500	50
Maine	14	2	475	1,800	442
Maryland	..	..	.....	......	17
Massachusetts	8	5	2,050	11,500	457
Michigan	33	6	1,750	4,325	1,540
Minnesota	4	..	.....	......	224
Mississippi	2	1	100	150	74
Missouri	42	18	5,000	58,650	3,189
Montana	2	2	400	1,500	122
Nebraska	20	7	1,060	7,500	1,058
Nevada............	4	..	.....	......	108
New Jersey........	1	..	.....	......	21
New Mexico.......	..	..	.....	......	3
New York.........	2	..	.....	......	102
Ohio	18	6	3,050	43,000	678
Oregon	3	..	.....	......	95
Pennsylvania	10	1	300	1,000	373
Rhode Island......	3	1	150	800	233
South Dakota......	4	..	.....	......	88
Tennessee	3	3	275	325	64
Texas	12	6	1,025	1,900	437
Utah	14	1	150	3,700	561
Virginia	1	..	.....	......	34
Washington.......	1	..	.....	......	34
West Virginia	10	1	300	1,400	325
Wisconsin	6	3	320	1,200	309
Wyoming	..	..	.....	......	14
Total	431	122	30,790	$226,285	21,773

The two branches of Latter-Day Saints aggregate 856 organizations, 388 church edifices, with a seating capacity of 122,892, and a value of $1,051,791, and 166,125 communicants. Of the latter 118,201 are in Utah, and the next largest number, 14,972, in Idaho.

CHAPTER XXVII.

THE EVANGELICAL LUTHERANS.

THE earliest Lutherans in America came from Holland to Manhattan Island in 1623 with the first Dutch colony. For some years they had great difficulty in establishing worship of their own, the Dutch authorities, ecclesiastical and civil, having received instructions " to encourage no other doctrine in the New Netherlands than the true Reformed " and " to allure the Lutherans to the Dutch churches and matriculate them in the Public Reformed religion." A Lutheran pastor, the Rev. John Ernest Goetwater, was sent to this country in 1657 by the Lutheran Consistory of Amsterdam to minister to two Lutheran congregations, one at New York, the other at Albany. He was not allowed, however, to enter upon his ministrations, but was sent back to Holland by representatives of the Reformed faith. When the English took possession of New York the Lutherans were allowed full liberty of worship.

The Lutheran faith was also established on the banks of the Delaware by a Swedish colony, who erected the first Lutheran church in America near Lewes in 1638. Swedish immigration was soon checked, and the large Lutheran influx from Germany did not begin until early in the eighteenth century, the first German congregation of Lutherans having been organized at about that time in Montgomery

County, Pa., with the Rev. Justus Falckner, who was ordained in this country by the Swedes, as its first pastor. In 1710 a large number of exiled Palatines settled in New York and Pennsylvania, and in 1734 a colony of Salzburgers planted the Lutheran faith in Georgia.

While immigration brought many Lutherans to this country, they were in a scattered and unorganized condition until the arrival of the Rev. Henry M. Muhlenburg, who drew them closer together, formed them into congregations, and inspired them with new life. In 1748 he, with six other ministers and lay delegates from congregations, organized the first Lutheran synod in this country, the Synod or Ministerium of Pennsylvania. In 1786 the second synod, the Ministerium of New York, was formed.

The recent extraordinary growth of the Lutheran communion in this country is due in part to immigration from Lutheran countries. A large proportion of Lutherans are either German immigrants or the offspring of German immigrants. There are also large bodies of Swedish, Norwegian, and Danish Lutherans, with a number from Finland and other European countries.

The system of faith held by all Lutherans is set forth in the Augsburg Confession and in a number of other symbols, known as Luther's Catechisms, the Apology of the Augsburg Confession, the Smalcald Articles, and the Formula of Concord. The cardinal doctrine of the system is that of justification by faith alone. The ordinances of baptism and the Lord's Supper are held by Lutherans to be not mere signs or memorials, but channels of grace. Their view of the Lord's Supper is peculiar. They believe that " in the Holy Supper there are present with the elements and are received sacramentally and supernaturally the body and blood of the Lord Jesus Christ," but reject both transubstantiation as held by the Roman Catholic Church, and consubstantiation as attributed by some writers to the Lutheran Church. They observe the various festivals of the Christian year, and have a liturgical form of worship.

In polity, while the sovereignty of the individual congregation, which includes the office of preaching the gospel and administering the sacraments, is recognized, in the synodical system as it prevails a measure of judicial and executive authority is conferred upon the individual synods by the individual congregations. General bodies, such as the General Synod, General Council, etc., are formed by the union of a number of synods and have chiefly advisory powers. Synods may withdraw from the General Synod, General Council, and other general bodies, and may afterward rejoin the body they withdrew from or join another body, or take an independent position.

Arranging the various synods as nearly as possible according to speech, we find that seven languages are represented, if the Norwegian be considered as different from the Danish. The United Synod of the South is wholly, and the General Synod mostly, English. The General Council, the Synodical Conference, and the independent synods have but a small percentage of English organizations. The following is a summary, omitting the independent congregations, which cannot well be classified:

SUMMARY BY LANGUAGES.

LANGUAGES.	Number of organizations.	Communicants.
English	1,816	198,997
German	2,691	460,706
German-English	1,178	232,512
Swedish	688	88,700
Norwegian	1,786	190,154
Danish	181	13,674
Icelandic	13	1,991
Finnish	11	1,385
Total	8,364	1,188,119

I.—THE GENERAL SYNOD.

This is the oldest general body of Lutherans. It was organized in 1820 by representatives of the Ministerium of Pennsylvania, the oldest synod; the Ministerium of New York, the next oldest; the Synod of North Carolina, the third oldest; and the Synod of Maryland and Virginia. The General Synod was the only general body until the Civil War cut off its Southern synods and led to the organization of the General Synod, South, now known as the United Synod in the South. It never had, however, the adherence of all the synods. One withdrew and afterward joined again; some held aloof from it for many years, so that from the first there has scarcely been a period in which there have not been synods in an independent attitude.

The chief cause of the changes which synods have made in their attachments to the general bodies, and also of the organization of the General Council and Synodical Conference, has been differences concerning the acceptance and interpretation of the doctrinal symbols. There have been no secessions or divisions among Lutherans on account of questions arising in church government, except several instances among the Germans, when charges of hierarchical tendencies were broached. The reception in 1864 of the Franckean Synod by the General Synod led to a division on confessional grounds. It was objected by many that the Franckean Synod had not announced its acceptance of the Augsburg Confession and it was thought to be doctrinally unsound. It was contended in behalf of those who adhered to the General Synod that the Franckean Synod had accepted the Augsburg Confession in accepting the constitution of the General Synod, in which is set forth the confessional basis. The minority, including the representatives of the Ministerium of Pennsylvania, presented a protest against the admission of the Franckean Synod, and the representatives of the Ministerium withdrew. Two years later, however, at the next meeting of the General Synod, delegates from the Ministerium were in attendance, but, not being allowed to participate in the election of officers, on the ground that the Ministerium must be considered as " in a state of practical withdrawal from the governing functions of the General Synod," they retired, and their example was subsequently followed by the Pittsburg, English Ohio, Minnesota, and Texas synods, and the Ministerium soon after led in a movement for the formation of another general body.

The following is the confessional basis of the General Synod:

" We receive and hold with the Evangelical Lutheran Church of our fathers the Word of God, as contained in the canonical Scriptures of the Old and New Testaments, as the only infallible rule of faith and practice, and the

Augsburg Confession as a correct exhibition of the fundamental doctrines of the divine Word and of the faith of our
church founded upon that Word."

The General Synod Lutherans affiliate more readily with
other evangelical denominations than the Lutherans attached to the General Council, the Synodical Conference,
or the Ohio Synod. They do not refuse to exchange pulpits with ministers of evangelical churches, as do their
stricter brethren, who condemn these relations under the
general term " unionism."

The General Synod has connected with it 23 synods, the
oldest of which, that of Maryland, was organized in 1820,
and the newest, that of Middle Tennessee, in 1878. It is
represented in twenty-five States and in the District of
Columbia and Territory of New Mexico. Nearly one half
of its communicants, or 78,938, are to be found in the
State of Pennsylvania. Of its 1424 organizations, Pennsylvania has 596. There are 1322 edifices, valued at
$8,919,170. This indicates an average value for each
edifice of $6745, which is extraordinary. The average
seating capacity of the edifices is 357. Only 72 of the
1424 organizations meet in other than church buildings.
The 72 halls have a seating capacity of 10,730.

The boundaries of Lutheran synods are very irregular.
Those of the synods belonging to the General Synod are
more regular than those of any of the other Lutheran general bodies, but only 5 of the 23 do not cross one or more
State lines.

SUMMARY BY STATES.

STATES.	Organizations.	Church Edifices.	Seating Capacity.	Value of Church Property.	Communicants.
Alabama..........	1	1	300	$2,000	175
California	6	3	1,700	87,000	743
Colorado..........	7	5	1,025	64,500	220
Connecticut	2	1	400	7,000	190
District of Columbia	6	6	3,000	301,000	1,038
Illinois............	93	83½	24,803	344,050	7,438
Indiana	86	88	23,600	243,300	6,090
Iowa	30	28	8,585	127,200	2,043
Kansas	53	43	10,245	171,000	2,835
Kentucky	11	11	3,700	43,700	1,627
Maryland	96	97	43,430	843,050	17,288
Massachusetts	2	2	275	2,700	103
Michigan	9	9	2,450	37,500	679
Minnesota.........	1	1	300	1,200	26
Missouri	14	13	4,125	132,850	1,576
Nebraska	73	55	12,185	330,420	3,731
New Jersey........	16	16	5,175	126,100	2,415
New Mexico.......	2	...	.....	....	64
New York.........	95	100¼	36,925	1,224,700	15,611
Ohio	189	182	59,310	1,039,950	18,437
Pennsylvania	596	545¾	219,516	3,672,650	78,938
South Dakota	3	3	370	7,700	64
Tennessee	11	11	4,600	8,900	749
Virginia	3	3	1,050	7,000	450
West Virginia	5	5	1,800	69,000	1,108
Wisconsin.........	11	8½	2,600	17,600	861
Wyoming.........	3	2	350	6,100	141
Total.........	1,424	1,322	471,819	$8,919,170	164,640

SUMMARY BY SYNODS.

SYNODS.					
Allegheny	138	131	42,456	$539,925	12,806
Central Illinois	25	24½	7,415	147,100	2,187
Central Pennsylvania..............	83	77½	29,280	372,100	8,680
East Ohio.........	75	72	24,425	412,800	6,360
East Pennsylvania..	109	102½	47,560	1,141,650	17,994
Franckean	29	28	8,225	100,200	2,147
Hartwick	34	35	13,404	286,400	4,578
Iowa	25	24	7,160	153,700	1,727
Kansas	47	38	10,275	242,650	2,924

SUMMARY BY SYNODS.—*Continued.*

SYNODS.	Organizations.	Church Edifices.	Seating Capacity.	Value of Church Property.	Communicants.
Maryland	108	109	48,905	$1,198,050	19,864
Miami	45	42	13,310	295,000	4,604
Middle Tennessee..	11	11	4,600	8,900	749
Nebraska	102	77	16,175	415,870	5,064
New York and New Jersey	50	54	20,096	955,900	11,234
North Illinois......	46	41	12,900	198,050	3,147
North Indiana.....	67	71	19,475	184,100	4,650
Olive Branch	37	35	9,675	135,100	3,577
Pittsburg	81	75	24,850	330,125	7,740
South Illinois......	19	15½	4,450	20,250	1,234
Susquehanna	59	58	26,540	483,850	10,643
Wartburg.	29	24	7,313	90,800	3,320
West Pennsylvania.	131	106	50,855	868,000	21,575
Wittenberg	74	71	22,475	338,650	7,836
Total	1,424	1,322	471,819	$8,919,170	164,640

2.—THE UNITED SYNOD IN THE SOUTH.

Soon after the beginning of the Civil War the four synods of North and South Carolina and of Virginia and southwest Virginia withdrew from the General Synod because of the adoption by that body, at its convention in 1862, of resolutions concerning the war which gave offense to the South. These synods and the Synod of Texas were not represented in the convention of 1862 on account of the outbreak of hostilities and the condition of the country. The next year (1863) the four synods above mentioned and the Synod of Georgia constituted the General Synod, South. A few other Southern synods afterward became connected with it. In 1886 a new organization, known as the United Synod in the South, took its place, consisting of six synods which had belonged to the General Synod, South, and the independent Tennessee and Holston synods.

The type of Lutheranism represented by the United Synod in the South is similar to that of the General Synod, though perhaps a little stricter. Its confessional basis is as follows:

"The Holy Scriptures, the inspired writings of the Old and New Testaments, the only standard of doctrine and church discipline.

"As a true and faithful exhibition of the doctrines of the Holy Scriptures in regard to matters of faith and practice, the three ancient symbols, the Apostolic, the Nicene, and the Athanasian Creeds, and the Unaltered Augsburg Confession of Faith; also, the other symbolical books of the Evangelical Lutheran Church, viz., the Apology, the Smalcald Articles, the Smaller and Larger Catechisms of Luther, and the Formula of Concord, consisting of the Epitome and full Declaration as they are set forth, defined, and published in the Christian Book of Concord, or the Symbolical Books of the Lutheran Church, published in the year 1580, as true and Scriptural developments of the doctrines taught in the Augsburg Confession and in perfect harmony of [*sic*] one and the same pure Scriptural faith."

The United Synod in the South is represented in nine of the Southern States, including Tennessee and West Virginia. It has 414 organizations and 379 church edifices, of an average value of $2938, and an average seating capacity of 365; 29 halls, with a seating capacity of 4225, are occupied.

SUMMARY BY STATES.

STATES.	Organi- zations.	Church Edifices.	Seating Ca- pacity.	Value of Church Property.	Com- muni- cants.
Alabama..........	3	1	250	$1,200	75
Florida	2	2	460	5,450	143
Georgia	16	15	4,825	99,150	1,477
Mississippi	11	10	2,750	4,650	533
North Carolina	119	107	44,463	263,690	11,759
South Carolina	74	78	27,525	339,250	8,757
Tennessee.........	23	20	7,410	52,750	1,999
Virginia	145	124	45,090	314,200	11,196
West Virginia	21	22	5,680	33,725	1,518
Total.........	414	379	138,453	$1,114,065	37,457

SUMMARY BY SYNODS.

SYNODS.					
Alpha Synod of Freedmen........	5	3	550	$1,750	94
Georgia...........	17	16	4,885	92,600	1,535
Holston...........	27	22	7,835	53,650	2,129
Mississippi	11	10	2,750	4,650	533
North Carolina	56	53	21,050	188,800	6,163
South Carolina	61	66	21,975	337,150	7,013
Southwest Virginia.	65	48	17,502	114,050	4,379
Tennessee.........	107	97	41,976	143,790	10,086
Virginia	65	64	19,930	177,625	5,525
Total.........	414	379	138,453	$1,114,065	37,457

3.—THE GENERAL COUNCIL.

This was the third general body to be organized in the order of time. When the General Synod consented in 1864 to the admission of the Franckean Synod, which was regarded by the minority of the General Synod as un-Lutheran and as not having definitely accepted the Augsburg Confession, the delegates of the Ministerium of Pennsylvania protested (a number of others joining in the protest) and withdrew. At the next session of the Gen-

eral Synod, being excluded from participation in its organization, they retired from the body. The Pittsburg, the
New York, the English Ohio, the Minnesota, and the
Texas synods also dissolved their connection with the
General Synod. The withdrawal of the delegates of the
Ministerium of Pennsylvania was approved by that body
at its next session, and a committee was appointed to issue
a "fraternal address to all Evangelical Lutheran synods,
ministers, and congregations in the United States and
Canada which confess the Unaltered Augsburg Confession,
inviting them to unite in a convention for the purpose
of forming a union of Lutheran synods." The proposed
convention was held in December, 1866, representatives
of the synods of Pennsylvania, New York, English Ohio,
Pittsburg, Wisconsin, English district of Ohio, Michigan,
Minnesota, Canada, Illinois, and the Joint Synod of Ohio
participating. "Principles of Faith and Church Polity"
were adopted, and the next year the first convention of
the new body was held. Thus was the General Council
organized.

In the first year of its history the Joint Synod of Ohio
withdrew and the German Synod of Iowa assumed a semi-
independent position, sending delegates and participating
in the debate but taking no part in the voting. This body
still sustains this relation. The withdrawal of the Joint
Synod of Ohio, and, a few years later, of the synods of
Wisconsin, Illinois, and Minnesota, and the semi-independ-
ent position taken by the German Synod of Iowa, were on
account of the refusal of the General Council to give a satisfactory declaration on what are called the "Four Points."
It was the desire of these bodies that some expression
should be given concerning chiliasm, and that the admis-

sion of non-Lutherans to communion, the exchange of "pulpits with sectarians," and membership in secret societies should be unequivocally condemned. The council would not commit itself fully at that time on these points, though it has since practically done so, especially on the questions of pulpit and altar fellowship.

The confessional basis of the General Council is as follows:

"We accept and acknowledge the doctrine of the Unaltered Augsburg Confession in its original sense as throughout in conformity with the pure truth, of which God's Word is the only rule. We accept its statements of truth as in perfect accordance with the canonical Scriptures. We reject the errors it condemns, and believe that all which it commits to the liberty of the church of right belongs to that liberty.

"In thus formally accepting and acknowledging the Unaltered Augsburg Confession we declare our conviction that the other confessions of the Evangelical Lutheran Church, inasmuch as they set forth none other than its system of doctrine and articles of faith, are of necessity pure and Scriptural. Preëminent among such accordant, pure, and Scriptural statements of doctrine, by their intrinsic excellence, by the great and necessary ends for which they were prepared, by their historical position, and by the general judgment of the church, are these: The Apology of the Augsburg Confession, the Smalcald Articles, the Catechisms of Luther, and the Formula of Concord, all of which are, with the Unaltered Augsburg Confession, in perfect harmony of one and the same Scriptural faith."

One of the most perplexing questions Lutherans have

had to deal with in this country has been that of language. It is agreed that the communion sustained very heavy losses down almost to the middle of this century by insisting that synodical proceedings and church services generally should be in the German tongue. The children, having learned English, desired to have the services conducted in that language; failing in this, they joined other denominations. The General Council proposed from the beginning that the different languages and nationalities " should be firmly knit together in this New World in the unity of one and the same pure faith," and declared that " no distinction of language " must be allowed " to interfere with the great work" before the church in this country. It includes American, German, and Scandinavian elements, but English is the official language of the General Council, though the German and Scandinavian tongues are also used. It has many large English churches in the eastern cities, but a majority of the congregations are German and Scandinavian and employ those languages. But few of the ministers are incapable of speaking and writing in English. All the correspondence of the Census Office with Lutherans of whatever synodical connection was in English, and scarcely a score out of the thousands of letters received were in any other tongue.

There are nine synods connected with the General Council, including one in Canada, which, of course, is not given in these tables. While the General Council, the General Synod, and, indeed, most other denominations of this country, have churches and communicants in other countries, these churches and communicants are omitted in the census reports. Only those congregations are included which are within the territorial limits of the United States.

The General Council has 2044 organizations, with 1554 edifices and 324,846 communicants. Of the latter, 107,-025 are attached to the Ministerium of Pennsylvania, the oldest Lutheran synod in the United States. Some 367 organizations hold worship in halls, etc., having a seating capacity of 30,904. The total value of church property is $11,119,286, or an average for each edifice of $7155, which is even higher than the extraordinary average of houses of worship owned by the General Synod. The average seating capacity of the edifices is 378.

While there are only eight synods, there are congregations in thirty-two States and one Territory, Pennsylvania, of course, maintaining the lead, with 616, or nearly one third of the whole number, and 124,163 communicants. The next largest number of communicants, 39,430, is found in New York, Minnesota coming third, with 27,906, and Illinois fourth, with 26,860. The Synod of Texas is the only synod that does not cross State lines. The Swedish Augustana Synod, though second in numbers to the Ministerium of Pennsylvania, embraces in its territory no fewer than thirty States, being, in fact, almost as widespread as the entire General Council. Delaware and Kentucky are the only two States covered by the General Council which are not also covered by the Augustana Synod. This body of wide boundaries was organized in 1860 with only about 5000 communicants, and is composed of Swedish Lutherans. The synod is subdivided into seven conferences, or sub-synods, which meet semi-annually. The synod itself is assembled yearly. The German Iowa Synod has five districts, and covers several States.

SUMMARY BY STATES.

STATES.	Organizations.	Church Edifices.	Seating Capacity.	Value of Church Property.	Communicants.
California	7	5	1,175	$62,300	603
Colorado	7	6	1,436	65,800	519
Connecticut	24	15	5,820	122,400	3,767
Delaware	2	1	335	10,000	296
Dist. of Columbia	1	2	1,400	40,000	600
Florida	1	...	......	......	17
Idaho	3	2	180	2,450	139
Illinois	143	122	42,335	809,150	26,860
Indiana	38	34	10,335	148,100	3,887
Iowa	174	132	34,771	420,680	20,009
Kansas	62	43	11,294	136,830	6,269
Kentucky	4	3	570	6,800	299
Maine	1	1	300	2,600	179
Massachusetts	12	6	2,110	55,900	1,743
Michigan	70	58	14,305	153,350	8,710
Minnesota	223	175	52,445	624,120	27,906
Missouri	18	16	3,584	101,800	1,857
Nebraska	88	55	12,181	206,001	7,204
New Hampshire	2	2	750	13,500	395
New Jersey	30	20	8,785	339,500	7,940
New York	113	109	43,764	1,915,510	39,430
North Dakota	38	7	1,210	15,400	1,582
Ohio	118	108	35,510	483,100	15,915
Oregon	4	3	675	13,650	305
Pennsylvania	616	486	268,885	4,993,355	124,163
Rhode Island	3	1	300	5,250	420
South Dakota	100	31	5,070	40,125	4,770
Texas	42	39	9,810	128,740	7,140
Vermont	2	...	......	......	174
Washington	7	5	1,400	33,950	446
West Virginia	1	1	800	10,000	650
Wisconsin	85	66	17,290	158,925	10,072
Wyoming	5	...	......	......	580
Total	2,044	1,554	588,825	$11,119,286	324,846

SUMMARY BY SYNODS.

SYNODS.					
English Synod of Ohio	64	58	20,375	$273,600	8,273
Indiana	31	27	9,010	169,000	3,058
Ministerium of New York	115	117	47,319	1,942,410	42,029

SYNODS.	Organizations.	Church Edifices.	Seating Capacity.	Value of Church Property.	Communicants.
Ministerium of Pennsylvania	456	347	227,555	$4,319,355	107,025
Pittsburg	167	149	47,825	961,800	20,755
Scandinavian Augustana	688	515	156,664	2,600,550	88,700
Texas	39	35	8,485	112,740	6,643
German Synod of Iowa	484	306	71,592	739,831	47,363
Total	2,044	1,554	588,825	$11,119,286	324,846

4.—THE SYNODICAL CONFERENCE.

The latest and largest of the Lutheran general bodies is the Synodical Conference, organized in 1872 by representatives of the Missouri, Ohio, Wisconsin, Minnesota, Illinois, and Norwegian synods. Four of these synods, the Ohio, Wisconsin, Minnesota, and Illinois, had taken part in the organization of the General Council, but had withdrawn. The conference was intended to represent a type of Lutheran confessionalism stricter than that of the General Council, as that of the General Council was stricter than the General Synod. The following is its confessional basis:

"The Synodical Conference acknowledges the canonical Scriptures of the Old and New Testaments as God's Word, and the Confession of the Evangelical Lutheran Church of 1580, called the Concordia, as its own."

The central body of the Synodical Conference, and the influence which constitutes the peculiar type of Lutheranism which it stands for, is the synod of Missouri, Ohio, and other States, which was organized in 1847. The nucleus of this synod was a Saxon colony of Lutherans who settled in Missouri in 1839. When the synod was constituted it embraced 12 congregations and 22 ministers, but, proclaiming a Lutheranism of the most positive character, it attracted to itself hosts of German immigrants who were dissatisfied with the result of the union of the Lutheran and Reformed religions in the Fatherland, and were pleased with the absolute and unreserved acceptance of the Augsburg Confession required by the synod and with its stern antagonism to every form of syncretism (union services, union communions, union congregations), and its insistence on pure Lutheran literature, pure Lutheran services, and a pure and positive Lutheranism. Some questions which most other Lutheran bodies might consider open questions are not so held by the " Missourians," as they are called. For example, they maintain that Antichrist is the Roman pontiff; that their doctrine as to the ministry and the church is the true and settled Scriptural doctrine, and that all forms of chiliasm or millenarianism are to be condemned. They allow no differences on these and some other extra-confessional points; therefore their type of doctrine and practice has become known, both in this country and Germany, where it has obtained some favor, as " Missourian."

In 1881 the Joint Synod of Ohio withdrew from the Synodical Conference as the result of a controversy which arose on the doctrine of predestination, and was followed in 1882 by the Norwegian Synod. The synod of Missouri maintained that predestination to salvation is not due to God's foresight of faith in man, but faith and perseverance in faith are included in the decree. The adherents of the Ohio party opposed this as Calvinistic, and a division was the result.

The Missouri is by far the largest Lutheran synod in the United States, and embraces in its territory thirty-one States and the District of Columbia. It is divided into 13 districts, or sub-synods, and reports 1589 organizations, with 1261 church edifices, valued at $6,759,535, and 293,-211 communicants.

The Synodical Conference has 1934 organizations, 1531 church edifices, and 357,153 communicants. The average seating capacity of its edifices is 289, and their average value $5098. Only 67 halls, with a seating capacity of 4362, are occupied. The constituency of the Synodical Conference is almost wholly German. Services in English are, however, being extensively introduced, and exclusively English congregations have been founded.

SUMMARY BY STATES.

STATES.	Organizations.	Church Edifices.	Seating Capacity.	Value of Church Property.	Communicants.
Alabama..........	5	5	1,300	$12,200	534
Arkansas	17	13	2,165	39,345	1,311
California	12	7	2,075	101,800	1,702
Colorado..........	6	2	475	22,500	394
Connecticut	8	4	1,900	33,500	1,405
District of Columbia	1	1	400	30,000	375
Florida	3	2	270	4,400	209
Idaho	1	...	......	....	27
Illinois...........	250	223	80,144	1,456,630	69,033
Indiana	102	96	32,299	632,260	24,666
Iowa	139	82	18,452	194,715	13,252
Kansas	71	47	8,974	95,030	5,906
Kentucky	3	3	900	9,800	468
Louisiana	11	11	3,375	59,400	2,452
Maryland	14	12	4,862	129,975	3,208
Massachusetts	10	6	1,575	54,000	1,717
Michigan	137	109	33,731	488,880	27,472
Minnesota	217	159	36,346	443,700	30,398
Missouri	118	112	32,820	613,940	22,121
Montana..........	2	1	225	10,000	130
Nebraska	135	93	16,788	168,570	12,339
New Jersey........	5	5	1,320	32,000	699

SUMMARY BY STATES.—*Continued.*

STATES.	Organizations.	Church Edifices.	Seating Capacity.	Value of Church Property.	Communicants.
New York.........	67	65	24,406	$1,055,455	22,642
North Dakota......	18	5	650	6,050	1,136
Ohio	54	55	18,330	409,975	15,440
Oregon	5	3	340	6,300	274
Pennsylvania	26	25	9,697	284,915	6,559
South Dakota	71	24	4,368	20,770	3,097
Tennessee	2	2	550	30,110	227
Texas	28	21	4,680	30,675	3,498
Virginia	4	5	1,275	20,815	399
West Virginia	4	2	300	300	121
Wisconsin.........	388	331	98,193	1,306,303	83,942
Total.........	1,934	1,531	443,185	$7,804,313	357,153

SUMMARY BY SYNODS.

SYNODS.					
Minnesota	90	58	14,523	$218,990	12,655
Missouri, Ohio, and other States	1,589	1,261½	366,507	6,759,535	293,211
Wisconsin........	237	198¾	58,855	794,988	50,095
English Conference of Missouri.....	18	12¾	3,300	30,800	1,192
Total........	1,934	1,531	443,185	$7,804,313	357,153

INDEPENDENT LUTHERAN SYNODS.

There are twelve Lutheran synods which are not connected with any of the four general bodies, and are therefore called independent bodies. They occupy this attitude for various reasons. In at least two cases, those of the Suomai Synod, a body of Finns, and the Icelandic Synod, the reason doubtless is peculiarity of language; in other cases it is differences of view on various doctrinal and practical questions and in national peculiarities. Some of these bodies are small, three of them having less than 5000 communicants each, but some of them are large enough to constitute separate denominations. In 1892 the Michigan Synod united with the Wisconsin and Minnesota synods of the Synodical Conference, and a new general body was thus formed. In 1893 the Joint Synod of Ohio and the German Synod of Iowa agreed upon terms of pulpit and altar fellowship, without becoming organically united.

5.—THE JOINT SYNOD OF OHIO AND OTHER STATES.

This body was organized in 1818. It occupied an independent attitude until 1867, when it assisted in constituting the General Council, but only to withdraw in the following year, because it was not fully satisfied with the position of the council concerning the question of pulpit and altar fellowship with other denominations. It has ever been conservative and strictly confessional in character, and it was for nine years connected with the Synodical Conference, from which it withdrew in 1881 because it could not accept the views of the majority concerning the doctrine of predestination. Since then it has occupied an independent position. Its constituency is for the most part German, but in about a third of its congregations both German and English are used. Like other large Lutheran synods, it is divided into a number of districts.

While its chief strength is in the State of Ohio, it has many communicants in Wisconsin, Michigan, Pennsylvania, and Indiana. It embraces twenty-three States and the District of Columbia, New York constituting the most easterly and northerly portion of its territory, Texas the most southerly, and Oregon the most westerly. It has 421 organizations, 443 edifices, valued at $1,639,087, and 69,505 communicants. Only ten of its organizations hold services in other than church edifices. The average value of its edifices is $3700, and their average seating capacity 337. Only 10 halls, with a seating capacity of 785, are occupied.

SUMMARY BY STATES.

STATES.	Organizations.	Church Edifices.	Seating Capacity.	Value of Church Property.	Communicants.
District of Columbia	1	1	250	$13,000	150
Idaho	1	1	300	1,000	80
Illinois............	16	16	6,950	60,000	2,695
Indiana...........	34	32	11,825	160,950	5,095
Iowa	5	8	1,850	10,500	650
Kansas	5	5	1,500	2,750	472
Louisiana	1	1	700	5,000	500
Maryland.........	12	12	3,620	38,900	1,545
Michigan	21	20	7,672	125,700	6,217
Minnesota	21	23	8,700	37,250	3,180
Missouri	1	1	200	600	30
Nebraska	7	7	1,800	4,600	440
New York.........	2	2	330	2,700	198
North Carolina	12	11	2,550	6,315	567
North Dakota	1	1	300	750	70
Ohio	191	197½	67,537	839,272	31,261
Oregon	1	1	200	600	50
Pennsylvania	32	32	10,429	206,100	5,552
South Dakota	3	3	1,000	2,700	327
Texas	4	7	2,850	20,000	1,730
Virginia	5	4	750	2,900	175
Washington.......	4	6	1,250	11,400	386
West Virginia	16	10½	2,025	5,500	779
Wisconsin.........	25	41	14,750	80,600	7,356
Total.........	421	443	149,338	$1,639,087	69,505

6.—THE BUFFALO SYNOD.

This synod was organized in 1845 by the Rev. J. A. A. Grabau, who came from Germany, where he had suffered for his opposition to the union of the Reformed and Lutheran religions. The synod has announced views concerning the ministerial office which other Lutherans have considered as hierarchical. It insists that ordination, unless by ordained ministers, is not valid; that ministers created by congregations have no divine authority to pronounce absolution or to consecrate the elements of bread and wine; that congregations may not pronounce excommunication; that obedience is due to ministers; and that the synod is the supreme tribunal in the church.

The synod has congregations in six States, with 25 church edifices, valued at $84,410, and 4242 communicants. The average value of its edifices is $3376, and their average seating capacity 232. Two halls, with a seating capacity of 275, are occupied.

SUMMARY BY STATES.

STATES.	Organizations.	Church Edifices.	Seating Capacity.	Value of Church Property.	Communicants.
California	1	1	150	$500	26
Illinois............	1	1	300	2,500	136
Michigan	4	4	848	10,100	342
Minnesota.........	2	2	300	3,700	312
New York.........	12	10	2,715	48,010	2,268
Wisconsin	7	7	1,480	19,600	1,158
Total	27	25	5,793	$84,410	4,242

7.—HAUGE'S SYNOD.

This is a body of Norwegian Lutherans organized in the period 1846–50 by immigrants from Norway. It took its name from Hauge, a leader of a strong spiritual movement in that country. Its followers lay much stress upon conversion and are noted for their earnestness. The laymen participate in prayer and exhortation in public assemblies, contrary to the practice of some other bodies of a more churchly character. This synod has always occupied an independent attitude.

It has 175 organizations, divided among eleven States,

but with two thirds of its strength in Minnesota, South Dakota, and Wisconsin, and 100 church edifices having an average seating capacity of 306 and an average value of $2149; 75 halls, with a seating capacity of 4436, are occupied.

SUMMARY BY STATES.

STATES.	Organizations.	Church Edifices.	Seating Capacity.	Value of Church Property.	Communicants.
Illinois............	10	8	2,875	$40,400	863
Indiana...........	1	1	250	800	29
Iowa	17	14	3,450	27,200	1,593
Kansas	1	..	.....	......	26
Michigan	1	1	200	4,000	62
Minnesota	55	41	13,285	99,345	6,534
Nebraska	8	4	725	4,950	438
North Dakota	16	5	1,700	4,850	576
South Dakota......	36	11	2,955	11,700	2,239
Washington	2	1	350	1,000	205
Wisconsin.........	28	14	4,710	20,150	2,165
Total	175	100	30,500	$214,395	14,730

8.—THE NORWEGIAN CHURCH IN AMERICA.

This body was organized by Norwegian immigrants a few years later than Hauge's Synod. Like the latter, it has always maintained an independent position, except for the short period when it was connected with the Synodical Conference. A few years ago a controversy over the doctrine of predestination caused a division in its ministry and congregations, resulting in the formation of what was known as the Anti-Missouri Brotherhood. The synod accepted the views of the Missouri Synod, which its type of Lutheranism resembles, while the brotherhood rejected these views as Calvinistic.

The synod is divided into three districts. Its territory

embraces twenty-two States, stretching from ocean to ocean and from the Lakes to the Gulf. Two thirds of its communicants, however, are in the States of Minnesota and Wisconsin. The average value of its church edifices is $2929, and their average seating capacity is 287. It occupies 182 halls, which have a seating capacity of 12,115.

SUMMARY BY STATES.

STATES.	Organizations.	Church Edifices.	Seating Capacity.	Value of Church Property.	Communicants.
California	3	1	300	$14,000	189
Colorado..........	1	1	300	2,000	75
Idaho	1	1	150	1,000	45
Illinois............	14	6	3,150	95,500	1,688
Indiana...........	2	1	300	6,000	182
Iowa	49	26	9,275	97,800	7,059
Kansas	1	1	100	200	30
Massachusetts	2	...	.....	......	375
Michigan	14	7	1,125	9,900	758
Minnesota.........	164	112½	32,843	267,950	21,832
Missouri	2	1	200	400	50
Montana..........	3	1	250	1,200	165
Nebraska	21	7	1,520	12,200	544
New Jersey........	1	1	225	4,000	180
New York.........	5	3	1,050	33,000	784
North Dakota	53	8	2,200	22,975	2,784
Ohio	4	1	150	3,000	184
Oregon	3	1	200	2,500	95
South Dakota	46	13	3,240	25,700	3,030
Texas	4	5	950	6,700	350
Washington.......	1	...	.....	......	16
Wisconsin	95	77½	21,460	200,800	15,037
Total........	489	275	78,988	$806,825	55,452

9.—THE MICHIGAN SYNOD.

This is a German body organized in 1860. It helped to organize the General Council, and was connected with it until 1888, when it withdrew because the position of the council on the question of pulpit and altar fellowship with other denominations was not sufficiently decided.

The synod is represented in the States of Michigan and Indiana, having in all 11,482 communicants. Its church edifices have an average value of $3109 and an average seating capacity of 276. There are 12 halls, with a seating capacity of 550.

SUMMARY BY STATES.

STATES.	Organizations.	Church Edifices.	Seating Capacity.	Value of Church Property.	Communicants.
Indiana............	3	3	1,150	$7,500	441
Michigan	62	50	13,463	157,270	11,041
Total.........	65	53	14,613	$164,770	11,482

10.—THE DANISH CHURCH IN AMERICA.

This is the oldest body of Danish Lutherans in this country, having been organized in 1872. It is connected with the Church of Denmark, which sent missionaries to this country, who helped to organize Danish congregations and a little later to form them into a synod.

It has congregations in fourteen States and in the Territory of Utah. Its territory stretches from Maine to California, forming a belt across the northern portion of the country. It has 131 organizations, with 75 edifices, having an average seating capacity of 198 and an average value of $1741. The total number of communicants is 10,181, more than half of whom are to be found in the States of Iowa, Wisconsin, Illinois, and Minnesota. The synod is divided into 9 districts. There are 42 halls, with a seating capacity of 2175, used as places of worship.

Summary by States.

STATES.	Organizations.	Church Edifices.	Seating Capacity.	Value of Church Property.	Communicants.
California.........	4	1	300	$1,200	125
Connecticut	2	2	300	2,000	200
Illinois............	9	5	1,330	15,100	1,314
Iowa	23	14	3,390	24,800	2,211
Kansas	1	1	125	800	120
Maine	2	2	400	......	200
Massachusetts	3	..	.....	......	119
Michigan	9	8	1,900	13,700	588
Minnesota	17	8	1,230	11,300	1,032
Nebraska	19	11	1,510	20,100	888
New Jersey........	8	5	1,000	6,000	565
New York.........	5	4	475	11,000	410
South Dakota	11	1	200	1,500	285
Utah	2	..	.....	......	48
Wisconsin	16	13	2,600	22,200	2,076
Total.........	131	75	14,760	$129,700	10,181

11.—THE GERMAN AUGSBURG SYNOD.

This body was formed in 1875. It has 23 organizations, distributed among nine States. These organizations own 23 church edifices, with an average seating capacity of 329 and an average value of $4829.

Summary by States.

STATES.	Organizations.	Church Edifices.	Seating Capacity.	Value of Church Property.	Communicants.
Arkansas	1	..	.....	......	75
Illinois............	4	4	700	$9,450	631
Indiana.	2	2	600	5,000	370
Iowa	1	1	100	1,000	70
Michigan	1	1	300	5,000	174
Missouri	2	3	1,360	40,000	1,199
New York.........	1	1	700	3,500	800
Ohio	1	1	1,000	26,800	1,700
Wisconsin	10	10	2,800	20,310	1,991
Total.........	23	23	7,560	$111,060	7,010

12.—THE DANISH ASSOCIATION IN AMERICA.

This association was formed in 1884, chiefly by Danish ministers, who withdrew from what was then called the Norwegian-Danish Conference, not because of doctrinal or ecclesiastical differences, but because of reasons growing out of differences of nationality.

It embraces 50 organizations, with 33 church edifices, having an average seating capacity of 173 and an average value of $1357. There are 15 halls, with a seating capacity of 480.

SUMMARY BY STATES.

STATES.	Organizations.	Church Edifices.	Seating Capacity.	Value of Church Property.	Communicants.
California	4	2	375	$3,000	144
Illinois............	1	..	.....	4,000	50
Iowa	6	2	350	3,800	413
Minnesota	14	9	1,675	10,150	1,524
Nebraska	16	14	2,200	14,625	754
Oregon	1	..	.....	......	20
South Dakota......	2	2	250	2,200	153
Washington	2	..	.....	......	40
Wisconsin	4	4	850	7,000	395
Total	50	33	5,700	$44,775	3,493

13.—THE ICELANDIC SYNOD.

The Synod of Icelanders was organized in 1885. By far the larger part of this synod is in Manitoba.

It has in this country 13 organizations, 4 church edifices, with an average seating capacity of 325 and an average value of $1800, and 1991 communicants. It is represented in two States only, Minnesota and North Dakota. There are 9 halls, with a seating capacity of 750.

SUMMARY BY STATES.

STATES.	Organi- zations.	Church Edifices.	Seating Ca- pacity.	Value of Church Property.	Com- muni- cants.
Minnesota..........	5	..	.....	......	221
North Dakota	8	4	1,300	$7,200	1,770
Total..........	13	4	1,300	$7,200	1,991

14.—THE IMMANUEL SYNOD.

This is a small German body whose organization dates from 1886. It is represented in seven States and the District of Columbia, having 21 organizations, 19 church edifices, with an average seating capacity of 279 and an average value of $4958, and 5580 communicants.

SUMMARY BY STATES.

STATES.	Organi- zations.	Church Edifices.	Seating Ca- pacity.	Value of Church Property.	Com- muni- cants.
District of Columbia	1	1	300	$15,000	500
Illinois............	1	1	300	10,000	300
Indiana	1	1	150	1,200	180
Michigan	1	1	600	15,000	500
New Jersey........	2	2	550	7,000	700
New York	5	3	600	6,000	600
Ohio	6	6	1,600	25,500	1,350
Pennsylvania	4	4	1,200	14,500	1,450
Total.	21	19	5,300	$94,200	5,580

15.—THE SUOMAI SYNOD.

This is a body of Finnish Lutherans constituted in 1889. It has 11 organizations, 8 church edifices, with an average seating capacity of 230 and an average value of $1548, and 1385 communicants, of whom 1265 are in Michigan and 120 in South Dakota.

SUMMARY BY STATES.

STATES.	Organizations.	Church Edifices.	Seating Capacity.	Value of Church Property.	Communicants.
Michigan	10	7	1,715	$10,973	1,265
South Dakota	1	1	200	1,925	120
Total	11	8	1,915	$12,898	1,385

16.—THE UNITED NORWEGIAN CHURCH.

This body was constituted in 1890 by the union of three synods, viz., the Norwegian Augustana Synod, organized in 1860, the Conference of the Norwegian-Danish Church, organized in 1870, and the Norwegian Anti-Missouri Brotherhood, organized in 1887. The Brotherhood separated from the Norwegian Synod because they could not accept the latter's views respecting the doctrine of absolute predestination. The union of these three bodies was due to a movement to bring together, as far as possible, all Norwegian Lutherans in one body. Hauge's Synod and the Norwegian Synod, however, still maintain a separate attitude.

The United Synod embraces eighteen States in its territory. It has 1122 organizations, 670 church edifices, and 119,972 communicants, of whom 49,541 are in the single State of Minnesota. The average seating capacity of the churches is 277, and the average value $2312. There are 393 halls, with a seating capacity of 29,185.

SUMMARY BY STATES.

STATES.	Organizations.	Church Edifices.	Seating Capacity.	Value of Church Property.	Communicants.
Idaho............	1	1	300	$2,500	110
Illinois...........	27	24	6,445	68,400	3,298
Iowa	113	85	25,335	220,100	14,891
Kansas	7	3	650	5,300	314

SUMMARY BY STATES.—*Continued.*

STATES.	Organi- zations.	Church Edifices.	Seating Ca- pacity.	Value of Church Property.	Com- muni- cants.
Maine	2	1	200	$2,000	225
Maryland	1	..	....	......	42
Michigan	27	23	5,973	69,450	3,011
Minnesota	405	283	76,791	608,200	49,541
Missouri	1	..	....	......	14
Montana.........	2	..	....	......	87
Nebraska	13	1	100	250	285
New Hampshire ..	1	1	250	2,500	125
New York........	1	..	....	......	84
North Dakota.....	162	44	10,380	77,550	10,283
Oregon	5	2	650	9,500	204
South Dakota	148	41	8,150	54,655	7,922
Washington......	19	10	2,575	29,600	819
Wisconsin	187	151	47,443	394,450	28,717
Total	1,122	670	185,242	$1,544,455	119,972

' INDEPENDENT CONGREGATIONS.

Besides the independent synods there are a number of independent Lutheran congregations—that is, congregations which do not belong to any synod. In most cases the reason is not doctrinal, but simply a love of independence. Not infrequently the pastor of an independent congregation is himself a member of some synod. They are found in most of the States and Territories. They aggregate 231 organizations, 188 church edifices, with a seating capacity of 62,334, and valued at $1,249,745, and 41,953 communicants.

SUMMARY BY STATES OF ALL LUTHERANS.

STATES.	Organi- zations.	Church Edifices.	Seating Ca- pacity.	Value of Church Property.	Com- muni- cants.
Alabama........	10	7	1,850	$15,400	791
Arkansas	18	13	2,165	39,345	1,386
California	39	21	6,575	364,800	4,267
Colorado........	21	14	3,236	154,800	1,208

SUMMARY BY STATES OF ALL LUTHERANS—*Continued.*

STATES.	Organizations.	Church Edifices.	Seating Capacity.	Value of Church Property.	Communicants.
Connecticut	37	23	8,820	$172,900	5,762
Delaware	2	1	335	10,000	296
Dist. of Columbia	11	13	6,100	414,000	2,997
Florida	6	4	730	9,850	369
Georgia	18	17	5,825	124,150	1,932
Idaho	7	5	930	6,950	401
Illinois..........	590	511	175,037	3,021,850	116,807
Indiana	279	266	82,609	1,220,410	41,832
Iowa	567	400	107,708	1,150,795	63,725
Kansas	205	147	33,688	418,410	16,262
Kentucky	18	17	5,170	60,300	2,394
Louisiana	12	12	4,075	64,400	2,952
Maine	6	5	1,300	8,600	904
Maryland	131	129	55,602	1,081,925	24,648
Massachusetts ...	30	15	4,260	114,400	4,137
Michigan	380	307	86,132	1,109,058	62,897
Minnesota.......	1,141	827	227,925	2,143,805	145,907
Mississippi	11	10	2,750	4,650	533
Missouri	160	148	42,689	890,090	27,099
Montana........	8	2	475	11,200	394
Nebraska	387	253	49,949	774,816	27,297
New Hampshire..	3	3	1,000	16,000	520
New Jersey......	68	53	18,080	526,750	12,878
New Mexico.....	2	....	......	....	64
New York.......	317	306	117,115	4,693,375	89,046
North Carolina ..	131	118	47,013	270,005	12,326
North Dakota ...	298	75	18,040	136,275	18,269
Ohio	588	573	192,537	3,007,097	89,569
Oregon	21	12	2,515	59,050	1,080
Pennsylvania	1,292	1,105	515,827	9,258,020	219,725
Rhode Island	4	2	600	7,750	590
South Carolina ..	74	78	27,525	339,250	8,757
South Dakota ...	432	138	27,783	183,575	23,314
Tennessee	36	33	12,560	91,760	2,975
Texas	88	80	20,840	210,915	14,556
Utah	4	....	......	....	84
Vermont........	2	....	......	....	174
Virginia	157	136	48,165	344,915	12,220
Washington.....	35	22	5,575	75,950	1,912
West Virginia ...	47	41	10,605	118,525	4,176
Wisconsin.......	894	757	223,570	2,328,138	160,919
Wyoming	8	2	350	6,100	721
Total........	8,595	6,701	2,205,635	$35,060,354	1,231,072

CHAPTER XXVIII.

THE MENNONITES.

THE Mennonites take their name from Menno Simons, born in Witmarsum, Holland, in 1492. He entered the priesthood of the Roman Catholic Church, and in 1524 was appointed chaplain in Pingium. Two years later he began to read the Scriptures, which he had hitherto ignored. Becoming a close student of them, his views on various doctrines soon changed, and he was known as an evangelical preacher. Upon hearing of the decapitation of a devout Christian because he had renewed his baptism, Menno Simons began to examine into the Scriptural teaching on that subject, and was convinced that there was no Scriptural warrant for infant baptism. He remained in connection with the Church of Rome for several years, during which he wrote a book against the Münsterites. He renounced Catholicism early in 1536, and was baptized at Leeuwarden. In the course of the following year he was ordained a minister in what was then known as the Old Evangelical or Waldensian Church. From this time on to his death, in 1559, he was active in the cause of evangelical truth, traveling through northern Germany, and preaching everywhere. The churches which he organized as a result of his labors rejected infant baptism and held to the principle of non-resistance. A severe persecution began to make itself felt against his followers, the Mennonites; and, having heard accounts of the colony established in the New World by William Penn, they began to emigrate to Pennsylvania near the close of the seventeenth century, that they might have opportunity to worship in peace.

The first Mennonite church in this country was established in Germantown. Upon the site occupied by that church a plain stone meeting-house, erected in 1770, now stands. The colony of Germantown, which had secured a tract of about six thousand acres of land, was increased from time to time by immigration from Europe. In 1688 the Mennonite meeting at Germantown adopted a protest against traffic in slaves, said to have been the first ever made on this continent. In this protest they say that many negroes are brought hither against their will, and though they are black "we cannot conceive there is more liberty to have them slaves than it is to have other white ones." The protest, which was sent to the Friends, asserted that "those who steal or rob men and those who buy or purchase them" are all alike. The protest was finally sent up to the Yearly Meeting of Friends, where, after some consideration, it was voted not to be proper for the meeting to give a positive judgment in the case. The minute of the Yearly Meeting refers to the Mennonites as "German Friends."

Successive immigrations from Holland, Switzerland Germany, and, in the last twenty-five years, from southern Russia, have resulted in placing the great majority of Mennonites in the world on American soil, in the United States and Canada. According to the census reports for 1890, the number of members in this country, exclusive of Canada, is less than 42,000. This is the first complete statistical statement that has been made of the Mennonites, and the number of members returned is much smaller than was expected. In 1860 there was a general meeting of Mennonites in Iowa, and the minutes of that conference estimated the number of Mennonites in the United States at 128,000. That estimate must have been a great deal too high, or the denomination has suffered extraordinary losses since.

The doctrines held by the Mennonites are set forth in eighteen articles of faith, which were adopted at a conference held in Dordrecht, Holland, in 1632. The first article treats of the Trinity and of God's work in creation; the second of the fall of man through the disobedience of Adam and Eve, who were " separated and estranged from God, that neither they themselves, nor any of their posterity, nor angel, nor man, nor any other creature in heaven or on earth, could help them, redeem them, or reconcile them to God." They would have been eternally lost had not God interposed in their behalf with love and mercy. The third article shows how the first man and his posterity are restored through the sacrifice of the Son of God. The next ten articles set forth the doctrines of salvation, the ordinances, and treat of marriage and the magistracy. The fourteenth article declares one of the prominent principles of the Mennonites, namely, non-resistance. It enjoins believers not to provoke or do violence to any man, but to promote the welfare and happiness of all; to flee when necessary for the Lord's sake from one country to another, " take patiently the spoiling of our goods," and " when we are smitten on one cheek to turn the other, rather than take revenge or resent evil." Enemies are to be prayed for, and, when hungry and thirsty, to be fed and refreshed. The fifteenth article interprets Christ as forbidding the use of all oaths, judicial and otherwise. The sixteenth treats of the ban, which is for amendment and not for destruction. Those who have been received into the company of saints, if they sin voluntarily or presumptuously against God, or unto death, must as offending members be reproved and excommunicated. The seventeenth article enjoins the duty of avoiding those who are separated from God and the church, not only in eating and drinking, but in all similar temporal matters; although if an offending member is hungry or thirsty or in distress of any kind, it is lawful to relieve him. The eighteenth article pertains to the resurrection of the dead and the last judgment. The righteous are to reign with Christ forever, and the wicked are to be thrust down into the everlasting pains of hell.

The Mennonites believe in baptism on profession of faith, but they do not baptize by immersion except in one or two branches, but by pouring. Candidates after having been under suitable instruction are catechized as to their faith in God and their desire to be received into the Church, and then receive baptism kneeling, the minister taking water with both hands from a vessel and putting it upon their heads and saying, " Upon the confession of thy faith which thou hast made before God and these witnesses, I baptize thee in the name of the Father, and of the Son, and of the Holy Ghost." Each candidate is then given the right hand of fellowship and the kiss of peace, the wife of the minister or deacon or some other sister giving the kiss to the female converts. Persons received from other denominations are not re-baptized unless they earnestly desire it.

In some cases candidates are baptized in the water, kneeling therein, the minister taking up water in both hands and pouring it upon their heads.

The Lord's Supper is observed twice a year, usually in the spring and fall. Church examinations are held before communion in order to inquire into the standing and condition of each member. Each member is examined privately, and asked whether he is at peace with God, with the church, and with all men, and desirous to partake of the Lord's Supper. If there are any difficulties between members an effort is made to have them all settled before the communion takes place. As the bread and wine are passed, those who receive them rise to their feet one after another. Sometimes the communicant goes forward to receive the bread and wine; in other cases the minister goes from seat to seat and from person to person. After the Lord's Supper the ceremony of feet-washing is performed. The deacons bring in vessels of water, and the members proceed to wash and wipe one another's feet and to give the kiss of peace, the sexes separating for this purpose. The polity is of the Presbyterian type.

Ministers are chosen from the congregations to be served. A request is made to the conference, and a day is appointed for the purpose of making the choice. The bishop preaches an appropriate sermon, and then retires to the council-room with two fellow-ministers. All the members who desire to do so visit the council-room, one by one, and indicate the person of their choice. If only one brother has been chosen in this way, ordination is immediately proceeded with. When more than one is nominated, a day is appointed in which to make choice by lot between those nominated. When choice by lot is made, the deacons take as many hymn-books as there are candidates, and, retiring to the council-room, place in one of these books a slip of paper on which is written the words: "The lot is cast into the lap, but the whole disposing thereof is of the Lord;" or, "Herewith God has called thee to the ministry of the Gospel." The books are then taken into the audience-room and placed on the desk or table. After prayer has been made each of the brethren nominated takes a book, and the bishop proceeds to look for the lot. The one in whose book it is found is considered chosen, and the bishop then proceeds to ordain him with laying on of hands. The ceremony is concluded with the kiss of peace, which is given by the bishop and the other ministers.

Deacons are chosen from the congregation in the same manner as ministers. Their office is to care for the poor and sick, to assist in administering the ordinances, and to take charge of public meetings in the absence of the minister or bishop. Bishops or elders are ministers having pastoral charge of a district, in which there may be one or several places of worship. All the ministers in the district are under the direction of the bishop or elder. A bishop is selected in the same manner as a minister or deacon, and is consecrated in the same way. When difficulties arise between brethren they are settled by arbitration. Those who refuse to submit to arbitration are excommunicated, and the names of the excommunicated are publicly announced. The Mennonites do not accept public offices except in connection with the management of schools. They are a sober, industrious, and thrifty people, simple in their habits, and conscientious, devout, and faithful Christians. More than a third of them are found in Pennsylvania, the great German State. They are also strong in Ohio, Kansas, Illinois, and Indiana. The Russian Mennonites have formed several settlements in the Northwest and across the northern border in Manitoba.

There are twelve branches of Mennonites, as follows:

1. Mennonite,	7. General Conference,
2. Bruederhoef,	8. Church of God in Christ,
3. Amish,	9. Old (Wisler),
4. Old Amish,	10. Brueder-Gemeinde,
5. Apostolic,	11. Defenseless,
6. Reformed,	12. Brethren in Christ.

I.—THE MENNONITE CHURCH.

This may be regarded as the parent body. It has nearly 18,000 communicants, considerably more than one third of the total of Mennonites in this country. Many of its congregations are very small, the average number of communicants to each congregation in Kansas being only about 25. There are 12 conferences, besides 23 congregations which sustain no conference relations. There are 29 halls, with a seating capacity of 1030.

SUMMARY BY STATES.

STATES.	Organizations.	Church Edifices.	Seating Capacity.	Value of Church Property.	Communicants.
Illinois	8	6	1,195	$6,250	273
Indiana	14	10	3,175	11,940	700
Iowa	3	..	.....	......	28
Kansas	20	5	1,033	3,030	513
Maryland	5	5	1,700	6,600	336
Michigan	5	3	875	2,200	155
Minnesota	6	4	1,400	3,700	725
Missouri	6	3½	900	2,900	199
Nebraska	8	5	1,190	7,250	751
North Dakota	1	..	.....	......	41
Ohio	27	22½	8,360	35,450	1,736

SUMMARY BY STATES.—*Continued.*

STATES.	Organizations.	Church Edifices.	Seating Capacity.	Value of Church Property.	Communicants.
Oregon	3	2	400	$1,100	115
Pennsylvania	114	110	41,952	221,100	10,077
South Dakota	7	6	1,000	2,500	655
Tennessee	1	1	150	200	28
Virginia	16	13	6,675	10,925	666
West Virginia	2	2	600	900	80
Total.........	246	198	70,605	$317,045	17,078

2.—THE BRUEDERHOEF.

Jacob Huter, of Innspruck, in the Tyrol, is considered the founder of this branch. Huter was burned at the stake in 1536. He instituted the communistic idea, which is still maintained, the members "having all things in common." His followers were driven from Moravia into Hungary, thence to Roumania, and in 1769 to Russia. The entire community came to the United States from Russia in 1874. They are a German-speaking community, and their books, which are in manuscript, are written in that language. They are all settled in three counties in South Dakota.

SUMMARY.

STATE.	Organizations.	Church Edifices.	Seating Capacity.	Value of Church Property.	Communicants.
South Dakota	5	5	600	$4,500	352

3.—THE AMISH.

The Amish constitute the second largest Mennonite branch. They take their name from Jacob Ammen, who separated from the main body of Mennonites about two centuries ago, on account of differences respecting the enforcement of church discipline. He and his followers insisted that the ban should be more rigorously observed. In Pennsylvania they are very numerous. They used to be called "Hookers," because they wore hooks instead of buttons on their coats. They are represented in fourteen States, being most numerous in Illinois, Pennsylvania, and Ohio. There are 33 halls, with a seating capacity of 960.

SUMMARY BY STATES.

STATES.	Organizations.	Church Edifices.	Seating Capacity.	Value of Church Property.	Communicants.
Arkansas	1	1	75	$300	65
Colorado..........	1	1	80	500	75
Illinois............	18	13	3,640	19,600	2,305
Indiana...........	10	9	2,000	9,800	929
Iowa	7	5	1,210	6,700	903
Kansas	12	3	375	1,700	291
Maryland	2	2	350	1,400	125
Missouri..........	3	2	830	4,100	316
Nebraska	5	2	470	1,200	504
New York	3	2	400	3,000	299
Ohio	12	11	3,725	17,850	1,965
Oregon	2	1	300	500	60
Pennsylvania	20	9	1,975	9,800	2,234
Tennessee	1	..	.....	......	30
Total.........	97	61	15,430	$76,450	10,101

4.—THE OLD AMISH.

This branch was the result of a division among the Amish about twenty-five years ago on the question of enforcing church discipline. The Old Amish are very strict in adhering to the ancient forms and practices, opposing the innovations in forms of worship and manner of conducting church work introduced during the present century. There are only about 2000 of them, and they have but one church edifice. Their meetings are all held in private houses, except in one case.

SUMMARY BY STATES.

STATES.	Organizations.	Church Edifices.	Seating Capacity.	Value of Church Property.	Communicants.
Illinois............	1	1	200	$1,500	105
Indiana..........	8	..	...	.....	853
Kansas	3	..	...	.....	145
Missouri	1	..	...	.....	24
Ohio	5	..	...	.....	694
Oregon	3	..	...	.....	73
Pennsylvania	1	..	...	.....	144
Total.........	22	1	200	$1,500	2,038

5.—THE APOSTOLIC.

This is properly a branch of the Amish Mennonites, differing from them chiefly in being less strict in the observance of the rules of discipline and forms of worship. There are only 209 of them, belonging to two congregations in Ohio.

SUMMARY.

STATE.	Organizations.	Church Edifices.	Seating Capacity.	Value of Church Property.	Communicants.
Ohio	2	1	225	$1,200	209

6.—THE REFORMED.

In 1812 a movement was begun among the Mennonites for "the restoration of purity in teaching and the maintenance of discipline" under the leadership of John Herr.

The "Herrites," as they are sometimes called, are very strict in their observances, severe in the use of the ban, and decline fellowship with other denominations. They are represented in seven States, more than half of their communicants, however, being found in Pennsylvania. Services are held in 4 private houses and in 1 hall, with a seating capacity of 50.

SUMMARY BY STATES.

STATES.	Organi- zations.	Church Edifices.	Seating Ca- pacity.	Value of Church Property.	Com- muni- cants.
Illinois..............	1	1	400	$2,500	60
Indiana	2	1	100	700	38
Maryland...........	2	2	400	1,800	64
Michigan	3	..	.....	.....	52
New York...........	3	3	500	2,200	125
Ohio	7	6	1,350	6,350	426
Pennsylvania	16	16	4,655	39,100	890
Total..........	34	29	7,465	$52,650	1,655

7.—THE GENERAL CONFERENCE.

The beginning of this body is traced to a difficulty which arose in Pennsylvania in 1848, in a matter of discipline. John Oberholzer was charged with attempting to introduce new practices and new doctrines. As the result of the controversy which arose over the matter an organization was formed, called the New Mennonites. This body is less strict than most other branches of Mennonites, and is in favor of an educated and paid ministry. The General Conference was organized in 1860 at West Point, Ia. At its third meeting, in 1863, a plan for an educational institute was adopted, and a theological school was begun at Wadsworth, O. It flourished for a number of years and was then discontinued. The General Conference has missions among the Arapahoe and Cheyenne Indians, in Indian Territory. It also conducts a number of home missions. There are three district conferences, the Central, the Eastern, and the Western. The General Conference meets once every three years. There are 5670 communicants, scattered over ten States. The average seating capacity of the edifices is 323, and the average value $2776. One hall, with a seating capacity of 50, is reported.

SUMMARY BY STATES.

STATES.	Organizations.	Church Edifices.	Seating Capacity.	Value of Church Property.	Communicants.
Illinois..............	1	1	350	$1,000	169
Indiana............	1	1	800	3,000	405
Iowa	5	5	1,075	5,950	509
Kansas	14	15	5,630	33,000	2,547
Minnesota	1	1	400	1,500	70
Missouri	2	1	200	1,000	133
New York.........	2	..	.....	.....	46
Ohio	2	2	350	2,000	139
Pennsylvania	15	15	4,325	69,500	1,426
South Dakota	2	2	750	2,400	226
Total.........	45	43	13,880	$119,350	5,670

8.—THE CHURCH OF GOD IN CHRIST.

This branch was organized by John Holdeman in 1859. Holdeman claimed by the spirit of prophecy " to understand the foreknowledge of God, to know mysteries, to settle difficulties, to keep peace, and to interpret visions and dreams." This branch has only 18 congregations, with 471 members. It is represented in eight States. There are 2 halls, with a seating capacity of 150.

SUMMARY BY STATES.

STATES.	Organizations.	Church Edifices.	Seating Capacity.	Value of Church Property.	Communicants.
Illinois............	1	..	....	.....	3
Indiana...........	1	..	....	.....	3
Kansas	6	2	250	$1,400	274
Michigan	3	1	150	200	60
Missouri	2	..	....	.....	58
Nebraska	1	..	....	.....	13
Ohio	2	..	....	.....	38
West Virginia	2	..	....	.....	22
Total.........	18	3	400	$1,600	471

9.—THE OLD (WISLER).

This branch, which has only 610 communicants, consists of those who are opposed to Sunday-schools and evening meetings and other practices, which they regard as innovations. They are represented by 15 congregations, in Indiana, Michigan, and Ohio.

SUMMARY BY STATES.

STATES.	Organizations.	Church Edifices.	Seating Capacity.	Value of Church Property.	Communicants.
Indiana...........	3	3	900	$1,550	146
Michigan	2	1	150	700	40
Ohio	10	8	3,070	5,765	424
Total.........	15	12	4,120	$8,015	610

10.—DER BRUEDER-GEMEINDE.

This body originated in Russia half a century ago, and emigrated to this country in 1873–76. They baptize by immersion and emphasize the importance of evidence of conversion. They are very active and zealous in the performance of their religious duties. They are represented

in Kansas, Minnesota, Nebraska, and South Dakota by 12
congregations, with 1388 communicants.   One hall, with a
seating capacity of 40, is reported.

SUMMARY BY STATES.

STATES.	Organi-zations.	Church Edifices.	Seating Ca-pacity.	Value of Church Property.	Com-muni-cants.
Kansas	5	5	1,650	$4,700	685
Minnesota	2	2	700	2,000	172
Nebraska	3	2	1,120	3,900	381
South Dakota	2	2	250	750	150
Total.........	12	11	3,720	$11,350	1,388

11.—THE DEFENSELESS.

The Defenseless Mennonites, sometimes called Eglyites,
are really a branch of the Amish.   They lay particular
stress upon the importance of conversion and regeneration.
Henry Egli was the leader of this movement.   It is represented in Illinois, Indiana, Kansas, Missouri, and Ohio, by
9 congregations, with 856 communicants.

SUMMARY BY STATES.

STATES.	Organi-zations.	Church Edifices.	Seating Ca-pacity.	Value of Church Property.	Com-muni-cants.
Illinois............	2	1	175	$1,000	99
Indiana...........	3	3	1,025	4,875	467
Kansas	1	1	270	1,300	140
Missouri	1	1	150	565	18
Ohio	2	2	450	2,800	132
Total.........	9	8	2,070	$10,540	856

12.—THE MENNONITE BRETHREN IN CHRIST.

This body, which originated about 1878, is Methodistic
in its form of organization, in its usages, and its discipline.

Applicants for baptism are baptized in any form they may prefer. It has two annual conferences in the United States, and there are also a number of churches in Canada. There are 45 churches, with 1113 communicants. Eight halls, with a seating capacity of 660, are occupied as places of worship.

SUMMARY BY STATES.

STATES.	Organizations.	Church edifices.	Seating Capacity.	Value of Church Property.	Communicants.
Arkansas	1	..	....	......	35
Indiana	9	6	2,050	$3,500	191
Iowa	1	1	300	500	14
Kansas	1	..	....	......	25
Michigan	2	2	400	2,400	49
Nebraska	1	..	....	......	15
Ohio	8	8	3,300	6,100	225
Pennsylvania	22	17½	4,575	27,100	559
Total	45	34½	10,625	$39,600	1,113

SUMMARY BY STATES OF ALL MENNONITES.

STATES.	Organizations.	Church edifices.	Seating Capacity.	Value of Church Property.	Communicants.
Arkansas	2	1	75	$300	100
Colorado	1	1	80	500	75
Illinois	32	23	5,960	31,850	3,014
Indiana	51	33	10,050	35,365	3,732
Iowa	16	11	2,585	13,150	1,454
Kansas	62	31	9,208	45,130	4,620
Maryland	9	9	2,450	9,800	525
Michigan	15	7	1,575	5,500	356
Minnesota	9	7	2,500	7,200	967
Missouri	15	7	2,080	8,565	748
Nebraska	18	9	2,780	12,350	1,664
New York	8	5	960	5,200	470
North Dakota	1	..	....	......	41
Ohio	77	60	20,830	77,515	5,988
Oregon	8	3	700	1,600	248
Pennsylvania	188	168	57,482	366,600	15,330
South Dakota	16	15	2,600	11,150	1,383
Tennessee	2	1	150	200	58
Virginia	16	13	6,675	10,925	666
West Virginia	4	2	600	900	102
Total	550	406	129,340	$643,800	41,541

CHAPTER XXIX.

THE METHODISTS.

METHODISM, which counts many branches in Great Britain, America, and elsewhere, is the result of a movement begun at Oxford University, England, as early as 1729, by John and Charles Wesley. Their own account of its origin is given in these words:

"In 1729 two young men in England, reading the Bible, saw they could not be saved without holiness, followed after it, and incited others so to do. In 1737 they saw likewise that men are justified before they are sanctified, but still holiness was their object. God then thrust them out to raise a holy people."

The Wesleys, with two others, began to meet together at Oxford for religious exercises in 1729. In derision they were called the "Holy Club," "Bible Bigots," "Methodists," etc. The last term was intended to describe their methodical habits, and it seems to have been accepted by them almost immediately, as the movement they led was soon widely known as the Methodist movement.

John and Charles Wesley and George Whitefield were ordained ministers of the Church of England, and it was as Church of England clergymen that they began and carried forward their stirring evangelistic work. Being excluded, as preachers of "new doctrines," from many of the pulpits of the Established Church, they held meetings in private houses, halls, barns, and fields, receiving many converts, who were organized into societies for worship. As their work expanded they introduced an order of lay preachers and established class-meetings for the religious care and training of members. In 1744 the first conference was held, and thereafter Wesley and his helpers met together annually. Thus was organized the annual conference, one of the distinctive institutions of Methodism. Wesley grouped together several appointments and put them in charge of one of his helpers. This was the beginning of the circuit system. He then conceived the idea of increasing the efficiency of his preachers by frequent changes in their appointments. This is how the itinerancy came into existence. The itinerancy is maintained in nearly all the branches of Methodism throughout the world, though it has been greatly modified in many cases.

Though the Wesleyan movement was a movement within the Church of England, and the Wesleys lived and died in full ministerial relations with it, serious differences arose between the Church and the Methodists. In 1745 John Wesley wrote that he was willing to make any concession which conscience would permit, in order to live in harmony with the clergy of the Established Church, but he could not, he said, give up the doctrines he was preaching, dissolve the societies, suppress lay preaching, or cease to preach in the open air. For many years he refused to sanction the administration of the sacraments by any except those who had been ordained by a bishop in the apostolic succession, and he himself hesitated to assume authority to ordain; but the Bishop of London having refused to ordain ministers for the Methodist societies in America, which were left by the Revolutionary War without the sacraments, Wesley, in 1784, by the imposition of hands, appointed or ordained men and gave them authority to ordain others. He ordained Thomas Coke, LL.D., who was already a presbyter of the Church of England, to be superintendent of the Methodist societies in America, and set apart for a similar purpose in Great Britain Alexander Mather, who had not been episcopally ordained. In England, Methodism continued to be a non-ecclesiastical religious movement within the Church of England till after John Wesley's death, March 2, 1791. In America the separation took place several years previous to that event.

The peculiarities of Methodism are: (1) The probationary system, by which converts are received for six months or more on trial; if the test results favorably, they are then taken into " full connection," and have all the rights and privileges of full members. (2) The class-meeting. The members and probationers of each church are divided into companies called classes, and meet under the care of a leader for prayer, testimony, and spiritual examination and advice. (3) Exhorters. Members licensed to hold meetings for prayer and exhortation. (4) Local preachers. Laymen adjudged to have " gifts, graces, and usefulness " sufficient to justify the issuance of a license, subject to annual renewal, to preach as occasion offers, without giving up their secular business; they may also be ordained as deacons and elders. (5) The itinerancy. There are rules requiring the bishop or a conference committee to station the regular ministers every year, and limiting the pastoral term to a fixed period. In the English Wesleyan Church it is three years; in the Methodist Episcopal Church in the United States it is five years, having been successively advanced from two to three and from three to five. No pastor can serve the same church or circuit in the Methodist Episcopal Church more than five years successively, nor can he be returned to it until after the expiration of another period of five years. (6) Presiding elders. In most American Methodist branches, each annual conference is divided into districts, two or more, and a presiding elder placed over each. His duty is to travel over his district, preside at quarterly conferences in each charge, report to the annual conference, and assist the presiding bishop in making out the list of appointments each year. His term of office is limited in the Methodist Episcopal Church to six years. (7) Bishops. The Episcopal branches have bishops, elected by the general conference for life. They ordain ministers, preside over the annual conferences and at the general conference, and station the ministers, with the advice of the presiding elders; they are itinerant and general, not diocesan, officers.

Methodism also has a system of conferences: (1) The quarterly conference is held four times a year in each church. It is composed of the pastor, local preachers, trustees, stewards, class leaders, and other church officers. (2) The annual conference consists of all the itinerant preachers (and in some branches of representatives of the churches) within its bounds. It examines the characters of the ministers, elects candidates to deacon's and elder's orders, and transacts various other business. (3) The general conference, composed of representatives, clerical and lay, from the various annual conferences, meets once in four years. It is the chief legislative and judicial court. It elects bishops and other general officers, creates new conferences, changes conference boundaries, and controls the administration of the general and benevolent interests of the church. In some branches a district conference is also provided for. It is composed of the pastors and representatives of the churches of a district, the presiding elder being the chairman.

In theology, Methodism, excepting the Welsh branch, is Arminian. Most of the American branches have adopted as their doctrinal symbol "Articles of Religion," twenty-five in number, prepared by John Wesley from the Thirty-nine Articles of the Church of England. In common with other Arminian bodies, Methodists emphasize the doctrine of the freedom of the will and universal atonement, and deny the Calvinistic ideas of predestination and reprobation. Their more distinctive doctrines are those which Wesley revived, restated, and specially emphasized, namely: (1) present personal salvation by faith; (2) the witness of the Spirit; (3) sanctification. Upon the latter point Wesley taught that sanctification is obtainable instantaneously, between justification and death, and that it is not "sinless perfection," but perfection in love, so that those who possess it " feel no sin, nothing but love."

There are seventeen branches of Methodism, as follows:

1. Methodist Episcopal,
2. Union American Meth. Epis.,
3. African Meth. Epis.,
4. African Union Meth. Prot.,
5. African Meth. Epis. Zion,
6. Zion Union Apostolic,
7. Methodist Protestant,
8. Wesleyan Methodist,
9. Methodist Episcopal, South,
10. Congregational,
11. Congregational, Colored,
12. New Congregational,
13. Colored Meth. Epis.,
14. Primitive,
15. Free,
16. Independent,
17. Evangelist Missionary.

I.—THE METHODIST EPISCOPAL CHURCH.

Though John and Charles Wesley crossed the ocean in 1735 and labored in Georgia, the latter about one year, the former two years, the beginnings of Methodism in this country are dated from 1766, in New York and Maryland. In that year a Wesleyan local preacher from Ireland, Philip Embury, gathered a few Methodists in the lower part of New York City for regular worship. Robert Strawbridge, likewise a Wesleyan local preacher and Irish immigrant, preached to a small number of people in Frederick County, Md., at about the same time. The first meetings in New York were held in Mr. Embury's house; then they were transferred to a sail-loft, and in 1768 an edifice was erected at a cost of $3000. This was the first Methodist church in the United States. Its site in John Street is still occupied by a Methodist edifice. Captain Thomas Webb of the British Army was an efficient colaborer with Mr. Embury. Mr. John Wesley sent over two missionaries in 1769, Richard Boardman and Joseph Pilmoor, to assist in the work of establishing Methodism in this country. Seven others subsequently arrived. Two became Presbyterians, and only one, Francis Asbury, remained through the Revolutionary War.

The first annual conference was held in Philadelphia in 1773, Thomas Rankin, one of Wesley's missionaries, presiding. At the close of 1784 a general conference met in Baltimore, December 24th, and the Methodist Episcopal Church was formally organized. This was in accordance with the plan of John Wesley himself. The societies had increased, and the number of members had swelled from 1160 in 1773 to 14,988, notwithstanding the adverse influences of the Revolutionary War; and these societies were without an ordained ministry and consequently without the sacraments during the period of the war, the clergy of the Church of England, from whom baptism and the Lord's Supper had previously been received, having in many cases left their parishes. Representations being made to Mr. Wesley concerning the condition of the Methodist societies, he set apart Dr. Thomas Coke, a presbyter of the Church of England, to be superintendent of the societies, and sent with him to America Francis Asbury and two others, directing him to organize the societies into a separate ecclesiastical body, and to have Asbury associated with him in the office of superintendent.

When the conference was assembled in Baltimore a letter from Mr. Wesley was read, stating that he had "appointed Dr. Coke and Mr. Francis Asbury to be joint-superintendents over our brethren in North America, as also Richard Whatcoat and Thomas Vasey to act as elders among them by baptizing and ministering the Lord's Supper"; that he had prepared a liturgy to be used by the traveling preachers; and that as " our American brethren are now totally disentangled both from the State and from the English hierarchy," he dared not " entangle them again, either with the one or with the other. They are now," he added, " at full liberty simply to follow the Scriptures and the Primitive Church."

The conference then proceeded to "form a Methodist Episcopal Church," electing both Coke and Asbury as superintendents or bishops. Asbury was successively ordained deacon, elder, and bishop. The order of worship and Articles of Religion prepared by Mr. Wesley were adopted, his rules and discipline were revised and accepted, a number of preachers were ordained, and the work of the conference was completed. The constitution of the church is generally held to consist of the general rules of conduct prepared by Mr. Wesley, the Articles of Religion, and six Restrictive Rules, limiting the powers of the general conference, which is the supreme legislative body and the final court. The general conference elects bishops, who hold office for life or during good behavior, and who preside over its sessions, but have no vote or veto in its proceedings. They are not diocesan, but general and itinerant, visiting and presiding over the annual conferences successively, and appointing, with the aid and advice of the presiding elders, the preachers to the pastorates.

The progress of Methodism in the new and growing nation was extremely rapid. Bishop Asbury (Dr. Coke returned after a few years to England), who had large organizing and administrative power, was intensely active in extending the work as an evangelistic movement. He changed his preachers frequently, appointed them to large circuits including several appointments, and raised up a body of class leaders, exhorters, local and itinerant preachers, by whom the gospel was propagated with great success. In 1800 Richard Whatcoat was elected to the bishopric, and in 1808 William McKendree also, the latter being the first native American to occupy that office. In the conference of 1808 a plan was adopted providing for a general conference to be composed of delegates elected by the annual conferences, and to meet once every four years. In 1812, when the first delegated general conference was held, there were upward of 195,000 communicants. In 1872 lay delegates appeared for the first time in the gen-

eral conference. Though the Methodist Episcopal Church
has suffered heavy losses at various times by secessions
and divisions, it has grown very rapidly, and is by far the
most numerous Methodist body in the world. It has in
this country 102 annual conferences, besides 12 in mission
fields in Europe, Asia, Africa, and Mexico, with missions
in South America, Korea, and other countries.

It is represented in all the States and Territories, excepting Alaska. In the following States it has congregations in
every county:

	No. of counties.		No. of counties.
Connecticut	8	Montana	16
Delaware	3	New Hampshire	10
Illinois	102	New Jersey	21
Indiana	92	New York	60
Iowa	99	Ohio	88
Kansas	106	Pennsylvania	67
Maine	16	Rhode Island	5
Maryland	24	Vermont	14
Massachusetts	14		

Of the 2790 counties in the various States and Territories, it has organizations in all save 585. This number
is made up chiefly of counties in the South where conferences of the Methodist Episcopal Church were not formed
after 1844, when the division occurred which resulted in
the organization of the Methodist Episcopal Church, South,
until the close of the late war. In the States of Alabama,
Arkansas, Florida, Georgia, Kentucky, Louisiana, Mississippi, North Carolina, South Carolina, Tennessee, Texas,
and Virginia, the Methodist Episcopal Church, South, is in
fuller occupancy than the Methodist Episcopal Church.

The total of communicants, including both members and

probationers (but not itinerant ministers), is 2,240,354. The total of organizations is 25,861, and there are 22,844 church edifices, with an aggregate seating capacity of 6,302,708, and a total valuation of $96,723,408. In addition to the church edifices, there are 2873 halls, etc., with a seating capacity of 275,444, used as places of worship. The average seating capacity of the churches is 276, and the average value $4234.

An examination of the table by States shows that the largest number of communicants in any one State is to be found in New York, 242,492; Ohio comes second, with 240,650; Pennsylvania third, with 222,886; Illinois fourth, with 165,191; and Indiana fifth, with 162,989. There are six States in which there are more than 100,000 members, and six other States in which the number is more than 50,000. In the number of organizations and church edifices Ohio leads and New York stands second. Of the 102 annual conferences, not including 11 missions, the largest numerically is the Philadelphia conference, which is also the oldest. The Philadelphia conference reports 61,645 communicants. The East Ohio comes second, with 59,666; the Ohio third, with 58,089; the New York East fourth, with 55,724; and the New York fifth, with 53,644. There are 7 conferences which have 50,000 and upward each, and 30 which have between 25,000 and 50,000.

The lines of these conferences do not correspond with those of the States. The New York East conference, for example, includes parts of New York, Connecticut, and New Jersey; the Troy conference includes appointments in New York, Massachusetts, and Vermont; the Wilmington conference, in Delaware, Maryland, and Virginia; the Baltimore conference, in Maryland, Pennsylvania, Virginia,

West Virginia, and the District of Columbia. The conferences are not arranged on a plan similar to that of dioceses in the Protestant Episcopal and the Roman Catholic churches. Each diocese occupies its own territory exclusively; but the same territory in the Methodist Episcopal Church is often covered by different conferences. For example, there are white conferences, in which the English language is spoken, and there are German, Swedish, and other conferences having foreign constituencies, which cover parts of the same territory. The Northwest Swedish conference covers portions of Illinois, Indiana, Iowa, Kansas, Michigan, Minnesota, Missouri, Nebraska, New York, Pennsylvania, and Wisconsin. The Norwegian and Danish conference covers portions of the same territory. So, also, do the St. Louis German, the West German, the Northwest German, the Chicago German, and the following English-speaking conferences: Rock River, St. Louis, Upper Iowa, West Nebraska, West Wisconsin, Wisconsin, Northwest Indiana, Northwest Iowa, Northwest Kansas, Central Illinois, Central Missouri, Des Moines, Detroit, Illinois, Iowa, Kansas, Minnesota, and Nebraska. White English-speaking conferences are also overlapped in many States by conferences composed of colored members.

In the German conferences and missions there are 928 organizations, with 57,105 communicants; in the Scandinavian, 308 organizations and 17,820 communicants. There are also 25 Spanish organizations, with 1475 members, and congregations of Bohemians, Finns, Portuguese, French, Italians, Welsh, Chinese, and Japanese.

SUMMARY BY STATES.

STATES.	Organizations.	Church Edifices.	Seating Capacity.	Value of Church Property.	Communicants.
Alabama........	318	289	72,580	$248,300	18,517
Arizona.........	12	11	3,550	46,100	320
Arkansas	226	167	38,243	162,360	10,076
California	337	306½	93,110	2,053,371	25,527
Colorado........	90	77	23,314	931,900	8,560
Connecticut	219	217	67,527	2,123,380	29,411
Delaware	187	188	49,455	956,300	20,412
Dist. of Columbia	30	29	20,450	772,500	9,630
Florida	117	105	22,620	219,000	5,739
Georgia.........	320	302	73,415	255,940	25,400
Idaho...........	31	26	5,225	69,200	941
Illinois..........	1,903	1,779	523,698	7,046,785	165,191
Indiana.........	1,618	1,585	453,035	4,243,180	162,989
Indian Territory .	32	15	3,925	9,750	838
Iowa	1,342	1,215	317,406	3,344,245	111,426
Kansas	1,249	734	179,230	1,912,015	83,288
Kentucky	435	341½	77,400	762,090	29,172
Louisiana	218	191	39,500	303,302	15,073
Maine	355	290	87,301	1,152,875	22,996
Maryland	925	887	234,856	3,771,717	82,069
Massachusetts ...	394	383	153,722	5,180,825	58,477
Michigan	1,085	894	250,747	3,739,850	86,958
Minnesota.......	534	424	92,400	1,725,843	30,837
Mississippi	398	388	81,038	245,624	31,142
Missouri	905	742	199,044	1,835,840	58,285
Montana........	48	39	8,535	159,850	1,901
Nebraska	649	461	112,603	1,242,200	41,086
Nevada.........	12	12	2,700	78,800	418
New Hampshire .	134	129	40,505	614,350	12,354
New Jersey......	579	554½	185,485	5,009,075	82,955
New Mexico.....	32	21	4,625	71,200	1,750
New York.......	2,123	2,038	614,501	16,944,350	242,492
North Carolina ..	287	238	64,487	195,645	16,433
North Dakota ...	131	61	11,100	139,985	4,804
Ohio	2,340	2,296	685,319	8,749,970	240,650
Oklahoma.......	36	13	3,100	21,400	1,224
Oregon	203	150	34,430	614,625	9,436
Pennsylvania	2,042	1,931	595,734	12,642,104	222,886
Rhode Island	39	37	16,835	495,000	6,064
South Carolina ..	335	337	81,810	292,235	43,200
South Dakota ...	254	140	31,674	375,260	11,371
Tennessee	609	549	146,470	665,460	42,873
Texas	407	346	73,790	592,835	27,453

SUMMARY BY STATES.—*Continued.*

STATES.	Organizations.	Church Edifices.	Seating Capacity.	Value of Church Property.	Communicants.
Utah	31	29	6,205	$223,650	1,048
Vermont........	228	195	55,851	758,800	17,268
Virginia	316	271	42,925	329,144	16,764
Washington.....	200	146	37,230	652,425	11,592
West Virginia ...	827	629½	146,900	902,153	48,925
Wisconsin	706	623	134,913	1,791,900	41,360
Wyoming	13	11	2,190	48,700	773
Total.......	25,861	22,844	6,302,708	$96,723,408	2,240,354

SUMMARY BY CONFERENCES.

CONFERENCES.					
Alabama........	171	151½	32,845	$128,800	7,455
Arkansas	134	95	26,200	114,220	6,295
Austin..........	33	25	6,605	219,900	1,485
Baltimore	411	403	137,966	3,221,060	41,195
Blue Ridge......	172	130	42,930	77,850	7,492
California	195	183	55,450	1,263,321	14,429
California German Mission	16	16	3,610	121,400	829
Central Alabama.	153	143	41,135	130,360	11,317
Central German..	177	176½	38,370	771,000	14,391
Central Illinois...	412	384½	103,147	1,148,700	29,754
Central Missouri .	158	136	35,305	177,580	8,559
Central New York	313	308	95,375	1,662,650	35,591
Central Ohio	408	396½	118,235	1,260,250	38,893
Central Pennsylvania	581	530	152,200	2,319,495	50,773
Central Tennessee	136	120	28,725	97,435	5,584
Chicago German.	122	115	21,890	369,400	7,873
Cincinnati	371	369	113,660	2,057,200	46,188
Colorado........	85	73	22,614	903,900	8,325
Columbia River..	132	84	19,845	254,250	5,792
Dakota	201	119	27,794	325,200	9,774
Delaware	236	228	50,534	315,970	16,877
Des Moines	392	355	96,010	965,900	36,927
Detroit	495	402½	118,750	1,920,600	40,189
East German	61	62	17,085	589,900	5,239
East Maine......	190	141½	42,105	471,150	10,444
East Ohio	539	535	160,510	2,385,700	59,666
East Tennessee ..	77	70	12,300	105,900	4,235
Erie	414	410½	114,014	1,487,314	36,796

SUMMARY BY CONFERENCES.—*Continued.*

CONFERENCES.	Organizations.	Church Edifices.	Seating Capacity.	Value of Church Property.	Communicants.
Florida	67	69	14,790	$86,365	4,425
Genesee	372	356½	98,095	2,080,150	34,946
Georgia	88	87	15,000	53,350	3,547
Holston.........	308	274	83,275	368,925	24,419
Idaho	31	26	5,000	66,000	1,173
Illinois..........	597	539	156,813	1,657,775	52,934
Indiana	424	408	122,425	858,650	41,424
Indian Mission...	68	28	7,025	31,150	2,062
Iowa	335	311	85,665	725,400	25,059
Kansas	242	201	54,810	654,150	21,534
Kentucky	333	249½	56,015	476,715	20,653
Lexington.......	151	137	33,785	286,125	10,437
Little Rock......	92	72	12,043	48,140	3,781
Louisiana	216	189	39,060	296,102	14,911
Maine	171	153	46,326	697,225	12,689
Michigan	540	445½	122,327	1,701,000	43,898
Minnesota	378	300	70,570	1,340,643	23,768
Mississippi	195	192	48,023	124,319	14,869
Missouri	328	282	74,860	453,875	19,799
Montana........	51	42	9,260	165,350	1,991
Nebraska	195	196	59,493	567,250	19,220
Newark..........	299	276½	89,045	3,067,575	42,198
New England ...	246	238	102,891	3,989,175	40,884
New England, Southern......	207	203	67,288	1,653,200	24,371
New Hampshire .	139	136	44,765	748,850	14,335
New Jersey......	303	300	101,870	2,181,900	44,488
New York.......	466	424½	131,608	4,731,900	53,644
New York East ..	325	327	117,343	5,609,380	55,724
North Carolina ..	115	108	21,557	117,795	8,941
North Dakota ...	117	59	10,650	136,185	4,509
Northern German	111	85½	12,800	257,950	4,643
Northern New York	312	302	85,205	1,309,650	27,540
North Indiana ...	463	452	131,315	1,291,500	47,144
North Nebraska..	117	112	25,205	395,650	9,481
North Ohio......	323	318	98,979	1,177,880	30,435
Northwest German..........	94	56½	9,160	130,850	4,371
NorthwestIndiana	343	339	89,720	977,030	33,167
Northwest Iowa ..	180	166	41,440	469,800	16,292
Northwest Kansas	329	112	25,495	228,790	13,902

SUMMARY BY CONFERENCES.—*Continued.*

CONFERENCES.	Organizations.	Church Edifices.	Seating Capacity.	Value of Church Property.	Communicants.
Northwest Swedish	144	116	27,675	$397,100	9,236
Norwegian and Danish	93	63	14,320	173,600	4,782
Ohio	588	570	167,985	1,453,340	58,089
Oregon	131	96	24,915	488,625	7,051
Philadelphia	371	374	156,921	5,014,220	61,645
Pittsburg	353	345	101,639	2,619,150	45,485
Puget Sound	97	78	19,875	368,125	6,615
Rock River	337	324½	115,529	2,946,400	38,674
Saint John River.	43	30	6,330	121,125	1,034
Saint Louis	359	260	77,225	945,185	24,543
Saint Louis German	161	154	31,760	491,490	11,100
Savannah	232	215	58,415	202,590	21,853
South Carolina	335	337	81,810	292,235	21,853
Southeast Indiana	304	303½	91,575	884,450	43,200
Southern California	114	94½	31,700	633,650	35,038
Southern Illinois.	405	388	112,110	637,310	9,836
Southern German	42	36½	6,800	72,700	30,322
South Kansas	306	206½	51,210	429,375	2,470
Southwest Kansas	289	160	37,050	490,700	22,800
Tennessee	115	112	26,620	129,850	21,899
Texas	238	197	40,340	202,005	10,065
Troy	355	339	104,006	2,417,525	14,531
Upper Iowa	317	289½	77,320	970,455	43,578
Upper Mississippi	202	195	32,955	120,505	27,493
Vermont	177	148	42,510	496,600	16,265
Virginia	202	158½	24,725	116,100	12,621
Washington	324	311	66,930	870,522	8,718
West German	126	96½	16,669	265,650	32,976
West Nebraska	274	104½	19,425	175,100	5,554
West Texas	95	89	20,245	97,730	9,743
West Virginia	740	533½	130,500	702,375	8,932
West Wisconsin	336	268	55,879	655,550	42,795
Wilmington	376	372	89,731	1,510,837	16,345
Wisconsin	234	234	58,014	886,200	35,592
Wyoming	413	360	93,820	1,657,150	17,702
					38,731

SUMMARY BY MISSIONS.

MISSIONS.	Organizations.	Church Edifices.	Seating Capacity.	Value of Church Property.	Communicants.
Arizona.........	12	11	3,550	$46,100	320
Black Hills......	23	17	3,550	47,060	831
Nevada.........	25	26	5,300	116,800	878
New Mexico English	10	8	1,900	42,000	540
New Mexico Spanish	25	15	3,225	38,700	1,475
North Pacific German..........	18	17	2,850	52,750	635
Northwest Norwegian and Danish	17	13	2,675	87,500	548
Utah	34	32	6,730	228,150	1,066
Wyoming.......	13	11	2,190	48,700	773
Total.......	25,861	22,844	6,302,708	$96,723,408	2,240,354

2.—THE UNION AMERICAN METHODIST EPISCOPAL CHURCH.

This is a body of colored Methodists having the same general doctrines and usages as other branches of Methodism. It was organized in 1813 in Wilmington, Del., by a number of colored members of the Methodist Episcopal Church, led by Rev. Peter Spencer, a colored preacher.

The church has 42 organizations, with 35 church edifices, valued at $187,600, and 2279 communicants; 2 halls, with a seating capacity of 250, are occupied as places of worship. There are three annual conferences, with two general superintendents or bishops, who are elected for life.

Summary by States.

STATES.	Organizations.	Church Edifices.	Seating Capacity.	Value of Church Property.	Communicants.
Connecticut	1	1	350	$2,000	80
Delaware	8	7	2,650	57,500	507
Maryland	4	4	1,000	6,400	124
Mississippi	1	1	200	2,000	80
New Jersey........	6	6	1,725	14,700	385
New York.........	5	3	975	37,400	288
Pennsylvania	16	12	4,300	65,800	765
Rhode Island......	1	1	300	1,800	50
Total.........	42	35	11,500	$187,600	2,279

Summary by Conferences.

CONFERENCES.					
Eastern District....	13	11	3,350	$55,900	803
Mississippi	1	1	200	2,000	80
Southern District ..	28	23	7,950	129,700	1,396
Total.........	42	35	11,500	$187,600	2,279

3.—THE AFRICAN METHODIST EPISCOPAL CHURCH.

This branch of American Methodism was organized in Philadelphia in 1816 by a number of colored members of the Methodist Episcopal Church. They withdrew from the parent body in order that they might have larger privileges and more freedom of action among themselves than they believed they could secure in continued association with their white brethren. The Rev. Richard Allen was elected the first bishop of the new church by the same convention that organized it. In the year 1787 Mr. Allen had been made the leader of a class of forty persons of his own color. A few years later he purchased a lot at the corner of Sixth and Lombard Streets, Philadelphia, where the first church erected in this country for colored Methodists was occupied in 1794. This site is now covered by an edifice, dedicated in 1890, valued at $50,000.

In doctrine, government, and usage the church does not essentially differ from the body from which it sprang. It has an itinerant and a local or non-itinerant ministry; its territory is divided into annual conferences; it has a general conference, meeting once every four years; has bishops or itinerant general superintendents, elected for life, who visit the annual conferences in the episcopal districts to which they are assigned; has presiding elders who exercise sub-episcopal oversight in the districts into which the annual conferences are divided; and has the probationary system for new members, with exhorters, class leaders, stewards, stewardesses, etc.

The church in its first half-century grew slowly, chiefly in the Northern States, until the close of the war. At the end of the first decade of its existence it had two conferences and about 8000 members. In 1856 it had seven conferences and about 20,000 members; in 1866, ten conferences and 75,000 members. Bishop B. W. Arnett, the ardent and industrious statistician of the church, in noting a decrease of 343 members in the decade ending in 1836, in the Baltimore conference explains that it was due to the numerous sales of members as slaves. According to elaborate figures furnished by him, the increase in the value of church property owned by the denomination was not less than $400,000 in the decade closing in 1866, or nearly 50 per cent. In the succeeding ten years the increase was from $825,000 to $3,064,000, not including parsonages, which seem to have been embraced in the total for 1866. According to the returns for 1890, given herewith, the valuation is $6,468,280, indicating an increase of $3,404,-280 in the last fourteen years, or 111.11 per cent.

The church is widely distributed, having congregations in forty-one States and Territories. The States in which it is not represented are the two Dakotas, Idaho, Maine, Nevada, New Hampshire, and Vermont. Its members are most numerous in South Carolina, where there are 88,172. Georgia comes second, with 73,248; Alabama third, with 30,781; Arkansas fourth, with 27,956; Mississippi fifth, with 25,439. Tennessee has 23,718, Texas 23,392, and Florida 22,463. In no other State does the number reach 17,000. The eight Southern States above given report 315,169 members, or considerably more than two thirds of the entire membership of the church.

It will be observed that of the 2481 organizations only 31, with a seating capacity of 2200, worship in halls, schoolhouses, etc. All the rest, 2450, own the edifices in which their meetings are held. These edifices number 4124—a remarkable excess—and have a total seating capacity of 1,160,838, an average of 281 to each edifice. The average value of each edifice is $1568.

SUMMARY BY STATES.

STATES.	Organizations.	Church Edifices.	Seating Capacity.	Value of Church Property.	Communicants.
Alabama	145	274	77,600	$242,765	30,781
Arkansas	173	333	77,585	233,425	27,956
California	13	15	2,929	24,300	772
Colorado	8	6	2,300	63,500	788
Connecticut	4	4	1,275	16,000	158
Delaware	16	33	7,025	39,500	2,603
Dist. of Columbia	6	7	5,500	117,500	1,479
Florida	152	269	63,445	168,473	22,463
Georgia	334	654	184,592	601,287	73,248
Illinois	74	105	23,799	310,985	6,383

SUMMARY BY STATES.—*Continued.*

STATES.	Organizations.	Church Edifices.	Seating Capacity.	Value of Church Property.	Communicants.
Indiana	36	51	16,450	$138,280	4,435
Indian Territory .	14	22	1,680	2,618	489
Iowa	29	29	7,115	87,365	1,820
Kansas	48	58	14,309	153,530	4,678
Kentucky	90	106	39,100	181,201	13,972
Louisiana	81	115	36,150	193,115	13,631
Maryland	58	93	29,881	266,370	12,359
Massachusetts ...	12	11	5,950	119,200	1,342
Michigan	21	26	7,155	72,185	1,836
Minnesota.......	6	6	2,350	30,000	489
Mississippi	122	255	59,833	226,242	25,439
Missouri	87	126	27,870	281,289	9,589
Montana	3	2	350	14,000	32
Nebraska	4	4	1,350	62,000	399
New Jersey......	54	68	19,510	159,850	5,851
New Mexico.....	3	3	550	3,300	62
New York	34	29	12,900	231,500	3,124
North Carolina ..	61	147	42,350	112,998	16,156
Ohio	111	113	40,965	318,250	10,025
Oregon	1	...	......	......	16
Pennsylvania	87	112	39,900	605,000	11,613
Rhode Island	4	3	2,050	95,000	595
South Carolina...	229	491	125,945	356,362	88,172
Tennessee	144	236	61,800	461,305	23,718
Texas	138	208	82,850	233,340	23,392
Utah	1	...	......	......	7
Virginia	67	102	34,375	187,245	12,314
Washington	2	1	400	4,000	66
West Virginia ...	3	3	1,050	11,000	216
Wisconsin.......	3	3	400	40,000	118
Wyoming	3	1	200	4,000	139
Total	2,481	4,124	1,160,838	$6,468,280	452,725

SUMMARY BY CONFERENCES.

CONFERENCES.					
Alabama........	81	175	50,500	$124,345	18,398
Arkansas........	62	100	25,590	77,490	9,174
Baltimore	64	100	35,381	383,870	13,838
California	16	16	3,329	28,300	854

SUMMARY BY CONFERENCES.—*Continued.*

CONFERENCES.	Organizations.	Church Edifices.	Seating Capacity.	Value of Church Property.	Communicants.
Central Texas ...	20	29	11,700	$50,300	3,526
Columbia	133	271	65,065	197,415	42,840
East Florida.....	104	187	45,320	122,070	12,797
Florida	48	82	18,125	46,403	9,666
Georgia.........	124	260	67,882	127,412	26,963
Illinois..........	45	77	17,209	107,250	3,796
Indiana	36	51	16,550	138,280	4,435
Indian Territory .	14	22	1,680	2,618	489
Iowa............	67	66	16,455	361,100	5,014
Kansas	52	62	15,659	215,530	5,077
Kentucky	47	58	19,850	81,551	7,434
Louisiana	42	63	18,850	166,385	7,587
Macon..........	107	226	68,060	287,662	25,568
Michigan	21	26	7,155	72,185	1,836
Mississippi	42	80	23,275	57,300	10,270
Missouri	44	56	13,700	216,575	4,917
New England....	20	18	9,275	230,200	2,095
New Jersey......	54	68	19,510	159,850	5,851
New York	34	29	12,900	231,500	3,124
North Alabama..	64	99	27,100	118,420	12,383
North Carolina .	61	147	42,350	112,998	16,156
Northeast Texas .	42	56	19,000	56,575	6,076
North Georgia...	103	168	48,650	186,213	20,717
North Louisiana .	39	52	17,300	26,730	6,044
North Mississippi.	80	175	36,558	168,942	15,169
North Missouri ..	43	70	14,170	64,714	4,672
North Ohio......	66	63	22,940	229,825	4,446
Ohio............	45	50	18,025	88,425	5,579
Philadelphia.....	61	96	30,975	390,550	10,247
Pittsburg........	45	52	17,000	264,950	4,185
Rocky Mountain .	18	12	3,400	84,800	1,028
South Arkansas ..	64	137	27,725	75,616	9,686
South Carolina ..	96	220	60,880	158,947	45,332
Tennessee.......	83	130	36,275	338,219	13,423
Texas...........	32	48	21,400	67,465	6,461
Virginia.........	67	102	34,375	187,245	12,314
West Arkansas ..	47	96	24,270	80,319	9,096
West Kentucky..	43	48	19,250	99,650	6,538
West Tennessee..	61	106	25,525	123,086	10,295
West Texas	44	75	30,750	59,000	7,329
Total	2,481	4,124	1,160,838	$6,468,280	452,725

4.—THE AFRICAN UNION METHODIST PROTESTANT CHURCH.

This body, which has a few congregations divided among eight States, came into existence at about the same time the African Methodist Episcopal Church was organized (1816), differing from the latter chiefly in objection to the itinerancy, to a paid ministry, and to the episcopacy. It has 2 annual conferences, with 40 organizations, 27 church edifices, valued at $54,440, and 3415 communicants; 13 halls, with a seating capacity of 1883, are occupied.

SUMMARY BY STATES.

STATES.	Organizations.	Church Edifices.	Seating Capacity.	Value of Church Property.	Communicants.
Delaware	6	4	1,250	$9,600	368
Maine	1	..	.....	......	45
Maryland	8	7	2,255	5,600	1,546
New Jersey	8	6	836	5,940	281
New York.........	3	..	.....	......	60
Pennsylvania	8	8	2,140	32,100	852
Rhode Island......	1	..	.....	......	49
Virginia	5	2	680	1,200	214
Total.........	40	27	7,161	$54,440	3,415

SUMMARY BY CONFERENCES.

CONFERENCES.					
Baltimore	14	9	2,935	$6,800	1,805
Northern	26	18	4,226	47,640	1,610
Total.........	40	27	7,161	$54,440	3,415

5.—THE AFRICAN METHODIST EPISCOPAL ZION CHURCH.

A congregation of colored people, organized in New York City in 1796, was the nucleus of the African Methodist Episcopal Zion Church. This congregation originated in a desire of colored members of the Methodist Episcopal Church to hold separate meetings, in which they "might have an opportunity to exercise their spiritual gifts among themselves, and thereby be more useful to one another." They built a church, which was dedicated in 1800, the full name of the denomination subsequently organized being given to it. The church entered into an agreement in 1801 by which it was to receive certain pastoral supervision from the Methodist Episcopal Church. It had preachers of its own, who supplied its pulpit in part. In 1820 this arrangement was terminated, and in the same year a union of colored churches in New York, New Haven, Long Island, and Philadelphia was formed and rules of government adopted. Thus was the African Methodist Episcopal Zion Church formally organized.

The first annual conference was held in 1821. It was attended by 19 preachers, representing 6 churches and 1426 members. Next year James Varick was chosen superintendent of the denomination, which was extended over the States of the North chiefly until the close of the Civil War, when it entered the South to organize many churches.

In its polity lay representation has long been a prominent feature. Laymen are in its annual conferences as well as in its general conference, and there is no bar to the ordination of women. Until 1880 its superintendents, or bishops, were elected for a term of four years. In that year the term of the office was made for life or during good behavior. Its system is almost identical with that of the Methodist Episcopal Church, except the presence of laymen in the annual conference, the election of presiding elders on the nomination of the presiding bishop, instead of their appointment by the bishop alone, and similar small divergences. Its general conference meets quadrennially. Its territory is divided into seven episcopal districts, to each of which a bishop is assigned by the general conference. There are in all twenty-eight annual conferences, one of which is partly in this country and partly in Canada. There is also a missionary district in Africa.

The church is represented in twenty-nine States. It is strongest in North Carolina, where it has 111,949 communicants; Alabama comes next, with 79,231 communicants; South Carolina third, with 45,880; and Florida fourth, with 14,791. There are in all 1704 organizations, 1587 church edifices, which have accommodations for 565,577 worshipers and are valued at $2,714,128, and 349,788 communicants. The average seating capacity of the church edifices is 356 and their average value $1710; also 114 halls, with a seating capacity of 15,520, are occupied as meeting-places.

SUMMARY BY STATES.

STATES.	Organizations.	Church Edifices.	Seating Capacity.	Value of Church Property.	Communicants.
Alabama	336	315½	118,800	$305,350	79,231
Arkansas	29	23	8,800	17,250	3,601
California	13	6	2,600	37,200	2,627
Connecticut	12	10	2,900	79,350	1,012
Delaware	2	1	115	500	158
District of Columbia	6	6	3,400	298,800	2,495
Florida	61	61	23,589	90,745	14,791
Georgia	70	62	19,775	52,360	12,705
Illinois	5	5	2,000	13,400	434
Indiana	5	5	2,400	54,700	1,339
Kentucky	55	52	13,075	86,830	7,217
Louisiana	21	19	5,200	12,920	2,747
Maryland	13	10	2,375	17,350	1,211
Massachusetts	7	6	2,050	58,800	724
Michigan	6	4	650	3,200	702

SUMMARY BY STATES.—*Continued.*

STATES.	Organi-zations.	Church Edifices.	Seating Ca-pacity.	Value of Church Property.	Com-muni-cants.
Mississippi	64	50	22,350	$22,975	8,519
Missouri	6	6	3,900	6,000	2,037
New Jersey	25	24	7,400	107,700	2,954
New York	47	47	17,000	371,400	6,668
North Carolina	541	526½	171,430	485,711	111,949
Ohio	8	5	1,160	13,000	194
Oregon	2	2	300	20,000	275
Pennsylvania	62	55	17,625	256,150	8,689
Rhode Island	3	1	400	2,000	401
South Carolina	130	128	66,770	126,325	45,880
Tennessee	55	52	21,093	78,813	12,434
Texas	47	38	11,500	26,450	6,927
Virginia	72	66	16,770	68,449	11,765
Wisconsin	1	1	150	400	102
Total	1,704	1,587	565,577	$2,714,128	349,788

6.—THE ZION UNION APOSTOLIC CHURCH.

This body was organized at a meeting held at Boydton, Va., in 1869. It is said that most of those concerned in instituting it had not previously belonged to any regular body. Its discipline is very similar to that of the Methodist Episcopal Church, except that it is much briefer. Its system includes bishops, annual conferences and a general conference, itinerant ministers, local preachers, class-meetings, etc.; 1 hall, with a seating capacity of 100, is occupied.

SUMMARY BY STATES.

STATES.	Organi-zations.	Church Edifices.	Seating Ca-pacity.	Value of Church Property.	Com-muni-cants.
North Carolina	3	3	900	$1,900	135
Virginia	29	24	9,200	13,100	2,211
Total	32	27	10,100	$15,000	2,346

7.—THE METHODIST PROTESTANT CHURCH.

This branch of Methodism was organized in 1830 by ministers and members who had been expelled, or had seceded from the Methodist Episcopal Church. It was the outcome of a movement for a change in certain features of the government of the Methodist Episcopal Church. In 1824 a Union Society was formed in Baltimore having this object in view, and a periodical called *The Mutual Rights* was established to advocate it. The chief reform insisted upon was the admission of the laity to a share in the government of the church. The annual and general conferences were composed entirely of ministers, and the laymen had no place or voice in either. A convention held in 1827 resolved to present a petition to the general conference of 1828 asking for lay representation. The conference returned an unfavorable reply to the petitioners. This only served to intensify the feeling. The Union Society entered into a campaign for " equal rights," and so great an agitation resulted that the leaders of the movement came to be regarded as disturbers of the peace. Some of them were brought to trial and expelled from the church. All efforts to have them restored having failed, many sympathizers withdrew from the church, and in 1828 a convention of the disaffected was held in Baltimore, and a provisional organization formed. Two years later (November 2, 1830) another convention was held and the Methodist Protestant Church was constituted. It began its separate existence with 83 ministers, and about 5000 members. In the first four years it increased its membership enormously. While equal rights were insisted upon in the new constitution, as between ministers and laymen, the right of suffrage and eligibility to office was restricted to the whites. When the antislavery agitation began in the new branch some years later, the northern and western conferences raised an objection to the retention of the word "white" in the constitution. They also protested against any toleration of slavery by the church. Failing to secure such changes as they desired, they held a convention in Springfield, Ill., in 1858, and resolved to suspend all relations with the Methodist Protestant Church. Later they united with a number of Wesleyan Methodists and formed the Methodist Church. After the close of the war negotiations for a reunion were begun, and in 1877 the two branches—the Methodist and the Methodist Protestant —were made one under the old title.

The Methodist Protestant Church is strongest numerically in the States of Ohio, North Carolina, Maryland, and West Virginia. It is represented in most of the border and Southern States, but is not widely diffused among the Northern and Western States. At the reunion in 1877 there were in the Methodist branch 58,072 communicants; in the Methodist Protestant branch 58,470, making a total of 116,542. The increase since then has amounted to 25,447, the membership in 1890 aggregating 141,989. They have not, however, been incorporated in the discipline. The average seating capacity of its edifices is 297, and their average value $1914. There are 575 halls, with a seating capacity of 80,025, used as places of worship.

In doctrine, the Methodist Protestant does not differ from the Methodist Episcopal Church, except that it has twenty-nine instead of twenty-six articles of religion. The general conference of 1888 appointed a committee to revise the doctrinal symbol. The committee made the revision in 1890, adding five new articles, with the following titles: " Free Grace," " Freedom of the Will," " Regeneration," " Sanctification," and " Witness of the Spirit." The revised articles were submitted to the annual conferences for amendment and approval, but have not been adopted.

SUMMARY BY STATES.

STATES.	Organizations.	Church Edifices.	Seating Capacity.	Value of Church Property.	Communicants.
Alabama	77	72½	19,895	$79,850	4,432
Arkansas	118	51	14,650	15,360	3,946
Connecticut	3	3	530	5,000	154
Delaware	22	22	5,015	51,600	1,551
District of Columbia	9	8	3,225	168,825	831
Florida	11	5	1,300	2,400	350
Georgia	80	73	21,050	33,475	4,390
Illinois	135	94	25,840	115,765	5,502
Indiana	132	110½	33,885	142,875	7,033
Indian Territory	16	1	200	300	278
Iowa	61	55	11,325	84,900	5,645
Kansas	32	19	4,550	33,770	1,890
Kentucky	40	18	6,050	8,500	1,822
Louisiana	26	23	7,550	6,850	1,231
Maryland	174	171½	44,993	654,625	13,283
Michigan	120	94	23,035	161,702	4,512
Minnesota	5	5	1,000	3,000	137
Mississippi	75	73	17,095	16,175	3,147
Missouri	90	38	11,025	29,900	3,359
Nebraska	34	9	1,150	8,450	686
New Jersey	39	39	12,625	181,950	3,459
New York	90	78	27,690	293,000	4,759
North Carolina	199	189	70,205	126,800	14,351
Ohio	234	226½	68,945	441,000	18,931
Oregon	1	1	200	1,200	15
Pennsylvania	172	129	44,567	641,575	10,081
South Carolina	42	42	11,495	21,095	2,665
Tennessee	40	36½	11,350	25,950	2,880
Texas	158	31	9,800	16,700	5,536
Virginia	57	57	15,650	94,000	4,154
Washington	6	6	2,550	62,800	315
West Virginia	230	142½	42,676	153,545	10,652
Wisconsin	1	1	150	400	12
Total	2,529	1,924	571,266	$3,683,337	141,989

Summary by Conferences.

CONFERENCES.	Organizations.	Church Edifices.	Seating Capacity.	Value of Church Property.	Communicants.
Alabama.........	73	69	18,895	$78,850	3,932
Alabama Colored Mission.........	4	4	1,000	1,000	500
Arkansas	81	50	14,300	14,825	2,868
Baltimore Colored Mission........	7	5	1,300	16,125	230
Central Texas	62	6	3,100	6,000	2,163
Colorado-Texas...	71	5	1,650	1,900	1,424
Florida Mission...	11	5	1,300	2,400	350
Fort Smith Mission	51	7	2,200	2,335	1,522
Genesee	18	16½	3,935	43,900	936
Georgia	50	45	15,650	22,100	3,067
Georgia Colored ..	29	27	5,200	11,325	1,293
Indiana..........	130	107½	33,135	140,225	6,981
Indiana Mission...	16	1	200	300	278
Iowa	61	55	11,325	84,900	5,645
Kansas	32	19	4,550	33,770	1,890
Kentucky	36	12	4,800	6,300	1,585
Louisiana	20	17	5,700	5,050	917
Maryland	254	250½	68,183	1,031,025	19,473
Michigan	92	68½	16,635	121,777	3,352
Minnesota	5	5	1,000	3,000	137
Mississippi	50	48	9,495	8,125	1,910
Missouri	53	22	5,825	17,200	2,155
Muskingum	109	105½	34,255	216,800	9,996
Nebraska	34	9	1,150	8,450	686
New Jersey.......	35	35	10,775	125,450	3,028
New York........	27	27	9,535	172,475	2,179
North Carolina ...	193	183	68,205	124,100	13,876
North Illinois.....	58	45	11,465	76,450	2,470
North Mississippi .	27	26	8,150	8,400	1,335
North Missouri ...	29	16	5,200	12,700	1,074
Ohio	115	112	32,290	195,100	8,134
Onondaga........	54	43½	16,850	119,400	2,304
Oregon	7	7	2,750	64,000	330
Pennsylvania	59	27	8,450	41,000	1,346
Pittsburg.........	96	85	31,257	575,650	7,817
South Carolina ...	37	37	10,550	18,950	2,132
South Carolina Colored........	14	14	4,045	6,995	1,160
South Illinois.....	78	49½	14,525	39,715	3,044

SUMMARY BY CONFERENCES.—*Continued.*

CONFERENCES.	Organi-zations.	Church Edifices.	Seating Capacity.	Value of Church Property.	Com-muni-cants.
Tennessee	33	33	9,750	$18,000	1,850
Texas	25	19½	5,050	8,800	1,949
Virginia	34	31	7,500	18,450	2,943
West Michigan ...	32	29½	7,400	43,175	1,301
West Virginia	227	143½	42,736	136,845	10,427
Total	2,529	1,924	571,266	$3,683,337	141,989

8.—THE WESLEYAN METHODIST CONNECTION OF AMERICA.

In this title "Connection" is used in a sense common to Methodism, especially British Methodism. It indicates congregations bound together by the same doctrinal and ecclesiastical ties. This body was organized in 1843 by ministers and members of the Methodist Episcopal Church in consequence of dissatisfaction with the attitude of that body toward slavery and with some of the features of its governmental system. It began with about 6000 members, most of whom were in the State of New York. In doctrine it does not differ from other branches of Methodism. It refuses to receive as members those who belong to secret societies, and as long as the institution existed, it maintained the same bar against those connected with slavery. It has twenty-two annual conferences, with ministerial and lay members, and a general conference, the chief legislative body of the church, which meets quadrennially. There is no itinerancy, as in most other Methodist bodies, but pastorates are arranged by mutual agreement of ministers and congregations, and are not limited to a term of years. It has 565 organizations, in twenty-two States, with 16,492 members, of whom nearly one fourth, or 3913, are in New York; Michigan second, with 2942; and Indiana third, with 2199 members. The average value of the 342 houses of worship is $1151, and the average seating capacity is 252. There are 213 halls, with a seating capacity of 18,483.

SUMMARY BY STATES.

STATES.	Organi-zations.	Church Edifices.	Seating Ca-pacity.	Value of Church Property.	Com-muni-cants.
California	2	1	250	$750	41
Illinois	19	17	3,825	24,900	643
Indiana	58	44	13,030	37,900	2,199
Iowa	26	16½	4,015	16,500	840
Kansas	22	8	2,325	14,350	566
Massachusetts	1	..	....	......	8
Michigan	143	63½	14,120	58,475	2,942
Minnesota	5	4	625	1,300	207
Missouri	2	..	....	......	50
Nebraska	6	..	....	......	78
New Jersey........	3	2	500	2,650	65
New York..........	114	75	19,038	135,950	3,913
North Carolina	8	7	1,980	1,675	141
Ohio	45	40	11,391	46,500	1,657
Oregon	4	1	250	1,200	61
Pennsylvania	41	30	7,205	25,300	1,195
South Dakota	23	5	900	5,200	458
Tennessee	14	9	2,650	2,050	462
Vermont..........	6	5	1,225	6,850	259
Washington	3	1	200	600	35
West Virginia	1	1	500	1,500	245
Wisconsin	19	12	2,225	9,600	427
Total	565	342	86,254	$393,250	16,492

SUMMARY BY CONFERENCES.

CONFERENCES.					
Allegheny	34	30	7,530	$37,100	1,207
Central Ohio	19	18	5,141	13,800	784
Champlain	39	27	6,750	43,950	1,444
Dakota	23	5	900	5,200	458
Illinois...........	19	17	3,825	24,900	643
Indiana	58	44	13,030	37,900	2,199
Iowa	26	16½	4,015	16,500	840

SUMMARY BY CONFERENCES.—*Continued.*

CONFERENCES.	Organizations.	Church Edifices.	Seating Capacity.	Value of Church Property.	Communicants.
Kansas	18	6	1,525	$10,150	464
Lockport..........	30	21	5,350	27,750	896
Miami	17	15	4,325	15,400	714
Michigan	78	46	10,520	49,250	1,979
Minnesota	5	4	625	1,300	207
Nebraska	6	..	.....	......	78
New York.........	12	4	776	5,250	239
North Carolina	8	7	1,980	1,675	141
North Michigan ...	65	17½	3,600	9,225	963
Pacific............	9	3	700	2,550	137
Rochester.........	36	23	6,087	49,100	1,099
South Kansas	6	2	800	4,200	152
Syracuse..........	24	15½	3,900	26,400	959
Tennessee	14	9	2,650	2,050	462
Wisconsin.........	19	11½	2,225	9,600	427
Total.........	565	342	86,254	$393,250	16,492

9.—THE METHODIST EPISCOPAL CHURCH, SOUTH.

This body was organized at a convention held in Louisville, Ky., in 1845, by annual conferences in the South, which had accepted a plan of separation adopted by the general conference of the Methodist Episcopal Church at its meeting in New York in 1844. The cause of separation was the slavery question.

This question, which gave rise to much discussion and several divisions among Methodists, engaged their attention as early as 1780, four years before American Methodism was given organized form. A conference held in Baltimore in 1780 took action requiring traveling preachers who held slaves to set them free, and advising lay slaveholders to do likewise. In 1789 the following appeared in the discipline among the rules prohibiting certain things:

" The buying or selling the bodies and souls of men, women, or children, with an intention to enslave them."

The conference of 1784, which organized the Methodist Episcopal Church, deemed it a " bounden duty " to take effective measures to " extirpate this abomination from among us." It accordingly insisted that all those holding slaves should adopt a system of manumission, failing in which they should be excluded from the church, and that in future no slaveholder should be admitted to the church until he had ceased to hold slaves. In 1800 the discipline provided that any minister becoming a slaveholder must, if legally possible under the laws of the State in which he lived, emancipate his slaves or " forfeit his ministerial character." In 1816 the general conference declared slaveholders ineligible to any official station in the church, except in States where the laws did not " admit of emancipation and permit the liberated slave to enjoy freedom." These provisions could not be observed in some of the States in the South, and were not insisted on in the Carolinas, Georgia, and Tennessee. In 1808 the general conference directed that a number of disciplines, " with the section and rule on slavery left out," be printed for use in South Carolina.

About twenty-five years later the antislavery agitation in the North began to affect Methodism. The general conference of 1836 exhorted the members of the church " to abstain from all abolition movements and associations," and censured two of its members for taking part in an antislavery meeting. In the South the rule concerning the connection of ministers with slavery had not been enforced, except in six of the border conferences. The episcopacy, however, had been kept free from any conflict with slaveholding. While the Northern conferences would not have received a slaveholding bishop, the Southern conferences could not agree that slaveholders ought to be excluded from the episcopacy. A serious conflict arose, therefore, when Bishop Andrew, a Southern man who was elected bishop in 1832, became by marriage, in January, 1844, a slaveholder. At the general conference held in May of that year in New York City, after a long discussion, it was declared by a vote of 111 to 69 to be the sense of the conference that Bishop Andrew " desist from the exercise of his office so long as he is connected with slavery." The Southern delegates protested against this action, and insisted that under the circumstances the " continuance of the jurisdiction of this general conference " over the conferences in the slaveholding States was " inconsistent with the success of the ministry " in those States. The outcome was the adoption of a report of a committee of nine embodying a plan of separation to become operative, if the thirteen annual conferences in the slaveholding States should " find it necessary to unite in a distinct ecclesiastical connection, and if the various annual conferences by a three-fourths vote should so change the constitution as to allow of a division of the property of the Book Concern."

The action of the general conference was followed, in the South, by a convention in Louisville, Ky., in May, 1845, representing the thirteen annual conferences which had expressed their approval of the plan of separation. This convention declared the conferences represented a distinct body under the title, " The Methodist Episcopal Church, South." Two bishops, Andrew and Soule, cast their lot with the Southern church, the former in 1845, the latter at the first general conference in 1846. The Northern annual conferences disapproved the plan of separation, and the general conference of 1848 declared it null and void. A suit for a division of the property according to the plan of separation was prosecuted, and the Supreme Court of the United States, in 1854, decided it in favor of the Southern church. A fraternal messenger sent by the latter to the Northern general conference of 1848 was not received officially by that body. It was not until after the Civil War (1876) that fraternity was established between the two churches.

The Southern church lost more heavily during the years of the war than the Northern. The latter had in 1864 about 68,000 fewer members than in 1860, the decrease occurring chiefly in the border conferences. The former lost between the years 1860 and 1866 113,000 white members, while its colored membership, aggregating 207,-766, dwindled to 78,742. Most of the colored members went, at the close of the war, into the Methodist Episcopal Church (which extended its operations into the South), and into the African Methodist Episcopal and African Methodist Episcopal Zion churches. In 1870 nearly all the remaining colored members were organized into the Colored Methodist Episcopal Church. There are now only about 500 colored members in the Methodist Episcopal Church, South, and these are scattered among 27 annual conferences. In the Indian Mission Conference about 3500 of the 10,498 members are Indians. The Southern church reorganized its shattered forces at the close of the war, and in a few years was again in the full tide of prosperity. Its growth in the last decade has been rapid.

The Methodist Episcopal Church, South, has the same articles of religion, the same system of conferences, annual and general, and substantially the same discipline as the Methodist Episcopal Church. It differs from the latter in admitting lay delegates (four from each district) to the annual conferences; in making lay equal to ministerial representation in the general conference; in giving the bishops a modified veto over legislation which they may deem unconstitutional; and in abolishing the probationary term of six months for candidates for membership. The changes respecting lay delegation and the probationary system were adopted in 1866. The pastoral term was in the same year extended from two to four years.

There are 45 annual conferences, covering the entire country south of the 40th parallel of latitude, which nearly corresponds with Mason and Dixon's line, and also parts of Oregon, Montana, Idaho, and Washington; but the number of congregations in these States is not large. Nor are there many congregations in the southern portions of Indiana and Illinois. The church is strongest in Texas, where it has 139,347 members; in Georgia, where it has 134,600; and in Tennessee, where the number reaches 121,398. There are in all 1,209,976 members, with 15,017 organizations, and 12,688 edifices, which are valued at $18,775,362. Of the congregations, 1634 meet in halls, etc., which have a seating capacity of 190,777. The average seating capacity of the church edifices is 265, and the average value $1480.

SUMMARY BY STATES.

STATES.	Organizations.	Church Edifices.	Seating Capacity.	Value of Church Property.	Communicants.
Alabama........	1,101	1,050	243,735	$1,123,523	87,912
Arizona.........	11	6	1,150	12,000	336
Arkansas........	1,033	809	203,069	708,895	71,565
California	175	97½	23,210	446,010	7,497
Colorado........	26	16	3,411	100,300	1,299
Dist. of Columbia	4	3	1,675	61,400	953
Florida	389	347	61,338	333,824	25,362
Georgia.........	1,286	1,272½	322,856	1,661,410	134,600
Idaho...........	11	4	700	5,000	221
Illinois..........	154	108	26,450	123,183	7,109
Indiana	10	8	1,850	13,100	945
Indian Territory..	275	134	24,455	59,600	9,693
Iowa............	8	7	1,800	9,200	730
Kansas..........	83	40½	10,300	83,450	3,346
Kentucky	989	827	239,410	1,539,567	82,430
Louisiana	316	296½	49,755	483,470	24,874
Maryland	142	135½	30,470	361,990	10,604
Mississippi	903	854	207,760	903,563	74,785
Missouri	1,230	921	264,788	2,046,389	86,466
Montana........	23	13	2,920	74,000	492
Nebraska	8	6	1,275	10,800	206
New Mexico.....	25	18	2,850	32,600	548
North Carolina...	1,288	1,203½	380,500	1,471,135	114,385
Oklahoma.......	15	7	1,550	16,150	805
Oregon	70	40	7,960	50,850	1,936
Pennsylvania	14	12	2,475	11,400	635
South Carolina...	686	678	196,808	796,840	68,092
Tennessee.......	1,367	1,258	376,483	1,994,382	121,398
Texas...........	1,701	1,076	296,578	1,647,866	139,347
Virginia	1,172	1,107	285,735	2,183,565	105,892
Washington	20	11	2,385	27,650	449
West Virginia ...	482	321	83,765	382,250	25,064
Total	15,017	12,688	3,359,466	$18,775,362	1,209,976

SUMMARY BY CONFERENCES.

CONFERENCES.					
Alabama........	509	502	109,920	$567,360	39,574
Arkansas........	333	203	55,985	199,596	23,134
Baltimore	561	482	120,550	977,965	41,070
Columbia	44	29	5,260	32,650	1,280

SUMMARY BY CONFERENCES.—*Continued.*

CONFERENCES.	Organizations.	Church Edifices.	Seating Capacity.	Value of Church Property.	Communicants.
Denver	28	17	3,561	$101,100	1,395
East Columbia...	56	24½	5,585	48,850	1,301
East Texas	219	210	47,925	214,825	22,050
Florida	322	280	53,348	309,024	20,420
German Mission .	22	21½	4,600	42,350	1,325
Holston	624	542	165,370	904,890	43,014
Illinois..........	163	115	28,050	133,783	7,854
Indian Mission...	290	141	26,005	75,750	10,498
Kentucky	332	278½	80,565	692,900	27,114
Little Rock......	456	391	92,845	326,217	28,016
Los Angeles.....	46	31	6,900	157,735	2,072
Louisiana	250	242½	37,155	445,845	20,379
Louisville	488	419½	119,100	691,967	40,427
Memphis........	491	484	135,728	704,620	49,436
Mexican Border Mission	22	14	2,125	24,075	1,041
Mississippi	463	418	100,207	413,690	38,173
Missouri	468	401	107,520	740,264	36,965
Montana	24	14	3,120	76,000	517
New Mexico.....	27	19	2,950	38,200	535
North Alabama ..	657	613	141,255	580,513	53,210
North Carolina ..	602	557	169,715	712,975	52,643
North Georgia...	737	734	198,176	1,041,680	82,921
North Mississippi.	508	492	120,703	527,948	41,177
North Texas.....	458	285	83,800	417,928	42,013
Northwest Texas.	610	275	86,730	439,386	45,208
Pacific..........	139	72	17,310	298,275	5,722
Saint Louis......	339	225	72,965	615,975	20,684
South Carolina ..	686	678	196,808	796,840	68,992
South Georgia...	546	535½	122,980	617,230	51,395
Southwest Missouri	431	301½	86,103	699,350	29,547
Tennessee.......	608	558	166,460	881,832	59,999
Texas	190	157	43,860	335,777	15,237
Virginia	710	702	177,055	1,474,580	69,826
Western	91	46½	11,575	94,250	3,552
Western North Carolina	646	607	199,635	689,960	57,594
Western Virginia.	400	241	68,285	279,000	20,722
West Texas	177	113	27,438	169,125	12,429
White River.....	244	216	54,239	183,082	20,415
Total	15,017	12,688	3,359,466	$18,775,362	1,209,976

10.—THE CONGREGATIONAL METHODISTS.

Dissatisfaction with certain features of the system of polity led a number of ministers and members of the Methodist Episcopal Church, South, to withdraw and organize a body in which laymen should have an equal voice in church government and local preachers should become pastors. The new church was organized in Georgia in 1852, and called the Congregational Methodist Church. The first district conference was formed the same year. A number of churches in harmony with the principles of the movement were organized in Georgia, Mississippi, and other States of the South, to which it has been confined. In 1888 many of the churches and ministers went over into the Congregational denomination, which appeared in the South after the war.

The system of the Congregational Methodists is not purely congregational. The local church has large powers, but appeals from its decisions may be taken to the district conference, and thence to the State conference, and also to the general conference. These bodies have likewise the power of censure or approval. The district conference may "condemn opinions and practices contrary to the word of truth and holiness," and may cite offending parties for trial, and admonish, rebuke, suspend, or expel from the conference. Ministers and lay members have equal rights and privileges in the local church and all the conferences. The district conference is composed of representatives from the churches, the State conference of representatives of the district conferences, and the general conference of delegates chosen by the State conferences. District conferences meet semi-annually, State conferences annually, and the general conference quadrennially. The ministers are elders ordained after examination and approved by the district conference. The elder, as pastor of a church, presides at its monthly conference. The other officers of a church are class leader, deacon or steward, and clerk. The itinerancy is not in force. In doctrine this branch does not differ from other Methodist bodies.

This body has in all 214 organizations, 150 edifices, valued at $41,680, and 8765 communicants. Its chief strength lies in Alabama, where it has 2596 communicants. The average seating capacity of its church edifices is 310, and the average value $278. There are 60 halls, with a seating capacity of 7825.

SUMMARY BY STATES.

STATES.	Organizations.	Church Edifices.	Seating Capacity.	Value of Church Property.	Communicants.
Alabama..........	65	59	18,575	$14.050	2,596
Arkansas	10	4	1,675	2,525	223
Florida	7	1	550	250	179
Georgia	29	28	8,000	8,050	1,655
Illinois............	4	..	.....	.....	96
Mississippi	28	22	5,600	5,400	1,341
Missouri	38	13	4,400	3,000	1,450
Tennessee	7	4	1,150	780	196
Texas	26	19	6,450	7,625	1,029
Total.........	214	150	46,400	$41,680	8,765

SUMMARY BY CONFERENCES.

CONFERENCES.					
Arkansas	10	4	1,675	$2,525	223
Georgia...........	26	25	7,200	7,300	1,517
Illinois............	4	..	.....	.....	96
Mississippi	28	22	5,600	5,400	1,341
Missouri	38	13	4,400	3,000	1,450
North Alabama....	59	53	17,550	13,300	2,281
Tennessee	7	4	1,150	780	196
Texas	26	19	6,450	7,625	1,029
West Florida......	16	10	2,375	1,750	632
Total.........	214	150	46,400	$41,680	8,765

11.—THE CONGREGATIONAL METHODISTS, COLORED.

This body consists of congregations of colored members, organized into conferences by presidents of the Congregational Methodist Church, to which it corresponds in all particulars of doctrine, polity, and usage. The only difference between the churches of the two bodies is that they are composed of white and colored persons respectively. Four halls, with a seating capacity of 450, are occupied.

SUMMARY BY STATES.

STATES.	Organizations.	Church Edifices.	Seating Capacity.	Value of Church Property.	Communicants.
Alabama	7	5	585	$525	215
Texas	2	..	...	....	104
Total	9	5	585	$525	319

12.—THE NEW CONGREGATIONAL METHODISTS.

This branch originated in Ware County, Ga., in 1881. It was organized by members of the Methodist Episcopal Church, South, who were aggrieved by a certain action of a quarterly conference of that body, which action they regarded as arbitrary. It has the same doctrines and substantially the same practical system as the Congregational Methodist Church. A number of its churches united with the Congregational denomination in 1888.

There are in all 24 organizations, 17 edifices, valued at $3750, and 1059 members, found chiefly in Georgia. The average seating capacity of the church edifices is 294 and the average value $214. There are 6 halls, with a seating capacity of 450.

SUMMARY BY STATES.

STATES.	Organizations.	Church Edifices.	Seating Capacity.	Value of Church Property.	Communicants.
Florida	3	1	300	$150	113
Georgia...........	21	16	4,850	3,600	946
Total.........	24	17	5,150	$3,750	1,059

13.—THE COLORED METHODIST EPISCOPAL CHURCH.

The Colored Methodist Episcopal Church was organized in 1870 of colored members and ministers of the Methodist Episcopal Church, South. Before the Civil War the Methodist Episcopal Church, South, did a large evangelistic work among the negroes. Bishop H. N. McTyeire, of that body, in his " History of Methodism," says: "As a general rule negro slaves received the gospel by Methodism from the same preachers and in the same churches with their masters, the galleries or a portion of the body of the house being assigned to them. If a separate building was provided, the negro congregation was an appendage to the white, the pastor usually preaching once on Sunday for them, holding separate official meetings with their leaders, exhorters, and preachers, and administering discipline and making return of members for the annual minutes." For the negroes on plantations, who were not privileged to attend organized churches, special missions were begun as early as 1829. In 1845, the year which marks the beginning of the separate existence of the Methodist Episcopal Church, South, there were in the Southern conferences of Methodism, according to Bishop McTyeire, 124,000 members of the slave population, and in 1860 about 207,000.

In 1866, after the opening of the South to Northern churches had given the negro members opportunity to join the African Methodist Episcopal, the African Methodist Episcopal Zion, and other Methodist bodies, it was found that of the 207,742 colored members which the church, South, had in 1860, only 78,742 remained. The general conference of 1866 authorized these colored members, with their preachers, to be organized into separate congregations and annual conferences, and the general conference of 1870 appointed two bishops to organize the colored conferences into a separate and independent church. This was done in December, 1870, the new body taking the name "Colored Methodist Episcopal Church." Its rules limited the privilege of membership to negroes.

The Colored Methodist Episcopal Church has the same articles of religion, the same form of government, and the same discipline as its parent body. Its bishops are elected for life. One of them, Bishop L. H. Holsey, says that for some years the body encountered strong opposition from colored people because of its relation to the Methodist Episcopal Church, South, but that this prejudice has now almost entirely disappeared. He says a separate organization was made necessary by the change in the relation between master and slave. "The former, though divested of his slaves, carried with him all the notions, feelings, and elements in his religious and social life that characterized his former years. On the other hand, the emancipated slave had but little in common with the former master; in fact, he had nothing but his religion, poverty, and ignorance. With social elements so distinct and dissimilar the best results of a common church relation could not be expected." Bishop Holsey declares that the great aim of the church is (1) to evangelize the negroes, and (2) to educate and elevate them.

There are 23 annual conferences, with 129,383 members. It will be noticed that the church is almost entirely confined to the South. It is strongest in Georgia, where it has 22,840 members; Mississippi comes next, with 20,107; Tennessee third, with 18,968; and Alabama fourth, with 18,940. There are 1759 organizations, with 1653 church edifices, valued at $1,713,366. The average seating capacity of each edifice is 328, and the average value $1036. There are 64 halls, with a seating capacity of 6526.

SUMMARY BY STATES.

STATES.	Organizations.	Church Edifices.	Seating Capacity.	Value of Church Property.	Communicants.
Alabama............	222	220	69,200	$264,625	18,940
Arkansas	116	104	31,050	60,277	5,888
Delaware	6	3	430	1,125	187
District of Columbia	5	4	3,500	123,800	939
Florida	36	26	7,000	14,709	1,461
Georgia...........	266	256	100,495	167,145	22,840
Illinois............	2	2	800	1,250	56
Indian Territory ...	13	9	2,850	2,975	291
Kansas	17	15	3,625	14,400	713
Kentucky	91	63	16,600	140,330	6,908
Louisiana	138	131	43,220	134,135	8,075
Maryland	2	2	205	475	44
Mississippi	293	292	72,150	230,290	20,107
Missouri	35	31	5,554	22,140	953
New Jersey........	5	3	625	7,500	266
North Carolina	26	20	7,725	23,120	2,786
Pennsylvania	6	2	310	1,400	247
South Carolina	34	33	15,045	65,325	3,468
Tennessee	206	205	67,900	258,120	18,968
Texas	222	216	88,330	147,075	14,895
Virginia	18	16	4,850	33,150	1,351
Total.........	1,759	1,653	541,464	$1,713,366	129,383

Summary by Conferences.

CONFERENCES.	Organizations.	Church Edifices.	Seating Capacity.	Value of Church Property.	Communicants.
Alabama...........	180	178	53,800	$230,125	16,347
Arkansas	44	44	10,575	23,650	2,152
Central Alabama ..	31	31	11,900	27,900	2,061
East Texas........	147	147	68,200	84,100	10,795
Florida	36	26	7,000	14,709	1,461
Georgia	104	96	43,050	71,300	8,047
Indian Mission	11	7	2,600	2,675	239
Kentucky	91	63	16,600	140,330	6,908
Little Rock	75	62	20,725	36,927	3,860
Louisiana	138	131	43,220	134,135	8,075
Mississippi	108	110	23,100	94,000	7,446
Missouri and Kansas	43	37	6,029	31,040	1,309
New Jersey........	18	9	1,445	10,325	716
North Carolina	26	20	7,725	23,120	2,786
North Mississippi ..	185	182	49,050	136,290	12,661
South Carolina	34	33	15,045	65,325	3,468
Southeast Missouri and Illinois......	12	12	4,350	7,100	430
South Georgia.....	162	160	57,445	95,845	14,793
Tennessee	98	96	30,550	87,270	8,621
Texas	34	34	11,200	14,850	1,700
Virginia	24	21	8,475	157,125	2,318
West Tennessee ...	118	119	40,450	177,100	10,862
West Texas	40	35	8,930	48,125	2,328
Total.........	1,759	1,653	541,464	$1,713,366	129,383

14.—THE PRIMITIVE METHODIST CHURCH.

The Primitive Methodist Church is not a branch of American Methodism, but it came from England, being introduced first into Canada in 1843 and then into the United States. In England the Primitive Methodist Church came into existence in 1812. It was organized by ministers and members of the Wesleyan Methodist Church who believed in camp-meetings and persisted in holding them. The Wesleyan conference declared camp-meetings "highly improper and likely to be productive of considerable mischief." Primitive Methodism differs from Wesleyan Methodism chiefly in the larger use it makes of the lay element.

For many years there were in the United States two annual conferences, the Eastern and the Western. These were separate until 1889, when they united in organizing a general conference. There are now three annual conferences, the Eastern, the Pennsylvania, and the Western. Each conference is subdivided into districts, as is the custom in other branches of Methodism. They also have itinerant and local ministers, class leaders, etc.

The Primitive Methodists are represented only in eight States, nearly one half of the total of communicants, 4764, being found in Pennsylvania. They have 84 organizations, with 78 edifices, valued at $291,993. The average value of each edifice is $3743, and the average seating capacity is 268. There are 11 halls, with a seating capacity of 1670.

SUMMARY BY STATES.

STATES.	Organizations.	Church Edifices.	Seating Capacity.	Value of Church Property.	Communicants.
Illinois.............	8	7	1,710	$14,800	369
Iowa	2	3	500	3,150	29
Massachusetts	7	6	1,750	40,000	575
New York	5	4	1,750	47,650	496
Ohio	3	3	660	2,400	69
Pennsylvania	42	40	11,435	146,025	2,267
Rhode Island......	4	3	750	12,568	194
Wisconsin	13	12	2,375	25,400	765
Total.........	84	78	20,930	$291,993	4,764

SUMMARY BY CONFERENCES.

CONFERENCES.					
Eastern...........	16	13	4,250	$100,218	1,265
Pennsylvania	45	43	12,095	148,425	2,336
Western	23	22	4,585	43,350	1,163
Total.........	84	78	20,930	$291,993	4,764

15.—THE FREE METHODISTS.

This body was organized in 1860 at Pekin, N. Y., at a convention of ministers and members who had been expelled or had withdrawn from the Methodist Episcopal Church. The movement arose within the bounds of the Genesee conference of the Methodist Episcopal Church over differences concerning membership in secret societies, other questions of discipline, and the emphasis to be placed in preaching on certain doctrines, particularly sanctification. In the course of the controversy several ministers were tried and expelled from the church on charges of contumacy. A number of laymen were also excluded.

The new organization adopted the discipline of the mother church with important changes. There are no bishops, but general superintendents are elected every four years. District chairmen take the place of presiding elders. Persons are not received on probation simply on the expression of "a desire to flee the wrath to come," but are required to give evidence of conversion. Members are required to "lay aside gold, pearls, and costly array" and dress plainly, and are forbidden to join secret societies or to indulge in the use of intoxicants and tobacco. Attendance at class-meeting is a condition of membership. Church choirs and the pew system are not approved. Two new numbers were added to the Articles of Religion, one setting forth the doctrine of entire sanctification, which is described as salvation "from all inward sin, from evil thoughts and evil tempers," and as taking place instantaneously subsequently to justification. The second pertains to future rewards and punishments. There are quarterly, district, annual, and general conferences. Laymen are admitted to all on equal terms with ministers. The average seating capacity of the edifices is 266, and their average value $1298. There are 439 halls, with a seating capacity of 48,285.

SUMMARY BY STATES.

STATES.	Organizations.	Church Edifices.	Seating Capacity.	Value of Church Property.	Communicants.
Arkansas	4	2	550	$750	61
California	19	11	1,775	14,000	410
Colorado..........	22	18	3,175	10,000	203
District of Columbia	1	...	.....	......	7
Illinois	152	112	32,675	156,050	3,395
Indiana	42	29	8,950	26,200	673
Indian Territory ...	1	...	.....	......	12
Iowa	111	62	13,829	57,500	2,117
Kansas	78	19	5,500	18,750	1,300
Louisiana	10	4	1,150	1,200	62
Maryland	1	1	200	700	31
Massachusetts	1	...	.....	......	12
Michigan	197	115	33,350	107,815	4,592
Minnesota	41	9	1,425	4,350	529
Mississippi	1	...	.....	......	29
Missouri	19	11	1,720	7,870	325
Nebraska	37	10	2,925	13,025	486
New Jersey........	8	4	1,125	11,275	161
New York.........	142	114	29,495	243,950	3,751
North Dakota	9	...	.....	......	85
Ohio	54	29	10,300	28,900	897
Oregon	13	6	1,800	5,400	188
Pennsylvania	46	28	6,950	50,050	1,158
South Dakota......	29	3	600	3,600	287
Texas	15	6	1,030	5,500	207
Virginia	1	1	150	1,000	28
Washington.......	8	6	1,850	15,700	240
Wisconsin	40	20	4,480	21,500	864
Total.........	1,102	620	165,004	$805,085	22,110

SUMMARY BY CONFERENCES.

CONFERENCES.					
California	19	11	1,775	$14,000	410
Central Illinois ...	73	53	13,900	41,300	1,800
Colorado.........	22	18	3,175	10,000	203
Dakota	31	5	900	5,600	308

S<small>UMMARY BY</small> C<small>ONFERENCES.</small>—*Continued.*

CONFERENCES.	Organi-zations.	Church Edifices.	Seating Capacity.	Value of Church Property.	Communicants.
East Michigan	80	38	11,825	$41,050	1,792
Genesee	69	61½	16,990	126,450	1,943
Illinois...........	58	46	14,275	103,200	1,188
Iowa	46	30	8,200	26,500	1,003
Kansas	37	10	3,100	12,250	847
Louisiana	15	6	1,700	1,950	152
Michigan	54	39	9,325	33,850	1,168
Minnesota and North Iowa	41	10	2,164	12,350	609
Missouri	18	11	1,720	7,870	300
Nebraska	11	2	275	1,200	171
New York........	50	27	6,425	73,875	962
North Indiana	20	12	3,350	11,250	317
North Michigan ..	63	38	12,200	32,915	1,632
North Minnesota..	27	6	800	750	351
Ohio	54	29	10,300	28,900	897
Oregon and Washington	21	12	3,650	21,100	428
Pittsburg	22	13	3,650	24,350	713
Susquehanna.....	59	46½	10,855	82,300	1,530
Texas	16	6	1,030	5,500	219
Wabash	43	30	10,100	26,500	763
West Iowa	52	29	5,240	28,450	868
West Kansas	61	11	3,600	10,125	672
Wisconsin	40	20	4,480	21,500	864
Total........	1,102	620	165,004	$805,085	22,110

16.—THE INDEPENDENT METHODISTS.

These consist of congregations in Maryland, Tennessee, and the District of Columbia, which are not connected with any annual conference. They are members of an association which, however, has no ecclesiastical authority whatever. Each congregation is entirely independent. There is 1 hall, with a seating capacity of 100.

SUMMARY BY STATES.

STATES.	Organizations.	Church edifices.	Seating Capacity.	Value of Church Property.	Communicants.
District of Columbia	1	1	175	$175	35
Maryland	13	12	7,000	262,300	2,347
Tennessee	1	1	550	4,500	187
Total.........	15	14	7,725	$266,975	2,569

17.—THE EVANGELIST MISSIONARY CHURCH.

This organization of Colored Methodists was formed in 1886 by ministers and members in Ohio who withdrew from the African Methodist Episcopal Zion Church for various reasons. It has no creed but the Bible; but, according to its bishop, it inclines in belief to the doctrine that there is but one divine person, Jesus Christ, "in whom dwells all the Godhead bodily." It has 11 organizations, in the States of Ohio, Illinois, Michigan, and Wisconsin. Nine halls, with a seating capacity of 2650, are occupied.

SUMMARY BY STATES.

STATES.	Organizations.	Church Edifices.	Seating Capacity.	Value of Church Property.	Communicants.
Illinois..........	1	..	...	....	180
Michigan	6	2	850	$1,200	409
Ohio	3	1	200	800	314
Wisconsin.......	1	..	...	....	48
Total	11	3	1,050	$2,000	951

SUMMARY BY STATES OF ALL METHODISTS.

Alabama........	2,271	2,284	620,970	$2,278,988	242,624
Alaska	....	....	....	....	
Arizona.........	23	17	4,700	58,100	656
Arkansas	1,709	1,493	375,622	1,200,842	123,316
California	559	438	123,874	2,575,631	36,874
Colorado........	146	117	32,200	1,105,700	10,850
Connecticut	239	235	72,582	2,225,730	30,815
Delaware	247	258	65,940	1,116,125	25,786

Summary by States of All Methodists.—*Continued.*

STATES.	Organizations.	Church Edifices.	Seating Capacity.	Value of Church Property.	Communicants.
Dist. of Columbia	62	58	37,925	$1,543,000	16,369
Florida	776	816	180,142	829,551	70,458
Georgia	2,406	2,663	735,033	2,783,267	275,784
Idaho...........	42	30	5,925	74,200	1,162
Illinois..........	2,457	2,229	640,797	7,807,118	189,358
Indiana.........	1,901	1,832	529,600	4,656,235	179,613
Indian Territory .	351	181	33,110	75,243	11,601
Iowa	1,579	1,387	355,990	3,602,860	122,607
Kansas	1,529	894	219,839	2,230,265	95,781
Kentucky	1,700	1,408	391,635	2,718,518	141,521
Louisiana	810	780	182,525	1,134,992	65,693
Maine	356	290	87,301	1,152,875	23,041
Maryland	1,340	1,324	353,235	5,347,527	123,618
Massachusetts ...	422	406	163,472	5,398,825	61,138
Michigan	1,578	1,198	329,907	4,144,427	101,951
Minnesota.......	591	448	97,800	1,764,493	32,199
Mississippi	1,885	1,935	466,026	1,652,269	164,589
Missouri	2,412	1,888	518,301	4,232,428	162,514
Montana........	74	54	11,805	247,850	2,425
Nebraska	738	490	119,303	1,336,475	42,941
Nevada	12	12	2,700	78,800	418
New Hampshire .	134	129	40,505	614,350	12,354
New Jersey......	727	707	229,831	5,500,640	96,377
New Mexico	60	42	8,025	107,100	2,360
New York........	2,563	2,388	723,349	18,305,200	265,551
North Carolina ..	2,413	2,335	739,577	2,418,984	276,336
North Dakota....	140	61	11,100	139,985	4,889
Ohio	2,798	2,713	818,940	9,600,820	272,737
Oklahoma.......	51	20	4,650	37,550	2,029
Oregon	294	199	44,940	693,275	11,927
Pennsylvania	2,536	2,359	732,641	14,476,904	260,388
Rhode Island	52	45	20,335	606,368	7,353
South Carolina ..	1,456	1,709	497,873	1,658,182	251,477
South Dakota ...	306	148	33,174	384,060	12,116
Tennessee	2,443	2,351	689,446	3,491,360	223,116
Texas	2,716	1,940	570,328	2,677,391	218,890
Utah	32	29	6,205	223,650	1,055
Vermont........	234	200	57,076	765,650	17,527
Virginia	1,737	1,646	410,335	2,910,853	154,693
Washington.....	239	171	44,615	763,175	12,697
West Virginia ...	1,543	1,097	274,891	1,450,448	85,102
Wisconsin.......	784	672	144,693	1,889,200	43,696
Wyoming	16	12	2,390	52,700	912
Total	51.489	46,138	12,863,178	$132,140,179	4,589,284

CHAPTER XXX.

THE MORAVIANS.

THIS is the name by which the members of the *Unitas Fratrum* are generally known. The *Unitas Fratrum*, or Unity of Brethren, originated in Germany, and has no connection with the United Brethren in Christ, a denomination which sprang up in this country near the beginning of the present century.

The Moravians trace their rise back to the time of Huss. The fruit of the Huss reformation appeared in the National Church of Bohemia. The Bohemian Brethren were an organization formed within the Bohemian Church, pledged to take the Bible as their only rule of faith and practice and maintain a Scriptural discipline. The Bohemian Brethren were persecuted and their organization was overthrown in Bohemia and Moravia, but it was resuscitated in 1722-35, among a colony of refugees from Bohemia and Moravia, settled on the estate of Count Zinzendorf in Berthelsdorf, Saxony. There the colony built the town of Herrnhut, which became the center of the Renewed Brethren.

The first Moravians who came to the United States settled in Georgia in 1735, the year when the first bishop of the Renewed Church was consecrated. The colony left

Georgia five years later and founded Bethlehem, in Pennsylvania. At Bethlehem, and also at Nazareth and Lititz, in the same State, Moravian Church settlements were formed. "The lands were the property of the church, and the farms and the various departments of mechanical industry were stocked by it and worked for its benefit. In return the church provided the inhabitants with all the necessaries of life. Whoever had private means retained them." There was, however, no common treasury, and the settlements did not adopt a communal life. The economical system was abolished in 1762, having lasted twenty years. The Brethren, however, continued to maintain the church system of communal government until 1844–56, when it disappeared. This system, in a modified form, is still maintained in Germany.

The Unity of Brethren consists of three provinces, the German, British, and American. All are under a central government, the seat of which is in Herrnhut, Germany. There is a general synod, which meets once in ten years. It consists of delegates from each of the provinces and also from the various foreign mission fields, and is empowered "to consult and legislate upon those matters which are of general import." It decides as to all questions of doctrine, all essential points of the liturgy, all fundamental rules of discipline, conditions of membership, nomination and appointment of bishops, etc. In the interim between its meetings it is represented by the Unity's Elders' Conference, which is a sort of executive committee. Each province has a synod of its own, which legislates for and controls provincial affairs.

Bishops, presbyters, and deacons are recognized in the ministry of the Brethren. Bishops are general, not diocesan, in character. They are appointed by the general synod or under its authority. The American Province has the right to nominate those for this country. Bishops are members of the general synod and also of provincial synods. They are chosen almost invariably to sit on provincial boards and in the Unity's Elders' Conference. They have the exclusive right to ordain to the ministry. Deacons are those who assist in preaching the gospel, administering the sacraments, and other church services. When deacons are appointed to preside over congregations they are ordained as presbyters.

The lot is not now used in the selection of bishops and appointments to office. Formerly it was used in the appointment of ministers and in connection with marriage. Marriage by lot was abolished by the general synod in 1818, and it is long since it was used in the United States in the appointment of ministers.

In public worship a liturgy is used. In addition to prescribed forms for baptism, the Lord's Supper, confirmation, ordination, etc., there is a litany to be used every Sunday morning; also special liturgical services for ecclesiastical festivals. Love-feasts are held preparatory to the Lord's Supper.

The Moravians accept the Scriptures as the only rule of faith and practice. They hold that it is not for them to "define what Scripture has left undefined, or to contend about mysteries," such as the Holy Trinity and the sacraments, "which are impenetrable to human understanding." They emphasize the doctrine of the "total depravity of human nature"; the love of God in the gift of his Son as the Redeemer of the world; the real Godhead and manhood of Christ; the atonement and satisfaction made by

Christ as the ground for forgiveness of sins; the work of the Holy Ghost in convicting of sin, inspiring faith in Christ, and bearing witness of adoption as children of God; the fruits of faith as shown in willing obedience to God's commandments. Christ is the center of Moravian theology, and his death is proclaimed as " made of God unto us wisdom and righteousness and justification and redemption."

The Moravians have 94 organizations, scattered among seventeen States and the Indian and Alaska Territories. The total of members is 11,781. Of these, 4308 are in Pennsylvania, 1734 in North Carolina, and 1477 in Wisconsin. In no other State are there as many as 900. Half of the total valuation of church property, $681,250, is reported for the 24 edifices in Pennsylvania. The average seating capacity of the 114 edifices returned for the denomination is 277, the average value $5975; 4 halls, with a seating capacity of 715, are occupied.

SUMMARY BY STATES.

STATES.	Organizations.	Church Edifices.	Seating Capacity.	Value of Church Property.	Communicants.
Alaska............	2	2	100	$5,000	36
California	1	1	100	700	19
Illinois............	1	2	600	4,000	336
Indiana	2	3	1,150	17,600	346
Indian Territory ...	1	1	150	400	40
Iowa	3	3	650	4,500	101
Kansas	1	2	325	2,500	19
Maryland	3	3	620	3,950	150
Michigan	2	2	375	4,500	168
Minnesota	9	9	1,480	20,600	696
Missouri	3	3	500	5,500	59
New Jersey........	4	4	800	13,500	374
New York	7	10	2,500	127,200	852
North Carolina	13	20	6,750	58,900	1,734
North Dakota	2	2	440	6,500	199

SUMMARY BY STATES.—*Continued.*

STATES.	Organizations.	Church Edifices.	Seating Capacity.	Value of Church Property.	Communicants.
Ohio	6	6	2,200	$37,400	822
Pennsylvania	14	24	9,770	340,400	4,308
Virginia	1	1	200	200	45
Wisconsin	19	16	2,905	27,900	1,477
Total.........	94	114	31,615	$681,250	11,781

SUMMARY BY DISTRICTS.

DISTRICTS.					
Northern	79	92	24,515	$621,750	9,962
Southern..........	15	22	7,100	59,500	1,819
Total.........	94	114	31,615	$681,250	11,781

CHAPTER XXXI.

THE PRESBYTERIANS.

THE Presbyterians are those who hold to a system of ecclesiastical government by presbyters. They believe that bishops and presbyters, or elders, as spoken of in the New Testament, are of the same order, being different designations for the same office. Bishops were presbyters in charge of congregations. Presbyters both taught and governed. They were both in and over the congregations. The Presbyterians are Calvinistic in doctrine. The Cumberland Presbyterian Church, with its colored branch, holds to a modified Calvinism, rejecting a limited atonement and the Westminster statement respecting the decrees; but it is considered sufficiently in accord with what is called the Reformed system to be admitted to membership in the council of the Reformed churches, which includes the Continental Reformed churches and their branches, as well as the British, American, and other Presbyterian bodies.

The Presbyterian polity provides for the following courts: the session, the presbytery, the synod, and (usually) the general assembly, and recognizes as officers, bishops or pastors, ruling elders and deacons. Candidates are ordained to the ministry and installed as pastors by the presbytery. There is but one order in the ministry, that of presbyter. Ruling elders are laymen chosen by congregations to exercise government and discipline therein, together with the pastor. Deacons are also laymen chosen by congregations to care for the poor, raise and distribute alms, and manage the temporal affairs of the church. Elders and deacons are ordained by ministers. The session is the court of the congregation. It is composed of the pastor or pastors, and the ruling elders. The pastor is *ex officio* moderator. The session is charged with the care of the spiritual interests of the church. It receives members, inquires into their conduct, has power to admonish or suspend them for offenses, and elects representatives to the presbytery. The presbytery consists of all the ministers and one ruling elder from each church within its bounds. It has power to entertain and decide appeals from church sessions; examine and license candidates for the ministry; ordain, install, remove, and judge ministers; decide questions of discipline and doctrine; unite or divide congregations, or receive new congregations; condemn erroneous opinions; and in general to care for the welfare of the churches within its limits. The synod is constituted of delegates, ministerial and lay, elected by the presbyteries belonging to it. It hears and decides appeals from the presbyteries, constitutes new presbyteries, and in general exercises supervision over presbyteries and sessions. The general assembly is the supreme legislative and judicial court in the Presbyterian system. It is composed of commissioners, ministerial and lay (bishops and elders), elected by the presbyteries. It receives and decides appeals from presbyteries or synods, and decides all questions of doctrine and discipline. It meets yearly.

There are twelve Presbyterian bodies in the United States, as follows:

1. Presbyterian Church in U. S. of America (Northern),
2. Cumberland Presbyterian,
3. Cumberland Colored,
4. Welsh Calvinistic Methodist,
5. United Presbyterian,
6. Presbyterian Church in the United States (Southern),
7. Associate Church of North America,
8. Associate Reformed Synod of the South,
9. Reformed Presbyterian Church in the United States (Synod),
10. Reformed Presbyterian Church in N. America (General Synod),
11. Reformed Presbyterian (Covenanted),
12. Reformed Presbyterian Church in U. S. and Canada.

I.—THE PRESBYTERIAN CHURCH IN THE UNITED STATES OF AMERICA.

The earliest Presbyterian churches in this country go back to the first half of the seventeenth century. The elements composing them were chiefly English Puritans and Scotch and Irish immigrants. On Long Island a church was organized as early as 1640 by a Puritan minister named John Young. Another church was founded at Hempstead two years later. Presbyterian services were held on Manhattan Island in 1643 by Francis Doughty, and a Presbyterian church was established at Newark, N. J., in 1667. The claim has recently been advanced that the oldest Presbyterian church is the First Church of Norfolk, Va., which was established as a congregation on Elizabeth River in the first quarter of the seventeenth century. Rev. Francis Makemie, generally regarded as the father of American Presbyterianism, came to this country in 1683 from Ireland, where he had been a member of the Presbytery of Laggan. He organized a Presbyterian church at Snow Hill, Md., at the close of the century, and in 1706, with John Hampton, an Irishman, and George McNish, a Scotchman, and four other ministers— Jedediah Andrews (Philadelphia), Nathaniel Taylor (Maryland), and Samuel Davis and John Wilson (Delaware)—

organized the first presbytery in America, the Presbytery of Philadelphia. The last four were Puritan ministers who had come from New England; Makemie was Scotch-Irish; Hampton, Irish; and McNish, Scotch. The same year this presbytery ordained John Boyd at Freehold, N. J.

In 1716, the number of ministers having increased to seventeen and covering an extensive territory, a synod, the Synod of Philadelphia, was formed, and the presbytery was divided into three "subordinate meetings, or presbyteries." In 1741 there was a division in the synod in consequence of differences respecting subscription to the confession of faith and doctrines and practices, which an extensive revival movement brought into prominence. Those contending for a strict subscription and opposing what they regarded as errors of doctrine in the revival movement were known as Old Side, and the other party as New Side, Presbyterians. The latter organized the Synod of New York. In 1758 the two bodies were reunited as the Synod of New York and Philadelphia. At the opening of the Revolutionary War, in 1775, there were in connection with the synod 17 presbyteries and 170 ministers. The church suffered severely in the war for independence, but it became prosperous after peace was declared, and in 1788 the synod decided to organize a general assembly with four synods. It revised and adopted the Westminster Confession and Larger Catechism, form of government, book of discipline, and directory of worship. The first meeting of the general assembly was held in Philadelphia in 1789.

Early in the nineteenth century there was an extensive revival movement in the Cumberland Valley, Tennessee. Differences in doctrine and practice were developed by this movement, and the Cumberland Presbyterian Church was organized.

In 1837, a little more than a century after the division in the Synod of Philadelphia into Old Side and New Side Presbyterians, the church was again divided into Old School and New School Assemblies, chiefly as the result of doctrinal differences concerning the atonement, whether it was general or for the elect only, and of differences concerning creed subscription and polity and discipline. In 1840 the Old School body had about 126,583 communicants, and the New School 102,060. In 1869 the two assemblies agreed to a reunion, which was consummated in the same year.

At the outbreak of the Civil War, in 1861, the churches in the South separated from the churches in the North, adhering to the Old School Assembly. The Southern churches adhering to the New School Assembly had also separated from the Northern churches belonging to the New School Assembly in 1858 on the question of slavery. The two bodies created in the South by this division united in 1865 and formed what is popularly known as the Southern Presbyterian Church.

The church in the North has grown rapidly since the reunion in 1869, and has extended into the South, where it has organized a number of presbyteries, chiefly of colored people. It is represented in all the States except Mississippi, and in all the Territories, including the District of Columbia. The largest number of communicants reported for a single State is 161,386 in Pennsylvania; New York comes second, with 154,083; and Ohio is third, with 82,444. Though there are more communicants in Pennsylvania by 7303 than in New York, the value of the church property in the latter State is much greater than the value of the church property in the former. While the 1086 edifices in Pennsylvania have an aggregate valuation of $15,491,680, the 932 edifices in New York have an aggregate of $21,293,992. Only 26 buildings other than churches are occupied in these two States. The total valuation for the whole church is $74,455,200, indicating an average value for each edifice of $11,173. The average seating capacity is 334. There are 556 halls, with a seating capacity of 57,805.

The general assembly of 1890 appointed a committee to revise the Westminster Confession, so as to soften, without impairing the integrity of the Calvinistic system, some of its expressions, particularly those setting forth the doctrine of preterition. The committee reported a revised confession to the general assembly of 1891, and the draft was sent down to the presbyteries for suggestions. The revision ultimately failed.

There are in all 214 presbyteries, of which 18 are in foreign lands. Of the 196 in this country, given in these tables, that of New York reports the largest number of communicants, 23,873, with 54 organizations and 68 edifices, valued at $8,628,000. The second presbytery in numerical order, the Central Philadelphia, has 38 organizations and 46 edifices, valued at $2,470,500, and 17,600 communicants. The Presbytery of Brooklyn has 17,170 communicants, with 39 edifices, worth $1,536,927.

There are thirty synods, of which two are foreign, one being in India and one in China. Synods are composed of commissioners chosen by the presbyteries. Within a few years they have been rearranged, so that their boundaries correspond with those of the various States as far as possible. There are, however, notable exceptions to this rule. The Synod of the Atlantic includes South Carolina, Georgia, and Florida; that of Catawba, Virginia and North Carolina.

SUMMARY BY STATES.

STATES.	Organizations.	Church Edifices.	Seating Capacity.	Value of Church Property.	Communicants.
Alabama	5	4	1,050	$17,300	152
Alaska	5	4	1,100	7,750	481
Arizona	7	3	850	13,900	188
Arkansas	15	12	2,660	26,450	494
California	213	172	50,271	1,696,725	16,236
Colorado	74	56	14,595	556,250	5,902
Connecticut	7	9	3,800	433,500	1,680
Delaware	32	43	14,970	709,800	4,622
Dist. of Columbia	15	19	10,600	900,000	4,882
Florida	34	28	6,050	322,000	1,042
Georgia	16	9	3,000	13,850	1,370
Idaho	19	15	2,275	40,950	815
Illinois	472	475	158,181	4,045,350	54,744
Indiana	308	320½	104,143	2,338,900	35,464
Indian Territory	70	54	8,018	39,763	1,803
Iowa	369	347	95,148	1,503,400	29,994
Kansas	370	267½	69,929	1,078,860	24,050
Kentucky	82	73	25,045	748,375	6,917
Louisiana	1	1	300	8,000	70
Maine	2	3	800	8,000	205
Maryland	77	90	33,020	1,488,124	10,593
Massachusetts	18	18	10,125	365,500	3,570
Michigan	236	230	76,050	2,214,636	25,088
Minnesota	167	154	40,261	1,292,670	13,732
Missouri	207	193	54,815	1,328,700	17,272
Montana	24	18	4,150	88,000	1,232
Nebraska	228	154½	34,901	576,210	12,159
Nevada	8	4	865	11,400	275
New Hampshire	8	9	3,150	34,800	956
New Jersey	300	420	169,357	6,699,100	58,759
New Mexico	39	17	2,815	45,675	1,275
New York	784	932	378,411	21,293,992	154,083
North Carolina	109	103	26,650	89,180	6,516
North Dakota	99	48	9,500	126,425	3,036
Ohio	618	636	223,553	5,754,350	82,444
Oklahoma	17	9	1,850	14,000	450
Oregon	73	61	14,397	416,500	3,935
Pennsylvania	939	1,086⅓	427,059	15,491,680	161,386

SUMMARY BY STATES.—*Continued.*

STATES.	Organizations.	Church Edifices.	Seating Capacity.	Value of Church Property.	Communicants.
Rhode Island	4	4	1,385	$61,000	608
South Carolina ..	77	67	25,015	173,900	6,829
South Dakota ...	124	83	13,966	156,940	4,413
Tennessee.......	77	71½	18,435	216,520	4,399
Texas	61	44	9,525	164,850	2,812
Utah	20	31	5,180	212,975	688
Vermont........	2	1	300	4,000	230
Virginia	19	19	4,440	43,925	945
Washington.....	85	62	14,785	343,175	3,770
West Virginia...	44	40	13,135	308,200	4,275
Wisconsin	131	137½	34,204	877,400	11,019
Wyoming	6	5	960	52,250	364
Total.......	6,717	6,664	2,225,044	$74,455,200	788,224

SUMMARY BY PRESBYTERIES.

PRESBYTERIES.					
Aberdeen	36	17	3,085	$34,575	883
Alaska..........	5	4	1,100	7,750	481
Albany	51	63	28,135	1,133,670	10,016
Allegheny.......	42	46	17,420	672,600	7,444
Alton...........	41	43	11,480	182,500	3,776
Arizona.........	7	3	850	13,900	188
Athens	32	31	7,010	105,250	2,460
Atlantic.........	20	18	7,650	72,000	2,619
Austin..........	27	18	4,700	113,850	1,360
Baltimore	54	64	25,045	1,243,324	8,407
Bellefontaine	25	23	6,925	104,900	3,197
Benicia	40	27½	7,610	136,850	1,970
Binghamton.....	28	35	13,359	364,050	4,745
Birmingham.....	5	4	1,050	17,300	152
Bismarck	10	6	1,500	27,200	189
Black Hills......	15	10	1,545	20,825	250
Blairsville	36	36	13,925	283,800	6,169
Bloomington	55	56	16,010	233,900	5,704
Boston..........	34	35	15,760	473,300	5,569
Boulder.........	16	10	2,575	85,550	1,177
Brooklyn	33	39	24,555	1,536,927	17,170
Buffalo	42	50	23,425	1,383,950	8,018
Butler	36	34	11,675	135,800	4,487
Cairo...........	52	48	12,235	117,350	3,775
Cape Fear	30	26	6,605	27,450	1,585

SUMMARY BY PRESBYTERIES.—*Continued.*

PRESBYTERIES.	Organizations.	Church Edifices.	Seating Capacity.	Value of Church Property.	Communicants.
Carlisle	52	68	21,779	$775,700	7,751
Catawba	35	35	8,350	25,250	2,242
Cayuga	23	26	10,130	386,000	4,453
Cedar Rapids	36	37	11,175	216,250	3,422
Central Dakota	33	20	3,375	41,950	1,242
Champlain	20	25	7,102	236,000	2,159
Chemung	22	23	7,650	225,300	2,331
Cherokee Nation	28	16	2,867	14,800	727
Chester	46	58	19,515	544,700	7,207
Chicago	73	72	37,935	1,839,250	15,306
Chickasaw	22	12	2,650	20,000	558
Chillicothe	32	31	10,225	127,300	3,836
Chippewa	18	20	4,025	102,975	1,346
Choctaw	32	30	3,286	11,700	641
Cincinnati	61	67	24,418	1,186,500	9,394
Clarion	48	46	14,985	206,250	4,588
Cleveland	26	34	17,635	871,250	6,721
Columbia	19	24	7,060	176,000	2,112
Columbus	29	34	11,750	282,700	3,623
Council Bluffs	52	48	11,903	183,400	4,066
Crawfordsville	57	58	17,045	322,900	5,757
Dakota	20	19	2,475	20,690	1,083
Dayton	39	43	16,465	600,300	7,596
Denver	21	14	4,255	240,250	2,502
Des Moines	54	52	14,830	225,325	4,265
Detroit	43	47	22,320	1,056,100	8,488
Dubuque	36	32	8,500	138,100	2,979
Duluth	22	16	3,195	49,700	1,048
East Florida	15	14	3,550	296,500	589
East Oregon	17	13	3,000	33,000	543
Ebenezer	26	25	8,725	232,900	2,624
Elizabeth	32	47	21,734	793,000	7,782
Emporia	83	58	14,790	207,650	6,353
Erie	67	75	25,925	584,950	9,415
Fairfield	40	36	14,000	86,750	3,359
Fargo	38	18	3,415	41,800	1,071
Flint	42	34	8,870	116,075	2,286
Fort Dodge	73	61	14,685	235,850	4,824
Fort Wayne	27	26	9,910	308,300	3,750
Freeport	32	32	10,644	261,000	4,057
Genesee	22	22½	7,485	200,150	3,184
Geneva	23	29	12,430	416,800	4,896
Grand Rapids	17	16	5,575	115,800	1,936

SUMMARY BY PRESBYTERIES.—*Continued.*

PRESBYTERIES.	Organizations.	Church Edifices.	Seating Capacity.	Value of Church Property.	Communicants.
Gunnison	11	12	2,545	$70,700	628
Hastings	52	19	4,170	39,710	1,972
Highland	25	21	6,530	111,225	2,261
Holston	30	26	5,425	41,650	973
Hudson	43	48	16,860	479,500	5,910
Huntingdon	72	92	30,325	676,550	9,907
Huron	20	22	7,625	214,100	2,598
Indianapolis	35	38	14,205	482,100	6,198
Iowa	41	41	13,700	224,225	4,212
Iowa City	41	41	11,388	157,050	3,617
Jersey City	31	40	17,880	978,700	6,179
Kalamazoo	21	20	7,030	163,000	2,465
Kansas City	41	39	10,175	280,200	4,092
Kearney	36	23	5,440	69,400	1,720
Kingston	21	16	4,885	88,720	1,105
Kittanning	50	52	18,170	278,080	7,159
Knox	16	9	3,000	13,850	1,370
Lackawanna	93	98	33,112	1,111,800	10,936
Lacrosse	10	11	2,250	63,000	776
Lake Superior	20	21	4,515	128,750	1,441
Lansing	21	20	5,815	175,500	2,552
Larned	58	37	9,660	181,600	2,494
Lehigh	46	58	20,365	657,550	6,266
Lima	33	30	9,455	238,700	3,729
Logansport	42	38	11,850	273,100	4,100
Long Island	26	37	10,527	199,950	3,431
Los Angeles	69	57	14,766	448,900	5,203
Louisville	29	26½	9,665	399,725	2,808
Lyons	18	21	7,430	161,345	3,113
McClelland	17	13	3,365	15,150	851
Madison	40	43	9,775	190,800	3,113
Mahoning	31	33	11,950	422,900	5,484
Mankato	35	30	6,624	85,570	2,013
Marion	28	28	7,995	99,000	2,678
Mattoon	44	43½	12,130	143,300	3,700
Maumee	38	35	13,985	334,300	3,966
Milwaukee	28	27½	9,349	390,200	3,228
Monmouth	47	61	20,530	391,750	5,877
Monroe	19	22	8,325	195,911	2,371
Montana	23	18	4,150	88,000	1,220
Morris and Orange	41	59	22,615	1,103,600	8,826
Muncie	24	23	6,640	140,500	2,609
Muskogee	9	9	1,625	8,188	420
Nassau	24	35	10,215	255,700	3,085

SUMMARY BY PRESBYTERIES.—*Continued.*

PRESBYTERIES.	Organi-zations.	Church Edifices.	Seating Capacity.	Value of Church Property.	Communicants.
Nebraska City ...	55	47	11,961	$205,600	3,993
Neosho	64	53	14,215	149,750	4,724
New Albany.....	54	63	18,355	253,900	4,856
Newark.........	29	44	21,900	1,557,820	9,662
New Brunswick..	35	53	21,800	865,800	8,024
Newcastle.......	50	63	21,470	936,100	6,550
Newton	38	49	20,258	385,530	5,874
New York.......	54	68	48,350	8,628,000	23,873
Niagara.........	20	21	7,825	224,700	2,984
Niobrara........	38	25½	4,350	37,900	1,188
North River	28	35	13,040	535,500	5,528
North Texas	17	13	2,070	27,800	731
Northumberland .	46	52	17,278	588,500	5,927
Olympia	32	21	5,700	154,400	1,407
Omaha	47	40	8,980	223,600	3,286
Oregon	45	40	9,297	358,800	2,960
Osborne	43	23½	3,844	45,600	981
Otsego..........	26	29	9,420	231,600	2,992
Ottawa	23	21	6,415	97,600	2,042
Ozark..........	35	29	7,915	116,750	2,113
Palmyra	33	30	7,745	85,700	2,094
Pembina........	46	20	4,105	53,725	1,608
Peoria..........	38	41	14,295	351,800	4,518
Petoskey........	19	15	3,415	44,700	746
Philadelphia.....	33	42	36,925	2,628,000	13,344
Philadelphia Central...........	38	46	35,280	2,470,500	17,600
Philadelphia North	44	58	23,135	1,059,800	8,450
Pittsburg........	61	63	29,355	1,603,900	14,092
Platte...........	53	51	13,455	141,500	3,132
Portsmouth	34	31	12,050	182,900	3,437
Pueblo..........	30	23	5,970	205,800	1,886
Puget Sound.....	34	23	5,225	122,325	1,510
Red River	22	17	2,950	32,200	816
Redstone	34	48	16,475	293,850	4,447
Rio Grande	15	5	840	19,100	392
Rochester.......	45	57	22,525	932,400	10,565
Rock River......	36	36	11,220	221,000	3,481
Sacramento	33	24½	6,260	145,625	1,367
Saginaw	31	32	9,385	204,300	2,611
Saint Clairsville..	44	45	15,185	229,600	6,219
Saint Lawrence ..	30	32	12,910	323,500	3,978
Saint Louis	49	48	16,525	724,550	6,011

SUMMARY BY PRESBYTERIES.—*Continued.*

PRESBYTERIES.	Organizations.	Church Edifices.	Seating Capacity.	Value of Church Property.	Communicants.
Saint Paul	64	69	23,419	$1,047,600	8,391
San Francisco ...	35	31	13,170	786,500	5,178
San José	24	21	5,430	110,250	1,902
Santa Fé........	24	12	1,975	26,575	883
Schuyler	42	44	12,172	227,000	3,922
Shenango	26	29	10,915	179,750	5,270
Solomon	48	32	7,155	90,025	2,551
Southern Dakota.	28	23	4,151	43,800	1,169
Southern Oregon.	13	10	2,525	28,700	538
Southern Virginia	12	11	2,690	15,075	522
South Florida ...	19	14	2,500	25,500	453
Spokane	15	11	2,110	50,650	639
Springfield	36	38½	13,645	370,650	4,463
Steuben	26	26½	8,710	247,400	3,242
Steubenville.....	61	64	22,875	351,250	7,557
Stockton	20	15	3,900	80,000	891
Syracuse	42	43	16,985	766,400	6,399
Topeka.	49	43	13,735	293,010	4,686
Transylvania	27	21	6,655	115,750	1,485
Trinity	18	14	3,055	31,200	791
Troy	44	53	19,375	812,100	7,980
Union	32	35	9,125	90,500	2,464
Utah	21	32	5,330	218,975	753
Utica...........	47	51	20,158	715,450	7,410
Vincennes.......	32	34	10,913	300,900	3,483
Walla Walla ...	12	13	2,550	24,850	773
Washington	38	39	17,355	428,400	7,406
Washington City.	27	33	13,775	948,500	5,558
Waterloo	35	33	8,842	122,200	2,583
Wellsboro.......	16	18	4,970	89,200	1,059
Westchester	36	49	16,750	1,173,100	6,852
West Jersey	47	67	22,640	622,900	6,535
Westminster	29	42	14,805	401,000	5,141
West Virginia ...	29	25	6,305	111,200	1,696
White River.....	7	4	1,100	5,525	231
White Water	37	40½	15,225	257,200	4,711
Winnebago	37	38	9,405	140,425	2,722
Winona.........	25	23	4,273	82,100	1,490
Wood River.....	9	7	1,050	27,900	150
Wooster	39	37	11,730	151,400	4,541
Yadkin	38	37	10,745	30,980	2,551
Zanesville	46	48	16,275	252,000	5,408
Total	6,717	6,664	2,225,044	$74,455,200	788,224

2.—THE CUMBERLAND PRESBYTERIAN CHURCH.

The body owes its existence to a revival which began among the Presbyterian churches within the bounds of the Presbytery of Transylvania, Ky., in 1800. The awakening was first manifested in the congregation of the Rev. James McGready, at Gasper River, Logan County, and soon extended throughout the Cumberland Valley, in Kentucky and Tennessee. Existing congregations were enlarged and new congregations organized, and there being a lack of regular ministers to supply all the pulpits, men were received from the laity and licensed by the presbytery, without the full literary qualifications required. Some of the ministers looked upon the revival with disfavor, and opposed the licensing and ordaining of laymen to preach, and members of the revival party were cited to appear before the synod to answer to a complaint that the Cumberland Presbytery, which had been formed out of the Transylvania Presbytery, and to which they then mostly belonged, had committed irregularities. The synod ultimately decided to dissolve the Cumberland Presbytery, suspend some of its ministers, and attach its ministers and members to the Transylvania Presbytery. The outcome of the matter was the organization of an independent presbytery in 1810, which was called the Cumberland Presbytery. The new body grew rapidly, and was divided into three presbyteries in 1813. The same year the Cumberland Synod was constituted. The synod authorized an expression of dissent from the teaching of the Westminster Confession as to reprobation, a limited atonement, infant salvation, and the calling of the elect only. The new church was rapidly extended. In 1822 it had 46 ordained ministers; in 1827, 114. Two years later a general assembly was constituted.

In polity, the Cumberland Church is distinctively Presbyterian, differing little from other Presbyterian branches. Its doctrines are embodied in a confession of faith, consisting of twenty-eight articles. It follows the Westminster Confession except as to the doctrines of the decrees. It is claimed that it represents the medium between Calvinistic and Arminian theology. It acknowledges the sovereignty of God, and declares the free agency of man. The atonement of Christ was made for all mankind, but only those who yield to the influences of the Spirit, which are coextensive with the atonement, will be saved. The salvation of those who thus yield is certain, because both divine and human agency coöperate to that end. The elect are those who believe on the Son, and the date of election is the beginning of regeneration and adoption— that is, when men are regenerated they are elected to eternal life, and will finally persevere, not by virtue of God's election alone, but by the concurrent choice of both God and the believer. No truly regenerated man will ever finally fall away. Grace is not "irresistible." It may be accepted or rejected. If accepted, it is the cause of election; if rejected, of reprobation. Election is therefore not unconditional, either to honor or dishonor. The divine decrees are regarded as immutable, but not as universal.

The Cumberland Church is not represented in many of the Northern States. Its chief strength lies in the States of the border. In Tennessee it has 39,477 members; in Missouri, 23,990; in Texas, 22,297; and in Kentucky, 15,458. In these four States three fifths of the membership of the church is found. The whole number of organizations is 2791; church edifices, 2024; seating capacity, 669,507; value of church property, $3,515,511; members, 164,940. The average seating capacity of church edifices is 330 and the average value $1751. There are 536 halls, with a seating capacity of 84,588.

SUMMARY BY STATES.

STATES.	Organizations.	Church Edifices.	Seating Capacity.	Value of Church Property.	Communicants.
Alabama..........	158	137	41,931	$187,705	7,390
Arkansas	300	178	57,735	158,250	12,282
California	37	29½	7,100	69,450	1,496
Colorado..........	5	5	980	19,300	231
Florida	6	1	200	200	88
Georgia...........	15	12	3,300	8,550	598
Illinois............	198	183	58,960	313,985	14,177
Indiana...........	42	53	18,075	160,700	4,826
Indian Territory ...	53	30	8,550	11,645	1,229
Iowa..............	24	23	5,650	34,550	1,167
Kansas	68	25	6,350	55,300	2,386
Kentucky	213	185	65,350	254,600	15,458
Louisiana	23	16	5,300	12,050	868
Mississippi	135	116	36,409	108,650	6,353
Missouri	393	271	98,096	571,363	23,990
Nebraska	7	4	790	10,000	416
Ohio	22	22	6,600	60,500	2,602
Oregon	23	10	3,365	22,200	897
Pennsylvania	52	48½	18,050	257,500	6,210
Tennessee.........	529	464	149,471	745,605	39,477
Texas	476	205½	75,395	436,108	22,297
Washington	11	4½	1,550	15,300	470
West Virginia.	1	1	300	2,000	32
Total	2,791	2,024	669,507	$3,515,511	164,940

SUMMARY BY PRESBYTERIES.

PRESBYTERIES.					
Alabama..........	27	24	6,925	$18,380	1,081
Albion............	16	17	5,075	19,785	1,299
Allegheny.........	19	17	4,900	52,400	1,576
Anderson	28	27	10,950	33,700	1,867
Arkansas	39	21	7,200	30,500	2,139
Atchison	7	2½	750	3,200	249

SUMMARY BY PRESBYTERIES.—*Continued.*

PRESBYTERIES.	Organizations.	Church Edifices.	Seating Capacity.	Value of Church Property.	Communicants.
Athens	11	12	3,600	$22,400	1,022
Bacon	23	11	6,400	32,800	966
Bartholomew	28	20	6,500	6,750	911
Bell	25	17	4,625	14,100	1,158
Bonham	27	11½	3,675	24,150	1,485
Buffalo Gap	15	3	1,000	5,750	788
Burrow	31	21	7,350	21,950	1,032
California	15	14½	3,150	30,400	485
Charlotte	34	28	8,600	23,265	1,354
Chattanooga	39	23½	7,000	56,300	2,139
Cherokee	15	4	1,300	5,550	466
Chillicothe	28	17½	5,175	18,613	1,443
Choctaw	24	24	6,850	4,945	446
Colesburg	6	6	1,200	14,600	385
Colorado........	19	6½	1,650	10,900	696
Corsicana	33	16	7,800	31,500	1,642
Cumberland	31	22	7,675	15,800	2,158
Dallas	23	15½	5,450	46,400	1,777
Davis...........	15	14½	3,925	28,050	1,261
Decatur.........	23	20	6,100	36,400	1,770
East Louisiana...	10	8	2,300	3,250	319
East Tennessee ..	27	21	7,850	37,250	2,033
Eden	10	4	800	10,500	331
Elk	53	50½	17,685	80,250	5,713
Ewing, Ark......	30	28	12,000	22,700	1,814
Ewing, Ill.......	27	27½	7,050	26,900	2,684
Florida	6	½	200	200	88
Foster	24	23	7,675	45,200	2,015
Georgia.........	21	8	4,850	12,450	908
Greenville.......	23	9	2,900	11,800	746
Gregory	30	1	800	8,608	998
Guadalupe	27	9	850	16,550	952
Guthrie.........	58	19	6,100	31,950	2,250
Hopewell	44	39	12,000	48,850	3,450
Illinois..........	23	16	6,700	10,550	1,141
Indiana	19	26½	9,125	118,500	2,767
Iowa............	11	12	2,600	13,150	544
Kansas	23	12	2,300	24,300	831
Kentucky	16	12	3,600	29,900	1,262
King	43	12	2,650	18,450	1,574
Kirksville	31	23	6,740	31,850	1,784
Knoxville	33	28½	7,200	45,050	2,162
Lebanon........	42	42	13,650	144,800	4.592

SUMMARY BY PRESBYTERIES.—*Continued.*

PRESBYTERIES.	Organizations.	Church Edifices.	Seating Capacity.	Value of Church Property.	Communicants.
Lexington	65	51	17,381	$130,900	4,220
Little River	26	8½	3,850	11,050	1,002
Logan	41	41	11,100	56,700	2,809
Louisiana	10	7	2,600	7,300	438
McGee	30	23	7,550	31,100	2,196
McGready	18	16½	5,656	13,700	1,078
McLin	16	13	5,500	14,250	794
McMinnville	31	31	9,500	48,100	2,055
Mackinaw	13	13	3,950	35,800	1,243
Madison	40	36	7,250	26,700	2,453
Marshall	23	15	4,825	43,600	978
Mayfield	30	29	11,400	22,700	2,100
Memphis	28	25	8,460	105,500	1,744
Miami	7	7	2,000	28,000	1,271
Mississippi	27	25	5,350	6,150	929
Morgan	14	17	6,450	20,500	1,242
Mound Prairie	28	17	4,450	13,700	1,178
Muskingum	4	3	1,000	10,100	309
Nebraska	7	4	790	10,000	416
Neosho	26	14½	7,150	16,950	1,188
New Hope	48	43	17,956	45,000	2,540
New Lebanon	32	30	15,600	89,100	2,735
Nolin	27	17	6,300	8,500	1,477
Obion	43	35	16,800	41,600	3,317
Oregon	9	3½	1,500	6,400	265
Ouachita	15	10	2,385	2,425	469
Owensboro	15	14	4,500	36,700	1,370
Oxford	26	22	6,900	36,550	1,154
Ozark	31	21	6,950	28,800	1,923
Parsons	20	4	1,800	5,900	733
Pennsylvania	23	21½	8,850	119,100	2,755
Platte	50	32	11,400	43,350	2,283
Princeton	16	15	7,550	25,750	1,568
Red Oak	33	14	5,500	61,400	2,048
Red River	23	12	3,475	21,300	1,610
Republican Valley	7	..	......	......	205
Richland	59	58	13,511	53,175	4,158
Robert Donnell	43	38	11,500	49,575	2,148
Rocky Mountain	5	5	980	19,300	231
Rushville	11	9	3,400	14,700	540
Sacramento	8	7	2,200	19,300	415
Saint Louis	2	2	1,400	80,000	305
Salem	15	7½	2,750	7,200	655

SUMMARY BY PRESBYTERIES.—*Continued.*

PRESBYTERIES.	Organizations.	Church Edifices.	Seating Capacity.	Value of Church Property.	Communicants.
Salt River	33	23	8,250	$55,550	2,840
Sangamon	26	26	6,710	50,400	1,575
San Jacinto......	8	3	800	15,550	215
San Saba	18	6	1,850	13,450	594
Searcy	30	16	5,000	21,900	1,207
Sparta	44	34	16,765	27,665	3,583
Springfield	19	13	2,575	29,200	1,095
Springville	30	30	9,550	83,900	1,419
Talladega	29	18	4,350	16,350	1,169
Tehuacana	16	7½	2,920	9,400	818
Texas	16	16	6,900	15,550	726
Trinity	15	11	4,950	11,850	809
Tulare	14	8	1,750	19,750	596
Union	11	11	4,600	88,000	1,911
Vandalia........	19	19	6,800	60,000	1,117
Wabash	9	10	2,500	21,700	817
Waco	15	10	2,800	9,600	791
Walla Walla	17	7	2,415	21,300	742
Washington	23	6	1,300	7,600	905
West Iowa	7	5	1,850	6,800	238
West Plains	12	6	2,600	6,000	362
West Prairie	21	9	3,075	8,800	684
White River.....	35	27½	8,800	11,925	1,178
Wichita.........	19	4½	2,000	11,300	728
Willamette......	8	4	1,000	9,800	360
Yazoo	20	19	5,534	12,650	1,067
Total.......	2,791	2,024	669,507	$3,515,511	164,940

3.—THE CUMBERLAND PRESBYTERIAN CHURCH, COLORED.

This body was organized in May, 1869, at Murfreesboro, Tenn., under the direction of the general assembly of the Cumberland Presbyterian Church. It was constituted of colored ministers and members who had been connected with that church. Its first presbytery, the Huntsville, was formed in 1870, its first synod, the Tennessee, in 1871, and its general assembly in 1874. It has the same doctrinal symbol as the parent body, and the same system of government and discipline, differing only in race.

It has 23 presbyteries, and is represented in nine States and one Territory. Of its 224 organizations, 34 only worship in buildings which they do not own. There are 12,956 communicants, and the total value of the church property is $195,826, making an average of $1070 to each edifice. The average seating capacity is 285. There are 34 halls, with a seating capacity of 3570.

SUMMARY BY STATES.

STATES.	Organizations.	Church Edifices.	Seating Capacity.	Value of Church Property.	Communicants.
Alabama...........	44	38	9,574	$26,200	3,104
Arkansas..........	2	..	....	......	255
Illinois............	7	4	1,300	5,375	195
Kansas	6	3	650	15,000	190
Kentucky	36	31	7,730	31,645	1,421
Mississippi	4	4	950	1,825	278
Missouri	10	9	3,425	17,900	471
Oklahoma.........	4	..	....	......	100
Tennessee	81	72	24,125	88,660	5,202
Texas	30	22	6,160	9,221	1,740
Total.	224	183	52,139	$195,826	12,956

SUMMARY BY PRESBYTERIES.

PRESBYTERIES.					
Alabama..........	7	5	1,850	$4,150	925
Angelina..........	7	5	1,750	2,350	435
Arkansas	2	..	....	....	255
Bowling Green	5	4	950	6,600	365
Brazos River	9	7	2,170	2,896	712
Cumberland.......	13	10	2,350	7,010	630
East Texas........	14	10	2,240	3,975	593
Elk River	11	11	3,700	10,100	625
Farmington	11	7	2,625	8,960	670
Florence..........	14	14	3,099	10,350	714
Green River.......	8	7	1,680	810	157

SUMMARY BY PRESBYTERIES.—*Continued.*

PRESBYTERIES.	Organizations.	Church Edifices.	Seating Capacity.	Value of Church Property.	Communicants.
Hartsville	5	4	450	$1,500	133
Hiwassee...........	12	11	2,700	10,125	400
Hopewell	10	9	3,350	14,500	530
Huntsville.........	18	15	2,925	8,500	1,160
Mississippi	4	4	950	1,825	278
New Hope	12	13	4,700	19,500	610
New Middleton	16	11	2,775	8,300	1,047
Oklahoma........ ..	4	..	.....	......	100
Pleasant Hill	5	4	1,700	3,200	305
Springfield........	5	5	1,200	16,400	338
Topeka	6	3	650	15,000	190
Walter............	26	24	8,325	39,775	1,784
Total	224	183	52,139	$195,826	12,956

4.—THE WELSH CALVINISTIC METHODIST CHURCH.

Historically this body is a part of the general Methodist movement of which the two Wesleys and Whitefield were the leaders in Great Britain. Doctrinally it is Calvinistic, its confession of faith being similar to that of Westminster. Until 1811 the Calvinistic Methodists in Wales were connected with the Church of England, as the followers of Wesley in England had been. Since that date they have been a distinct denomination.

The first Welsh Calvinistic Methodist Church in this country was organized in 1826 in Remsen, N. Y. Four years later a presbytery was constituted. A general assembly, which meets once in three years, was organized in 1869. The church system is very similar to that of the Presbyterian churches, with which it affiliates. There are six synods, as follows: Synod of New York and Vermont, Synod of Ohio, Synod of Pennsylvania, Synod of Wisconsin, Synod of Minnesota, and the Western Synod.

There are 19 presbyteries. The number of organizations is 187, with 12,722 communicants. The average seating capacity of the churches is 235, and their average value $3303. There are 14 halls, with a seating capacity of 1266.

The Welsh are, of course, the constituency of the church, and the Welsh language is used in its services and in the proceedings of its ecclesiastical judicatories.

SUMMARY BY STATES.

STATES.	Organizations.	Church Edifices.	Seating Capacity.	Value of Church Property.	Communicants.
Colorado	1	1	200	$8,000	156
Illinois	1	1	700	20,000	425
Iowa	8	7	1,220	7,650	348
Kansas	5	4	850	3,650	115
Minnesota	13	13	3,705	34,500	1,166
Missouri	6	4	555	2,500	154
Nebraska	7	4	780	6,800	267
New York	28	28	6,370	143,300	1,789
Ohio	31	34	8,050	111,575	2,463
Pennsylvania	34	33	10,000	153,700	2,461
South Dakota	6	4	730	4,200	306
Vermont	6	5	1,175	15,500	431
Wisconsin	41	52	10,110	114,500	2,641
Total	187	190	44,445	$625,875	12,722

SUMMARY BY PRESBYTERIES.

PRESBYTERIES.					
Columbus	12	12	3,460	$69,875	1,242
Dodgeville	5	7	1,525	17,800	271
Eastern New York and Vermont	8	8	1,825	26,500	701
First Kansas	5	4	850	3,650	115
First Minnesota	10	10	2,555	22,500	766
Jackson	11	14	2,770	18,600	855
Lacrosse	3	3	550	5,200	166
Lime Spring	5	4	1,210	12,800	465
Long Creek	6	6	1,160	6,850	283
Missouri	6	4	555	2,500	154

SUMMARY BY PRESBYTERIES.—*Continued.*

PRESBYTERIES.	Organizations.	Church Edifices.	Seating Capacity.	Value of Church Property.	Communicants.
Nebraska	8	5	980	$14,800	423
New York City	1	1	550	70,000	350
North Pennsylvania.	23	21	7,111	98,900	1,707
Oneida	25	24	5,170	62,300	1,169
Pittsburg	12	13	3,270	61,700	721
South Dakota......	6	4	730	4,200	306
Southern Pennsylvania	7	7	1,439	16,200	399
Waukesha	13	15	3,495	66,900	1,309
Welsh Prairie	21	28	5,240	44,600	1,320
Total	187	190	44,445	$625,875	12,722

5.—THE UNITED PRESBYTERIANS.

This body is not historically connected with the United Presbyterian Church of Scotland, though it was formed in a similar way and of similar elements. The Scottish body was organized in 1847 of Secession or Associate Burgher, and Relief Presbyterians. The American branch was constituted in 1858 of Associate and Associate Reformed Presbyterians. The Associate Presbyterians included both Burghers and Secession Presbyterians, and the Associate Reformed, Associate and Reformed Presbyterians. All these divisions were brought to the United States by Scotch immigrants. In 1858 most of the Associate and Associate Reformed Presbyterians agreed to unite, and the United Presbyterian Church in North America was the result. A number of each of the bodies, however, refused to enter the union, and hold still a separate existence.

The United Presbyterian Church accepts the Westminster Confession of Faith and catechisms as its doctrinal standards, modifying somewhat the chapters on the power of civil magistrates. Accompanying these standards as a part of the basis of union was a "Judicial Testimony," declaring the sense in which these symbols were received. It consisted of eighteen declarations, including one against human slavery, another against all secret oath-bound societies as "inconsistent with the genius and spirit of Christianity" and forbidden to church members, another opposed to extending the "communion in sealing ordinances" to those refusing adherence to the church's profession, subjection to its government and discipline, or abandonment of fellowship with those not in sympathy with the church's position; also another that it is the "will of God" that the songs contained in the Book of Psalms be sung, and these only, "to the exclusion of the devotional compositions of uninspired men," in public and private worship. In government and discipline the church is similar to other Presbyterian churches. It has presbyteries, synods, and a general assembly.

There are 56 presbyteries, not including three in foreign lands—one each in Canada, India, and Egypt. The number of organizations is 866, with 832 church edifices, valued at $5,408,084, and 94,402 communicants. In 1859, the year after the church was organized, it had 55,547 communicants. It has gained, therefore, in thirty-one years, 38,855 communicants, or about seventy per cent. The average seating capacity of its church edifices is 318, and their average value $6500. There are 50 halls, with a seating capacity of 5930.

SUMMARY BY STATES.

STATES.	Organizations.	Church Edifices.	Seating Capacity.	Value of Church Property.	Communicants.
California	13	10	2,400	$129,500	1,202
Colorado..........	5	5	1,450	55,500	537
Connecticut	1	1	500	10,000	184
Illinois............	62	61	18,363	231,300	6,529
Indiana	29	29	7,885	92,850	2,542
Iowa	101	98	25,960	274,200	7,769
Kansas	58	48	11,605	127,350	3,669
Maryland	1	1	500	25,000	171
Massachusetts	7	7	2,600	65,000	1,135
Michigan	14	11	2,850	21,600	646
Minnesota	1	..	....	......	12
Missouri	14	14	3,900	104,200	1,068
Nebraska	35	25	5,160	95,429	2,172
New Jersey........	6	6	2,175	98,500	685
New York	65	62	25,516	707,400	9,719
North Dakota	1	1	100	1,600	8
Ohio	136	136	43,132	697,550	14,710
Oregon	5	5	1,330	24,800	412
Pennsylvania	281	283	102,404	2,552,450	39,204
Rhode Island......	1	1	400	15,000	220
South Dakota......	4	2	200	1,700	59
Tennessee.........	7	6	1,300	6,000	465
Vermont..........	3	3	900	8,000	219
Washington	3	3	525	7,400	103
West Virginia	6	6	1,730	45,300	530
Wisconsin.........	7	8	1,413	10,455	432
Total.........	866	832	264,298	$5,408,084	94,402

SUMMARY BY PRESBYTERIES.

PRESBYTERIES.					
Albany	8	8	3,050	$77,000	915
Allegheny.........	31	30	13,205	443,200	5,856
Argyle............	12	12	6,250	108,000	2,268
Arkansas Valley ...	22	16	3,510	30,600	977
Beaver Valley	23	23	8,110	100,800	3,214
Big Spring	10	12	3,365	57,800	1,201
Boston	8	8	3,000	80,000	1,355
Brookville.........	18	15	4,275	31,800	1,174
Butler	32	32	10,330	161,400	3,748
Caledonia..........	14	13	4,525	139,300	2,273
Cedar Rapids......	11	10	2,685	45,000	834
Chartiers..........	17	17	6,580	133,200	2,745
Chicago	9	9	2,600	58,000	972

Summary by Presbyteries.—*Continued.*

PRESBYTERIES.	Organi- zations.	Church Edifices.	Seating Ca- pacity.	Value of Church Property.	Com- muni- cants.
Chillicothe	7	6	2,250	$10,000	694
Cleveland	11	9	3,130	65,300	1,235
College Springs	24	23	6,515	56,900	2,208
Colorado	5	5	1,450	55,500	537
Concordia	12	9	1,690	15,800	511
Conemaugh	18	19	6,370	92,600	2,230
Delaware	20	19	6,121	55,100	2,341
Des Moines	35	33	7,460	89,500	2,003
Detroit	13	10	2,600	19,300	591
First Ohio	11	13	4,900	130,000	1,386
Frankfort	17	17	5,631	87,100	2,117
Garnett	17	16	4,240	50,100	1,510
Illinois Central	11	10	2,500	26,500	646
Illinois Southern	21	21	7,105	82,100	2,284
Indiana	11	11	2,850	27,500	845
Indiana Northern	11	10	2,185	16,500	735
Iowa Northwestern	6	5	1,165	14,325	239
Kansas City	11	11	3,240	73,300	1,061
Keokuk	17	18	5,800	53,300	1,910
Lake	26	27	7,713	95,750	2,827
Le Claire	10	10	2,410	17,225	710
Los Angeles	7	5	750	25,000	296
Mansfield	15	15	4,255	78,050	1,424
Mercer	13	14	4,875	80,300	1,998
Monmouth	15	15	4,958	82,200	2,039
Monongahela	33	31	14,045	646,250	5,543
Muskingum	27	29	9,315	65,600	3,349
New York	18	17	8,245	436,500	2,791
Omaha	24	18	3,170	64,079	1,034
Oregon	8	8	1,855	32,200	515
Pawnee	17	11	2,530	37,000	1,259
Philadelphia	15	16	8,180	475,500	3,577
Princeton	9	10	3,100	40,450	1,010
Rock Island	11	11	3,110	38,250	876
San Francisco	6	5	1,650	104,500	906
Sidney	17	16	4,170	65,400	1,429
Steubenville	22	22	6,887	109,300	2,461
Tennessee	7	6	1,300	6,000	465
Vermont	3	3	900	8,000	219
Westmoreland	31	33	10,125	160,550	3,028
Wheeling	19	19	6,255	128,700	1,930
Wisconsin	7	8	1,413	10,455	432
Xenia	13	13	4,400	114,000	1,669
Total	866	832	264,298	$5,408,084	94,402

6.—THE PRESBYTERIAN CHURCH IN THE UNITED STATES (SOUTHERN).

In 1858 the Southern churches of the New School general assembly separated from the Northern churches because of differences on the slavery question. There were 4 synods with 15 presbyteries in the South, and these organized the United Synod, South. In 1861 there was a similar division in the Old School Presbyterian Church, resulting in the organization of the Presbyterian Church in the Confederate States of America, with 11 synods and 47 presbyteries. In 1864 this body and the United Synod, South, were united, and soon after the name Presbyterian Church in the United States was adopted. On account of similarity of titles this church is commonly called the Southern and the parent body the Northern Church.

When the union of 1864 took place the Southern Church had 87,000 communicants. A number of presbyteries which had been connected with the Northern Church joined it after the close of the Civil War, and it has increased rapidly. It now has 13 synods, 72 presbyteries, and 179,-570 communicants. In 1882 fraternity was formally established between the Northern and Southern bodies, and in 1888 the general assemblies, respectively, held a joint meeting in Philadelphia in celebration of the centenary of the adoption of the constitution of the church.

The Southern Church has 2391 organizations, with 2288 church edifices, valued at $8,812,152. The average seating capacity is 302, and the average value $3851. There are 143 halls, with a seating capacity of 19,895.

SUMMARY BY STATES.

STATES.	Organizations.	Church Edifices.	Seating Capacity.	Value of Church Property.	Communicants.
Alabama	172	141½	42,920	$573,400	10,560
Arkansas	92	75	21,830	165,685	4,478
District of Columbia	1	1	1,000	50,000	246
Florida	67	66	16,015	162,450	3,444
Georgia	162	164	52,764	737,725	12,096
Indiana	2	2	650	1,750	79
Indian Territory	13	22	5,250	7,750	629
Kentucky	171	168½	48,745	996,750	16,915
Louisiana	64	55	18,435	433,985	4,926
Maryland	14	17	4,785	224,300	1,654
Mississippi	208	174	47,585	415,315	11,055
Missouri	143	116	38,705	753,490	10,363
North Carolina	282	275	96,485	678,565	27,477
South Carolina	226	243½	68,185	652,335	16,561
Tennessee	155	150	53,030	927,320	15,954
Texas	242	171	45,977	627,806	10,774
Virginia	290	345½	100,977	1,180,576	26,515
West Virginia	87	101	27,505	222,950	5,995
Total	2,391	2,288	690,843	$8,812,152	179,721

SUMMARY BY PRESBYTERIES.

PRESBYTERIES.					
Abingdon	38	35	11,107	$117,350	2,634
Albemarle	26	27	7,850	80,400	1,608
Arkansas	22	19	5,530	68,800	1,130
Athens	34	35	11,700	43,125	1,775
Atlanta	39	40	11,875	203,750	4,100
Augusta	19	20½	7,950	189,600	1,413
Bethel	46	53	17,185	106,800	4,796
Brazos	22	19½	5,625	134,400	1,404
Central Alabama	10	8	1,850	6,300	357
Central Mississippi	60	52	12,450	104,150	3,024
Central Texas	49	27	6,882	112,600	2,450
Charleston	28	33	9,025	268,020	2,243
Cherokee	28	28	9,767	63,400	2,127
Chesapeake	17	20	7,925	110,900	1,452
Chickasaw	25	25	8,250	17,500	1,266
Columbia	26	27	9,255	78,700	1,965
Concord	43	47	17,415	101,750	4,511
Dallas	59	42	12,980	175,064	2,848

SUMMARY BY PRESBYTERIES.—*Continued.*

PRESBYTERIES.	Organizations.	Church Edifices.	Seating Capacity.	Value of Church Property.	Communicants.
Eastern Texas	56	43	9,965	$50,442	1,479
Eastern Hanover..	53	67	21,195	402,700	5,720
Ebenezer.........	29	29	7,545	170,100	2,730
Enoree	44	45	14,605	94,500	2,898
Fayetteville	64	53	23,140	70,690	7,388
Florida	20	21	5,425	47,100	1,064
Greenbrier	45	45	12,455	98,550	3,023
Harmony	32	35	8,890	55,465	1,932
Holston..........	16	15½	6,775	43,200	2,705
Indian	13	22	5,250	7,750	629
Knoxville	24	19	6,225	133,100	2,012
Lafayette	36	26	7,540	72,700	2,194
Lexington........	59	73	19,320	158,950	7,451
Louisiana	21	19	5,100	44,900	808
Louisville	43	45	14,200	339,450	4,433
Macon...........	21	18	5,775	144,850	1,261
Maryland	13	16	4,385	209,300	1,607
Mecklenburg	71	70	21,125	194,700	7,299
Memphis.........	34	30	9,100	203,350	2,807
Mississippi	24	22	6,865	115,000	1,957
Missouri	28	24	7,250	79,750	2,330
Montgomery	48	61	16,990	230,011	4,202
Muhlenberg......	16	16	3,475	52,950	959
Nashville.........	37	42	16,325	433,920	5,013
New Orleans	29	24	10,565	362,700	3,635
North Alabama...	55	35	11,145	226,800	3,427
North Mississippi .	35	24	6,680	76,590	1,721
Orange	39	38	14,920	140,500	3,949
Ouachita.........	22	19	5,400	41,100	1,198
Paducah	16	17	5,400	107,600	1,750
Palmyra	23	20½	5,950	49,350	1,598
Paris	21	15	4,170	33,000	920
Peedee	24	24	6,975	47,200	1,489
Pine Bluff........	18	17	5,300	23,950	1,131
Potosi	17	13	4,400	37,800	961
Red River........	30	26	6,835	65,085	1,202
Roanoke.........	40	44	11,330	95,200	2,805
Saint John	25	25	5,650	40,700	1,103
Saint Louis.......	21	17	5,515	283,940	1,472
Savannah	21	22	5,697	93,000	1,420
South Alabama...	55	48	16,100	210,925	3,783
South Carolina ...	52	53	11,505	80,350	3,203
Suwanee	22	20	4,940	74,650	1,277

Summary by Presbyteries.—*Continued.*

PRESBYTERIES.	Organi-zations.	Church Edifices.	Seating Ca-pacity.	Value of Church Property.	Com-muni-cants.
Tombeckbee	48	38	9,275	$63,375	2,368
Transylvania	29	26	8,750	151,000	2,949
Tuscaloosa	52	50	13,825	129,375	2,993
Upper Missouri...	18	16	8,050	229,950	1,808
Washburn........	27	18	5,050	30,585	922
Western District ..	23	20½	6,500	41,800	1,664
Western Texas ...	35	24	6,355	122,300	1,673
West Hanover....	36	41½	11,410	76,165	2,100
West Lexington ..	40	37½	10,025	177,400	4,173
Wilmington......	39	40	12,035	90,525	2,722
Winchester.......	41	59½	17,550	173,200	3,301
Total.	2,391	2,288	690,843	$8,812,152	179,721

7.—THE ASSOCIATE CHURCH OF NORTH AMERICA.

The Associate Presbyterians began with a secession in 1733 of Ebenezer Erskine and three other ministers from the Church of Scotland. Twenty years later the first associate presbytery in this country, that of Pennsylvania, was organized. In 1782 most of these Presbyterians, who held what are known as the Marrow doctrines, united with Reformed Presbyterians, whence came, in course of time, various bodies of Associate Reformed Presbyterians. There were Associate Presbyterians, however, who did not join this union, and these organized in 1801 a synod, embracing several presbyteries. In 1858 there was a union of Associate and Associate Reformed Presbyterians, resulting in the United Presbyterian Church. Some Associate Presbyterians, however, remained separate still. These are known as the Associate Church of North America.

The Associate Presbyterians were very pronounced against slavery. As early as 1800 the Associate Presbytery denounced slavery as immoral and unjustifiable. In 1811 it repeated this declaration, and in 1831 it resolved to exclude slaveholders from its communion, losing thereby its Southern congregations.

There are now 4 presbyteries, with 31 organizations and 1053 communicants, scattered among eight States, the majority of them being in Pennsylvania and Iowa. They have 23 edifices, with an average seating capacity of 211, and an average value of $1270; 8 halls, with a seating capacity of 345, are occupied.

SUMMARY BY STATES.

STATES.	Organizations.	Church Edifices.	Seating Capacity.	Value of Church Property.	Communicants.
Illinois............	1	1	175	$1,000	17
Indiana...........	3	3	600	2,600	112
Iowa	5	5	974	5,300	233
Kansas	4	3	650	3,300	160
New Jersey........	1	1	200	2,400	20
New York.........	1	..	...	.....	14
Ohio	4	3	625	6,800	77
Pennsylvania	12	7	1,625	7,800	420
Total.	31	23	4,849	$29,200	1,053

SUMMARY BY PRESBYTERIES.

PRESBYTERIES.					
Clarion	16	10	2,200	$12,000	501
Iowa	5	5	974	5,300	233
Kansas	4	3	650	3,300	160
Northern Indiana ..	6	5	1,025	8,600	159
Total.	31	23	4,849	$29,200	1,053

8.—THE ASSOCIATE REFORMED SYNOD OF THE SOUTH.

The union of Associate and Reformed Presbyterians in 1782 resulted in a body called Associate Reformed Presbyterians. There have been various divisions bearing this name, but all have ceased to exist, having joined with Associate Presbyterians to form the United Presbyterian Church, or been absorbed by other Presbyterian bodies, except the Associate Reformed Synod of the South. In consequence of differences in the general synod of the Associate Reformed Church, which had been formed in 1804, on the psalmody and communion questions, the Associate Reformed Synod of the Carolinas withdrew in 1821 and became the next year an independent body, under the title of The Associate Reformed Synod of the South.

The synod accepts the Westminster Confession of Faith, with those sections treating of the power of civil magistrates in ecclesiastical matters changed so as to eliminate their " Erastian doctrine." In 1871 the synod also adopted a " summary of doctrines," consisting of thirty-five articles, together with a brief declaration of church order and terms of communion. Its distinctive principles are contained in the sections concerning psalmody and the communion. Psalms only and not uninspired hymns may be used in worship, and persons " holding to error or corrupt worship, or notoriously belonging to societies which so hold," may not be admitted to the Lord's Table.

Connected with the synod are 8 presbyteries, with 116 organizations, the same number of edifices, and 8501 communicants. The average seating capacity of the edifices is 319; their average value, $1826. The main body of communicants is to be found in the two Carolinas and Tennessee. Five halls, with a seating capacity of 540, are occupied.

SUMMARY BY STATES.

STATES.	Organi-zations.	Church Edifices.	Seating Capacity.	Value of Church Property.	Communicants.
Alabama..........	5	5	1,700	$13,150	220
Arkansas	10	9	1,900	7,300	513
Georgia	8	8	2,500	15,900	474
Kentucky	5	6	1,150	14,500	169
Mississippi	5	5	1,425	4,500	564
Missouri	1	1	350	1,500	92
North Carolina	20	21	7,650	51,000	2,109
South Carolina	36	37	12,800	70,400	2,728
Tennessee	14	14	3,975	18,100	1,058
Texas	7	4	1,650	3,500	188
Virginia	4	5	1,550	10,000	286
West Virginia	1	1	400	2,000	100
Total.........	116	116	37,050	$211,850	8,501

SUMMARY BY PRESBYTERIES.

PRESBYTERIES.					
Arkansas	10	9	1,900	$7,300	513
First	38	39	14,125	84,900	3,686
Kentucky	6	7	1,500	16,000	261
Memphis	13	13	3,250	11,100	1,200
Second	26	27	8,825	52,400	1,625
Tennessee and Alabama...........	11	11	3,850	24,650	642
Texas	7	4	1,650	3,500	188
Virginia	5	6	1,950	12,000	386
Total.........	116	116	37,050	$211,850	8,501

THE REFORMED PRESBYTERIANS.

The Reformed Presbyterians of the United States, of whom there are several branches, are ecclesiastically descended from the Cameronians, or Reformed Presbyterians of Scotland, otherwise called Covenanters. The first presbytery in Scotland was organized in 1743. Eight years later the first Covenanter minister arrived in this country, and in 1774 the first presbytery of this church in America was constituted. A few years later the members of this presbytery, joining with a number of seceders, as they were called, also a Scottish Presbyterian division, organized the Associate Reformed Church. A division in this body resulted in the formation of the Reformed Dissenting Presbytery, and the original Presbytery being resuscitated, there were before the close of the century three branches of Reformed Presbyterians.

The question of the relation of the Christian Church to civil government has ever been a prominent one among Reformed Presbyterians. All accept the Westminster Confession of Faith and form of church government, and all occupy an attitude of protest against civil governments which do not recognize the headship of Christ and the authority of God and his law. They differ, however, among themselves as to the extent to which this protest should be carried. Some refuse, because the Constitution of the United States does not acknowledge the existence of Almighty God, the supremacy of Christ, and the authority of the Scripture, to " incorporate with the political body," and hence do not participate in elections and in certain other political rights and duties. Others continue to protest against " a godless government," but do not refrain from voting. The Reformed Presbyterians deem the influence of secret societies pernicious, and forbid communicants all connection with them. They do not use modern hymns, but sing psalms only. They were always opposed to slavery. In 1800, when attention was called to the fact that some of the members owned slaves, the presbytery enacted, without a dissenting voice, that " no slaveholder should be allowed the communion of the church."

9.—THE SYNOD OF THE REFORMED PRESBYTERIAN CHURCH.

In 1809 a synod was organized. A motion brought before this body in 1825 to open fraternal correspondence with the general assembly of the Presbyterian Church being defeated, a number of ministers subsequently withdrew and joined the latter body. In 1833 a division occurred, resulting in two organizations, both of which retained the same subordinate standards unchanged, but differed in the application of them. The one, allowing its members to vote and hold office under the government, is known as the Reformed Presbyterian Church (New Light) or General Synod; the other, still adhering to the old practice, as the Reformed Presbyterian Church (Old Light) or Synod.

The synod's "terms of ecclesiastical communion" embrace an acknowledgment of the Scriptures as the word of God and only rule of faith and manners; of the whole doctrine of the Westminster Confession and catechisms as founded upon the Scriptures; of the divine right of one unalterable form of church government as set forth by the Westminster Assembly; of the obligation upon the church of the covenant entered into in 1871, in which are embodied the engagement of the national covenant and of the solemn league and covenant, so far as applicable in this land. The covenant of 1871 declares that those accepting it are pledged to labor for " a constitutional recognition of God as the source of all power, of Jesus Christ as the ruler of nations, of the Holy Scriptures as the supreme rule, and of the true Christian religion," and to refuse to " incorporate by any act with the political body until this blessed reformation is secured." The members of this branch, therefore, do not take part in state or national elections. They neither vote nor hold office.

The synod embraces 11 presbyteries, with 115 organizations and edifices, 10,574 communicants, and church property valued at $1,071,400. The average value of its edifices is $9317, and the average seating capacity 323. Though it is represented in nineteen States, more than half of its communicants are in Pennsylvania and New York. Three halls, with a seating capacity of 600, are occupied.

SUMMARY BY STATES.

STATES.	Organizations.	Church Edifices.	Seating Capacity.	Value of Church Property.	Communicants.
Alabama	1	1	300	$1,500	76
Colorado	3	2	650	4,500	142
Illinois	5	5	1,575	16,000	536
Indiana	3	3	850	11,000	246
Iowa	9	9	2,760	21,900	984
Kansas	9	7	1,750	15,000	758
Maine	1	1	300	4,000	19
Maryland	1	1	250	15,000	65
Massachusetts	2	2	1,350	100,000	400
Michigan	2	2	550	6,000	197
Minnesota	4	3	1,000	2,800	145
Missouri	2	1	350	10,000	100
Nebraska	1	1	350	3,500	51
New York	18	19	8,030	459,500	2,328
Ohio	14	16	4,160	55,600	951
Pennsylvania	33	35	11,180	324,500	3,272
Vermont	5	5	1,240	17,900	222
West Virginia	1	1	200	700	20
Wisconsin	1	1	250	2,000	62
Total	115	115	37,095	$1,071,400	10,574

SUMMARY BY PRESBYTERIES.

PRESBYTERIES.	Organizations.	Church Edifices.	Seating Capacity.	Value of Church Property.	Communicants.
Illinois............	9	9	2,775	$35,000	776
Iowa	12	11	3,310	19,700	916
Kansas	16	12	3,450	30,000	1,291
Lakes	9	9	2,730	35,000	768
Maine	1	1	300	4,000	19
New York.........	15	16	7,900	517,500	2,351
Ohio	8	10	2,180	25,800	472
Philadelphia.......	5	5	1,880	88,000	789
Pittsburg	30	32	9,850	256,500	2,593
Rochester.........	5	5	1,480	42,000	377
Vermont..........	5	5	1,240	17,900	222
Total	115	115	37,095	$1,071,400	10,574

10.—THE GENERAL SYNOD OF THE REFORMED PRESBYTERIAN CHURCH.

This is the other body resulting from the division of the Reformed Presbyterian Church in 1833. They used to be popularly distinguished as "New Lights." The general synod holds equally with the synod to the Westminster standards, to the headship of Christ over nations, to the doctrine of "public social covenanting," to the exclusive use of the psalms in singing, to restricted communion in the use of the sacraments, and to the principle of "dissent from all immoral civil institutions," but allows its members to decide for themselves whether the government of this country should be regarded as an immoral institution, and thus determine what duties of citizenship devolve upon them. They may therefore exercise the franchise and hold office, provided they do not in these civil acts violate the principle that forbids connection with immoral institutions. Many of them do participate in elections. Negotiations for the union of the general synod and the synod failed in 1890, because the latter would not agree to a basis which interpreted the phrase "incorporate with the political body" as meaning "such incorporation as involves sinful compliance with the religious defects of the written constitution as it now stands, either in holding such offices as require an oath to support the constitution or in voting for men to administer such offices."

The general synod embraces 5 presbyteries, with 33 organizations, the same number of edifices, valued at $469,000, and 4602 communicants. The average seating capacity of its edifices is 375, and their average value $14,212, which is an extremely high figure. One hall, with a seating capacity of 100, is occupied.

SUMMARY BY STATES.

STATES.	Organizations.	Church Edifices.	Seating Capacity.	Value of Church Property.	Communicants.
Illinois	6	6	2,150	$16,400	590
Indiana	2	2	450	2,400	82
Iowa	2	1	180	1,000	33
Kansas	1	1	150	800	65
New York	6	6	2,650	123,000	624
Ohio	2	2	1,100	36,500	340
Pennsylvania	11	12	4,900	283,500	2,685
Tennessee	1	1	200	400	18
Vermont	2	2	600	5,000	165
Total	33	33	12,380	$469,000	4,602

SUMMARY BY PRESBYTERIES.

PRESBYTERIES.					
Northern	8	8	3,250	$128,000	789
Ohio	3	3	1,300	38,000	400
Philadelphia	6	6	3,250	185,500	2,103
Pittsburg	5	6	1,650	98,000	582
Western	11	10	2,930	19,500	728
Total	33	33	12,380	$469,000	4,602

11.—THE REFORMED PRESBYTERIAN CHURCH (COVENANTED).

This body was organized in 1840 by two ministers and three elders who withdrew from the synod, or the branch known as the "Old Lights," on the ground that the latter maintained sinful ecclesiastical relations and patronized or indorsed moral reform societies with which persons of any religion or no religion were connected. Its terms of communion are somewhat stricter than those of the synod. It is a small body, having only 4 organizations, with 37 members, divided among three States.

SUMMARY BY STATES.

STATES.	Organizations.	Church Edifices.	Seating Capacity.	Value of Church Property.	Communicants.
New York.........	1	..	...	......	7
Ohio	1	1	200	......	20
Pennsylvania	2	..	...	......	10
Total.	4	1	200	......	37

12.—THE REFORMED PRESBYTERIAN CHURCH IN THE UNITED STATES AND CANADA.

This body was organized in 1883, in consequence of dissatisfaction with the treatment of a question of discipline by the general synod of the Reformed Presbyterian Church (New Lights). In the matter of participation in elections it holds with the general synod, and contrary to the synod, that Christians may vote and be voted for, regarding the republic as essentially a Christian republic. It has but 600 members in the United States, who belong to one congregation in Allegheny County, Pennsylvania.

SUMMARY.

PRESBYTERY.	Organizations.	Church Edifices.	Seating Capacity.	Value of Church Property.	Communicants.
Pittsburg	1	1	800	$75,000	600

SUMMARY BY STATES OF ALL PRESBYTERIANS.

STATES.					
Alabama........	385	327	97,475	$819,255	21,502
Alaska..........	5	4	1,100	7,750	481
Arizona.........	7	3	850	13,900	188
Arkansas	419	274	84,125	357,685	18,022
California	263	211	59,771	1,895,675	18,934
Colorado........	88	69	17,875	643,550	6,968
Connecticut	8	10	4,300	443,500	1,864
Delaware	32	43	14,970	709,800	4,622
Dist. of Columbia	16	20	11,600	950,000	5,128
Florida	107	95	22,265	484,650	4,574
Georgia.........	201	193	61,564	776,025	14,538
Idaho...........	19	15	2,275	40,950	815
Illinois..........	752	736	241,404	4,649,410	77,213
Indiana	389	412	132,653	2,610,200	43,351
Indian Territory .	136	106	21,818	59,158	3,661
Iowa	518	490	131,892	1,848,000	40,528
Kansas	521	359	91,934	1,299,260	31,393
Kentucky	507	464	148,020	2,045,870	40,880
Louisiana	88	72	24,035	454,035	5,864
Maine	3	4	1,100	12,000	224
Maryland	93	109	38,555	1,752,424	12,483
Massachusetts ...	27	27	14,075	530,500	5,105
Michigan	252	243	79,450	2,242,236	25,931
Minnesota.......	185	170	44,966	1,329,910	15,055
Mississippi	352	299	86,369	530,290	18,250
Missouri	776	609	198,421	2,789,652	53,510
Montana........	24	18	4,150	88,000	1,232
Nebraska	278	189	41,981	691,939	15,065
Nevada	8	4	865	11,400	275
New Hampshire .	8	9	3,150	34,800	956
New Jersey......	307	427	171,732	6,800,000	59,464
New Mexico	39	17	2,815	45,675	1,275
New York.......	903	1,047	420,977	22,727,192	168,564

SUMMARY BY STATES OF ALL PRESBYTERIANS.—*Continued.*

STATES.	Organizations.	Church Edifices.	Seating Capacity.	Value of Church Property.	Communicants.
North Carolina ..	411	399	130,785	$818,745	36,102
North Dakota ...	100	49	9,600	128,025	3,044
Ohio	828	849	287,420	6,722,875	103,607
Oklahoma.......	21	9	1,850	14,000	550
Oregon	101	76	19,092	463,500	5,244
Pennsylvania	1,365	1,506	576,018	19,146,130	216,248
Rhode Island....	5	5	1,785	76,000	828
South Carolina ..	339	347	106,000	896,635	26,118
South Dakota....	134	89	14,896	162,840	4,778
Tennessee.......	864	779	250,536	2,002,605	66,573
Texas...........	816	446	138,707	1,241,485	37,811
Utah	20	31	5,180	212,975	688
Vermont........	18	16	4,215	50,400	1,267
Virginia	313	369	106,967	1,234,501	27,746
Washington	99	70	16,860	365,875	4,343
West Virginia ...	140	150	43,270	581,150	10,952
Wisconsin.......	180	199	45,977	1,004,355	14,154
Wyoming	6	5	960	52,250	364
Total	13,476	12,469	4,038,650	$94,869,097	1,278,332

CHAPTER XXXII.

PROTESTANT EPISCOPAL BODIES.

I.—THE PROTESTANT EPISCOPAL CHURCH.

THE beginnings of the Church of England in this country reach back into the sixteenth century, although the Protestant Episcopal Church was not formally organized as an independent branch until 1785. Clergymen of the Church of England accompanied the early colonists of North Carolina across the sea, one of whom baptized an Indian chief in 1587 in a colony unsuccessfully begun by Sir Walter Raleigh, and also, about the same time, the first white Christian born in that colony. It is probable that the Rev. Francis Fletcher, who accompanied, as chaplain, the expedition of Sir Francis Drake to the Pacific Coast, held services on California soil as early as 1579. He officiated for six weeks in the neighborhood of Drake's Bay. In 1607 worship according to the Anglican ritual was established in the new colonies at Jamestown, Va., and Kennebec, Me. It was soon discontinued in Maine, but in Virginia it was not interrupted. An Episcopal congregation was gathered in New Hampshire in 1631, and parishes were formed in other parts of New England and the Middle States in the early colonial days, Trinity parish, New York City, being constituted in 1693, and Christ Church parish, in Philadelphia, in 1695. The church became the established church in New York, New

Jersey, Maryland, Virginia, South Carolina, and Georgia. In Virginia, for a considerable period, no other form of worship was tolerated. In Massachusetts, on the other hand, the Anglican service was not allowed until liberty for it was secured by royal proclamation in 1662. The Episcopal Church received considerable assistance from England, particularly from the Society for the Propagation of the Gospel, organized in 1701, which sent over many missionaries. It is said that at the beginning of the Revolutionary War the society was maintaining about eighty missionaries in the colonies.

At the close of the struggle resulting in American independence many of the parishes were without ministerial oversight. Some of the clergymen had left the country during the war, returning to England or going north to the British provinces. In Virginia, where at the outbreak of the war there had been 164 churches and chapels and 91 clergymen, it was found in 1784 that 95 parishes were either extinct or forsaken, and only 28 clergymen remained. At a conference of clergymen and laymen from New York, New Jersey, and Pennsylvania, held in New Brunswick, N. J., in May, 1784, steps were taken to form " a continental representation of the Episcopal Church." In the following October a convention, representing Delaware and Maryland, in addition to the three States above named, assembled in New York City, and resolved to " recommend to the clergy and congregations of their communion " that " there be a general convention of the Episcopal Church "; that the first meeting of the convention be held in Philadelphia in September, 1785 ; and that clerical and lay deputies be appointed by the Episcopal churches in the several States, " duly instructed and authorized " to take part in its deliberations. At the convention of 1785 a committee was appointed to draft a constitution, to prepare such alterations in the liturgy as were necessary, and to report a plan for securing the consecration of bishops. All of these matters were considered by the committee, and the convention acted upon the several reports it made. The first Episcopal consecration was that of Bishop Seabury, of Connecticut, which took place in Aberdeen, Scotland, in 1784, the Scottish bishops officiating. In 1787 Drs. William White and Samuel Provoost were consecrated bishops in London, by the Archbishop of Canterbury. The consecration of Bishop Seabury was recognized by the general convention of 1789, and the church was thus fully organized and fully equipped, with bishops of the Scottish and English succession, a constitution, a general convention, and a prayer-book. When the general convention of 1792 was held, it was estimated that there were in this country about 200 clergymen. The church developed quite slowly until after the first quarter of the present century. The clerical list reported at the convention of 1832 contained nearly 600 names; three years later it had swelled to 763, and in 1838 it reached 951. In the next thirty years this number was considerably more than doubled. It now has 52 dioceses and 13 missionary jurisdictions, besides 5 missionary jurisdictions in foreign lands. The number of its bishops is 75.

The doctrinal symbols of the Protestant Episcopal Church are the Apostles' and the Nicene creeds, together with the Thirty-nine Articles of the Church of England slightly altered.

The legislative authority of the church is vested in a general convention, which meets triennially. The convention consists of two houses, the house of bishops and the house of clerical and lay deputies. The deputies are elected by diocesan conventions. Every diocese, regardless of the number of clergymen and communicants within its bounds, is entitled to eight deputies, four clerical and four lay. The concurrence of both orders in the house of deputies and the consent of both houses are necessary to the enactment of legislation. The general convention has the power to adopt, alter, or repeal canons pertaining to the regulation of the general affairs of the church, to ratify measures for the erection of new dioceses, and to make alterations in the constitution and Book of Common Prayer under certain restrictions. It is the supreme legislative, executive, and judicial power. The legislation of the general convention is in the form of canons, which are arranged under four titles:

" I. Of the orders in the ministry and of the doctrine and worship of the church.

" II. Of discipline.

" III. Of the organized bodies and officers of the church.

" IV. Miscellaneous provisions."

There is in each diocese a convention consisting of the clergy and representatives of the laity. The bishop of the diocese is the presiding officer. The diocesan convention has power to provide by legislation for such diocesan matters as are not regulated by the general canons of the church. The unit of the diocese is the parish, with its rector, churchwardens, vestrymen, and congregation. The vestrymen are the trustees and hold the property for the corporation. The wardens, of whom there are usually two, represent the body of the parish, and have charge of the records, collect the alms, and look after the repairs of the church. Vestry meetings, to be valid, require the presence of at least one warden. The rector, who must be a priest, presides, and has exclusive direction of the spiritual affairs of the church.

Three orders are recognized in the ministry: bishops, priests, deacons. A bishop is elected by the diocesan convention and consecrated by bishops after consent has been given by the standing committees of the various dioceses and by the bishops. He licenses lay readers, ordains deacons and priests, administers the ~~right~~ rite of confirmation to members, institutes rectors, and is required to visit every parish in his diocese at least once in three years.

The number of organizations is 5019; of church edifices, 5019, which have an aggregate value of $81,220,317. Worship is also held in 312 halls, etc., with an aggregate seating capacity of 28,007. There are in all 532,054 communicants. Of these New York reports the largest number (127,218) among the States. Pennsylvania comes second, with 54,720; New Jersey third, with 30,103; Massachusetts fourth, with 26,855; and Connecticut fifth, with 26,652. Maryland has more than Virginia, and the District of Columbia a larger number than Alabama, Arkansas, Florida, Georgia, Kentucky, Louisiana, Mississippi, or any of the other Southern States, excepting only North Carolina and Virginia. The church is represented in all the States and Territories. The largest diocese is that of New York, with 53,593 communicants. Pennsylvania comes second, with 33,459; Maryland third, with 28,273; and Massachusetts fourth, with 26,855. There are 51 dioceses, besides a number of missions and missionary jurisdictions. The multiplication of dioceses has been quite rapid in the last quarter of a century.

The average seating capacity of the church edifices is 266, and the average value $16,182.

SUMMARY BY STATES.

STATES.	Organizations.	Church Edifices.	Seating Capacity.	Value of Church Property.	Communicants.
Alabama.........	58	59	16,755	$655,752	6,085
Alaska	1	1	200	1,200	6
Arizona..........	9	4	800	24,216	179
Arkansas	30	28	7,575	196,122	2,381
California	103	95	19,700	1,019,695	9,221
Colorado.........	52	44	8,663	700,065	3,814
Connecticut	161	187	64,275	3,403,170	26,652
Delaware	38	44	11,215	371,500	2,719
Dist. of Columbia .	18	28	10,825	790,500	7,476
Florida	100	84	13,569	390,561	4,225
Georgia..........	46	50	13,282	492,300	5,515
Idaho............	13	..	.....	......	364
Illinois...........	186	179	47,523	2,117,275	19,099
Indiana	65	61	15,660	537,600	5,185
Iowa	105	77	17,385	887,400	6,481
Kansas	96	48	9,090	316,225	3,593
Kentucky	47	57	34,935	758,800	7,161
Louisiana	85	65	15,099	387,950	5,162
Maine	38	37	10,342	406,590	3,291
Maryland	166	244	62,553	2,381,406	23,938
Massachusetts	166	172	57,613	4,676,193	26,855
Michigan	189	175	46,639	1,645,551	18,034
Minnesota	171	148	27,070	931,100	11,142
Mississippi	68	61	13,589	322,960	3,560
Missouri	111	84	23,035	952,600	8,828
Montana.........	30	22	2,375	165,450	1,104
Nebraska	110	68	11,665	580,145	4,036
Nevada..........	9	9	1,825	19,500	535
New Hampshire ..	44	46	10,550	541,400	2,911
New Jersey.......	184	234	62,125	3,815,850	30,103
New Mexico......	16	6	1,140	41,165	373
New York........	731	827	252,343	30,862,213	127,218
North Carolina ...	178	161	34,721	545,010	8,186
North Dakota.....	39	...	.....	......	892
Ohio	166	184	49,419	2,069,787	17,454
Oklahoma........	4	2	325	4,000	105
Oregon	31	25	4,014	361,930	1,849
Pennsylvania	369	418	134,967	10,854,131	54,720
Rhode Island.	50	61	20,949	1,189,700	9,458
South Carolina ...	94	88	21,041	571,833	5,742
South Dakota	83	69	9,295	234,532	2,649
Tennessee	69	63	16,275	575,900	5,671

SUMMARY BY STATES.—*Continued.*

STATES.	Organi-zations.	Church Edifices.	Seating Ca-pacity.	Value of Church Property.	Com-muni-cants.
Texas	139	110	23,120	$624,900	7,097
Utah	10	10	1,525	71,250	751
Vermont.........	63	56	13,087	472,050	4,335
Virginia	245	330	79,340	1,697,375	20,371
Washington......	23	18	3,731	242,800	1,698
West Virginia	61	63	13,898	276,687	2,906
Wisconsin	133	117	21,830	1,035,978	10,457
Wyoming........	16	...	......	....	467
Total........	5,019	5,019	1,336,952	$81,220,317	532,054

SUMMARY BY DIOCESES AND MISSIONS.

DIOCESES.

Alabama.........	58	59	16,755	$655,752	6,085
Albany	143	153	41,796	2,323,600	18,556
Arkansas	30	28	7,575	196,122	2,381
California	76	70	15,375	900,353	8,107
Central New York.	152	158½	40,362	1,873,500	16,159
Cent'l Pennsylvania	117	141	37,870	2,211,115	10,658
Chicago..........	90	88	26,688	1,721,050	13,597
Colorado.........	52	44	8,663	700,065	3,814
Connecticut	161	187	64,275	3,403,170	26,652
Delaware.........	38	44	11,215	371,500	2,719
East Carolina.....	51	49	13,125	243,910	3,351
Easton...........	37	68	12,636	338,762	3,141
Florida	100	84	13,569	390,561	4,225
Fond du Lac	57	42	9,105	190,150	3,751
Georgia..........	46	50	13,282	492,300	5,515
Indiana..........	65	61	15,660	537,600	5,185
Iowa.............	105	77	17,385	887,400	6,481
Kansas...........	96	48	9,090	316,225	3,593
Kentucky	47	57	34,935	758,800	7,161
Long Island......	110	147	43,642	4,868,500	23,690
Louisiana	85	65	15,099	387,950	5,162
Maine	38	37	10,342	406,590	3,291
Maryland	147	204	60,742	2,833,144	28,273
Massachusetts	166	172	57,613	4,676,193	26,855
Michigan.........	126	123	33,771	1,301,580	13,559
Milwaukee	76	75	12,725	845,828	6,706
Minnesota........	171	148	27,070	931,100	11,142
Mississippi	68	61	13,589	322,960	3,560

SUMMARY BY DIOCESES AND MISSIONS.—*Continued.*

DIOCESES.	Organi- zations.	Church Edifices.	Seating Ca- pacity.	Value of Church Property.	Com- muni- cants.
Missouri	111	84	23,035	$952,600	8,828
Nebraska	56	50	9,285	492,725	2,916
Newark..........	78	98	29,343	2,370,300	15,805
New Hampshire...	44	46	10,550	541,400	2,911
New Jersey.......	106	136	32,782	1,445,550	14,298
New York........	210	251	91,240	19,662,450	53,593
North Carolina ...	127	112	21,596	301,100	4,835
Ohio	99	109	30,515	1,101,100	9,946
Oregon	31	25	4,014	361,930	1,849
Pennsylvania	139	165	70,202	6,868,971	33,459
Pittsburg.........	113	112	26,895	1,774,045	10,603
Quincy...........	40	39	10,960	172,500	2,201
Rhode Island.....	50	61	20,949	1,189,700	9,458
South Carolina....	94	88	21,041	571,833	5,742
Southern Ohio....	67	75	18,904	968,687	7,508
Springfield.......	56	52	9,875	223,725	3,301
Tennessee........	69	63	16,275	575,900	5,671
Texas	51	47	11,130	305,200	3,229
Vermont.........	63	56	13,087	472,050	4,335
Virginia	245	330	79,340	1,697,375	20,371
Western Michigan.	63	52	12,868	343,971	4,475
Western New York	116	117	35,303	2,134,163	15,220
West Virginia	61	63	13,898	276,687	2,906
MISSIONS.					
Alaska...........	1	1	200	1,200	6
Montana.........	30	22	2,375	165,450	1,104
Nevada and Utah..	19	19	3,350	90,750	1,286
New Mexico and Arizona........	25	10⅓	1,940	65,381	552
North Dakota.....	39	..	.....	......	892
Northern California	27	25	4,325	119,342	1,114
Northern Texas...	39	31	6,060	187,350	2,037
Oklahoma and In- dian Territory ..	4	2	325	4,000	105
South Dakota	86	72	9,625	244,632	2,937
The Platte	51	15	2,050	77,320	832
Washington	23	18	3,731	242,800	1,698
Western Texas ...	49	32	5,930	132,350	1,831
Wyom'g and Idaho	29	..	.....	......	831
Total.	5,019	5,019	1,336,952	$81,220,317	532,054

2.—THE REFORMED EPISCOPAL CHURCH.

This body was organized in 1873. Bishop Cummins, of Kentucky, withdrew from the ministry of the Protestant Episcopal Church that year, in consequence of certain criticisms which had been uttered respecting his participation in a union communion service in connection with the Sixth Conference of the Evangelical Alliance. Bishop Cummins met, in December, 1873, with seven clergymen and twenty laymen in the city of New York, and it was resolved to inaugurate a separate movement. Bishop Cummins was chosen presiding officer of the new church, and the Rev. C. E. Cheney, D.D., of Chicago, was elected bishop, and subsequently consecrated by Bishop Cummins. A declaration of principles was adopted setting forth the views of the new body respecting doctrine, polity, worship, and discipline. These principles were as follows:

"I. The Reformed Episcopal Church, holding ' the faith once delivered unto the saints,' declares its belief in the Holy Scriptures of the Old and New Testaments as the Word of God and the sole rule of faith and practice; in the creed ' commonly called the Apostles' Creed '; in the divine institution of the sacraments of baptism and the Lord's Supper; and in the doctrines of grace substantially as they are set forth in the Thirty-nine Articles of Religion.

"II. This church recognizes and adheres to Episcopacy, not as of divine right, but as a very ancient and desirable form of church polity.

"III. This church, retaining a liturgy which shall not be imperative or repressive of freedom in prayer, accepts the Book of Common Prayer, as it was revised, proposed, and recommended for use by the general convention of the Protestant Episcopal Church, A.D. 1785, reserving full liberty to alter, abridge, enlarge, and amend the same, as may seem most conducive to the edification of the people, 'provided that the substance of the faith be kept entire.'

" IV. This Church condemns and rejects the following erroneous and strange doctrines as contrary to God's Word:

" First, that the Church of Christ exists only in one order or form of ecclesiastical polity;

" Second, that Christian ministers are 'priests' in another sense than that in which all believers are 'a royal priesthood';

" Third, that the Lord's Table is an altar on which the oblation of the body and blood of Christ is offered anew to the Father;

" Fourth, that the presence of Christ in the Lord's Supper is a presence in the elements of bread and wine;

" Fifth, that regeneration is inseparably connected with baptism."

At a general council of the Reformed Episcopal Church, held at Chicago, Ill., in May, 1874, articles of religion were adopted, thirty-five in number. They follow closely the Anglican articles of religion, with such changes as are indicated by the principles adopted in 1873. At the same meeting of the general council a revised Book of Common Prayer was also adopted. The church recognizes but two orders in the ministry, that of presbyter and that of deacon. It holds that the episcopate is not an order but an office, the bishop being simply first presbyter. The bishops do not constitute a separate house in the general council as in the general convention of the Protestant Episcopal Church. They preside over synods or jurisdictions, which correspond more or less closely to dioceses and jurisdictions of the Protestant Episcopal Church.

The Reformed Episcopal Church has 83 organizations, 84 church edifices, valued at $1,615,101, and 8455 communicants. It is represented in twelve States, including Virginia and South Carolina, and it has two synods and three missionary jurisdictions. The average seating capacity of the edifices is 285, and their average value $19,227. There are 2 halls, with a seating capacity of 300.

SUMMARY BY STATES.

STATES.	Organizations.	Church Edifices.	Seating Capacity.	Value of Church Property.	Communicants.
Delaware..........	2	2	650	$16,500	139
Illinois............	10	10	4,250	225,800	1,755
Maryland	4	5	1,375	46,000	285
Massachusetts	2	2	850	44,000	311
Michigan	2	2	350	8,100	102
Missouri	2	2	650	25,000	125
New Jersey........	2	2	725	44,500	326
New York..........	4	4	1,775	280,400	743
Ohio	3	2	1,100	33,700	257
Pennsylvania	13	15	5,800	870,000	2,640
Virginia	2	2	425	2,700	49
South Carolina (colored)	37	36	5,975	18,401	1,723
Total.	83	84	23,925	$1,615,101	8,455

SUMMARY BY SYNODS.

SYNODS.					
Chicago...........	13	12	4,850	$220,800	1,684
New York and Philadelphia	23	25	9,800	1,255,400	4,159
Missionary Jurisdiction of the South.	6	7	1,800	48,700	334
Missionary Jurisdiction of the West and Northwest...	4	4	1,500	71,800	555
Special Missionary Jurisdiction of the South (colored)..	37	36	5,975	18,401	1,723
Total.........	83	84	23,925	$1,615,101	8,455

The totals of the two bodies are: Organizations, 5102; church edifices, 5103; seating capacity, 1,360,877; value of church property, $82,835,418; communicants, 540,509.

The Reformed Episcopal Church adds no considerable number to the communicants of the Protestant Episcopal Church, except in Pennsylvania (2640), Illinois (1755), and South Carolina (1723). It contributes to the total valuation of church property upward of $1,600,000.

CHAPTER XXXIII.

THE REFORMED BODIES.

THERE are three Reformed churches in the United States, the chief of which are the Reformed Church in America and the Reformed Church in the United States. The Reformed churches belong to the Presbyterian family in polity and doctrine, though their standards are not those of Westminster and their ecclesiastical terms differ somewhat from those generally used by the Presbyterian churches. They have consistories instead of sessions, classes instead of presbyteries, and general synods instead of general assemblies. The origin of the Reformed Church in America is traced to the Reformed Church of Holland; that of the Reformed Church in the United States to the Reformed Church in Germany. For the sake of distinction the former is popularly called the Reformed Dutch and the latter the Reformed German Church. These two bodies, both of which looked for aid and direction to the classis of Amsterdam until late in the eighteenth century, agreed in 1891, through their general synods, upon a plan of federal union, by which, if it should be ratified by the classes, while each retained its autonomy, a community of interest would be established respecting missionary and educational matters, and a federal synod, representing both churches and having advisory powers, would be held annually. The plan, however, failed, the classes of the Reformed Dutch

Church declining to ratify it, and the general synod of that body regretfully declaring the fact, in 1893.

I.—THE REFORMED CHURCH IN AMERICA.

The Rev. Jonas Michaelius organized in New Amsterdam, in 1628, the first church of this order in this country. It embraced fifty communicants, "Walloons and Dutch." As the Dutch immigrants settled along the Hudson, on Long Island, and in New Jersey, congregations of their faith were gathered. A number of these churches are still in existence upward of two centuries old. The first organization, termed the "cœtus," was formed in 1747 by permission of the classis of Amsterdam. It had no ecclesiastical power, but was merely advisory, the classis reserving all power to itself. In 1755 a minority of the "cœtus," dissatisfied with the assumption by that body of larger powers, formed a "conferentie." This was the beginning of a sharp controversy, which was ended in 1770 in the union of the two bodies in a self-governing organization. This system was further developed in 1793, and finally perfected in the present ecclesiastical government of the church.

The stream of Dutch immigration ceased to flow in the latter half of the seventeenth century. This fact, with certain peculiar difficulties encountered by the church, accounts for its failure to attain to greater numerical strength. The Dutch language having ceased to be the language of its worship many years ago, the word " Dutch " was eliminated from its title in 1867. In consequence of a considerable immigration from Holland in late years, which has settled in Michigan and other Western States, there are many congregations in that section in which the Dutch tongue is now used.

The Reformed Church accepts the Apostles', the Nicene, and the Athanasian creeds, the Belgic Confession, the canons of the Synod of Dort, and the Heidelberg Catechism as its doctrinal symbols. It is a distinctively Calvinistic body. The church has a liturgy for use in public worship, including an order of Scripture lessons, an order of worship, and forms of prayer. These, however, are not obligatory, and are not generally used. Forms for the administration of baptism and the Lord's Supper, for the ordination of ministers, etc., are imperative.

The church has thirty-three classes in this country. There are also four particular synods, which consist of representatives from classes. Above the particular synods is a general synod, which meets annually. The particular synod of New York embraces 8 classes; that of Albany, 9; that of Chicago, 7; and that of New Brunswick, 9.

The largest classis is that of New York, which has 8881 communicants, with church property valued at $3,308,000. The total number of communicants is 92,970. These belong to 572 organizations, and own 670 edifices, only 8 halls, with a seating capacity of 751, being rented for public worship. These church edifices have a total value of $10,340,159, which indicates an average for each church of $15,439. The average seating capacity is 385.

The denomination is represented only in fourteen States. New York has 52,228 communicants, and New Jersey 24,057. In these two States, therefore, are more than four fifths of the entire number of communicants, with church property valued at $9,536,309, or within $803,850 of the entire valuation for the denomination.

SUMMARY BY STATES.

STATES.	Organi-zations.	Church Edifices.	Seating Ca-pacity.	Value of Church Property.	Com-muni-cants.
Illinois............	25	27	9,895	$169,800	2,820
Indiana...........	3	3	700	9,000	172
Iowa..............	26	28	8,104	90,900	2,605
Kansas	2	2	400	2,500	46
Michigan	45	50	17,229	262,800	6,609
Minnesota	3	3	750	10,000	145
Nebraska	4	3	960	7,500	344
New Jersey........	124	155	65,445	2,091,029	24,057
New York.........	302	358	142,380	7,445,280	52,228
North Dakota	2	2	205	750	89
Ohio	2	2	600	8,100	156
Pennsylvania	8	10	4,930	178,500	1,756
South Dakota......	15	14	2,899	23,900	594
Wisconsin	11	13	3,425	40,100	1,349
Total.	572	670	257,922	$10,340,159	92,970

SUMMARY BY CLASSES.

CLASSES.					
Albany	17	18	8,250	$360,000	3,340
Bergen	19	22	9,200	316,000	2,764
Bergen (South Classis)	12	14	6,100	327,500	3,094
Dakota	18	17	3,604	30,850	749
Grand River.......	21	23	8,455	131,400	3,327
Greene	7	8	3,150	73,500	1,603
Holland...........	19	22	6,024	72,000	2,530
Hudson...........	14	13½	5,235	121,150	2,087
Illinois............	17	19	4,985	65,000	984
Iowa	23	25	6,944	85,700	2,395
Kingston..........	19	17½	7,150	146,800	2,766
Long Island (North Classis)	22	35	15,090	547,500	4,062
Long Island (South Classis)	20	28	13,345	896,500	4,443
Michigan	9	10	4,050	76,000	1,013
Monmouth........	10	12	4,200	94,079	1,417
Montgomery	31	33	11,025	338,500	3,513
Newark...........	17	21	9,105	538,500	4,175
New Brunswick....	12	16	8,805	189,600	2,708
New York.........	30	33	19,179	3,308,000	8,881

SUMMARY BY CLASSES.—*Continued.*

CLASSES.	Organizations.	Church Edifices.	Seating Capacity.	Value of Church Property.	Communicants.
Orange	26	28	10,790	$235,150	3,649
Paramus	24	34	11,355	358,800	3,966
Passaic	12	14	5,975	153,250	2,272
Philadelphia	13	17	8,025	216,300	2,880
Poughkeepsie	14	17	6,475	234,000	2,262
Raritan	14	19	9,080	161,000	3,423
Rensselaer	14	18	5,330	124,380	2,090
Rochester	13	17	5,380	89,200	2,415
Saratoga	13	13	4,775	144,800	1,973
Schenectady	11	18	6,585	186,500	2,506
Schoharie	17	17	5,286	60,150	1,138
Ulster	18	20	6,740	187,250	2,593
Westchester	15	20	7,125	306,400	2,021
Wisconsin	31	31	11,105	164,400	3,931
Total.	572	670	257,922	$10,340,159	92,970

2.—THE REFORMED CHURCH IN THE UNITED STATES.

The original source of this body was the Reformed Church established in the Palatinate, one of the provinces of Germany. On account of severe persecutions the Palatine reformers were scattered, many finding refuge in this country in the early part of the eighteenth century. There were Germans among the American colonists, however, before this period. From 1700 to 1746 many thousand settled in Pennsylvania and elsewhere, and a number of Reformed congregations having been gathered, a " cœtus " (an ecclesiastical organization having advisory powers) was formed in 1747, the same year that the Reformed Dutch organized their " cœtus " in New York.

In response to most earnest appeals from the Rev. Michael Schlatter, who was a sort of general missionary and organizer, gathering scattered members together and ministering to pastorless organizations, the Reformed Church of Holland raised nearly $60,000, the interest of which was devoted to the erection of churches and school-houses and the support of ministers. Help was also received for the education of youth from a society in London.

In 1793 the " cœtus " became a synod and the Reformed German Church an entirely independent body. There are now 8 synods, 6 of which are English and 2 German. The Eastern Synod embraces 11 classes; that of Ohio, 6; that of the Northwest, 10; that of Pittsburg, 5; that of the Potomac, 9; the German Synod of the East, 5; the Central Synod, 4; and the Synod of the Interior, 5.

Below the synods are classes, corresponding to presbyteries in the Presbyterian churches, and above the synods is a general synod, which is the supreme legislative and judicial body of the church. It meets once every three years, and was organized in 1863.

Like the Reformed (Dutch) Church, the Reformed (German) Church is Calvinistic in doctrine. Its symbol is the Heidelberg Catechism, which is also accepted by the former body. In substance the Heidelberg Catechism is Augustinian, says Prof. T. G. Apple, respecting the doctrines of natural depravity and salvation by free grace alone; but it does not, like some other Calvinistic symbols, teach a decree of reprobation as well as a decree of election. The Reformed Church has a liturgical system of worship, but its use is optional with congregations.

The Reformed (German) Church (it dropped the word " German " from its title in 1869) has fifty-five classes. It is represented in twenty-eight States and in the District of Columbia, and has many congregations in foreign mission fields. Half its organizations and considerably more than half its communicants are in the State of Pennsylvania. It is also particularly strong in the State of Ohio, Maryland ranking third. The total value of its church property is $7,975,583. Its 1510 organizations own 1304 edifices, with an average seating capacity of 410 and an average value of $6115. There are 61 halls, with accommodations for 6504.

SUMMARY BY STATES.

STATES.	Organizations.	Church Edifices.	Seating Capacity.	Value of Church Property.	Communicants.
California	3	2	300	$11,000	68
Colorado.	1	1	250	20,000	35
Connecticut	1	1	450	18,000	150
Delaware	1	1	200	2,000	69
Dist. of Columbia.	2	2	375	31,000	301
Illinois............	30	25½	7,500	73,200	1,783
Indiana..........	60	56	16,080	231,775	6,269
Iowa	34	31	7,635	66,350	2,513
Kansas	25	14	3,257	49,900	984
Kentucky	10	6	1,630	37,500	1,350
Maryland	67	63	27,320	484,225	10,741
Massachusetts	1	1	450	56,000	62
Michigan	17	12	3,675	47,900	1,013
Minnesota.	10	8	,511	17,820	730
Missouri	11	7	1,475	18,800	586
Nebraska	14	10	1,500	14,100	968
New Jersey.......	5	5	1,309	23,800	830
New York........	13	13	5,850	204,200	3,432
North Carolina ...	39	36	14,150	49,000	2,903
North Dakota	3	1	200	600	161
Ohio	294	283	89,879	1,128,275	35,846
Oregon	10	6	1,000	29,300	298
Pennsylvania	754	618	322,173	5,121,328	122,944
South Dakota	16	13	2,700	11,750	1,000
Tennessee	3	3	450	2,500	236
Virginia	20	22	7,260	44,800	1,819
Washington......	5	4	550	11,410	167
West Virginia	6	5	1,850	25,300	794
Wisconsin........	55	54½	13,275	143,750	5,966
Total.	1,510	1,304	534,254	$7,975,583	204,018

SUMMARY BY CLASSES.

CLASSES.	Organi- zations.	Church Edifices.	Seating Ca- pacity.	Value of Church Property.	Com- muni- cants.
Allegheny........	13	13	4,502	$124,100	1,767
Carlisle..........	21	17½	6,780	82,900	2,212
Chicago.........	7	7	2,050	35,500	645
Cincinnati........	18	18	7,030	216,100	3,635
Clarion..........	29	26½	8,740	74,600	2,999
Eastern Ohio.....	28	23½	8,950	46,600	3,389
East Pennsylvania.	49	31	27,690	393,450	10,021
East Susquehanna.	45	31½	18,600	187,000	4,751
Erie.............	27	27	7,369	136,500	4,521
German Maryland.	8	7	3,625	94,525	2,463
German Philadelp'a	18	18	9,539	376,800	6,116
Gettysburg.......	24	24	11,500	145,600	4,987
Goshenhoppen....	31	23	18,020	285,500	7,306
Heidelberg.......	27	33	8,735	114,000	4,642
Illinois...........	21	16	4,850	31,700	776
Indiana..........	31	27	6,550	138,450	3,530
Iowa............	18	15	4,050	25,500	846
Juniata..........	50	48	15,110	168,036	5,400
Kansas..........	15	9	2,250	31,700	678
Lancaster (Ohio)..	29	25	8,300	77,500	2,656
Lancaster (Penn.)	40	32	16,575	257,100	5,508
Lebanon..........	54	33	30,650	180,300	11,456
Lehigh..........	35	37	20,750	408,100	9,208
Lincoln..........	4	2	400	11,200	169
Maryland........	57	55	23,220	412,500	8,112
Mercersburg......	25	23½	9,945	134,667	3,029
Miami...........	55	54	17,539	176,300	5,678
Milwaukee.......	20	20	5,320	57,650	2,611
Minnesota.......	21	19	3,536	37,420	1,450
Missouri.........	9	6	1,075	6,800	541
Nebraska........	14	11	1,750	34,100	973
New York........	8	8	3,320	215,200	1,871
North Carolina....	39	36	14,150	49,000	2,903
Philadelphia......	30	28½	12,225	509,600	5,454
Portland (Oregon).	18	12	1,850	51,710	533
Saint John's......	24	22½	7,475	111,550	4,440
Saint Joseph's....	42	33	10,825	100,600	2,332
Saint Paul's......	20	19½	5,750	84,000	2,585
Schuylkill........	45	32	21,490	517,900	11,282
Sheboygan.......	28	28	6,805	74,600	3,007
Somerset.........	36	33	8,926	100,650	3,169
South Dakota.....	16	14	2,900	12,350	1,098
Tiffin............	34	31	9,186	104,750	2,396

SUMMARY BY CLASSES.—*Continued.*

CLASSES.	Organizations.	Church Edifices.	Seating Capacity.	Value of Church Property.	Communicants.
Tohickon	39	24½	21,235	$257,350	7,636
Tuscarawas.......	45	42	13,650	144,500	4,665
Ursinus..........	12	10	2,360	24,050	1,306
Virginia	24	26	8,560	64,100	2,283
Westmoreland....	31	28	10,550	200,400	3,962
West New York...	9	9	4,350	86,000	2,583
West Pennsylvania	6	6	1,925	23,300	905
West Susquehanna	50	39½	14,840	182,000	4,236
Wichita..........	12	6	1,407	30,200	351
Wyoming.........	37	34	12,070	179,250	5,257
Zion's (Ind.)......	28	28	7,205	90,600	3,435
Zion's (Penn.)	34	22	16,200	259,725	4,254
Total.	1,510	1,304	534,254	$7,975,583	204,018

3.—THE CHRISTIAN REFORMED CHURCH.

This body is a branch of an organization of the same name in Holland. In 1835 there was a secession from the Reformed Church of Holland of ministers and others who were dissatisfied with the prevailing tone of the doctrinal teaching of the State church and with some features of its government. This was the origin of the Christian Reformed Church of Holland. It has been represented in this country many years. In 1882 its numbers were increased by a secession of ministers and members of the particular synod of Chicago, Reformed (Dutch) Church, because of the refusal of the general synod of the latter body to denounce freemasonry and to make connection with that order a subject of church discipline. Finding the position of the Christian Reformed Church more to their mind, they united with it. In 1889 the church was still further increased by the accession of a number of congregations belonging to the True Reformed Church, organized in 1822 by a number of ministers who had seceded from the Reformed Dutch Church.

The Christian Reformed Church has seven classes and one synod. Connected with the classes are 99 organizations, with 106 edifices, valued at $428,500, and 12,470 communicants. More than half of the latter are to be found in the State of Michigan. The average value of the church edifices is $4042, and the average seating capacity 318. There are 4 halls, with accommodations for 200 persons.

SUMMARY BY STATES.

STATES.	Organizations.	Church Edifices.	Seating Capacity.	Value of Church Property.	Communicants.
Illinois............	7	8	2,250	$29,000	782
Indiana...........	1	2	300	3,000	320
Iowa..............	6	6	1,950	19,000	623
Kansas...........	2	2	225	3,000	109
Michigan.........	44	52	19,380	174,100	7,782
Minnesota........	4	1	100	800	93
Nebraska.........	2	1	100	1,200	96
New Jersey.......	13	14	4,725	115,500	1,323
New York.........	8	8	1,995	48,800	313
North Dakota......	1	1	125	500	37
Ohio.............	3	3	750	19,500	253
South Dakota.....	4	4	830	6,000	289
Wisconsin........	4	4	1,025	8,100	450
Total.........	99	106	33,755	$428,500	12,470

SUMMARY BY CLASSES.

CLASSES.					
Grand Rapids.....	16	18	8,630	$85,900	2,900
Hackensack.......	13	14	4,245	127,500	531
Holland..........	17	19	6,340	47,500	3,088
Hudson..........	8	8	2,475	36,800	1,105
Illinois............	12	13	3,725	49,100	1,637
Iowa.............	20	17	3,530	33,500	1,292
Muskegon.........	13	17	4,810	48,200	1,917
Total.........	99	106	33,755	$428,500	12,470

SUMMARY BY STATES OF ALL REFORMED BODIES.

STATES.	Organizations.	Church Edifices.	Seating Capacity.	Value of Church Property.	Communicants.
California	3	2	300	$11,000	68
Colorado.........	1	1	250	20,000	35
Connecticut	1	1	450	18,000	150
Delaware.........	1	1	200	2,000	69
Dist. of Columbia .	2	2	375	31,000	301
Illinois...........	62	61	19,645	272,000	5,385
Indiana..........	64	61	17,080	243,775	6,761
Iowa	66	65	17,689	176,250	5,741
Kansas..........	29	18	3,882	55,400	1,139
Kentucky	10	6	1,630	37,500	1,350
Maryland	67	63	27,320	484,225	10,741
Massachusetts	1	1	450	56,000	62
Michigan.........	106	114	40,284	484,800	15,404
Minnesota........	17	12	2,361	28,620	968
Missouri	11	7	1,475	18,800	586
Nebraska	20	14	2,560	22,800	1,408
New Jersey.......	142	174	71,749	2,230,329	26,210
New York.........	323	379	150,225	7,698,280	55,973
North Carolina ...	39	36	14,150	49,000	2,903
North Dakota	6	4	530	1,850	287
Ohio	299	288	91,229	1,155,875	36,255
Oregon	10	6	1,000	29,300	298
Pennsylvania	762	628	327,103	5,299,828	124,700
South Dakota	35	31	6,429	41,650	1,883
Tennessee........	3	3	450	2,500	236
Virginia	20	22	7,260	44,800	1,819
Washington......	5	4	550	11,410	167
West Virginia	6	5	1,850	25,300	794
Wisconsin........	70	71	17,725	191,950	7,765
Total.	2,181	2,080	825,931	$18,744,242	309,458

CHAPTER XXXIV.

THE SALVATION ARMY.

THIS body was organized in London, England, in 1876, by William Booth. He had been engaged for several years previously in evangelistic work in the east of London, chiefly among those who were beyond the reach of ordinary religious influences. He was formerly a minister of the Methodist New Connection, withdrawing from the regular ministry in 1861 for independent evangelistic work. The new organization was speedily introduced into various countries of Europe, into the United States, Australia, and elsewhere.

In doctrine the Salvation Army is thoroughly evangelical. Its teachings are given in a book which has been prepared by the "general" of the Army, Mr. Booth. This book of doctrine and discipline sets forth the ordinary doctrines respecting God and Christ; the sinfulness of man; the work of redemption; the atonement, which is described as general; election, of which the Arminian view is taken; the Holy Ghost; repentance and faith as conditions of salvation; the forgiveness of sins; conversion; the two natures of man; assurance, setting forth the Methodist view; sanctification, which is emphasized as one of the more important doctrines. Entire sanctification is described as a "complete deliverance." "Sin is destroyed out of the soul, and all the powers, faculties, possessions, and influences of the soul are given up to the service and glory of

340

God." No fewer than seven sections of the Book of Discipline are given to the doctrine of sanctification; backsliding also forms a section, and so also do final perseverance, " death and after," hell, the Bible, and baptism. The Army recognizes women's right to preach, and full directions are given how to proceed " in getting men saved."

The government is military in form, and military titles are used in designating the various officers, and military terms in describing the various departments of the work. The officers are: (1) the commander-in-chief, who has the general direction of the entire army; (2) the chief of staff, who has the oversight of all the business at the war office, known as headquarters; (3) a lieutenant-general, who travels under the direction of the commander-in-chief and inspects various divisions; (4) a general, who has command of a division; (5) a captain, who commands a single corps; (6) a lieutenant, who is under the direction of the captain; (7) a color sergeant, who has charge of the colors and carries them in procession; (8) a paymaster-sergeant, or treasurer, who cares for all the moneys of a corps; (9) a paymaster-secretary. There are also sergeants who lead bands, and there are various other officers. The sergeants are appointed by the captains. The treasurers and secretaries are recommended for appointment to the generals of divisions, and the commissions are issued by the general-in-chief. The term of office is indefinite.

All members of the Salvation Army on active duty wear a uniform. The places where meetings are regularly held are usually called " barracks."

The Salvation Army in the United States is represented in thirty States, also in the territory of Utah and the District of Columbia. It has 329 organizations, with 27 church edifices, or barracks, which are valued at $38,150. Of halls, etc., 300, with a seating capacity of 87,101, are occupied. There are in all 8742 communicants or members. It is not the chief aim of the army to make converts for membership in its own organization. Many of those who are converted through its labors join various other denominations.

SUMMARY BY STATES.

STATES.	Organizations.	Church Edifices.	Seating Capacity.	Value of Church Property.	Communicants.
California	29	3	1,500	$9,188	340
Colorado	10	1	700	2,000	214
Connecticut	6	2	600	2,235	203
Delaware	1	..	.....	......	153
District of Columbia.	1	..	.....	......	23
Illinois.............	28	1	250	......	922
Indiana	4	..	.....	......	104
Iowa	16	..	.....	......	397
Kansas	12	..	.....	......	307
Maine	9	..	.....	......	265
Maryland	7	4	2,025	5,130	213
Massachusetts	14	1	1,300	1,000	656
Michigan	28	5	1,720	7,575	1,099
Minnesota..........	13	3	1,110	800	460
Missouri	12	..	.....	......	340
Montana...........	3	..	.....	......	30
Nebraska	1	..	.....	......	19
New Hampshire.....	1	..	.....	......	26
New Jersey.........	4	..	.....	......	156
New York..........	32	..	.....	......	625
North Carolina	2	2	1,000	2,200	59
Ohio	30	1	150	875	655
Oregon	3	..	.....	......	44
Pennsylvania	30	3	1,250	5,997	772
Rhode Island.......	2	..	.....	......	31
South Dakota	2	..	.....	......	41
Texas	4	..	.....	......	35
Utah	1	..	.....	......	4
Virginia	3	1	450	1,150	54
Washington........	5	..	.....	......	156
West Virginia	2	..	.....	......	7
Wisconsin	14	..	.....	......	322
Total..........	329	27	12,055	$38,150	8,742

SUMMARY BY DIVISIONS.

DIVISIONS.	Organizations.	Church Edifices.	Seating Capacity.	Value of Church Property.	Communicants.
Colorado and Wyoming	10	1	700	$2,000	214
Central	22	..	....	....	538
East Pennsylvania	16	3	1,250	5,997	405
Iowa and Dakota	18	..	....	....	438
Illinois and Indiana	22	..	....	....	759
Kansas, Missouri, and Nebraska	25	..	....	....	666
Massachusetts, Connecticut, and Rhode Island	22	3	1,900	3,235	890
Maine and New Hampshire	10	..	....	....	291
Michigan	28	5	1,720	7,575	1,099
New York State	16	..	....	....	284
Northwestern	37	4	1,360	800	1,049
Ohio	32	1	150	875	662
Pittsburg and West Pennsylvania	12	..	....	....	326
Pacific Coast	41	3	1,500	9,188	574
Southern	14	7	3,475	8,480	502
Texas	4	..	....	....	35
Total	329	27	12,055	$38,150	8,742

CHAPTER XXXV.

THE SCHWENKFELDERS.

KASPAR VON SCHWENKFELD, a nobleman of Germany, born in the fifteenth century, differed from other Reformers of the period on a number of points concerning the Lord's Supper, the efficacy of the external Word, and Christ's human nature. He did not form a separate sect, but his followers did so after his death, taking his name. Early in the eighteenth century they were scattered by persecution. Some fled to Denmark, whence they came to this country near the close of the first half of that century. They settled in Pennsylvania, where a remnant of them still exist. They celebrate the arrival from Denmark annually, making it a kind of festival.

They hold in general to the doctrines of the German Reformation, with a few peculiarities. The words of Christ, " This is my body," they interpret as meaning, " My body is this," i.e., such as this bread, which is broken and consumed, and affords true and real food for the soul. The external Word, as they believe, has no power to renew ; only the internal Word, which is Christ himself. The human nature of Christ was not a created substance. Being associated with the divine essence, it had a majestic dignity of its own.

Among the customs peculiar to the Schwenkfelders is a service of prayer and exhortation over newly born infants, repeated in church when the mother and child appear. The churches are Congregational in government, each electing its minister and officers annually. The former is chosen by lot.

SUMMARY.

STATE.	Organizations.	Church Edifices.	Seating Capacity.	Value of Church Property.	Communicants.
Pennsylvania	4	6	1,925	$12,200	306

CHAPTER XXXVI.

THE SOCIAL BRETHREN CHURCH.

THIS is a small body of about twenty congregations in Arkansas and Illinois, which had its beginning in 1867. In that year a number of members of various bodies, whose views concerning certain passages of Scripture and certain points of discipline were not in harmony with the churches to which they belonged, came together and organized a church and subsequently an association of churches. In 1887 a discipline, containing a statement of doctrine and rules for the government of the churches and the ordination of ministers, was adopted. The Confession of Faith, which consists of ten articles, sets forth the commonly received doctrine of the Trinity, the Holy Scriptures, the evangelical doctrine of redemption, regeneration, and sanctification, declaring that he that endures unto the end the same shall be saved; holding that baptism and the Lord's Supper are ordinances made binding by Christ, and none but true believers are the proper subjects. Three modes of administering baptism are recognized, and candidates are allowed to choose between them. The eighth, ninth, and tenth articles declare the right of lay members to free suffrage and free speech, that candidates shall be received into full membership by the voice of the church, and that ministers are called to preach the gospel, and not to preach politics or anything else. The associations correspond in general usage to Baptist associations. There are two classes in the ministry, ordained and licensed, also exhorters and stewards, as in the Methodist churches, and ordained deacons, as in the Baptist. It is quite evident that the denomination was originally formed of Baptists and Methodists, the ideas of both these denominations and some of their usages being incorporated in the new body.

There are 20 organizations, with 11 edifices, valued at $8700, and 913 members; 6 halls, with accommodations for 600, are occupied.

SUMMARY BY STATES.

STATES.	Organi- zations.	Church Edifices.	Seating Ca- pacity.	Value of Church Property.	Com- muni- cants.
Arkansas..........	4	1	800	$1,000	83
Illinois............	16	10	7,900	7,700	830
Total	20	11	8,700	$8,700	913

SUMMARY BY ASSOCIATIONS.

ASSOCIATIONS.					
Northw'n Arkansas.	4	1	800	$1,000	83
Southern Illinois ...	10	8	7,100	6,900	675
Wabash..........	6	2	800	800	155
Total.........	20	11	8,700	$8,700	913

CHAPTER XXXVII.

THE SOCIETY FOR ETHICAL CULTURE.

THIS society was founded in New York in 1876 by Prof. Felix Adler. It was announced as " the new religion of morality, whose God is The Good, whose church is the universe, whose heaven is here on earth, and not in the clouds." Its aims have been thus defined by Professor Adler:

" I. To teach the supremacy of the moral ends above all other human ends and interests.

" II. To teach that the moral law has an immediate authority not contingent on the truth of religious beliefs or of philosophical theories.

" III. To advance the science and art of right living."

Meetings are held on Sunday, at which addresses or lectures are delivered. Societies having been organized in Chicago, Philadelphia, and St. Louis, as well as in New York, a convention was held in 1886, and " The Union of the Societies for Ethical Culture" formed, with a constitution calling for annual meetings. The four societies report an aggregate of 1064 members. The New York society has a cash fund in hand of $60,000. The 5 halls occupied have a seating capacity of 6260.

In connection with the New York Society considerable educational and philanthropic work is carried on, both by men and women, who seek the necessitous and endeavor both to relieve and elevate them, and also to prepare them to get their own living.

SUMMARY BY STATES.

STATES.	Organizations.	Church Edifices.	Seating Capacity.	Value of Church Property.	Communicants.
Illinois	1	..	....	....	175
Missouri	1	..	....	....	150
New York	1	..	....	....	600
Pennsylvania	1	..	....	....	139
Total	4	..	....	....	1,064

CHAPTER XXXVIII.

THE SPIRITUALISTS.

WHAT is known as modern spiritualism began with "demonstrations" in the Fox family in Hydesville, N. Y., in March, 1848. The same phenomena had been common in Shaker communities before that date, and, indeed, in almost all ages and among many different peoples; but it was then that these demonstrations, generally in the form of rappings, began to be interpreted as communications from the disembodied spirits of men and women who had, in the ordinary course of nature, passed away, but whose spirits were still in a living and active state. From this time individuals began to investigate these spirit manifestations, circles began to be formed, mediums were discovered, lecturers recognized, and a literature established.

Spiritualists claim that the miracles of Christ are explained by the central doctrine of their belief, and they regard the demonstrations of spiritualism as establishing by evidence the fact of a future life. They do not hold that God is a personal being, but that he exists in all things. Eternal progression is the law of the spirit world, and every individual will attain supreme wisdom and unalloyed happiness.

A few spiritualist societies employ permanent speakers, but usually they appoint lecturers for limited terms, varying from a week to several months. A large proportion of the lecturers are mediums, who are believed to speak under the influence or direction of the spirit who guides or controls them. They follow the Scriptural injunction: "Take no thought how or what ye shall speak, for it shall be given you in that same hour what ye shall speak." When a lecturer appears before an audience, therefore, he asks that a subject be given him, and when he receives it begins to speak upon it without hesitation. Summer gatherings or camp meetings, which continue from one to ten weeks, have become prominent among the spiritualists. In 1891 twenty-two such meetings were held.

The spiritualists report 334 organizations, with 30 regular church edifices, not including halls, pavilions, and other places owned or occupied by them. There are 45,030 members, and the value of the property reported, which includes camp grounds as well as church edifices, pavilions, etc., is $573,650. Not many of the halls are owned by them. There are members in thirty-six States, besides the District of Columbia and the Territories of Oklahoma and Utah. Among the States Massachusetts has the greatest number, 7345; New York stands second, with 6351; and Pennsylvania third, with 4569. There are 307 halls, with accommodations for 72,522.

SUMMARY BY STATES.

STATES.	Organizations.	Church Edifices.	Seating Capacity.	Value of Church Property.	Communicants.
Arkansas............	1	1	300	$1,000	25
California	20	1	250	19,325	1,869
Colorado..........	2	..	....	600	275
Connecticut	19	4	1,650	20,810	2,354
District of Columbia	3	..	....	......	475
Florida	2	..	....	750	65
Georgia...........	2	..	....	......	169

SUMMARY BY STATES.—*Continued.*

STATES.	Organi-zations.	Church Edifices.	Seating Ca-pacity.	Value of Church Property.	Com-muni-cants.
Illinois............	7	1	350	$10,500	1,314
Indiana...........	5	..	....	4,850	715
Iowa	13	..	....	23,075	2,613
Kansas	9	..	....	......	627
Kentucky	1	..	....	......	300
Louisiana	3	..	....	400	120
Maine	21	..	....	15,650	2,562
Maryland	6	..	....	......	665
Massachusetts	61	4	4,250	269,710	7,345
Michigan	27	1	500	11,500	2,565
Minnesota.........	3	..	....	......	500
Missouri	5	3	2,500	13,100	853
Montana..........	1	..	....	......	20
Nebraska	4	..	....	......	290
New Hampshire ...	6	..	....	......	672
New Jersey........	2	..	....	......	100
New York.........	34	1	1,500	33,250	6,351
Ohio	25	2	1,000	3,350	2,174
Oklahoma.........	1	..	....	......	26
Oregon	6	..	....	930	751
Pennsylvania	12	7	5,650	58,600	4,569
Rhode Island......	4	..	....	......	150
South Carolina	1	..	....	......	20
Tennessee.........	6	4	2,000	36,000	1,075
Texas	1	..	....	......	29
Utah	1	..	....	......	80
Vermont..........	10	1	500	23,250	1,966
Virginia	1	..	....	......	12
Washington	4	..	....	......	565
West Virginia	1	..	....	......	65
Wisconsin.........	3	..	....	27,000	354
Wyoming..........	1	..	....	......	50
Total	334	30	20,450	$573,650	45,030

CHAPTER XXXIX.

THE THEOSOPHICAL SOCIETY.

THE first branch of this society in the United States was founded in New York in November, 1875. Its declared objects are :

" First, to form a nucleus of a Universal Brotherhood of Humanity, without distinction of race, creed, or color.

" Second, to promote the study of Aryan and other Eastern literatures, religions, and sciences, and demonstrate the importance of that study.

" Third, to investigate unexplained laws of nature and the psychical powers latent in man.".

A circular, issued for the information of inquirers by the general secretary of the American section, states that the society is unsectarian and interferes with no person's religious belief. Another circular, entitled "An Epitome of Theosophy," issued by the secretary of the executive committee of the Pacific Coast, states that some of the fundamental propositions of Theosophy, or " Wisdom Religion," are : That the spirit in man is the only real and permanent portion of his being; that between the spirit and the intellect is a " plane of consciousness in which experiences are noted," and that this spiritual nature is " as susceptible of culture as the body or intellect " ; that spiritual culture is only attainable as the grosser interests and passions of the flesh are subordinate ; that men, systematically trained,

353

may, by their interior faculties, " attain to clear insight into the immaterial, spiritual world "; that, as a result of this spiritual training, men become able to perform works usually called " miraculous."

The Theosophical Society has branches in seventeen States and the District of Columbia. Forty organizations are reported, with 695 members. Of the 40 organizations 14 are in California. There are 38 halls, with accommodations for 1815.

SUMMARY BY STATES.

STATES.	Organizations.	Church Edifices.	Seating Capacity.	Value of Church Property.	Communicants.
California	14	1	200	$500	216
Connecticut	1	..	. . .	. . . .	13
District of Columbia	1	..	. . .	75	9
Illinois	2	..	. . .	. . . .	68
Indiana	1	..	. . .	. . . .	5
Iowa	2	..	. . .	. . . .	48
Louisiana	1	..	. . .	. . . .	10
Maryland	1	..	. . .	. . . .	5
Massachusetts	2	..	. . .	. . . .	57
Michigan	1	..	. . .	. . . .	8
Minnesota	1	..	. . .	. . . .	10
Missouri	2	..	. . .	. . . .	13
Nebraska	4	..	. . .	. . . .	41
New York	2	..	. . .	. . . .	97
Ohio	2	..	. . .	. . . .	52
Pennsylvania	1	..	. . .	. . . .	25
Washington	1	..	. . .	25	9
Wisconsin	1	..	. . .	. . . .	9
Total	40	1	200	$600	695

CHAPTER XL.

THE UNITED BRETHREN.

THE United Brethren in Christ are sometimes con-founded with the *Unitas Fratrum* or Moravian Brethren. Though some of the historians of the former body claim that it was connected in some way with the Ancient and Renewed Brethren of Bohemia and Moravia, the United Brethren in Christ and the Moravians are wholly separate and distinct, and have no actual historical relations. The Moravians were represented in this country long before the United Brethren in Christ arose, which was about the year 1800.

Philip William Otterbein, a native of Prussia and a min-ister of the German Reformed Church, and Martin Boehm, a Mennonite pastor in Pennsylvania, of Swiss descent, were the chief founders of the church of the United Brethren in Christ. These men, preaching with great earnestness and fervency, had revivals of religion in Pennsylvania and Maryland, resulting in many accessions to membership of the churches they served. Others of like mind assisted them in the ministry, and they met occasionally in con-ference concerning their work. The first of these informal conferences was held in Baltimore, Md., in 1789. The movement, though meeting with some opposition, gradu-ally developed into a separate denomination. At a con-ference held in Frederick County, Md., in 1800, attended by Otterbein, Boehm, Geeting, Newcomer, and nine others, an organization was formed under the title " United Brethren in Christ," and Otterbein and Boehm were elected superintendents or bishops. The preachers increased and new churches arose, and it soon became necessary to have two annual conferences, the second one being formed in the State of Ohio. In 1815 the denomination completed its organization by the adoption at a general conference of a discipline, rules of order, and a confession of faith. For some years the work of the church was mainly among the German element. It still has German conferences, but the great bulk of its members are English-speaking people.

In doctrine, practice, and usage the United Brethren are Methodistic. They have classes and class leaders, stewards, exhorters, local and itinerant preachers, presiding elders, circuits, quarterly and annual conferences, and other Methodist features. Their founders were in fraternal intercourse with the fathers of American Methodism, and in spirit and purpose the two bodies were not dissimilar. The United Brethren, though not historically a Methodist branch, affiliate with the Methodist churches, sending representatives to the œcumenical Methodist conferences.

Their annual conferences are composed of itinerant and local preachers, and lay delegates representing the churches. The bishops preside in turn over these conferences, and in conjunction with a committee of presiding elders and preachers fix the appointments of the preachers for the ensuing year. The pastoral term is three years, but in particular cases it may be extended with the consent of the conference. There is but one order among the ordained preachers, that of elder. Since 1889 it has been lawful to license and ordain women. Bishops are elected by the general conference, not to life service, but for a quadrennium. They are, however, eligible to reëlection. The general conference, which is composed of ministerial and lay delegates, elected by the annual conferences, meets once in every four years, and has full authority, under certain constitutional restrictions, to legislate for the whole church, to hear and decide appeals, etc.

Their doctrines, which are Arminian, are expressed in a confession of faith, consisting of thirteen brief articles, which set forth the generally accepted view of the Father, Son, and Holy Ghost, the Scriptures, justification and regeneration, the Christian Sabbath, and the future state. Concerning the sacraments, it holds that baptism and the Lord's Supper should be observed by all Christians, but the mode of baptism and the manner of celebrating the Lord's Supper should be left to the judgment of individuals. The baptism of children is also left to the choice of parents. Sanctification is described as the " work of God's grace through the word and the Spirit, by which those who have been born again are separated in their acts, words, and thoughts from sin and are enabled to live unto God."

I.—THE UNITED BRETHREN IN CHRIST.

The confession, first adopted in 1815, was revised in 1889 and slightly enlarged. The constitution was also changed in the same year, resulting in a division, those who held that the changes were not effected in a constitutional way withdrawing from the general conference of 1889 and holding a separate session. The latter hold to the unchanged confession and constitution, and insist that they are the legal body known as the United Brethren in

Christ. Many cases to settle the validity of the action of the general conference of 1889 have been before the courts, and considerable church property is involved in the final decision, which may not be reached for some years to come. As both bodies claim the same title, it has been deemed necessary to put after it, in parentheses, in one case, for the sake of distinction, the words "old constitution." This designates the smaller body, which refuses to recognize the constitutionality of the revision.

The general conference of 1885 created a commission to revise the confession of faith and the constitution, expressing at the same time its opinion that two clauses in the existing constitution, one forbidding the changing of or doing away with the confession, and the other likewise forbidding any change in the constitution except upon "request of two thirds of the whole society," were "in their language and apparent meaning so far-reaching as to render them extraordinary and impracticable as articles of constitutional law." The commission submitted a revised confession and constitution to the churches, as directed, for their approval. A number of members of the general conference of 1885 protested against the act creating the commission as unconstitutional and revolutionary. When the work of the commission was submitted for approval they and those who agreed with them refused to vote on it, insisting that the matter was not legally before the church. Of those who voted, more than two thirds approved the revised documents, and they were accordingly formally proclaimed by the general conference of 1889 as the "fundamental belief and organic law of the church." The vote of the conference was 111 to 21. When the chairman announced that the conference would proceed under the amended constitution, Bishop Milton Wright and eleven delegates withdrew to meet elsewhere for legislation under the old constitution. The majority claim that the constitution of 1841 was never submitted to the members of conferences or of the church, but was adopted by the general conference only.

Two important changes were made in the constitution, one admitting laymen to the general conference, and one modifying the section prohibiting membership in secret societies. The old constitution had this section: "There shall be no connection with secret combinations." The new constitution modifies this by providing that all secret combinations which infringe upon the rights of others and whose principles are injurious to the Christian character of their members are contrary to the Word of God, and Christians should have no connection with them. The new section also empowers the general conference to enact "rules of discipline concerning such combinations."

There are in this country 45 annual conferences; also, one in Canada, and mission districts in Africa and Germany. The denomination is not represented in any of the New England States, nor in any of the States south of Virginia, Tennessee, and Missouri. It is strongest in members in the three States of Ohio (47,678), Indiana (35,824), and Pennsylvania (33,951). Its total membership is 202,-474, divided among 3731 organizations, with 2836 church edifices, valued at $4,292,643. The average seating capacity of the edifices is 288, and the average value $1513. There are 780 halls, with accommodations for 93,035.

SUMMARY BY STATES.

STATES.	Organizations.	Church Edifices.	Seating Capacity.	Value of Church Property.	Communicants.
California	24	15	3,825	$28,400	588
Colorado..........	18	8	1,800	32,800	585
Idaho..............	2	...	.....	......	100
Illinois............	320	245	67,495	260,075	15,429
Indiana	569	476	154,762	551,636	35,824
Iowa	213	148	29,810	211,323	10,401
Kansas	322	128½	33,200	183,770	13,768
Kentucky	13	11	2,400	4,700	567
Maryland	57	55	14,300	113,789	4,736
Michigan	138	93	27,405	133,250	5,201
Minnesota.........	35	23	4,975	23,375	803
Missouri	105	45½	14,150	47,825	4,361
Nebraska	147	75	16,775	84,950	5,673
New York.........	35	23	5,975	34,650	953
Ohio	745	692	205,755	1,198,870	47,678
Oregon	13	8	2,100	11,100	493
Pennsylvania	526	467	147,036	1,086,135	33,951
South Dakota	27	7	1,175	4,150	493
Tennessee.........	27	18	5,600	13,985	1,141
Virginia	71	66	11,500	65,940	5,306
Washington	18	13	3,400	22,000	494
West Virginia	259	175	54,170	140,645	12,242
Wisconsin.........	47	45	8,850	39,275	1,687
Total	3,731	2,837	816,458	$4,292,643	202,474

SUMMARY BY CONFERENCES.

CONFERENCES.					
Allegheny.........	153	135	41,375	$323,475	9,709
Arkansas Valley ...	74	28	7,090	48,500	4,100
Auglaize	125	116½	39,150	145,150	6,187
California	24	15	3,825	28,400	588
Central Illinois	62	52½	15,590	67,900	3,052
Central Ohio	68	66	20,845	91,850	4,076
Colorado	18	8	1,800	32,800	585
Des Moines	99	61½	15,000	82,070	4,521
East German	83	77½	25,925	208,700	5,715
East Nebraska.....	67	49½	11,075	66,200	3,807
East Ohio	127	124	32,900	204,570	8,531
East Pennsylvania..	76	73	23,661	227,700	7,030
Elkhorn and Dakota	39	12	1,800	3,700	743
Erie	117	83	21,025	100,435	3,552

SUMMARY BY CONFERENCES.—*Continued.*

CONFERENCES.	Organi-zations.	Church Edifices.	Seating Ca-pacity.	Value of Church Property.	Com-muni-cants.
Illinois.............	69	61	20,500	$72,950	2,784
Indiana...........	174	116	52,000	92,885	9,180
Iowa	114	86	14,810	129,253	5,880
Kansas	97	36½	9,835	47,700	3,051
Kentucky	12	10	2,250	3,500	507
Lower Wabash	164	113	26,630	74,225	9,547
Maryland	39	38	9,150	62,889	3,236
Miami	101	94	30,700	303,950	10,957
Michigan	39	30	9,155	45,900	1,213
Minnesota.........	42	25	5,350	25,425	910
Missouri	67	33½	10,400	34,775	2,927
Neosho	96	39½	10,675	45,700	3,763
North Michigan ...	56	24	8,000	25,950	2,499
North Ohio........	109	96½	28,385	142,550	4,206
Northwest Kansas..	54	22½	5,300	40,270	2,794
Ohio German......	46	43½	8,400	100,450	2,317
Oregon	14	7	1,800	7,900	284
Parkersburg	206	144	48,115	116,095	10,377
Pennsylvania	148	137	45,625	311,375	10,234
Rock River........	29	25½	3,100	40,450	1,104
Saint Joseph	144	130	41,947	206,315	10,112
Sandusky	122	115	37,775	252,560	7,424
Scioto	148	130½	35,550	92,990	8,510
South Missouri	38	12	3,750	13,050	1,434
Tennessee	27	18	5,600	13,985	1,141
Upper Wabash	83	75	21,875	83,175	6,654
Virginia...........	127	99	18,355	91,490	7,346
Walla Walla	19	14	3,700	25,200	803
West Nebraska	60	17½	4,550	16,150	1,476
White River.......	108	96	23,265	102,811	5,921
Wisconsin.........	47	45	8,850	39,275	1,687
Total.........	3,731	2,837	816,458	$4,292,643	202,474

2.—THE UNITED BRETHREN IN CHRIST (OLD CON-STITUTION).

This body consists of those who hold that the act of the general conference of 1885, creating a commission to revise the confession of faith and constitution, was unconstitutional, and that all proceedings under it were null and void. Bishop Milton Wright and eleven delegates withdrew from the general conference of 1889 because of the announcement that its proceedings would conform to the revised constitution. They immediately convened in conference and proceeded to legislate and elect bishops and general church officers under the old constitution. The division, begun in this way, was soon widely extended, involving many of the conferences and placing the ownership and occupancy of much church property in dispute. The " Liberals," as the majority are called, continued in possession of the general church property and offices, and also of most of the churches and parsonages. The " Radicals," those who adhere to the old confession and constitution, have churches, ministers, and members in many of the conferences, the titles of which they have preserved. There are therefore two sets of conferences bearing the same names and covering the same territory. Many suits have been entered in the courts to test the control of the property involved. A final decision has not yet been reached. Those who adhere to the unamended constitution insist that the general conference of 1885 had no constitutional power to provide for the revision of the constitution and confession; that the general conference of 1889 had no right to act under the revised constitution, and that the existing constitution was and still is the organic law of the church. They maintain an exclusive attitude toward all secret societies, according to the provision of the old constitution forbidding connection with any of them.

When the statistics for the eleventh census were obtained, the line of division had not in all cases become distinct, and it was difficult to get returns from some of the districts. A number of presiding elders reported that much of the church property in their respective districts was in dispute, being claimed by both parties. In tabulating from the schedules returned by the presiding elders of each branch, care was taken not to count the same edifices and property twice. It is possible, however, that in some cases duplication has not been prevented.

The total number of members is 22,807, and there are 795 organizations. The average seating capacity of the church edifices is 302, and their average value $1116. There are 209 halls, with accommodations for 23,285.

SUMMARY BY STATES.

STATES.	Organizations.	Church Edifices.	Seating Capacity.	Value of Church Property.	Communicants.
California	9	6	1,595	$8,600	118
Illinois	39	33	7,895	33,400	1,193
Indiana	160	143	51,420	169,550	6,873
Iowa	23	20	6,900	19,200	272
Kansas	33	11	3,450	10,200	588
Michigan	164	90	25,325	119,550	5,602
Nebraska	29	8	3,730	10,600	358
Ohio	250	235	66,460	237,940	5,822
Oregon	49	20	5,505	24,700	1,203
South Dakota	6	4	800	2,300	109
Washington	29	8	1,600	8,900	606
Wisconsin	4	. .	. . . . .	. . . . . .	63
Total	795	578	174,680	$644,940	22,807

SUMMARY BY CONFERENCES.

CONFERENCES.

Arkansas Valley . . .	12	7	1,850	$6,400	232
Auglaize	126	121	40,450	135,990	2,800
California	9	5½	1,595	8,600	118
Central Illinois	19	16	3,905	17,700	369
East Des Moines . . .	19	16	5,950	15,700	142
East Nebraska	7	. .	. . . . . .	2,800	205

SUMMARY BY CONFERENCES.—*Continued.*

CONFERENCES.	Organizations.	Church Edifices.	Seating Capacity.	Value of Church Property.	Communicants.
Elkhorn and Dakota	15	6	930	$3,400	156
Indiana	10	2	800	2,000	180
Iowa	4	4	950	3,500	130
Kansas	15	4½	1,600	3,800	303
Michigan	58	35	9,900	56,200	2,192
Minnesota.........	2	1	200	400	23
North Michigan ...	82	34	11,350	40,250	2,388
North Ohio........	84	80⅓	16,465	84,850	3,356
Oregon	38	17¾	5,105	21,600	1,029
Rock River........	20	17	3,990	15,700	824
Sandusky	34	16½	3,760	15,200	565
Scioto	81	87½	23,775	73,100	1,685
Walla Walla	40	10	2,000	12,000	780
West Kansas	6	..	......	......	53
West Nebraska	11	5½	3,400	6,300	83
White River.......	99	91½	36,705	119,450	5,131
Wisconsin.........	4	..	......	......	63
Total	795	578	174,680	$644,940	22,807

The totals for the two bodies are as follows: organizations, 4526; edifices, 3415; seating capacity, 991,138; value of church property, $4,937,583; communicants, 225,281.

CHAPTER XLI.

UNITARIANISM, as its name indicates, is distinguished from other systems of Christian belief chiefly by its rejection of the doctrine of the Trinity and the deity of Jesus Christ. It denies that three persons—the Father, the Son, and the Holy Spirit—are united in one God, and holds that God is one, that he is *uni-*, not *tri-*personal. This view is not modern. Arius, a presbyter of Alexandria in the fourth century, held that Christ, though the greatest of created beings, was not equal in nature and dignity to God.

Unitarian organizations were formed in Poland and Hungary as early as the middle of the sixteenth century, and in the United States and England in the first quarter of the present century. King's Chapel, Boston, a Protestant Episcopal congregation, adopted in 1785 a liturgy so revised as to exclude all recognition of the Trinity, and ordained in 1787, as its pastor, on the refusal of the bishop of the diocese to do so, James Freeman, who was Unitarian in his views. Arian ideas began to influence ministers and laymen in the Congregational churches in New England at the beginning of the present century. In 1805 a Unitarian, Dr. Henry Ware, was elected to the divinity chair in Harvard University, and in 1819 a separate divinity school was organized in connection with the university with a Unitarian faculty.

Those holding Arian views became generally known as Unitarians in 1815, which is usually given as the beginning of the Unitarian denomination in America. In 1819 a Unitarian congregation was formed in Baltimore. William Ellery Channing preached the installation sermon, in which he clearly defined the differences between Orthodox and Unitarian doctrines. Many Congregational churches in eastern Massachusetts, including the oldest, that of Plymouth, the church founded by the Pilgrims in 1620, became Unitarian without changing their covenants or names. In the course of the controversy, 120 Congregational churches in New England, founded before the War of the Revolution, went over to the Unitarians. In 1830 there were, in all, 193 churches of the Unitarian faith; in 1865, 340. The present number is 421.

The Unitarians acknowledge no binding creed. They contend for the fullest liberty in belief, and exclude no one from their fellowship for difference in doctrinal views. Unitarianism is declared to be "not a fixed dogmatic statement, but a movement of ever-enlarging faith," welcoming "inquiry, progress, and diversity of individual thought in the unity of spiritual thought." In the denomination are included those who stand upon a simple basis of Theism, and are represented in the Western Unitarian Conference, for example, and those who accept the Messiahship of Jesus Christ. In general terms they believe in God as the All-in-All, " in eternal life as the great hope, in the inspiration of all truth, in man's great possibilities, and in the divineness of sanctified humanity."

The Unitarian churches are Congregational in polity, each congregation being independent in the management of its own affairs. There are societies for the conduct of missionary work, such as the American Unitarian Association, organized in 1825, the Western Unitarian Conference, which attends to the general interests of the societies represented in it, and the Western Unitarian Association, whose object is to " diffuse the knowledge and promote the interests of pure Christianity." There are also conferences, national and state and local. The national conference, which is biennial, declares in its constitution its " allegiance to the gospel of Jesus Christ " and its " desire to secure the largest unity of spirit and the widest practical coöperation " in the cause of Christian faith and work. It confines itself to recommending to existing Unitarian organizations " such undertaking and methods as it judges to be in the heart of the Unitarian denomination." It is composed of delegates from the churches and representatives of certain Unitarian organizations. The conference provides for a committee of fellowship, for the consideration of applications of persons not graduates of Unitarian schools to enter the Unitarian ministry.

The 421 organizations report 424 edifices, valued at $10,335,100, and with an aggregate seating capacity of 165,090. Of the 67,749 communicants, or, more properly, members, as the Unitarian custom is to admit any one to the communion, a little more than half are in Massachusetts. New York has the second largest number, 4470; California is third, with 3819; and New Hampshire fourth, with 3252. The denomination has organizations in thirty-two States and the District of Columbia. In the Southern States it has scarcely half a dozen churches.

The average value of its church edifices is very high, reaching $24,725; their average seating capacity, 389. There are 55 halls, with accommodations for 10,370.

SUMMARY BY STATES.

STATES.	Organizations.	Church Edifices.	Seating Capacity.	Value of Church Property.	Communicants
California	16	8	5,100	$366,040	3,819
Colorado..........	4	2	1,300	157,500	644
Connecticut	2	2	975	38,000	179
Delaware	1	1	250	14,000	60
District of Columbia	1	1	850	80,000	600
Georgia...........	1	1	300	10,000	75
Illinois............	16	15	5,650	406,000	1,932
Indiana	3	3	1,100	8,500	320
Iowa..............	10	9	2,500	83,100	1,238
Kansas	5	2	525	20,500	278
Kentucky	1	1	650	70,000	100
Louisiana	1	1	400	40,000	110
Maine	22	25	7,800	216,700	2,421
Maryland	2	3	1,450	107,000	603
Massachusetts	189	217	86,346	5,278,370	34,610
Michigan	12	13	4,850	168,500	1,904
Minnesota.........	12	9	2,750	126,600	1,349
Missouri	6	8	2,850	230,800	1,135
Nebraska	3	3	800	44,000	190
New Hampshire ...	26	25	9,386	357,200	3,252
New Jersey........	5	2	700	23,500	363
New York.........	18	22	9,423	1,117,500	4,470
North Dakota......	1	..	....	90	55
Ohio	5	3	1,350	80,000	907
Oregon	5	4	2,050	139,500	890
Pennsylvania	7	8	2,585	276,200	1,171
Rhode Island......	6	6	3,650	393,500	1,595
South Carolina	1	1	400	30,000	150
South Dakota	2	1	400	10,000	105
Tennessee	1	2	400	16,000	60
Vermont..........	9	8	2,480	112,500	968
Washington	12	4	1,570	75,000	802
Wisconsin.........	16	14	4,250	238,500	1,394
Total.........	421	424	165,090	$10,335,100	67,749

CHAPTER XLII.

THE UNIVERSALISTS.

THE first regular preacher in America of the distinctive doctrines of Universalism was Rev. John Murray, a disciple of James Relly, who had gathered a congregation of Universalists in London. The names of a number of ministers of different denominations are included in the list of those who held or published Universalist views before Murray arrived from England in 1770. Among these was Dr. George de Benneville, of Pennsylvania. Mr. Murray preached at various places, settling at Gloucester, Mass., in 1774, and at Boston in 1793. By him and a few others a number of Universalist churches were established. At the close of the eighteenth century there were about a score of Universalist ministers.

The Rev. Hosea Ballou, whose name is honored as the father of Universalism in its present form, became prominent in the movement at the beginning of the present century. His views differed radically from those of Mr. Murray. In a " Treatise on Atonement," published in 1795, he denied the doctrine of the vicarious sacrifice, and insisted that punishment for the sins of mortality is confined to this life. If there were any punishment in the future life it would be, he contended, for sins committed in that life. Some years later he expressed the belief that there is no sin beyond the grave and consequently no punishment. Mr.

Murray had held that Christ himself bore the punishment due the sins of mankind, and therefore there would be no further punishment. Of the early Universalists, Murray had been a Methodist, Winchester and Ballou Baptists.

There being quite a number of Universalists who held, contrary to the views of Mr. Ballou, to a limited future punishment, a division occurred in 1830, and an association was organized in the interests of the doctrine of restoration. This association existed for about eleven years and then became extinct; some of its preachers returning to the Universalist denomination, others becoming Unitarians. The Restorationists held that there would be a future retribution, but that God would, in his own time, " restore the whole family of mankind to holiness and happiness."

The symbol of the Universalist faith is the Winchester " Profession of Belief," which was adopted in 1803 by the New England Convention, held in Winchester, N. H. It is as follows:

"ARTICLE 1. We believe that the Holy Scriptures of the Old and New Testaments contain a revelation of the character of God, and of the duty, interest, and final destination of mankind.

"ARTICLE 2. We believe that there is one God, whose nature is love, revealed in one Lord Jesus Christ, by one Holy Spirit of Grace, who will finally restore the whole family of mankind to holiness and happiness.

"ARTICLE 3. We believe that holiness and true happiness are inseparably connected, and that believers ought to be careful to maintain order and practice good works; for these things are good and profitable unto men."

This profession of belief has remained unaltered since it was formulated. It is regarded as a sufficient general declaration of the fundamental doctrine of Universalists for the purpose of fellowship. A more particular knowledge of their general belief may be gathered from the utterances of leading Universalist writers.

Universalists believe that God is not only almighty, all-wise, and omniscient, but that he is perfectly holy. As a holy God he is hostile to sin. He forbade it at the first, has never consented to it, and can never be reconciled to it. His power, wisdom, goodness, and holiness are all pledges that there " shall be an end of it in the moral universe," and that " universal righteousness " shall be established. Sin is to be ended through the conversion and salvation of all sinners, who are to come ultimately into holiness and perfection. This is to be done by Jesus Christ, whose function it is to bring man into harmony with God. In Christ God has set forth in a single human life his great scheme of reconciliation. There was perfect harmony between this life and God; and Christ, the derived from the underived, most intimately shared the nature of God and represents him to man in complete fullness. There is no shadow of variance between Christ and God. Christ's work in the world is to bring men to light and strengthen the will in resolution against sin. He helps to overcome and destroy sin in the individual soul. Salvation is not from the demands of justice, nor from punishment, endless or otherwise. The demands of justice must be met, the consequences of sin cannot be avoided. It is the bondage of present sin from which salvation is necessary. Salvation is not exemption from the consequences of sin, but redemption from the disposition to sin; also from imperfection. Beginning with repentance and receiving God's forgiveness for past sins, the soul must put off the old man with all his sins and put on the new man created in God's likeness. Punishment is a necessary penalty for violated law. Divine punishment is "not the manifestation of hatred but the sign and instrument of love." The punishment of sin is its inevitable consequences—"the wounds, the damage, the shame which sin impresses" upon the individual consciousness. It is wholly within the soul. The purpose of punishment is to deter from sin and to recover from sin. It is therefore beneficent, whence it follows that it cannot be endless, for endless punishment would be vindictive and not beneficent. The soul is immortal. It survives death and enters upon the disembodied state in the same condition in which it quits the embodied. If it has been "dwarfed" in the present life "by neglect," or "weakened" by abuse, or "corrupted" by sin, then dwarfed, weakened, corrupt, it must enter the next life. Disciplinary processes will be continued in that life, and the soul that goes into it unrepentant must suffer the "thraldom or retribution" until the "will consents to the divine order." Even the penitent will be subject to "such discipline and chastening experiences as contribute to moral progress."

These are not to be taken as authoritative expressions of denominational belief. The Winchester Profession is the only acknowledged symbol. They simply represent the current teaching of the Universalist ministry. Probably some Universalists would differ from them in some respects.

The Universalist system of government is a modified Presbyterianism. The parish manages its own financial and general interests, and calls or dismisses a pastor; but it "acknowledges allegiance both to the State and general conventions, and is bound to observe the laws they enact."

No State conventions can be formed " without a constituency of at least four parishes." Such conventions exercise authority in their own territory under rules and limitations prescribed by the general convention. They are composed of all Universalist ministers in fellowship, and of lay delegates from the parishes. They meet every year.

The general convention, which is held in October biennially, consists of clerical and lay delegates from each State convention, in the proportion of one of the former to two of the latter. Every convention is entitled to send at least one clerical and two lay delegates. If it has fifty parishes and clergymen it can send twice as many delegates, with an additional three for every additional twenty-five parishes and clergymen. The general convention " exercises ecclesiastical authority throughout the United States and Canada. It is the court of final appeal in cases of dispute between State conventions, and in all cases of discipline not provided for and settled by subordinate bodies," and has original jurisdiction in States and Territories where subordinate conventions have not been organized. The general convention is an incorporated body and controls various denominational funds. Ministers are ordained by councils, consisting of ten ordained ministers and lay delegates from ten parishes, called by the parish desiring the ordination, with the consent of the convention (State) committee on fellowship, ordination, and discipline. There are also licentiates, both of the clerical and lay order.

Among the usages of the church is the observance of the second Sunday in June as " Children's Sunday." The churches are decorated with flowers and children are baptized. Christmas and Easter are generally observed, and a Sunday in October is set apart for services in memory of members who have died during the year. The sacraments observed are baptism and the Lord's Supper. The mode of baptism is left to the choice of the applicant.

There are forty State conventions, besides those of Canada and Scotland, the oldest of which, that of New York, was organized in 1825. New York leads in the number of members, reporting 8526; Massachusetts comes second, with 7142; Ohio third, with 4961; and Maine fourth, with 3750. The total of members is 49,194, and the aggregate value of church property $8,054,333. The average value of the church edifices is $9750, and the average seating capacity 294.

SUMMARY BY STATES.

STATES.	Organi-zations.	Church Edifices.	Seating Capacity.	Value of Church Property.	Communicants.
Alabama	10	6	625	$3,500	365
Arkansas	1	..	.....	......	16
California	9	5	1,950	96,000	1,382
Colorado	1	..	.....	500	15
Connecticut	18	18	6,325	367,000	2,129
District of Columbia	1	1	500	47,000	128
Florida	3	1	150	2,000	45
Georgia	15	12	2,250	3,140	533
Idaho	1	1	200	3,000	25
Illinois	54	49½	13,400	523,850	3,424
Indiana	50	37	8,850	138,900	1,950
Iowa	22	23	6,550	118,300	829
Kansas	14	8	1,875	20,200	571
Kentucky	23	12	3,200	16,525	434
Maine	86	83	26,405	542,900	3,750
Maryland	1	1	700	30,000	382
Massachusetts	121	119½	40,550	2,110,193	7,142
Michigan	27	26	6,600	221,800	1,549
Minnesota	13	10	3,500	192,900	1,093
Mississippi	3	2	200	800	120
Missouri	16	4	1,600	4,800	711
Nebraska	5	5	775	38,800	161
New Hampshire	33	34	9,600	203,025	1,204

SUMMARY BY STATES.—*Continued.*

STATES.	Organizations.	Church Edifices.	Seating Capacity.	Value of Church Property.	Communicants.
New Jersey........	6	6	1,720	$112,300	541
New York	168	147	44,600	1,798,250	8,526
North Carolina	3	3	500	1,200	255
Ohio	91	91	24,950	344,800	4,961
Oregon	5	3	550	9,500	84
Pennsylvania	42	36	9,850	417,500	2,209
Rhode Island	10	10	4,035	301,500	998
South Carolina.....	2	1	100	1,200	101
Tennessee.........	1	1	100	750	20
Texas	18	2	450	5,800	514
Vermont..........	65	57	18,010	285,000	2,409
Virginia	1	1	300	5,000	18
West Virginia	2	1	100	1,200	56
Wisconsin.........	15	15	3,545	85,200	544
Total	956	832	244,615	$8,054,333	49,194

CHAPTER XLIII.

INDEPENDENT CONGREGATIONS.

THESE are congregations having no connection with any of the denominations. Some are akin to Presbyterian, others to Methodist and other bodies. Some are organized on a union basis and receive part of their support from members of several denominations. There are 54 halls, with accommodations for 10,445.

SUMMARY BY STATES.

STATES.	Organizations.	Church Edifices.	Seating Capacity.	Value of Church Property.	Communicants.
Alabama...........	1	..	....	......	150
Alaska............	1	..	....	......	766
California	11	2	550	$70,575	717
Connecticut	4	3	425	3,600	353
District of Columbia	5	3	1,100	17,100	386
Georgia...........	1	1	150	......	25
Illinois............	8	7	3,970	140,000	1,640
Indiana	16	11	3,200	8,450	918
Iowa	1	1	200	1,000	75
Kansas	9	5	1,090	7,550	271
Maine	3	3	850	17,500	170
Maryland	2	2	2,200	40,000	500
Massachusetts	18	12	3,105	121,350	684
Michigan..........	2	2	375	6,000	170
Minnesota.........	1	1	100	700	31
Missouri	3	1	200	1,500	156
New Hampshire ...	3	1	200	1,500	150
New Jersey........	8	6	2,150	52,300	552
New York.........	26	23	10,255	722,400	4,232
Ohio	5	6	2,025	22,800	298
Pennsylvania	17	15	4,650	140,900	948
Rhode Island	6	4	1,750	89,200	768
South Carolina	1	1	200	8,000	....
Vermont...........	4	2	600	13,575	166
Total	156	112	39,345	$1,486,000	14,126

1890

GENERAL STATISTICAL SUMMARIES.

1. Summary by States of all denominations.
2. Summary by denominations.
3. Summary by denominational families.
4. Summary of denominations according to number of communicants.
5. Summary of denominational families according to number of communicants.
6. Summary of denominations classified according to polity.
7. Summary of colored organizations.
8. Summary of churches in cities.

TABLE I.—*(a)* SUMMARY BY STATES

STATES.	Organizations.	Edifices.
Alabama	6,383	6,013
Alaska	26	34
Arizona	131	70
Arkansas	4,874	3,791
California	1,996	1,505
Colorado	647	463
Connecticut	1,149	1,175
Delaware	382	401
District of Columbia	217	205
Florida	1,971	1,793
Georgia	6,899	7,008
Idaho	247	143
Illinois	8,296	7,352
Indiana	6,480	5,944
Indian Territory	806	429
Iowa	5,539	4,539
Kansas	4,927	2,859
Kentucky	5,555	4,768
Louisiana	2,701	2,520
Maine	1,610	1,346
Maryland	2,328	2,369
Massachusetts	2,547	2,458
Michigan	4,798	3,761
Minnesota	3,429	2,619
Mississippi	5,194	5,009
Missouri	8,064	6,121
Montana	273	164
Nebraska	2,797	1,822
Nevada	64	41
New Hampshire	783	774
New Jersey	2,085	2,204
New Mexico	463	381
New York	8,237	7,942
North Carolina	6,824	6,512
North Dakota	868	335
Ohio	9,384	8,896
Oklahoma	123	41
Oregon	969	592
Pennsylvania	10,175	9,624
Rhode Island	402	386
South Carolina	3,815	3,967
South Dakota	1,589	774
Tennessee	6,351	5,794

(a) For summary by States for 1906 see p.   *(b)* This column shows the percentage

OF ALL DENOMINATIONS.

Seating Capacity.	Value of Church Property.	Communicants.	Per cent. of Population (b).
1,702,527	$6,768,477	559,171	36.96
4,800	203,650	14,852	. . . . .
19,230	270,816	26,972	. . . . .
1,041,040	3,266,663	296,208	45.24
422,609	11,961,914	280,619	26.26
120,862	4,743,317	86,837	23.23
443,979	16,985,036	309,341	21.07
111,172	2,708,825	48,679	41.45
114,420	6,313,625	94,203	28.89
391,132	2,424,423	141,734	40.89
2,108,566	8,228,060	679,051	36.21
29,527	281,310	24,036	36.96
2,260,619	39,715,245	1,202,588	28.48
1,890,300	18,671,131	693,860	31.43
79,583	182,266	29,275	31.65
1,203,185	16,056,786	556,817	. . . . .
708,134	7,452,269	336,729	29.12
1,504,736	12,112,320	606,397	23.58
617,245	5,032,194	399,991	32.63
408,767	6,198,400	160,271	35.76
718,459	15,445,946	379,418	24.24
1,102,772	46,835,014	942,751	36.40
1,097,069	18,682,971	569,504	42.11
691,631	12,940,152	532,590	27.20
1,332,442	4,392,473	430,746	40.91
1,859,589	19,663,737	735,839	33.40
33,942	885,950	32,478	27.47
409,462	6,443,689	194,466	24.57
9,890	208,225	5,877	18.36
250,035	4,457,225	102,941	12.84
803,017	29,490,414	508,351	27.34
107,925	531,925	105,749	35.18
2,868,490	140,123,008	2,171,822	68.85
2,192,835	7,077,440	685,194	36.21
69,590	780,775	59,496	42.35
2,827,113	42,159,762	1,216,469	32.56
8,605	61,575	4,901	33.13
142,843	2,829,150	70,524	7.58
3,592,019	85,917,370	1,726,640	22.48
166,384	7,583,110	148,008	32.84
1,199,908	5,636,236	508,485	42.84
149,728	1,761,277	85,490	44.17
1,812,942	9,890,443	552,658	26.00
			31.26

of population represented by the number of communicants in each State.

TABLE I.—SUMMARY BY STATES

STATES.	Organizations.	Edifices.
Texas...........................	8,766	5,638
Utah	427	280
Vermont	904	802
Virginia	4,998	4,894
Washington	892	532
West Virginia	3,045	2,216
Wisconsin	3,726	3,290
Wyoming	141	43
Total	165,297	142,639

TABLE II.—SUMMARY

DENOMINATIONS.	Ministers.	Organizations.
ADVENTISTS:		
1. Evangelical	34	30
2. Advent Christians	883	580
3. Seventh-Day.....................	284	995
4. Church of God.	19	29
5. Life and Advent Union	50	28
6. Churches of God in Jesus Christ .	94	95
Total Adventists	1,364	1,757
BAPTISTS:		
1. Regular (North)................	6,685	7,907
2. Regular (South)................	8,957	16,238
3. Regular (Colored)	5,468	12,533
4. Six-Principle...................	14	18
5. Seventh-Day....................	115	106
6. Freewill	1,493	1,586
7. Original Freewill	118	167
8. General	332	399
9. Separate........................	19	24
10. United	25	204
11. Baptist Church of Christ	80	152
12. Primitive	2,040	3,222
13. Old Two-Seed-in-the-Spirit Predes-tinarian	300	473
Total Baptists.................	25,646	43,029

(*a*) This column shows the percentage of population

OF ALL DENOMINATIONS.—*Continued.*

Seating Capacity.	Value of Church Property.	Communicants.	Per cent. of Population (*a*).
1,567,745	$8,682,337	677,151	30.30
89,695	1,493,791	128,115	61.62
237,000	4,643,800	106,315	31.98
1,490,675	10,473,943	569,235	34.37
126,109	2,408,625	58,798	16.83
601,238	3,723,383	192,477	25.23
846,408	14,525,841	556,483	32.98
8,385	368,625	11,705	19.28
43,596,378	$679,694,439	20,618,307	32.92

BY DENOMINATIONS.

Church Edifices.	Seating Capacity.	Value of Church Property.	Communicants.
23	5,855	$61,400	1,147
294	80,286	465,605	25,816
418	94,627	645,075	28,991
1	200	1,400	647
8	2,250	16,790	1,018
30	7,530	46,075	2,872
774	190,748	$1,236,345	60,491
7,070	2,180,773	$49,530,504	800,450
13,502	4,349,407	18,196,637	1,280,066
11,987	3,440,970	9,038,549	1,348,989
14	3,600	19,500	937
78	21,467	265,260	9,143
1,225	349,309	3,115,642	87,898
125	41,400	57,005	11,864
209	71,850	201,140	21,362
19	5,650	9,200	1,599
179	60,220	80,150	13,209
135	40,885	56,755	8,254
2,849	899,273	1,649,851	121,347
397	134,730	172,230	12,851
37,789	11,599,534	$82,392,423	3,717,969

represented by the number of communicants in each State.

TABLE II.—Summary by

DENOMINATIONS.	Ministers.	Organizations.
Brethren (River):		
1. Brethren in Christ	128	78
2. Old Order or Yorker	7	8
3. United Zion's Children	20	25
Total River Brethren	155	111
Brethren (Plymouth):		
Brethren (I.)	....	109
Brethren (II.)	....	88
Brethren (III.)	....	86
Brethren (IV.)	....	31
Total Plymouth Brethren	....	314
Catholics:		
1. Roman Catholic	9,157	10,231
2. Greek Catholic (Uniates)	9	14
3. Russian Orthodox	13	12
4. Greek Orthodox	1	1
5. Armenian	7	6
6. Old Catholic	1	4
7. Reformed Catholic	8	8
Total	9,196	10,276
Catholic Apostolic	95	10
Chinese Temples	....	47
Christadelphians	....	63
Christians:		
1. Christians (Christian Connection)	1,350	1,281
2. Christian Church South	85	143
Total Christians	1,435	1,424
Christian Missionary Association	10	13
Christian Scientists	26	221
Christian Union	183	294
Church of God (Winebrennerian)	522	479
Church Triumphant (Schweinfurth)	...	12
Church of the New Jerusalem	119	154

DENOMINATIONS.—*Continued.*

Church Edifices.	Seating Capacity.	Value of Church Property.	Communicants.
45	19,005	$73,050	2,688
..	......	......	214
25	3,100	8,300	525
70	22,105	$81,350	3,427
..	......	......	2,289
..	......	$1,265	2,419
..	......	200	1,235
..	......	......	718
..	......	$1,465	6,661
8,776	3,365,754	$118,069,746	6,231,417
13	5,228	63,300	10,850
23	3,150	220,000	13,504
1	75	5,000	100
....	....	......	335
3	700	13,320	665
....	....	......	1,000
8,816	3,374,907	$118,371,366	6,257,871
3	750	$66,050	1,394
47	....	62,000	....
4	950	2,700	1,277
963	301,692	$1,637,202	90,718
135	46,005	138,000	13,004
1,098	347,697	$1,775,202	103,722
11	3,300	$3,900	754
7	1,500	40,666	8,724
184	68,000	234,450	18,214
338	115,530	643,185	22,511
..	....	15,000	384
88	20,810	1,386,455	7,095

TABLE II.—Summary by

DENOMINATIONS.	Ministers.	Organizations.
COMMUNISTIC SOCIETIES (*a*):		
1. Shakers	..	15
2. Amana	..	7
3. Harmony	..	1
4. Separatists	..	1
5. New Icaria	..	1
6. Altruists	..	1
7. Adonai Shomo	..	1
8. Church Triumphant (Koreshan Ecclesia)	..	5
Total Communistic Societies	..	32
Congregationalists	5,058	4,868
Disciples of Christ	3,773	7,246
DUNKARDS:		
1. Dunkards or German Baptists (Conserv.)	1,622	720
2. Dunkards or German Baptists (Old Order)	237	135
3. Dunkards or German Baptists (Progressive)	224	128
4. Seventh-Day Baptists (German)	5	6
Total Dunkards	2,088	989
Evangelical Association	1,235	2,310
FRIENDS:		
1. Friends (Orthodox)	1,113	794
2. Friends (Hicksite)	115	201
3. Friends (Wilburite)	38	52
4. Friends (Primitive)	11	9
Total Friends	1,277	1,056
Friends of the Temple	4	4
German Evangelical Protestant	44	52
German Evangelical Synod	680	870
JEWS:		
1. Jewish Congregations (Orthodox)	125	316
2. Jewish Congregations (Reformed)	75	217
Total Jews	200	533

(*a*) The Bruederhoef Mennonites also observe a communal life. They

DENOMINATIONS.—*Continued*.

Church Edifices.	Seating Capacity.	Value of Church Property.	Communicants.
16	5,650	$36,800	1,728
22	2,800	15,000	1,600
1	500	10,000	250
1	500	3,000	200
..	....	......	21
..	....	......	25
..	....	6,000	20
..	....	36,000	205
40	9,450	$106,800	4,049
4,736	1,553,080	$43,335,437	512,771
5,324	1,609,452	12,206,038	641,051
854	353,586	$1,121,541	61,101
63	25,750	80,770	4,411
96	32,740	145,770	8,089
3	1,960	14,550	194
1,016	414,036	$1,362,631	73,795
1,899	479,335	$4,785,680	133,313
725	215,431	$2,795,784	80,655
213	72,568	1,661,850	21,992
52	13,169	67,000	4,329
5	1,050	16,700	232
995	302,218	$4,541,334	107,208
5	1,150	$15,300	340
52	35,175	1,187,450	36,156
785	245,781	4,614,490	187,432
122	46,837	$2,802,050	57,597
179	92,397	6,952,225	72,899
301	139,234	$9,754,275	130,496

are reported in connection with the other Mennonite branches.

TABLE II.—SUMMARY BY

DENOMINATIONS.	Ministers.	Organizations.
LATTER-DAY SAINTS:		
1. Church of Jesus Christ of Latter-Day Saints	543	425
2. Reorganized Church of Jesus Christ of Latter-Day Saints	1,500	431
Total Latter-Day Saints	2,043	856
LUTHERANS:		
General Bodies.		
1. General Synod	966	1,424
2. United Synod in the South	201	414
3. General Council	1,153	2,044
4. Synodical Conference	1,282	1,934
Independent Synods.		
5. Joint Synod of Ohio, etc.	297	421
6. Buffalo	20	27
7. Hauge's	58	175
8. Norwegian in North America	194	489
9. Michigan	37	65
10. Danish in America	108	131
11. German Augsburg	49	23
12. Danish Church Association	40	50
13. Icelandic Synod	1	13
14. Immanuel	21	21
15. Suomai Synod	8	11
16. United Norwegian of America	109	1,122
Independent Congregations	47	231
Total Lutherans	4,591	8,595
MENNONITES:		
1. Mennonite	336	246
2. Bruederhoef (*a*)	9	5
3. Amish	228	97
4. Old Amish	71	22
5. Apostolic	2	2
6. Reformed	43	34
7. General Conference	95	45
8. Church of God in Christ	18	18
9. Old (Wisler)	17	15

(*a*) The Bruederhoef Mennonites observe a communal

DENOMINATIONS.—*Continued.*

Church Edifices.	Seating Capacity.	Value of Church Property.	Communicants.
266	92,102	$825,506	144,352
122	30,790	226,285	21,773
388	122,892	$1,051,791	166,125
1,322	471,819	$8,919,170	164,640
379	138,453	1,114,065	37,457
1,554	588,825	11,119,286	324,846
1,531	443,185	7,804,313	357,153
443	149,338	$1,639,087	69,505
25	5,793	84,410	4,242
100	30,500	214,395	14,730
275	78,988	806,825	55,452
53	14,613	164,770	11,482
75	14,760	129,700	10,181
23	7,560	111,060	7,010
33	5,700	44,775	3,493
4	1,300	7,200	1,991
19	5,300	94,200	5,580
8	1,915	12,898	1,385
669	185,242	1,544,455	119,972
188	62,344	1,249,745	41,953
6,701	2,205,635	$35,060,354	1,231,072
198	70,605	$317,045	17,078
5	600	4,500	352
61	15,430	76,450	10,101
1	200	1,500	2,038
1	225	1,200	209
29	7,465	52,650	1,655
43	13,880	119,350	5,670
3	400	1,600	471
12	4,120	8,015	610

life and constitute properly a communistic society.

TABLE II.—SUMMARY BY

DENOMINATIONS.	Ministers.	Organizations.
MENNONITES—*Continued :*		
10. Bundes Conference	37	12
11. Defenseless	18	9
12. Brethren in Christ	31	45
Total Mennonites	905	550
METHODISTS :		
1. Methodist Episcopal	15,423	25,861
2. Union American Methodist Episcopal.....	32	42
3. African Methodist Episcopal	3,321	2,481
4. African Union Methodist Protestant	40	40
5. African Methodist Episcopal Zion	1,565	1,704
6. Methodist Protestant.....................	1,441	2,529
7. Wesleyan Methodist	600	565
8. Methodist Episcopal, South	4,801	15,017
9. Congregational Methodist	150	214
10. Congregational Methodist (Colored)	5	9
11. New Congregational Methodist...........	20	24
12. Zion Union Apostolic	30	32
13. Colored Methodist Episcopal.............	1,800	1,759
14. Primitive Methodist......................	60	84
15. Free Methodist..........................	657	1,102
16. Independent Methodist...................	8	15
17. Evangelist Missionary....................	47	11
Total Methodists	30,000	51,489
Moravians......................................	114	94
PRESBYTERIANS :		
1. Presbyterian in the United States of America (Northern)	5,934	6,717
2. Cumberland Presbyterian.................	1,861	2,791
3. Cumberland Presbyterian (Colored)	393	224
4. Welsh Calvinistic........................	100	187
5. United Presbyterian	731	866
6. Presbyterian in the United States (Southern)	1,129	2,391
7. Associate Church of North America	12	31
8. Associate Reformed Synod of the South ...	133	116
9. Reformed Presbyterian in the United States (Synod)	124	115

DENOMINATIONS.—*Continued.*

Church Edifices.	Seating Capacity.	Value of Church Property.	Communicants.
11	3,720	$11,350	1,388
8	2,070	10,540	856
34	10,625	39,600	1,113
406	129,340	$643,800	41,541
22,844	6,302,708	$96,723,408	2,240,354
35	11,500	187,600	2,279
4,124	1,160,838	6,468,280	452,725
27	7,161	54,440	3,415
1,587	565,577	2,714,128	349,788
1,924	571,266	3,683,337	141,989
342	86,254	393,250	16,492
12,688	3,359,466	18,775,362	1,209,976
150	46,400	41,680	8,765
5	585	525	319
17	5,150	3,750	1,059
27	10,100	15,000	2,346
1,653	541,464	1,713,366	129,383
78	20,930	291,993	4,764
620	165,004	805,085	22,110
14	7,725	266,975	2,569
3	1,050	2,000	951
46,138	12,863,178	$132,140,179	4,589,284
114	31,615	$681,250	11,781
6,664	2,225,044	$74,455,200	788,224
2,024	669,507	3,515,510	164,940
183	52,139	195,826	12,956
189	44,445	625,875	12,722
832	264,298	5,408,084	94,402
2,288	690,843	8,812,152	179,721
23	4,849	29,200	1,053
116	37,050	211,850	8,501
115	37,095	1,071,400	10,574

TABLE II.—Summary by

DENOMINATIONS.	Ministers.	Organizations.
PRESBYTERIANS—*Continued :*		
10. Reformed Presbyterian in North America (General Synod)	29	33
11. Reformed Presbyterian (Covenanted)	1	4
12. Reformed Presbyterian in the United States and Canada	1	1
Total Presbyterians	10,448	13,476
PROTESTANT EPISCOPAL:		
1. Protestant Episcopal	4,146	5,019
2. Reformed Episcopal	78	83
Total Episcopal	4,224	5,102
REFORMED:		
1. Reformed in America	558	572
2. Reformed in United States	880	1,510
3. Christian Reformed......................	68	99
Total Reformed	1,506	2,181
Salvation Army	...	329
Schwenkfelders	3	4
Social Brethren	17	20
Society for Ethical Culture	...	4
Spiritualists...............................	...	334
Theosophical Society	...	40
UNITED BRETHREN:		
1. United Brethren in Christ	2,267	3,731
2. United Brethren (Old Constitution).......	531	795
Total United Brethren...............	2,798	4,526
Unitarians.................................	515	421
Universalists...............................	708	956
Independent Congregations	54	156
Grand Total.......................	111,036	165,297

DENOMINATIONS.—*Continued.*

Church Edifices.	Seating Capacity.	Value of Church Property.	Communicants.
33	12,380	$469,000	4,602
1	200	. . . .	37
1	800	75,000	600
12,469	4,038,650	$94,869,097	1,278,332
5,019	1,336,952	$81,220,317	532,054
84	23,925	1,615,101	8,455
5,103	1,360,877	$82,835,418	540,509
670	257,922	$10,340,159	92,970
1,304	534,254	7,975,583	204,018
106	33,755	428,500	12,470
2,080	825,931	$18,744,242	309,458
27	12,055	$38,150	8,742
6	1,925	12,200	306
11	8,700	8,700	913
. .	. . . . .	. . . . . .	1,064
30	20,450	573,650	45,030
1	200	600	695
2,837	816,458	$4,292,643	202,474
578	174,680	644,940	22,807
3,415	991,138	$4,937,583	225,281
424	165,090	$10,335,100	67,749
832	244,615	8,054,333	49,194
112	39,345	1,486,000	14,126
142,639	43,596,378	$679,694,439	20,618,307

TABLE III.—SUMMARY BY

DENOMINATIONS.	Ministers.	Organizations.
Adventists (6 bodies)	1,364	1,757
Baptists (13 bodies)	25,646	43,029
Brethren (River) (3 bodies).................	155	111
Brethren (Plymouth) (4 bodies).............	....	314
Catholics (7 bodies)	9,196	10,276
Catholic Apostolic..........................	95	10
Chinese Temples............................	....	47
Christadelphians	....	63
Christians (2 bodies)	1,435	1,424
Christian Missionary Association............	10	13
Christian Scientists........................	26	221
Christian Union............................	183	294
Church of God (Winebrennerian)...........	522	479
Church Triumphant (Schweinfurth).........	....	12
Church of the New Jerusalem...............	119	154
Communistic Societies (8 bodies)............	....	32
Congregationalists	5,058	4,868
Disciples of Christ..........................	3,773	7,246
Dunkards (4 bodies)........................	2,088	989
Evangelical Association	1,235	2,310
Friends (4 bodies)..........................	1,277	1,056
Friends of the Temple......................	4	4
German Evangelical (Protestant)	44	52
German Evangelical Synod..................	680	870
Jewish Congregations (2 bodies)	200	533
Latter-Day Saints (2 bodies)...............	2,043	856
Lutherans (16 bodies) and independent congregations..............................	4,591	8,595
Mennonites (12 bodies)	905	550
Methodists (17 bodies).....................	30,000	51,489
Moravians..................................	114	94
Presbyterians (12 bodies)...................	10,448	13,476
Protestant Episcopal (2 bodies)	4,224	5,102
Reformed (3 bodies)........................	1,506	2,181
Salvation Army	....	329
Schwenkfelders	3	4
Social Brethren	17	20
Society for Ethical Culture	....	4
Spiritualists	....	334
Theosophical Society	....	40
United Brethren (2 bodies).................	2,798	4,526
Unitarians.................................	515	421
Universalists...............................	708	956
Independent Congregations	54	156
Total	111,036	165,297

DENOMINATIONAL FAMILIES.

Church Edifices.	Seating Capacity.	Value of Church Property.	Communicants.
774	190,748	$1,236,345	60,491
37,789	11,599,534	82,392,423	3,717,969
70	22,105	81,350	3,427
. . . .	. . . . . .	1,465	6,661
8,816	3,374,907	118,371,366	6,257,871
3	750	66,050	1,394
47	. . . . . .	62,000	. . . . .
4	950	2,700	1,277
1,098	347,697	1,775,202	103,722
11	3,300	3,900	754
7	1,500	40,666	8,724
184	68,000	234,450	18,214
338	115,530	643,185	22,511
. . . .	. . . . . .	15,000	384
88	20,810	1,386,455	7,095
40	9,450	106,800	4,049
4,736	1,553,080	43,335,437	512,771
5,324	1,609,452	12,206,038	641,051
1,016	414,036	1,362,631	73,795
1,899	479,335	4,785,680	133,313
995	302,218	4,541,334	107,208
5	1,150	15,300	340
52	35,175	1,187,450	36,156
785	245,781	4,614,490	187,432
301	139,234	9,754,275	130,496
388	122,892	1,051,791	166,125
6,701	2,205,635	35,060,354	1,231,072
406	129,340	643,800	41,541
46,138	12,863,178	132,140,179	4,589,284
114	31,615	681,250	11,781
12,469	4,038,650	94,869,097	1,278,332
5,103	1,360,877	82,835,418	540,509
2,080	825,931	18,744,242	309,458
27	12,055	38,150	8,742
6	1,925	12,200	306
11	8,700	8,700	913
. . . .	. . . . . .	. . . . . .	1,064
30	20,450	573,650	45,030
1	200	600	695
3,415	991,138	4,937,583	225,281
424	165,090	10,335,100	67,749
832	244,615	8,054,333	49,194
112	39,345	1,486,000	14,126
142,639	43,596,378	$679,694,439	20,618,307

TABLE IV.—DENOMINATIONS ACCORDING TO NUMBER OF COMMUNICANTS.

DENOMINATIONS.	Communicants.
1. Roman Catholic	6,231,417
2. Methodist Episcopal	2,240,354
3. Regular Baptist (Colored)	1,348,989
4. Regular Baptist (South)	1,280,066
5. Methodist Episcopal (South)	1,209,976
6. Regular Baptist (North)	800,450
7. Presbyterian (North)	788,224
8. Disciples of Christ	641,051
9. Protestant Episcopal	532,054
10. Congregational	512,771
11. African Methodist Episcopal	452,725
12. Lutheran Synodical Conference	357,153
13. African Methodist Episcopal Zion	349,788
14. Lutheran General Council	324,846
15. Reformed in the United States	204,018
16. United Brethren in Christ	202,474
17. German Evangelical Synod	187,432
18. Presbyterian (South)	179,721
19. Cumberland Presbyterian	164,940
20. Lutheran General Synod	164,640
21. Latter-Day Saints	144,352
22. Methodist Protestant	141,989
23. Evangelical Association	133,313
24. Colored Methodist Episcopal	129,383
25. Primitive Baptist	121,347
26. United Norwegian Lutheran	119,972
27. United Presbyterian	94,402
28. Reformed in America	92,970
29. Christian	90,718
30. Freewill Baptist	87,808
31. Friends (Orthodox)	80,655
32. Jewish (Reformed)	72,899
33. Lutheran Synod of Ohio	69,505
34. Unitarian	67,749
35. Dunkards (Conservative)	61,101
36. Jewish (Orthodox)	57,597
37. Norwegian Lutheran	55,452
38. Universalist	49,194
39. Spiritualist	45,030
40. Lutheran United Synod in the South	37,457
41. German Evangelical Protestant	36,156
42. Seventh-Day Adventist	28,991

TABLE IV.—*Continued.*

DENOMINATIONS.	Communicants.
43. Advent Christian	25,816
44. United Brethren (Old Constitution)	22,807
45. Church of God	22,511
46. Free Methodist	22,110
47. Friends (Hicksite)	21,992
48. Latter-Day Saints (Reorganized)	21,773
49. General Baptist	21,362
50. Christian Union	18,214
51. Mennonite	17,078
52. Wesleyan Methodist	16,492
53. Hauge's Lutheran Synod	14,730
Independent Congregations	14,126
54. Russian Orthodox	13,504
55. United Baptist	13,209
56. Christian (South)	13,004
57. Cumberland Presbyterian (Colored)	12,956
58. Old Two-Seed Baptist	12,851
59. Welsh Calvinistic Methodist	12,722
60. Christian Reformed	12,470
61. Original Freewill Baptist	11,864
62. Moravian	11,781
63. Michigan Lutheran Synod	11,482
64. Greek Catholic (Uniates)	10,850
65. Reformed Presbyterian (Synod)	10,574
66. Danish Lutheran Church	10,181
67. Amish Mennonite	10,101
68. Seventh-Day Baptist	9,143
69. Congregational Methodist	8,765
70. Salvation Army	8,742
71. Christian Scientist	8,724
72. Associated Reformed Synod (South)	8,501
73. Reformed Episcopal	8,455
74. Baptist Church in Christ	8,254
75. Dunkards (Progressive)	8,089
76. New Jerusalem	7,095
77. Augsburg Lutheran Synod	7,010
78. General Conference Mennonite	5,670
79. Immanuel Lutheran Synod	5,580
80. Primitive Methodist	4,764
81. Reformed Presbyterian (General Synod)	4,602
82. Dunkards (Old Order)	4,411
83. Friends (Wilburite)	4,329
84. Buffalo Lutheran Synod	4,242
85. Danish Lutheran Association	3,493

TABLE IV.—*Continued.*

DENOMINATIONS.	Communicants.
86. African Union Methodist Protestant.........	3,415
87. Churches of God (Adventist)	2,872
88. Brethren in Christ	2,688
89. Independent Methodist	2,569
90. (Plymouth) Brethren II....................	2,419
91. Zion Union Apostolic	2,346
92. (Plymouth) Brethren I.....................	2,289
93. Union American Methodist Episcopal	2,279
94. Old Amish (Mennonite)	2,038
95. Icelandic Lutheran Synod	1,991
96. Shakers...................................	1,728
97. Reformed Mennonite.......................	1,655
98. Amana Society	1,600
99. Separate Baptist	1,599
100. Catholic Apostolic	1,394
101. Bundes Conference (Mennonite)	1,388
102. Suomai Lutheran Synod	1,385
103. Christadelphian	1,277
104. (Plymouth) Brethren III.	1,235
105. Evangelical Adventist	1,147
106. Brethren in Christ (Mennonite).............	1,113
107. Ethical Culture	1,064
108. New Congregational Methodist	1,059
109. Associate Church of North America.........	1,053
110. Life and Advent Union....................	1,018
111. Reformed Catholic.........................	1,000
112. Evangelist Missionary	951
113. Six-Principle Baptist	937
114. Social Brethren............................	913
115. Defenseless Mennonite.....................	856
116. Christian Missionary Association............	754
117. (Plymouth) Brethren IV.	718
118. Theosophical Society	695
119. Old Catholic	665
120. Church of God (Adventist).................	647
121. Old (Wisler) Mennonite	610
122. Reformed Presbyterian in the United States and Canada	600
123. United Zion's Children	525
124. Church of God in Christ (Mennonite).......	471
125. Church Triumphant (Schweinfurth)	384
126. Bruederhoef Mennonite.....................	352
127. Friends of the Temple.....................	340

TABLE IV.—*Continued.*

DENOMINATIONS.	Communicants.
128. Armenian Catholic	335
129. Congregational Methodist (Colored).........	319
130. Schwenkfelder	306
131. Harmony Society.........................	250
132. Friends (Primitive)	232
133. Old Order, or Yorker Brethren..............	214
134. Apostolic Mennonite.......................	209
135. Church Triumphant (Koreshan Ecclesia).....	205
136. Separatists................................	200
137. Seventh-Day Baptist, German...............	194
138. Greek Orthodox...........................	100
139. Reformed Presbyterian Covenanted..........	37
140. Altruists..................................	25
141. New Icarians..............................	21
142. Adonai Shomo	20
143. Chinese Temples (no members reported).	

TABLE V.—DENOMINATIONAL FAMILIES ACCORDING TO NUMBER OF COMMUNICANTS.

DENOMINATIONS.	Communicants.
1. Catholic.................................	6,257,871
2. Methodist	4,589,284
3. Baptist..................................	3,717,969
4. Presbyterian............................	1,278,332
5. Lutheran	1,231,072
6. Episcopalian............................	540,509
7. Reformed	309,458
8. United Brethren	225,281
9. Latter-Day Saints	166,125
10. Jewish	130,496
11. Friends	107,208
12. Christians	103,722
13. Dunkards	73,795
14. Adventist	60,491
15. Mennonite	41,541
16. (Plymouth) Brethren	6,661
17. Communistic Societies	4,049
18. (River) Brethren	3,427

TABLE VI.—DENOMINATIONS

CONGRE

DENOMINATIONS.	Ministers.	Organizations.
Adventist (4 bodies)	1,061	733
Baptist (12 bodies)	25,528	42,862
(River) Brethren (all)	155	111
(Plymouth) Brethren (all)	....	314
Catholic (Reformed)	8	8
Christians (all)	1,435	1,424
Christadelphian	....	63
Christian Missionary Association	10	13
Christian Scientist	26	221
Christian Union	183	294
Chinese Temples	....	47
Congregational	5,058	4,868
Disciples of Christ	3,773	7,246
Friends of the Temple	4	4
German Evangelical Protestant	44	52
Jewish Congregations (all)	200	533
Lutheran (2 bodies) (b)	1,626	2,586
Methodist Independent	8	15
Schwenkfelder	3	4
Social Brethren	17	20
Society for Ethical Culture	...	4
Spiritualist	...	334
Theosophical Society	...	40
Unitarian	515	421
Independent Congregations	54	156

EPIS

Catholic (6 bodies)	9,188	10,268
Catholic Apostolic	95	10
Evangelical Association	1,235	2,310
Latter-Day Saints (all)	2,043	856
Methodist (8 bodies)	27,019	46,907
Moravian	114	94
Protestant Episcopal (all)	4,224	5,102
United Brethren (all)	2,798	4,526

(a) For explanations, see page   of Introduction.

CLASSIFIED ACCORDING TO POLITY (*a*).

GATIONAL.

Church Edifices.	Seating Capacity.	Value of Church Property.	Communi- cants.
355	95,921	$589,870	30,853
37,664	11,558,134	82,335,418	3,706,105
70	22,105	81,350	3,427
. . . . .	. . . .	1,465	6,661
. . . . .	. . . .	. . . .	1,000
1,098	347,697	1,775,202	103,722
4	950	2,700	1,277
11	3,300	3,900	754
7	1,500	40,666	8,724
184	68,000	234,450	18,214
47	. . . .	62,000	. . . . . .
4,736	1,553,080	43,335,437	512,771
5,324	1,609,452	12,206,038	641,051
5	1,150	15,300	340
52	35,175	1,187,450	36,156
301	139,324	9,754,275	130,496
2,162	654,867	10,693,145	468,611
14	7,725	266,975	2,569
6	1,925	12,200	306
11	8,700	8,700	913
. . . .	. . . .	. . . .	1,064
30	20,450	573,650	45,030
1	200	600	695
424	165,090	10,335,100	67,749
112	39,345	1,486,000	14,126

COPAL.

8,816	3,374,907	$118,371,366	6,256,871
3	750	66,050	1,394
1,899	479,335	4,785,680	133,313
388	122,892	1,051,791	166,125
42,961	11,952,703	126,599,144	4,387,802
114	31,615	681,250	11,781
5,103	1,360,877	82,835,418	540,509
3,415	991,138	4,937,583	225,281

(*b*) Including independent congregations.

TABLE VI.—DENOMINATIONS CLASSIFIED

PRESBY

DENOMINATIONS.	Ministers.	Organizations.
Adventist (2 bodies)	303	1,024
Baptist, Original Freewill	118	167
Church of God (Winebrennerian)......	522	479
Church of the New Jerusalem	119	154
Dunkards (all).......................	2,088	989
Friends (all)	1,277	1,056
German Evangelical Synod	680	870
Lutheran (*a*) (14 bodies)	2,965	6,009
Mennonites (all)	905	550
Methodist (8 bodies)	2,973	4,567
Presbyterians (all)....................	10,448	13,476
Reformed (all).......................	1,506	2,181
Salvation Army.......................	.....	329
Universalist	708	956

RECAPIT

Congregational	39,708	62,373
Episcopal	46,716	70,073
Presbyterian.........................	24,612	32,807
Grand Total	111,036	165,253

TABLE VII.—SUMMARY OF

COLORED

DENOMINATIONS.	Organizations.
Regular Baptist (Colored)	12,533
Union American Methodist Episcopal	42
African Methodist Episcopal	2,481
African Union Methodist Protestant	40

(*a*) For explanations, see

ACCORDING TO POLITY.—*Continued.*

TERIAN.

Church Edifices.	Seating Capacity.	Value of Church Property.	Communicants.
419	94,827	$646,475	29,638
125	41,400	57,005	11,864
338	115,530	643,185	22,511
88	20,810	1,386,455	7,095
1,016	414,036	1,362,631	73,795
995	302,218	4,541,334	107,208
785	245,781	4,614,490	187,432
4,539	1,550,768	24,367,209	762,461
406	129,340	643,800	41,541
3,163	902,750	5,274,060	198,913
12,469	4,038,650	94,869,097	1,278,332
2,080	825,931	18,744,242	309,458
27	12,055	38,150	8,742
832	244,615	8,054,333	49,194

ULATION.

52,618	16,334,000	$175,001,891	5,802,614
62,699	18,314,217	339,328,282	11,723,076
27,282	8,938,711	165,242,466	3,088,184
142,599	43,586,928	$679,572,639	20,613,874

COLORED ORGANIZATIONS.

DENOMINATIONS.

Church Edifices.	Seating Capacity.	Value of Church Property.	Communicants.
11,987	3,441,880	$9,038,549	1,349,189
35	11,500	187,600	2,279
4,124	1,160,838	6,468,280	452,725
27	7,161	54,440	3,415

page   of Introduction.

TABLE VII.—COLORED

DENOMINATIONS.	Organizations.
African Methodist Episcopal Zion	1,704
Congregational Methodist (Colored)	9
Colored Methodist Episcopal	1,759
Zion Union Apostolic	32
Evangelist Missionary	11
Cumberland Presbyterian (Colored)	224
Total	18,835

COLORED ORGANIZATIONS

Regular Baptist (North)	406
Regular Baptist (South)	7
Freewill Baptist	5
Primitive Baptist	323
Old Two-Seed-in-the-Spirit Predestinarian Baptist	15
Roman Catholic	31
Christians (Christian Connection)	63
Congregational	85
Disciples of Christ	277
Lutheran (Synodical Conference)	5
Lutheran (United Synod in the South)	5
Methodist Episcopal	2,984
Methodist Protestant	54
Independent Methodist	2
Presbyterian (Northern)	233
Presbyterian (Southern)	45
Reformed Presbyterian (Synod)	1
Protestant Episcopal	49
Reformed Episcopal	37
Total	4,627

RECAPIT

Colored Denominations	18,835
Colored Organizations in other Denominations	4,627
Total	23,462

DENOMINATIONS.—*Continued.*

Church Edifices.	Seating Capacity.	Value of Church Property.	Communicants.
1,587	565,577	$2,714,128	349,788
5	585	525	319
1,653	541,464	1,713,366	129,383
27	10,100	15,000	2,346
3	1,050	2,000	951
183	52,139	195,826	12,956
19,631	5,792,294	$20,389,714	2,303,351

IN OTHER DENOMINATIONS.

324	92,660	$1,087,518	35,221
5	1,900	3,875	651
3	800	13,300	271
291	96,699	135,427	18,162
4	1,025	930	265
27	8,370	237,400	14,517
54	16,495	23,500	4,989
69	19,360	246,125	6,908
183	41,590	176,795	18,578
5	1,050	13,400	211
3	550	1,750	94
2,800	635,252	3,630,093	246,249
50	11,545	35,445	3,183
2	725	4,675	222
200	56,280	391,650	14,961
29	6,190	22,200	1,568
1	300	1,500	76
53	11,885	192,750	2,977
36	5,975	18,401	1,723
4,139	1,008,651	$6,236,734	370,826

ULATION.

19,631	5,792,294	$20,389,714	2,303,351
4,139	1,008,651	6,236,734	370,826
23,770	6,800,945	$26,626,448	2,674,177

TABLE VIII.—CHURCHES IN CITIES—FIRST CLASS (*a*).

ORGANIZATIONS.

DENOMINATIONS.	New York City.	Chicago, Ill.	Philadelphia, Pa.	Brooklyn, N. Y.	Total.
Baptist (4 bodies)	43	36	94	34	207
Roman Catholic	123	123	57	57	360
Congregational	8	47	3	20	78
Disciples of Christ	3	5	3	3	14
Evangelical Association	3	11	9	6	29
Friends (3 bodies)	3	2	10	3	18
Lutheran (11 bodies)	29	65	41	25	160
Jewish Congregations (2 bodies)	135	17	9	8	169
Methodist Episcopal	63	97	108	56	324
Other Methodist (9 bodies)	8	14	24	12	58
Presbyterian (6 bodies)	67	39	112	31	249
Protestant Episcopal	80	36	87	42	245
Reformed (3 bodies)	32	9	21	18	80
Unitarian	3	5	3	3	14
Universalist	4	5	2	5	16
Miscellaneous	40	62	27	37	166
Total	644	573	610	360	2,187

(*a*) Cities having 500,000 population and upward.

TABLE VIII.—Churches in Cities—First Class.—*Continued.*

CHURCH EDIFICES.

DENOMINATIONS.	New York City.	Chicago, Ill.	Phila-delphia, Pa.	Brook-lyn, N. Y.	Total.
Baptist (4 bodies)............	41	40	95	42	218
Roman Catholic.............	108	119	61	62	350
Congregational.............	10	48	4	27	89
Disciples of Christ...........	2	4	2	2	10
Evangelical Association	3	11	9	6	29
Friends (3 bodies)	2	1	15	3	21
Lutheran (11 bodies).........	24	58	40	25	147
Jewish Congregations (2 bodies)	41	10	8	8	67
Methodist Episcopal	63	75	107	55	300
Other Methodist (9 bodies) ...	6	13	20	11	50
Presbyterian (6 bodies).......	79	38	136	37	290
Protestant Episcopal	98	32	102	60	292
Reformed (3 bodies)	34	9	21	25	89
Unitarian...................	4	4	4	5	17
Universalist.................	4	4	2	5	15
Miscellaneous...............	15	34	38	10	97
Total	534	500	664	383	2,081

TABLE VIII.—Churches in

VALUE OF

DENOMINATIONS.	New York City.
Baptist (4 bodies)..............................	$3,878,800
Roman Catholic	8,124,750
Congregational	1,015,500
Disciples of Christ...........................	113,000
Evangelical Association	80,000
Friends (3 bodies)	448,000
Lutheran (11 bodies)	1,621,800
Jewish Congregations (2 bodies)	3,740,000
Methodist Episcopal	3,640,750
Other Methodist (9 bodies)	331,000
Presbyterian (6 bodies).......................	9,354,000
Protestant Episcopal..........................	16,393,000
Reformed (3 bodies)..........................	3,448,000
Unitarian....................................	630,000
Universalist.................................	565,000
Miscellaneous................................	1,287,000
Total	$54,670,600

COMMUNI

Population	1,515,301

DENOMINATIONS.	
Baptist (4 bodies).............................	14,510
Roman Catholic	386,200
Congregational	3,047
Disciples of Christ...........................	414
Evangelical Association	292
Friends (3 bodies)	835
Lutheran (11 bodies).........................	16,125
Jewish Congregations (2 bodies)	35,085
Methodist Episcopal	14,998
Other Methodist (9 bodies)	2,681
Presbyterian (6 bodies).......................	26,602
Protestant Episcopal	37,597
Reformed (3 bodies)..........................	8,942
Unitarian....................................	940
Universalist.................................	863
Miscellaneous................................	7,823
Total	556,954

Cities—First Class.—*Continued.*

Church Property.

Chicago, Ill.	Philadelphia, Pa.	Brooklyn, N. Y.	Total.
$1,053,350	$2,962,384	$1,858,000	$9,752,534
4,837,657	2,468,300	4,984,637	20,415,344
1,272,310	160,110	1,753,000	4,200,920
65,000	35,000	50,800	263,800
137,000	130,500	49,500	397,000
12,000	1,495,000	146,000	2,101,000
1,080,250	1,584,400	852,100	5,138,550
536,500	475,000	227,000	4,978,500
2,023,100	3,288,200	2,116,500	11,068,550
195,600	258,900	166,650	952,150
1,646,800	6,504,500	1,582,000	19,087,300
1,223,100	5,919,171	3,369,500	26,904,771
35,800	860,000	976,500	5,320,300
300,000	250,000	190,000	1,370,000
218,000	245,500	183,250	1,211,750
826,200	1,386,400	177,000	3,676,600
$15,462,667	$28,023,365	$18,682,437	$116,839,069

CANTS.

1,099,850	1,046,964	806,343	4,468,458
12,634	25,193	13,971	66,308
262,047	163,658	201,063	1,012,968
9,704	890	11,153	24,794
1,320	472	287	2,493
1,684	1,256	412	3,644
222	5,014	768	6,839
34,999	11,653	14,732	77,509
9,187	4,216	2,645	51,133
15,859	32,925	18,410	82,192
2,091	5,281	1,416	11,469
11,831	41,199	17,095	96,727
8,937	28,319	17,600	92,453
809	7,566	5,473	22,790
995	675	1,600	4,210
1,037	514	771	3,185
14,789	6,358	2,214	31,184
388,145	335,189	309,610	1,589,898

TABLE VIII.—Churches in

ORGANI

CITIES.	Baptist (5 bodies).	Catholic (6 bodies).	Congrega-tional.	Jews (2 bodies).	Lutheran (12 bodies).
St. Louis, Mo.	35	86	14	9	16
Boston, Mass.	29	60	30	7	7
Baltimore, Md.	38	42	2	11	25
San Francisco, Cal. . .	8	33	8	6	7
Cincinnati, O.	15	41	5	6	4
Cleveland, O.	16	26	16	11	12
Buffalo, N. Y.	12	29	4	4	13
New Orleans, La.	27	32	4	9	10
Pittsburg, Pa.	12	43	2	2	12
Washington, D. C. . . .	55	15	6	2	11
Detroit, Mich.	11	32	6	4	16
Milwaukee, Wis.	9	29	6	5	22
Newark, N. J.	12	19	2	7	4
Minneapolis, Minn. . . .	16	18	20	2	21
Jersey City, N. J.	8	15	3	2	7
Louisville, Ky.	25	22	1	4	6
Omaha, Neb.	8	9	10	5	11
Rochester, N. Y.	12	16	2	3	7
St. Paul, Minn.	11	25	9	3	20
Kansas City, Mo.	13	22	7	3	4
Providence, R. I.	19	18	13	4	1
Denver, Col.	11	12	10	4	5
Indianapolis, Ind. . . .	10	9	5	6	4
Allegheny, Pa.	5	13	2	1	12
Total	417	666	187	120	257

CHURCH

St. Louis, Mo.	36	80	12	5	15
Boston, Mass.	29	35	32	5	6
Baltimore, Md.	38	41	2	8	24
San Francisco, Cal. . .	6	33	9	5	6
Cincinnati, O.	12	40	5	5	3
Cleveland, O.	16	28	17	5	11
Buffalo, N. Y.	15	28	5	2	13
New Orleans, La.	26	32	4	4	10

(*a*) Cities having a population

CITIES—SECOND CLASS (a).

ZATIONS.

Methodist Episcopal.	Other Methodist (11 bodies)	Presbyterian (11 bodies).	Protestant Episcopal.	Reformed (3 bodies).	Miscellaneous.	Total.
21	21	25	20	..	42	289
24	2	9	27	1	74	270
87	42	27	40	10	47	371
16	4	19	7	..	42	150
33	2	21	11	5	36	179
18	4	14	16	12	45	190
20	3	13	17	8	33	156
22	26	13	11	..	11	165
27	12	45	13	2	24	194
23	30	16	17	2	18	195
16	5	15	21	2	24	152
13	3	7	5	2	20	121
17	4	23	11	7	9	115
24	3	11	8	..	31	154
14	2	10	9	11	8	89
9	17	16	12	2	15	129
10	2	15	10	..	15	95
10	3	13	12	4	16	98
28	2	13	12	1	15	139
19	10	12	5	1	27	123
12	7	2	13	..	26	115
12	5	10	8	1	20	98
18	6	16	7	3	21	105
7	5	25	2	..	6	78
500	220	390	314	74	625	3,770

EDIFICES.

21	18	26	17	..	33	263
23	2	8	35	1	59	235
86	37	35	52	10	38	371
16	3	16	9	..	22	125
31	2	24	11	5	30	168
20	3	21	20	12	42	195
20	3	17	19	8	24	154
20	26	13	13	..	6	154

TABLE VIII.—Church

CITIES.	Baptist (5 bodies).	Catholic (6 bodies).	Congrega-tional.	Jews (2 bodies).	Lutheran (12 bodies).
Pittsburg, Pa........	10	40	2	2	13
Washington, D. C...	45	15	6	2	13
Detroit, Mich.	12	32	6	4	16
Milwaukee, Wis.	9	22	6	3	22
Newark, N. J........	12	19	2	5	3
Minneapolis, Minn...	16	12	16	1	17
Jersey City, N. J.....	8	15	2	1	5
Louisville, Ky.	27	22	..	2	6
Omaha, Neb.	9	9	10	2	10
Rochester, N. Y.....	14	16	2	2	8
St. Paul, Minn.......	11	18	8	2	19
Kansas City, Mo.....	12	21	5	1	4
Providence, R. I.....	21	17	16	1	..
Denver, Col........	10	12	10	3	6
Indianapolis, Ind. ...	10	8	4	4	6
Allegheny, Pa.......	5	13	2	..	10
Total	409	608	183	74	246

VALUE OF CHURCH

CITIES.	Baptist (5 bodies).	Catholic (6 bodies).
St. Louis, Mo....................	$431,375	$1,602,835
Boston, Mass....................	1,537,000	3,296,700
Baltimore, Md...................	804,150	1,462,920
San Francisco, Cal...............	199,250	1,364,300
Cincinnati, O....................	348,500	1,934,900
Cleveland, O....................	363,500	832,000
Buffalo, N.Y.	412,000	2,176,500
New Orleans, La.................	137,850	970,400
Pittsburg, Pa....................	252,200	1,373,800
Washington, D. C...............	1,026,000	990,800
Detroit, Mich...................	344,200	1,050,800
Milwaukee, Wis.	200,800	891,200
Newark, N. J....................	547,000	783,049
Minneapolis, Minn...............	513,863	625,115
Jersey City, N. J.................	207,000	1,083,500
Louisville, Ky...................	686,650	889,200
Omaha, Neb.	124,300	549,000
Rochester, N. Y.................	424,607	1,057,000

EDIFICES.—*Continued.*

Methodist Episcopal.	Other Methodist (11 bodies).	Presbyterian (11 bodies).	Protestant Episcopal.	Reformed (3 bodies).	Miscellaneous.	Total.
26	12	46	18	2	16	187
22	27	20	27	2	7	186
17	3	17	29	2	18	156
14	2	8	8	2	11	107
18	4	35	16	12	6	132
23	2	14	8	..	17	126
14	2	11	12	12	7	89
9	18	20	19	2	19	144
10	2	16	10	..	6	84
11	2	14	16	6	11	102
30	2	13	13	1	11	128
13	9	15	5	1	15	101
11	5	2	14	..	14	101
12	4	7	7	1	9	81
19	6	16	7	3	13	96
7	5	26	4	..	5	77
493	199	440	389	82	439	3,562

PROPERTY.

Congregational.	Jews (2 bodies).	Lutheran (12 bodies).	Methodist Episcopal.
$333,000	$178,000	$422,400	$274,450
2,318,100	243,000	72,000	1,085,000
68,000	263,000	585,800	2,055,300
249,500	300,000	168,200	446,500
169,000	484,000	119,000	691,000
397,200	108,000	178,000	517,000
117,000	50,000	257,070	404,900
15,700	235,000	60,200	119,412
52,500	65,000	373,000	796,900
339,000	42,000	414,000	758,800
161,500	107,000	181,250	366,600
158,000	93,000	653,700	183,000
90,000	117,800	75,000	679,500
465,250	20,000	203,000	474,200
52,000	10,000	77,000	345,300
....	4,500	40,800	105,000
220,600	20,500	258,075	191,100
120,000	40,000	127,000	250,000

TABLE VIII.—VALUE OF

CITIES.	Baptist (5 bodies).	Catholic (6 bodies).
St. Paul, Minn....................	$250,400	$683,300
Kansas City, Mo.................	356,000	569,950
Providence, R. I.................	676,700	1,285,000
Denver, Col......................	254,600	513,042
Indianapolis, Ind.	93,600	243,700
Allegheny, Pa...................	37,400	337,500
Total	$10,228,945	$26,566,511

CONTINUATION OF VALUE

CITIES.	Other Methodist (11 bodies).	Presbyterian (11 bodies).
St. Louis, Mo.	$474,900	$980,700
Boston, Mass.....................	105,000	350,000
Baltimore, Md....................	686,100	1,191,324
San Francisco, Cal.	71,450	666,100
Cincinnati, O	18,000	963,700
Cleveland, O.....................	31,000	840,000
Buffalo, N. Y.....................	17,300	1,051,600
New Orleans, La.................	319,195	337,000
Pittsburg, Pa.....................	448,800	2,042,450
Washington, D. C.	760,100	950,000
Detroit, Mich....................	30,600	875,000
Milwaukee, Wis.	42,500	302,500
Newark, N. J.....................	58,500	1,339,720
Minneapolis, Minn...............	11,000	546,000
Jersey City, N. J.................	16,600	280,500
Louisville, Ky....................	268,500	575,500
Omaha, Neb.	53,000	195,700
Rochester, N. Y..................	16,000	670,000
St. Paul, Minn.	18,000	395,000
Kansas City, Mo.................	250,070	332,700
Providence, R. I.................	80,368	55,000
Denver, Col......................	110,000	236,150
Indianapolis, Ind.	87,500	360,000
Allegheny, Pa...................	123,000	831,600
Total	$4,097,483	$16,368,244

CHURCH PROPERTY—*Continued.*

Congrega-tional.	Jews (2 bodies).	Lutheran (12 bodies).	Methodist Episcopal.
$133,200	$50,000	$269,300	$389,200
164,500	50,000	95,000	397,385
585,500	25,000	. . . .	250,300
206,300	63,500	140,200	652,000
66,050	24,500	118,700	351,000
30,500	. . . . . .	201,400	197,000
$6,512,400	$2,593,800	$5,090,095	$11,980,847

OF CHURCH PROPERTY.

Protestant Episcopal.	Reformed (3 bodies).	Miscellaneous.	Total.
$502,000	. . . . . .	$677,300	$5,876,960
2,144,175	$56,000	3,464,400	14,671,375
1,418,544	185,500	808,200	9,528,838
385,000	. . . . . .	390,800	4,241,100
314,000	172,500	929,450	6,144,050
367,700	74,650	524,850	4,233,900
797,000	76,000	609,750	5,969,120
231,500	. . . . . .	126,850	2,553,107
939,500	70,000	499,600	6,913,750
788,500	31,000	270,375	6,370,575
621,600	13,000	367,600	4,119,150
493,700	24,500	162,500	3,205,400
426,000	426,500	179,000	4,722,069
246,200	. . . . . .	342,200	3,446,828
325,000	336,500	65,000	2,798,400
376,300	25,000	361,300	3,332,750
276,550	. . . . . .	102,000	1,990,825
330,500	46,000	297,000	3,378,107
193,700	8,000	109,200	2,499,300
200,500	12,000	244,250	2,672,355
627,300	. . . . . .	673,600	4,258,768
418,000	20,000	270,350	2,884,142
153,000	23,000	130,600	1,651,650
76,000	. . . . . .	203,000	2,037,400
$12,652,269	$1,600,150	$11,809,175	$109,499,919

TABLE VIII—Churches in

Communi

CITIES.	Population.	Baptist (5 bodies).	Catholic (6 bodies).	Congregational.	Jews (2 bodies).
St. Louis, Mo.........	451,770	5,654	75,908	2,670	3,022
Boston, Mass..........	448,477	11,885	185,188	10,076	2,300
Baltimore, Md.	434,439	18,728	77,047	268	3,500
San Francisco, Cal.....	298,997	1,228	70,670	2,121	4,075
Cincinnati, O..........	296,908	4,063	72,368	1,047	3,725
Cleveland, O..........	261,353	3,449	52,420	3,333	2,911
Buffalo, N. Y.	255,664	3,958	73,010	592	1,025
New Orleans, La......	242,039	2,941	67,156	431	2,750
Pittsburg, Pa..........	238,617	2,288	56,916	489	1,250
Washington, D. C.....	230,392	21,781	36,488	1,399	976
Detroit, Mich.........	205,876	3,078	45,795	1,268	2,700
Milwaukee, Wis.......	204,468	1,686	35,050	1,154	981
Newark, N. J.........	181,830	4,119	39,324	744	2,090
Minneapolis, Minn.....	164,738	3,687	37,855	3,372	474
Jersey City, N. J......	163,003	2,378	45,760	633	250
Louisville, Ky.........	161,129	13,753	33,740	56	515
Omaha, Neb..........	140,452	1,107	7,675	1,103	1,035
Rochester, N. Y.......	133,896	3,345	31,690	460	911
St. Paul, Minn........	133,156	1,867	51,215	1,354	950
Kansas City, Mo.......	132,716	4,490	11,900	1,076	825
Providence, R. I.......	132,146	5,382	44,065	3,766	875
Denver, Col..........	106,713	2,498	18,039	1,362	895
Indianapolis, Ind.	105,436	1,714	8,390	636	1,627
Allegheny, Pa.........	105,287	1,005	13,494	356	25
Total	5,229,432	126,184	1,191,163	39,766	39,687

RECAPIT

	Organizations.
Cities of the First Class (4)	2,187
Cities of the Second Class (24)	3,770
Cities of the Third Class (96)	4,284
Total (124)	10,241

CITIES—SECOND CLASS.—*Continued.*

CANTS.

Lutheran (12 bodies).	Methodist Episcopal.	Other Methodist (11 bodies).	Presbyterian (11 bodies).	Protestant Episcopal.	Reformed (3 bodies).	Miscellaneous.	Total.
7,458	3,871	6,440	5,727	3,536	....	16,900	131,186
1,959	5,963	737	2,243	8,167	62	15,468	244,048
10,902	22,258	10,879	6,505	12,193	3,695	9,920	175,995
2,096	3,115	1,125	3,421	2,446	....	2,575	92,872
1,252	6,262	587	5,110	2,253	2,018	17,092	115,777
7,162	4,440	543	5,553	3,257	2,611	8,706	94,385
13,460	3,785	210	4,240	3,387	2,163	9,330	115,160
2,777	3,938	4,679	3,023	2,910	....	5,111	95,716
4,868	6,701	2,926	12,066	3,545	630	14,078	105,757
2,997	9,144	6,526	5,128	7,315	301	2,517	94,572
8,609	4,696	875	5,343	5,693	220	5,120	83,397
18,892	2,403	119	1,467	1,952	380	4,165	68,249
1,387	6,199	568	7,606	3,076	2,178	2,697	60,988
5,906	4,432	189	3,653	2,465	....	3,151	65,184
2,230	3,805	231	2,000	2,755	3,033	790	63,865
1,483	1,613	6,271	3,981	3,651	600	7,692	73,355
1,277	1,859	204	2,150	1,228	....	1,020	18,658
4,847	3,008	360	6,137	3,263	952	4,064	59,037
5,608	3,290	190	2,772	2,140	120	1,607	71,113
838	3,195	1,960	2,272	1,143	31	3,870	31,600
75	2,886	859	525	4,251	....	4,031	66,715
540	2,858	706	2,319	1,820	35	2,541	33,613
2,588	5,829	2,053	3,806	1,120	560	3,833	32,156
2,804	2,538	1,107	6,985	484	....	3,868	32,666
112,015	118,088	50,344	104,032	84,050	19,589	150,146	2,035,064

ULATION.

Church Edifices.	Value of Church Property.	Communicants.	Population.
2,081	$116,839,069	1,589,898	4,468,458
3,562	109,499,919	2,035,064	5,229,432
4,079	87,198,259	1,677,056	4,291,048
9,722	$313,537,247	5,302,018	13,988,938

STATISTICAL SUMMARY BY STATES ACCORDING TO THE CENSUS OF 1906

SHOWING GAINS IN THE SIXTEEN YEARS IN NUMBER AND PERCENTAGE OF COMMUNICANTS

TABLE I.—Returns

STATES.	Organizations.	Edifices.	Seating Capacity.
Alabama	8,858	8,183	2,423,175
*Alaska	....	....	......
Arizona	236	181	40,954
Arkansas	6,144	5,192	1,446,892
California	2,840	2,521	694,510
Colorado	1,261	956	255,469
Connecticut	1,364	1,414	522,941
Delaware	467	478	130,267
District of Columbia	288	264	142,311
Florida	3,346	3,061	688,986
Georgia	10,026	9,624	3,063,866
Idaho	673	495	121,775
Illinois	9,308	8,626	2,685,352
Indiana	6,829	6,580	2,132,181
Iowa	6,259	5,921	1,617,467
Kansas	4,975	4,107	1,054,976
Kentucky	6,512	5,894	1,775,123
Louisiana	3,813	3,630	1,046,850
Maine	1,532	1,511	412,833
Maryland	2,756	2,814	810,701
Massachusetts	3,031	2,983	1,313,564
Michigan	5,605	4,882	1,353,180
Minnesota	4,721	4,280	1,104,317
Mississippi	7,361	6,997	2,041,665
Missouri	9,172	8,146	2,391,498
Montana	542	407	100,665
Nebraska	3,300	2,847	649,132
Nevada	86	67	15,015
New Hampshire	832	851	254,017
New Jersey	2,750	2,875	1,015,903
New Mexico	624	522	129,745
New York	9,227	9,193	3,191,267
North Carolina	8,554	8,188	2,715,567
North Dakota	1,961	1,325	262,251
Ohio	9,807	9,519	3,102,819
†Oklahoma	4,466	2,709	598,650
Oregon	1,290	1,086	270,329
Pennsylvania	12,748	12,780	4,646,929

* Not given in census of 1906.

BY STATES FOR 1906.

Value of Church Property.	Communicants.	Increase in Communicants, 1890–1906.	
		Actual.	Percentage.
$13,314,993	824,209	265,038	47
. . . .	. . . . . .	. . . . .	. .
798,975	45,057	18,085	67
6,733,375	426,179	129,971	44
28,065,261	611,464	330,845	118
7,723,200	205,666	118,829	137
29,196,128	502,560	193,219	62
3,250,105	71,251	22,572	46
10,025,122	136,759	42,556	45
5,795,859	221,318	79,584	56
17,929,183	1,029,037	349,986	52
1,726,734	74,578	50,542	210
66,222,514	2,077,197	874,609	73
31,081,500	938,405	244,545	35
30,464,860	788,667	231,580	42
14,053,454	458,190	121,461	36
18,044,389	858,324	251,927	42
10,456,146	778,901	378,909	95
9,955,363	212,988	52,717	33
23,765,172	473,257	93,839	25
84,729,445	1,562,621	619,870	66
27,144,250	982,479	412,975	73
26,053,159	834,442	301,852	57
9,482,229	657,381	226,635	53
38,059,233	1,199,239	463,400	63
2,809,779	98,984	66,236	202
12,114,817	345,803	151,337	78
402,350	14,944	9,056	154
7,864,991	190,298	87,307	85
50,907,123	857,548	349,197	69
956,605	137,009	31,260	30
255,166,284	3,591,974	1,420,152	65
14,053,505	824,385	139,191	20
4,576,157	159,053	99,557	167
74,670,765	1,742,873	526,407	43
4,933,843	257,100	222,924	652
4,620,793	120,229	49,705	70
173,605,141	2,977,022	1,250,382	72

† Includes Indian Territory, given separately in 1890.

TABLE I.—Returns by

STATES.	Organizations.	Edifices.	Seating Capacity.
Rhode Island..............	507	493	195,688
South Carolina............	5,373	5,290	1,774,437
South Dakota.............	1,798	1,461	285,197
Tennessee................	7,963	7,400	2,323,285
Texas....................	12,285	9,589	2,822,460
Utah.....................	537	516	169,369
Vermont.................	902	891	235,661
Virginia..................	6,605	6,480	1,974,332
Washington...............	1,759	1,416	341,812
West Virginia.............	4,019	3,428	949,812
Wisconsin................	4,880	4,562	1,206,385
Wyoming.................	226	160	35,250
Total for U. S. in 1906.....	210,418	192,795	58,536,830
*Total for U. S. in 1890.....	165,271	142,605	43,591,575
Increase in 16 years........	45,147	50,190	14,945,255

* Exclusive

STATES FOR 1906.—*Continued.*

Value of Church Property.	Communicants.	Increase in Communicants, 1890–1906.	
		Actual.	Percentage.
$9,533,543	264,712	116,704	79
10,209,043	665,933	157,448	31
4,538,013	161,961	76,471	89
14,469,012	697,570	144,912	26
22,949,976	1,226,906	549,745	81
3,612,422	172,814	44,699	35
5,939,492	147,223	40,908	40
19,699,014	793,546	224,311	38
8,082,986	191,976	133,178	227
9,733,585	301,565	109,088	57
27,277,837	1,000,903	444,420	80
778,142	23,945	12,240	105
$1,257,575,867	32,936,445	12,332,990	60
679,490,789	20,603,455		
$578,085,078	12,332,990		

of Alaska.

STATISTICAL TABLES FOR 1900 AND 1910
GAINS AND LOSSES OF TWO DECADES

STATISTICAL SUMMARIES

TABLE I.—Ministers, Churches, and Communi

DENOMINATIONS.	Ministers.	For the In the United Churches.
Adventists:		
1. Evangelical............................	34	30
2. Advent Christians.....................	912	610
3. Seventh-Day..........................	386	1,494
4. Church of God........................	19	29
5. Life and Advent Union.................	60	28
6. Churches of God in Jesus Christ.........	94	95
Total Adventists	1,505	2,286
Baptists:		
1. Regular (North).......................	7,535	9,295
2. Regular (South).......................	12,560	19,669
3. Regular (Colored).....................	9,856	14,786
4. Six-Principle.........................	8	12
5. Seventh-Day..........................	124	95
6. Free.................................	1,436	1,522
7. Freewill.............................	120	167
8. General..............................	484	423
9. Separate.............................	113	103
10. United...............................	25	204
11. Baptist Church of Christ...............	80	152
12. Primitive............................	2,130	3,530
13. Primitive (Colored) (1)................	.....	.....
14. Old Two-Seed-in-the-Spirit Predestinarian.	300	473
15. Church of God and Saints of Christ (Col.)..	.....	.....
Total Baptists.....................	34,771	50,431
Brethren (Dunkards or Dunkers):		
1. Conservative..........................	2,612	850
2. Old Order............................	140	80
3. Progressive...........................	231	145
4. Seventh-Day (German).................	5	6
Total (Dunkard) Brethren..........	2,988	1,081

(1) Not reported

FOR 1900 AND 1910

CANTS IN THE UNITED STATES ONLY

Year 1900. States Only. Communicants.	Ministers.	For the Year 1910. In the United States Only. Churches.	Communicants.
1,147	c 8	c 18	c 481
26,500	c 528	c 550	c 26,799
54,539	517	1,826	65,122
647	c 32	c 20	c 611
3,000	c 12	c 12	c 509
2,872	c 56	c 62	c 2,124
88,705	1,153	2,488	95,646
999,657	8,198	9,704	1,210,713
1,638,985	14,533	22,726	2,283,066
1,594,584	12,637	17,323	1,790,165
828	10	16	731
9,095	98	82	8,119
86,535	1,186	1,112	70,880
12,000	604	623	40,578
24,775	550	545	33,600
6,479	c 100	c 76	c 5,180
13,209	c 260	c 196	c 13,698
8,254	c 99	c 93	c 6,416
126,000	c 1,500	c 2,922	c 102,311
......	c 1,480	c 797	c 35,076
12,851	c 35	c 55	c 781
......	c 75	c 48	c 1,823
4,533,252	41,365	56,318	5,603,137
95,000	3,006	880	100,000
4,000	228	75	4,000
13,000	186	219	18,607
194	9	14	240
112,194	3,429	1,188	122,847

separately in 1890.   *c* Census of 1906.

TABLE I.—Ministers, Churches, and Communi

DENOMINATIONS.	For the In the United Ministers.	Churches.
BRETHREN (PLYMOUTH):		
1. Brethren (I.).............................	....	109
2. Brethren (II.)............................	....	88
3. Brethren (III.)..........................	....	86
4. Brethren (IV.)...........................	....	31
Total (Plymouth) Brethren..........	....	314
BRETHREN (RIVER):		
1. Brethren in Christ......................	152	78
2. Old Order, or Yorker...................	7	8
3. United Zion's Children.................	20	25
Total (River) Brethren..............	179	111
BUDDHISTS:		
1. Chinese Temples.........................	....	47
2. Japanese Temples (1)...................	....	....
Total Buddhists....................	....	47
CATHOLIC APOSTOLIC:		
1. Catholic Apostolic......................	95	10
2. New Apostolic...........................	....	....
Total Catholic Apostolic............	95	10
CATHOLICS, EASTERN ORTHODOX:		
1. Armenian Apostolic.....................	15	21
2. Russian Orthodox.......................	40	31
3. Greek Orthodox.........................	5	5
4. Syrian Orthodox (2).....................	....	....
5. Servian Orthodox (2)...................	....	....
6. Roumanian Orthodox (2)...............	....	....
7. Bulgarian Orthodox (2).................	....	....
Total Eastern Orthodox.............	60	57

(1) Not in existence in 1890. Most of the temples in California.

CANTS IN THE UNITED STATES ONLY.—*Continued.*

Year 1900. States Only.		For the Year 1910. In the United States Only.	
Communicants.	Ministers.	Churches.	Communicants.
2,289	....	*c* 134	*c* 2,933
2,419	....	*c* 128	*c* 4,752
1,235	....	*c* 81	*c* 1,724
718	....	*c* 60	*c* 1,157
6,661	....	403	10,566
4,000	174	65	3,675
214	*c* 24	*c* 9	*c* 423
525	*c* 22	*c* 28	*c* 749
4,739	220	102	4,847
....	*c* 1	*c* 62	......
....	*c* 14	*c* 12	*c* 3,165
....	15	74	3,165
1,491	*c* 14	*c* 11	*c* 2,907
.....	*c* 19	*c* 13	*c* 2,020
1,491	33	24	4,927
8,500	14	21	50,000
40,000	110	121	60,000
5,000	71	62	160,000
.....	21	18	40,000
.....	9	10	35,000
.....	5	5	20,000
.....	3	3	20,000
53,500	233	240	385,000

(2) Introduced in recent years by immigration.   *c* Census of 1906.

TABLE I.—Ministers, Churches, and Communi

DENOMINATIONS.	Ministers.	For the In the United Churches.
CATHOLICS, WESTERN:		
1. Roman Catholic	11,848	12,263
2. Polish National Catholic	19	18
3. Reformed Catholic	6	6
4. Old Catholic (1)	3	5
Total Western Catholics	11,876	12,292
CHRISTADELPHIANS	....	63
CHRISTIANS (2)	1,151	1,517
CHRISTIAN CATHOLIC (DOWIE)	55	50
CHRISTIAN MISSIONARY ASSOCIATION (1)	10	13
CHRISTIAN SCIENTISTS	940	470
CHRISTIAN UNION	183	294
CHURCHES OF GOD (WINNEBRENNERIAN)	460	580
CHURCHES OF THE LIVING GOD (COLORED) (3):		
1. Christian Workers for Friendship	....	....
2. Apostolic	....	....
3. Church of Christ in God	....	....
Total Churches of the Living God	....	....
CHURCHES OF THE NEW JERUSALEM:		
1. General Convention	143	173
2. General Church (4)	....	....
Total New Jerusalem Churches	143	173
COMMUNISTIC SOCIETIES:		
1. Shakers	....	15
2. Amana	....	7
3. Harmony (1)	....	1
4. Separatists (1)	....	1
5. Altruists (1)	....	1
6. Church Triumphant (Koreshan Ecclesia) (1)	....	5
7. Christian Commonwealth (1)	....	1
Total Communists	....	31

(1) Dissolved.   (2) Formerly reported in two branches.

CANTS IN THE UNITED STATES ONLY.—*Continued.*

Year 1900. States Only. Communicants.	For the Year 1910. In the United States Only.		
	Ministers.	Churches.	Communicants.
8,690,658	17,084	13,461	12,425,947
20,000	c 24	c 24	c 15,473
1,500	7	6	2,100
425	. . . . .	. . . .	. . . . . .
8,712,583	17,115	13,491	12,443,520
1,277	. . . .	c 70	c 1,412
109,278	993	1,329	87,478
40,000	c 35	c 17	c 5,865
754	. . . .	. . . .	. . . .
48,930	2,208	1,104	85,096
18,214	c 295	c 237	c 13,905
38,000	509	595	41,475
. . . . .	c 51	c 44	c 2,676
. . . . .	c 30	c 15	c 752
. . . . .	c 20	c 9	c 858
. . . . .	101	68	4,286
7,679	109	138	8,500
. . . . .	23	14	814
7,679	132	152	9,314
1,650	. . . .	c 15	c 516
1,600	. . . .	c 7	c 1,756
250	. . . .	. . . .	. . . .
200	. . . .	. . . .	. . . .
25	. . . .	. . . .	. . . .
205	. . . .	. . . .	. . . .
80	. . . .	. . . .	. . . .
4,010	. . . .	22	2,272

(3) Organized since 1899.   (4) Organized in 1897, as result of division.   *c* Census of 1906.

TABLE I.—Ministers, Churches, and Communi

| | | For the
In the United |
DENOMINATIONS.	Ministers.	Churches.
CONGREGATIONALISTS......................	5,625	5,624
DISCIPLES OF CHRIST:		
1. Disciples of Christ....................	6,348	10,528
2. Churches of Christ (1)..................	....	....
Total Disciples of Christ............	6,348	10,528
EVANGELICAL BODIES:		
1. Evangelical Association.................	877	1,617
2. United Evangelical Church..............	478	985
Total Evangelical bodies............	1,355	2,602
FAITH ASSOCIATIONS: (2)		
1. Apostolic Faith Movement..............	....	....
2. Peniel Missions.......................	....	....
3. Metropolitan Church Association........	....	....
4. Hepzibah Faith Association.............	....	....
5. Missionary Church Association..........	....	....
6. Heavenly Recruit Church...............	....	....
7. Apostolic Christian Church.............	....	....
8. Christian Congregation.................	....	....
9. Voluntary Missionary Society (Colored)..	....	....
Total Faith Associations............	....	....
FREE CHRISTIAN ZION CHURCH (COLORED) (3).	....	....
FRIENDS:		
1. Orthodox............................	1,279	830
2. "Hicksite"..........................	115	201
3. "Wilburite".........................	38	53
4. Primitive...........................	11	9
Total Friends....................	1,443	1,093

(1) Not reported separately in 1890 or 1900.   A division.   (2) All reported since 1900.

CANTS IN THE UNITED STATES ONLY.—*Continued.*

Year 1900. States Only. Communicants.	Ministers.	For the Year 1910. In the United States Only. Churches.	Communicants.
631,360	6,045	6,050	735,400
1,149,982	5,970	10,830	1,308,116
. . . .	c 2,100	2,649	c 156,658
1,149,982	8,070	13,479	1,464,774
96,345	980	1,657	108,666
60,993	509	997	73,399
157,338	1,489	2,654	182,065
. . . .	. . . .	c 6	c 538
. . . .	c 30	c 11	c 703
. . . .	c 29	c 6	c 466
. . . .	c 36	c 10	c 293
. . . .	c 35	c 32	c 1,256
. . . .	c 55	c 27	c 938
. . . .	c 19	c 42	c 4,558
. . . .	c 26	c 9	c 395
. . . .	c 11	c 3	c 425
. . . .	241	146	9,572
. . . .	c 20	c 15	c 1,835
92,468	1,302	830	100,072
21,992	97	211	19,595
4,468	c 47	c 48	c 3,880
232	c 10	c 8	c 171
119,160	1,456	1,097	123,718

(3) Organized in 1895 by withdrawals from Methodist and Baptist bodies.   *c* Census of 1906.

TABLE I.—Ministers, Churches, and Communi

DENOMINATIONS.	Ministers.	For the In the United Churches.
Friends of the Temple.....................	4	4
German Evangelical Protestant..........	45	55
German Evangelical Synod...............	909	1,129
Jewish Congregations (1).................	301	570
Latter-Day Saints:		
1. Utah Branch.........................	700	796
2. Reorganized........................	1,200	600
Total Latter-Day Saints............	1,900	1,396
Lutherans:		
1. General Synod.......................	1,216	1,576
2. United Synod, South.................	214	390
3. General Council.....................	1,205	1,882
4. Synodical Conference................	2,029	2,650
5. United Norwegian....................	361	1,121
Independent Synods.		
6. Ohio................................	457	604
7. Buffalo.............................	26	36
8. Hauge's.............................	95	212
9. Eielsen's...........................	9	52
10. Texas..............................	11	14
11. Iowa...............................	433	824
12. Norwegian..........................	252	739
13. Michigan (3).......................	53	78
14. Danish in America..................	47	66
15. Icelandic..........................	8	26
16. Immanuel...........................	45	50
17. Suomai (Finnish)...................	11	46
18. Finnish Apostolic (4)..............	...	...
19. Finnish National (4)...............	...	...
20. Norwegian Free.....................	112	300
21. Danish United......................	88	150
22. Slovakian (4)......................	...	...
23. Church of the Lutheran Brethren (4).....	...	...
24. Jehovah............................	6	6
Independent Congregations.............	85	200
Total Lutherans...................	6,763	11,022

(1) Reported in 1890 in two branches.   (2) Including only heads of families.

CANTS IN THE UNITED STATES ONLY.—*Continued.*

Year 1900. States Only. Communicants.	Ministers.	For the Year 1910. In the United States Only. Churches.	Communicants.
340	c 3	c 2	c 376
36,500	c 59	c 66	c 34,704
203,574	1,024	1,314	236,615
143,000 (2)	c 1,084	c 1,769	143,000(2)
300,000	1,223	780	350,000
43,824	1,260	570	50,650
343,824	2,483	1,350	400,650
199,589	1,333	1,785	302,440
38,639	248	468	48,921
356,401	1,507	2,298	459,224
581,029	2,713	3,356	766,281
130,000	550	1,464	161,964
77,362	585	784	127,430
5,000	28	42	5,200
12,540	150	347	36,357
2,800	6	26	1,130
1,700	21	32	2,800
74,058	527	940	106,593
66,927	382	1,000	100,000
9,547	....	....	......
10,000	58	119	13,052
5,559	13	39	4,700
6,118	12	6	2,500
11,048	32	170	17,500
......	62	73	11,000
......	20	40	6,000
38,000	175	375	20,000
8,500	114	176	11,994
......	17	30	9,500
......	12	16	1,800
350	9	11	1,100
25,000	85	205	26,000
1,660,167	8,659	13,802	2,243,486

(3) Dissolved.   (4) Organized since 1900.   c Census of 1906.

TABLE I.—Ministers, Churches, and Communi

DENOMINATIONS.	For the In the United Ministers.	Churches.
SCANDINAVIAN EVANGELICAL BODIES:		
1. Swedish Evangelical Mission Covenant (1)	265	270
2. Swedish Evangelical Free Mission........	....	....
3. Norwegian Evangelical Free.............	....	....
Total Scandinavian Evangelical bodies	265	270
MENNONITES:		
1. Mennonite............................	418	288
2. Bruederhoef..........................	9	5
3. Amish................................	265	124
4. Old Amish............................	75	25
5. Apostolic (2).........................	2	2
6. Reformed............................	43	34
7. General Conference...................	128	76
8. Church of God in Christ...............	18	18
9. Old (Wisler).........................	17	15
10. Bundes Conference....................	41	16
11. Defenceless..........................	20	11
12. Brethren in Christ....................	76	59
Separate Conferences (two).............	....	....
Total Mennonites..................	1,112	673
METHODIST:		
1. Methodist Episcopal...................	16,791	26,232
2. Union American Methodist Episcopal....	125	155
3. African Methodist Episcopal...........	5,852	5,630
4. African Union Methodist Protestant.....	106	88
5. African Methodist Episcopal Zion........	3,155	1,906
6. Methodist Protestant...................	1,629	2,394
7. Wesleyan Methodist...................	595	506
8. Methodist Episcopal, South............	5,989	14,212
9. Congregational Methodist..............	325	330
10. Congregational Methodist (Colored) (2)...	5	5
11. New Congregational Methodist..........	192	366
12. Zion Union Apostolic..................	30	27
13. Colored Methodist Episcopal...........	2,061	1,433
14. Primitive............................	74	90
15. Free.................................	922	944
16. Reformed Methodist Union Episcopal (3).	....	....
17. Independent Methodist.................	8	14
18. Evangelist Missionary (2)..............	48	13
Total Methodists..................	37,907	54,345

(1) Not reported in 1890.   (2) Dissolved.   (3) Result of secession in the

CANTS IN THE UNITED STATES ONLY.—*Continued.*

Year 1900. States Only. Communicants.	For the Year 1910. In the United States Only. Ministers.	Churches.	Communicants.
30,000	377	290	40,000
. . . . . .	151	133	18,000
. . . . . .	65	150	4,000
30,000	593	573	62,000
22,443	c 346	c 220	c 18,674
352	c 9	c 8	c 275
13,051	c 131	c 57	c 7,640
2,438	c 141	c 46	c 5,043
209	. . . .	. . . .	. . . . . .
1,680	c 34	c 34	c 2,079
10,395	c 143	c 90	c 11,661
471	c 17	c 18	c 562
610	c 18	c 9	c 655
2,950	c 36	c 19	c 2,533
1,176	c 26	c 14	c 967
2,953	c 70	c 68	c 2,801
. . . . .	c 35	c 21	c 1,908
58,728	1,006	604	54,798
2,746,191	18,280	28,436	3,186,862
15,500	138	255	18,500
675,462	6,353	5,527	500,000
3,563	200	125	4,000
536,271	3,488	3,298	547,216
183,714	1,393	2,432	188,437
17,201	598	571	19,178
1,468,390	6,611	16,332	1,851,149
20,000	337	333	15,529
319	. . . .	. . . . .	. . . . . .
4,000	c 59	c 35	c 1,782
2,346	c 33	c 45	c 3,059
204,972	2,901	2,857	234,721
6,549	74	101	7,346
27,292	1,119	1,163	32,112
. . . .	c 40	c 58	c 4,000
2,569	2	2	1,161
2,010	. . . .	. . . .	. . . . . .
5,916,349	41,626	61,570	6,615,052

South from African Methodist Episcopal Church in 1885.   c Census of 1906.

TABLE I.—Ministers, Churches, and Communi

DENOMINATIONS.	Ministers.	For the In the United Churches.
MORAVIAN BODIES:		
1. Moravian..............................	117	122
2. Union Bohemians and Moravians (1)	....	....
Total Moravian Bodies..............	117	122
NON-SECTARIAN BIBLE FAITH CHURCHES (2) ..	....	....
PENTECOSTAL BODIES:		
1. Pentecostal Church (3).................	....	....
2. Other Pentecostal Associations..........	....	....
Total Pentecostal Bodies............	....	....
PRESBYTERIANS:		
1. Northern.............................	7,170	7,459
2. Cumberland (4)........................	1,596	2,957
3. Cumberland (Colored)..................	450	400
4. Welsh Calvinistic......................	89	158
5. United...............................	918	911
6. Southern.............................	1,461	2,959
7. Associate.............................	12	31
8. Associate Reformed, South..............	104	131
9. Reformed (Synod)......................	124	113
10. Reformed (General Synod)..............	33	36
11. Reformed (Covenanted).................	1	1
12. Reformed in U. S. and Canada..........	1	1
Total Presbyterians................	11,959	15,157
PROTESTANT EPISCOPAL:		
1. Protestant Episcopal...................	4,811	6,421
2. Reformed Episcopal....................	100	78
Total Protestant Episcopal..........	4,911	6,499
REFORMED:		
1. Reformed (Dutch).....................	690	619
2. Reformed (German)....................	1,074	1,653
3. Christian Reformed....................	96	145
4. Hungarian Reformed (5)................	....	....
Total Reformed....................	1,860	2,417

(1) Organized in Texas in 1903 by immigrants.   (2) Not reported in 1890.
(3) Outcome of union of various Holiness associations at close of last century.

CANTS IN THE UNITED STATES ONLY.—*Continued.*

Year 1900. States Only. Communicants.	Ministers.	For the Year 1910. In the United States Only. Churches.	Communicants.
14,817	133	121	17,940
. . . . .	c 3	c 15	c 771
14,817	136	136	18,711
. . . . .	c 50	c 204	c 6,396
. . . .	700	428	20,000
. . . .	c 115	c 30	c 1,420
. . . .	815	458	21,420
983,433	8,980	9,926	1,328,714
180,192	917	1,570	115,000
30,000	c 375	c 196	c 18,066
12,152	91	148	13,759
115,901	1,012	990	135,010
225,890	1,694	3,324	281,920
1,053	c 12	c 22	c 786
11,344	106	142	14,017
9,790	136	115	9,455
5,000	17	19	3,400
37	. . . .	1	40
608	2	3	598
1,575,400	13,342	16,456	1,920,765
710,356	5,286	7,572	928,780
9,282	94	80	9,610
719,638	5,380	7,652	938,390
107,594	728	684	116,815
242,831	1,226	1,730	297,116
18,096	138	189	29,006
. . . . .	c 18	c 16	c 5,253
368,521	2,110	2,619	448,190

(4) Losses due to union in 1906 with Northern Presbyterian Church.
(5) Organized in 1904 by immigrants from Hungary.   c Census of 1906.

TABLE I.—MINISTERS, CHURCHES, AND COMMUNI

DENOMINATIONS.	For the In the United Ministers.	Churches.
SALVATIONISTS:		
1. Salvation Army..........................	2,361	663
2. American Salvation Army (1)............	....	....
Total Salvationists..................	2,361	663
SCHWENKFELDERS	3	4
SOCIAL BRETHREN............................	17	20
SOCIETY FOR ETHICAL CULTURE...............	....	5
SPIRITUALISTS..............................	....	334
THEOSOPHICAL SOCIETY......................	....	122
UNITARIANS.................................	544	453
UNITED BRETHREN:		
1. United Brethren........................	1,833	4,166
2. United Brethren (Old Constitution)......	619	786
Total United Brethren..............	2,452	4,952
UNIVERSALISTS..............................	730	770
INDEPENDENT CONGREGATIONS................	54	156
GRAND TOTAL.....................	143,401	190,805

TABLE II.—

DENOMINATIONS.	For the In the United Ministers.
Adventists (6 bodies)..............................	1,505
Baptists (15 bodies in 1910)...........................	34,771
Brethren (Dunkards) (4 bodies).....................	2,988
Brethren (Plymouth) (4 bodies).....................	....
Brethren (River) (3 bodies)........................	179
Buddhists (2 bodies in 1910).......................	....
Catholic Apostolic (2 bodies in 1910)...............	95
Catholic, Eastern Orthodox (7 bodies in 1910)........	60
Catholic, Western (3 bodies in 1910)................	11,876
Christadelphians...................................	....
Christians...	1,151
Christian Catholic (Dowie).........................	55

(1) Not reported in 1890.

CANTS IN THE UNITED STATES ONLY.—*Continued.*

Year 1900. States Only. Communicants.	Ministers.	For the Year 1910. In the United States Only. Churches.	Communicants.
19,490	3,137	896	25,839
......	c 59	c 20	c 436
19,490	3,196	916	26,275
306	6	8	850
913	c 15	c 17	c 1,262
1,300	7	6	2,450
45,030	....	1,000	150,000
3,000	....	114	3,100
71,000	558	482	70,542
239,639	1,890	3,721	283,682
26,296	303	545	19,637
265,935	2,193	4,266	303,319
52,739	730	881	52,150
14,126	267	879	48,673
27,383,804	170,499	218,507	35,145,296

SUMMARY.

Year 1900. States Only. Churches.	Communicants.	Ministers.	For the Year 1910. In the United States Only. Churches.	Communicants
2,286	88,705	1,153	2,488	95,646
50,431	4,533,252	41,365	56,318	5,603,137
1,081	112,194	3,429	1,188	122,847
314	6,661	....	403	10,566
111	4,739	220	102	4,847
47	....	15	74	3,165
10	1,491	33	24	4,927
57	53,500	233	240	385,000
12,292	8,712,583	17,115	13,491	12,443,520
63	1,277	....	c 70	c 1,412
1,517	109,278	993	1,329	87,478
50	40,000	35	17	5,865

c Census of 1906.

TABLE II.—

For the
In the United
Ministers.

DENOMINATIONS.	
Christian Missionary Association	10
Christian Scientists	940
Christian Union	183
Church of God (Winnebrennerian)	460
Churches of the Living God (3 bodies)	....
Churches of the New Jerusalem (2 bodies in 1910)	143
Communistic Societies (2 bodies in 1910)	....
Congregationalists	5,625
Disciples of Christ (2 bodies in 1910)	6,348
Evangelical bodies (2 bodies)	1,355
Faith Associations (9 bodies)	....
Free Christian Zion Church	....
Friends (4 bodies)	1,443
Friends of the Temple	4
German Evangelical Protestant	45
German Evangelical Synod	909
Jewish Congregations	301
Latter-Day Saints (2 bodies)	1,900
Lutherans (24 bodies in 1910)	6,763
Scandinavian Evangelical (3 bodies in 1910)	265
Mennonites (11 bodies in 1910)	1,112
Methodists (17 bodies in 1910)	37,907
Moravians (2 bodies in 1910)	117
Non-sectarian Bible Faith Churches	....
Pentecostal bodies (all bodies)	....
Presbyterians (12 bodies)	11,959
Protestant Episcopal (2 bodies)	4,911
Reformed (4 bodies in 1910)	1,860
Salvationists (2 bodies in 1910)	2,361
Schwenkfelders	3
Social Brethren	17
Society for Ethical Culture	....
Spiritualists	....
Theosophical Society	....
Unitarians	544
United Brethren (2 bodies)	2,452
Universalists	730
Independent Congregations	54
Total	143,401

SUMMARY.—*Continued.*

Year 1900. States Only.		For the Year 1910. In the United States Only.		
Churches.	Communicants.	Ministers.	Churches.	Communicants.
13	754	. . . .	. . . .	. . . .
470	48,930	2,208	1,104	85,096
294	18,214	295	237	13,905
580	38,000	509	595	41,475
. . . .	. . . .	101	68	4,286
173	7,679	132	152	9,314
31	4,010	. . . .	22	2,272
5,624	631,360	6,045	6,050	735,400
10,528	1,149,982	8,070	13,479	1,464,774
2,602	157,338	1,489	2,654	182,065
. . . .	. . . .	241	146	9,572
. . . .	. . . .	20	15	1,835
1,093	119,160	1,456	1,097	123,718
4	340	3	2	376
55	36,500	59	66	34,704
1,219	203,574	1,024	1,314	236,615
570	143,000	1,084	1,769	143,000
1,396	343,824	2,483	1,350	400,650
11,022	1,660,167	8,659	13,802	2,243,486
270	30,000	593	573	62,000
673	58,728	1,006	604	54,798
54,345	5,916,349	41,626	61,570	6,615,052
122	14,817	136	136	18,711
. . . .	. . . .	50	204	6,396
. . . .	. . . .	815	458	21,420
15,157	1,575,400	13,342	16,456	1,920,765
6,499	719,638	5,380	7,652	938,390
2,417	368,521	2,110	2,619	448,190
663	19,490	3,196	916	26,275
4	306	6	8	850
20	913	15	17	1,262
5	1,300	7	6	2,450
334	45,030	. . . .	1,000	150,000
122	3,000	. . . .	114	3,100
453	71,000	558	482	70,542
4,952	265,935	2,193	4,266	303,319
770	52,739	730	881	52,150
156	14,126	267	879	48,673
190,805	27,383,804	170,499	218,507	35,245,296

TABLE III.—ORDER OF ALL DENOMINATIONS ACCORDING TO NUMBER OF COMMUNICANTS, 1910.

DENOMINATIONS.	Communicants.
1. Roman Catholic	12,425,947
2. Methodist Episcopal	3,186,862
3. Southern Baptist	2,283,066
4. Methodist Episcopal, South	1,851,149
5. Colored Baptist	1,790,165
6. Northern Presbyterian	1,328,714
7. Disciples of Christ	1,308,116
8. Northern Baptists	1,210,713
9. Protestant Episcopal	928,780
10. Lutheran Synodical Conference	766,281
11. Congregational	735,400
12. African Methodist Episcopal Zion	547,216
13. African Methodist Episcopal	500,000
14. Lutheran General Council	459,224
15. Latter-Day Saints, Utah	350,000
16. Lutheran General Synod	302,440
17. Reformed (German)	297,116
18. United Brethren	283,682
19. Southern Presbyterian	281,920
20. German Evangelical Synod	236,615
21. Colored Methodist Episcopal	234,721
22. Methodist Protestant	188,437
23. Lutheran United Norwegian	161,964
24. Greek Orthodox	160,000
25. Churches of Christ, Disciple	156,658
26. Spiritualist	150,000
27. Jewish	143,000
28. United Presbyterian	135,010
29. Lutheran Synod of Ohio	127,430
30. Reformed (Dutch)	116,815
31. Cumberland Presbyterian	115,000
32. Evangelical Association	108,666
33. Lutheran Synod of Iowa	106,593
34. Primitive Baptist	102,311
35. Orthodox Friends	100,072
36. Conservative Brethren, Dunkard	100,000
37. Lutheran Norwegian	100,000
38. Christian	87,478
39. Christian Science	85,096
40. United Evangelical	73,399
41. Free Baptist	70,880
42. Unitarian	70,542

TABLE III.—Order of all Denominations according to
Number of Communicants, 1910.—*Continued.*

DENOMINATIONS.	Communicants.
43. Seventh-Day Adventist	65,122
44. Russian Orthodox	60,000
45. Universalist	52,150
46. Latter-Day Saints, Reorganized	50,650
47. Armenian Apostolic	50,000
48. Lutheran United Synod, South	48,921
49. Church of God (Winnebrennerian)	41,475
50. Freewill Baptist	40,578
51. Syrian Orthodox	40,000
52. Swedish Evangelical Mission Covenant	40,000
53. Lutheran Hauge's Synod	36,357
54. Primitive Baptist, Colored	35,076
55. Servian Orthodox	35,000
56. German Evangelical Protestant	34,704
57. General Baptist	33,600
58. Free Methodist	32,112
59. Christian Reformed	29,006
60. Advent Christian	26,799
61. Salvation Army	25,839
62. Roumanian Orthodox	20,000
63. Bulgarian Orthodox	20,000
64. Pentecostal Church	20,000
65. Lutheran Norwegian Free	20,000
66. United Brethren (O. C.)	19,637
67. Hicksite Friends	19,595
68. Wesleyan Methodist	19,178
69. Mennonite	18,674
70. Progressive Brethren, Dunkard	18,607
71. Union American Methodist Episcopal	18,500
72. Cumberland Presbyterian (Colored)	18,066
73. Swedish Evangelical Free Mission	18,000
74. Moravian	17,940
75. Lutheran Suomai Synod	17,500
76. Congregational Methodist	15,529
77. Polish National Catholic	15,473
78. Associate Reformed Synod, South	14,017
79. Christian Union	13,905
80. Welsh Calvinistic Presbyterian	13,759
81. United Baptist	13,698
82. Lutheran Danish in America	13,052
83. Lutheran Danish United	11,994
84. General Conference, Mennonite	11,661
85. Lutheran Finnish Apostolic	11,000

TABLE III.—ORDER OF ALL DENOMINATIONS ACCORDING TO NUMBER OF COMMUNICANTS, 1910.—*Continued*.

DENOMINATIONS.	Communicants.
86. Reformed Episcopal	9,610
87. Lutheran Slovakian Synod	9,500
88. Reformed Presbyterian (Synod)	9,455
89. General Convention, New Jerusalem	8,500
90. Seventh-Day Baptist	8,119
91. Amish, Mennonite	7,640
92. Primitive Methodist	7,346
93. Baptist Church of Christ	6,416
94. Non-sectarian Bible Faith	6,396
95. Lutheran Finnish National Synod	6,000
96. Christian Catholic (Dowie)	5,865
97. Hungarian Reformed	5,253
98. Lutheran Buffalo Synod	5,200
99. Separate Baptist	5,180
100. Old Amish, Mennonite	5,043
101. Plymouth Brethren II	4,752
102. Lutheran Icelandic Synod	4,700
103. Apostolic Christian, Faith	4,558
104. Norwegian Evangelical Free	4,000
105. Old Order Brethren, Dunkard	4,000
106. Reformed Methodist Union Episcopal	4,000
107. African Union Methodist Protestant	4,000
108. Wilburite Friends	3,880
109. Brethren in Christ (River)	3,675
110. Reformed Presbyterian (General Synod)	3,400
111. Japanese Buddhists	3,165
112. Theosophists	3,100
113. Zion Union Apostolic, Methodist	3,059
114. Plymouth Brethren I	2,933
115. Catholic Apostolic	2,907
116. Brethren in Christ, Mennonite	2,801
117. Lutheran Texas Synod	2,800
118. Christian Workers for Friendship	2,676
119. Bundes Conference, Mennonite	2,533
120. Lutheran Immanuel Synod	2,500
121. Ethical Culture Society	2,450
122. Churches of God in Jesus Christ, Adventist	2,124
123. Reformed Catholic	2,100
124. Reformed Mennonite	2,079
125. New Apostolic	2,020
126. Free Christian Zion Church (Colored)	1,835
127. Church of God and Saints of Christ (Colored)	1,823
128. Lutheran Brethren	1,800

TABLE III.—Order of all Denominations according to
Number of Communicants, 1910.—*Continued.*

DENOMINATIONS.	Communicants.
129. New Congregational Methodist	1,782
130. Amana Society	1,756
131. Plymouth Brethren III	1,724
132. Christadelphian	1,412
133. Social Brethren	1,262
134. Missionary Church Association, Faith	1,256
135. Independent Methodist	1,161
136. Plymouth Brethren IV	1,157
137. Lutheran Eielsen's Synod	1,130
138. Lutheran Jehovah Synod	1,100
139. Defenceless Mennonites	967
140. Heavenly Recruit	938
141. Church of Christ in God (Colored)	858
142. Schwenkfelders	850
143. General Church, New Jerusalem	814
144. Associate Presbyterian	786
145. Old Two-Seed-in-the-Spirit Baptist	781
146. Bohemian and Moravian Brethren	771
147. Apostolic, Living God	752
148. United Zion's Children (River)	749
149. Six-Principle Baptist	731
150. Peniel Missions, Faith	703
151. Old Mennonites	655
152. Church of God, Adventist	611
153. Reformed Presbyterian in U. S. and Canada	598
154. Church of God in Christ, Mennonite	562
155. Apostolic, Faith	538
156. Shaker	516
157. Life and Advent Union, Adventist	509
158. Evangelical Adventist	481
159. Metropolitan Church Association, Faith	466
160. American Salvation Army	436
161. Voluntary Missionary Association (Colored)	425
162. Old Order or Yorker (River)	423
163. Christian Congregation, Faith	395
164. Friends of the Temple	376
165. Hepzibah Faith	293
166. Bruederhoef, Mennonite, Faith	275
167. Seventh-Day German, Dunkard	240
168. Primitive Friends	171
169. Reformed Presbyterian Covenanted	40
170. Chinese Buddhists	....

TABLE IV.—Net

DENOMINATIONS.	Gains in Ten Years Ministers.	Churches.
ADVENTISTS:		
1. Evangelical............................	....	...
2. Advent Christians.....................	29	30
3. Seventh-Day...........................	102	499
4. Church of God.........................	....	....
5. Life and Advent Union.................	10	....
6. Churches of God in Jesus Christ........	....	....
Total............................	141	529
BAPTISTS:		
1. Regular (North).......................	850	1,388
2. Regular (South).......................	3,603	3,431
3. Regular (Colored).....................	4,388	2,253
4. Six-Principle.........................	d 6	d 6
5. Seventh-Day...........................	9	d 11
6. Free..................................	d 57	d 64
7. Freewill..............................	2	....
8. General...............................	152	24
9. Separate..............................	94	79
10. United...............................	....	....
11. Baptist Church of Christ.............	....	....
12. Primitive............................	90	308
13. Primitive (Colored)...................	....	....
14. Old Two-Seed-in-the-Spirit Predestinarian	....	....
15. Church of God and Saints of Christ (Colored)............................	....	....
Total............................	9,125	7,402
BRETHREN (DUNKARDS OR DUNKERS):		
1. Conservative..........................	990	130
2. Old Order.............................	d 97	d 55
3. Progressive...........................	7	17
4. Seventh-Day (German).................	....	....
Total............................	900	92

d Decrease.

GAINS IN TWO DECADES.

Ending in 1900. Communicants.	Ministers.	Gains in Ten Years Ending in 1910. Churches.	Communicants.
....	*d* 26	*d* 12	*d* 666
684	*d* 384	*d* 60	299
25,548	131	332	10,583
....	13	*d* 9	*d* 36
1,982	*d* 48	*d* 16	*d* 2,491
....	*d* 38	*d* 33	*d* 748
28,214	*d* 352	202	6,941
199,207	663	409	211,056
358,919	1,973	3,057	644,081
245,595	2,781	2,537	195,581
d 109	2	4	*d* 97
d 48	*d* 26	*d* 13	*d* 976
d 1,363	*d* 250	*d* 410	*d* 15,655
136	484	456	28,578
3,413	66	122	8,825
4,880	*d* 13	*d* 27	*d* 1,299
....	235	*d* 8	489
....	19	*d* 59	*d* 1,838
4,653	*d* 630	*d* 608	*d* 23,689
....	1,480	797	35,076
....	*d* 265	*d* 418	*d* 12,070
....	75	48	1,823
815,283	6,594	5,887	1,069,885
33,899	394	30	5,000
d 411	88	*d* 5	....
. 4,911	*d* 45	74	5,607
....	4	8	46
38,399	441	107	10,653

TABLE IV.—Net Gains in

DENOMINATIONS.	Gains in Ten Years Ministers.	Churches.
BRETHREN (PLYMOUTH):		
1. Brethren I................................	....	....
2. Brethren II...............................	....	....
3. Brethren III..............................	....	....
4. Brethren IV..............................	....	....
Total................................	....	....
BRETHREN (RIVER):		
1. Brethren in Christ........................	24	....
2. Old Order or Yorker......................	....	....
3. United Zion's Children...................	....	....
Total................................	24	....
BUDDHISTS:		
1. Chinese Temples..........................	....	....
2. Japanese Temples.........................	....	....
CATHOLIC APOSTOLIC:		
1. Catholic Apostolic........................	....	....
2. New Apostolic............................	....	....
Total................................	....	....
CATHOLICS, EASTERN ORTHODOX:		
1. Armenian Apostolic.......................	8	15
2. Russian Orthodox.........................	27	19
3. Greek Orthodox...........................	4	4
4. Syrian Orthodox..........................	....	....
5. Servian Orthodox.........................	....	....
6. Roumanian Orthodox......................	....	....
7. Bulgarian Orthodox.......................	....	....
Total................................	39	38

d Decrease.

Two Decades.—*Continued.*

Ending in 1900. Communicants.	Ministers.	Gains in Ten Years Ending in 1910.	
		Churches.	Communicants.
....	....	25	644
....	....	40	2,333
....	....	*d* 5	489
....	....	29	439
....	....	89	3,905
1,312	22	*d* 13	*d* 325
....	17	1	209
....	2	3	224
1,312	41	*d* 9	108
....	1	15	....
....	14	12	3,165
....	15	27	3,165
97	*d* 81	1	1,416
....	19	13	2,020
97	*d* 62	14	3,436
8,165	*d* 1	....	41,500
26,496	70	90	20,000
4,900	66	57	155,000
....	21	18	40,000
....	9	10	35,000
....	5	5	20,000
....	3	3	20,000
39,561	173	183	331,500

TABLE IV.—NET GAINS IN

DENOMINATIONS.	Gains in Ten Years Ministers.	Gains in Ten Years Churches.
CATHOLICS, WESTERN:		
1. Roman Catholic........................	2,682	2,018
2. Polish National Catholic................	19	18
3. Reformed Catholic.....................	d 2	d 2
4. Old Catholic..........................	2	1
Total...............................	2,701	2,035
CHRISTADELPHIANS...........................	....	....
CHRISTIANS	d 284	93
CHRISTIAN CATHOLIC (DOWIE)...............	55	50
CHRISTIAN MISSIONARY ASSOCIATION...........	....	....
CHRISTIAN SCIENTISTS......................	914	249
CHRISTIAN UNION...........................	....	....
CHURCHES OF GOD (WINNEBRENNERIAN).......	d 62	101
CHURCHES OF THE LIVING GOD (COLORED):		
1. Christian Workers for Friendship.........	....	....
2. Apostolic.............................	....	....
3. Church of Christ in God.................	....	....
Total...............................	....	....
CHURCH TRIUMPHANT (SCHWEINFURTH).......	....	d 12
CHURCHES OF THE NEW JERUSALEM:		
1. General Convention.....................	24	19
2. General Church........................	....	....
Total...............................	24	19
COMMUNISTIC SOCIETIES:		
1. Shakers...............................	....	....
2. Amana................................	....	....
3. Harmony.............................	....	....
4. Separatists............................	....	d 1
5. New Icaria............................	....	....
6. Altruists..............................	....	....
7. Adonai Shomo.........................	....	d 1
8. Church Triumphant (Koreshan Ecclesia)...	....	....
9. Christian Commonwealth................	....	1
Total...............................	....	d 1

d Decrease.

TWO DECADES.—*Continued.*

Ending in 1900. Communicants.	Gains in Ten Years Ending in 1910. Ministers.	Churches.	Communicants.
2,448,391	5,236	1,198	3,735,289
20,000	5	6	d 4,527
500	1	....	600
d 240	d 3	d 5	d 425
2,468,651	5,239	1,199	3,730,937
....	....	7	135
5,556	d 158	d 188	21,800
40,000	d 20	d 33	d 34,135
....	d 10	d 13	d 754
40,206	1,268	634	36,166
....	112	d 57	d 4,309
15,489	49	15	3,475
....	51	44	2,676
....	30	15	752
....	20	9	858
....	101	68	4,286
d 384	....	....	....
584	d 34	d 35	821
....	23	14	814
584	d 11	d 21	1,635
d 78	....	....	d 1,134
....	....	....	156
....	....	d 1	d 250
....	....	d 1	d 200
d 21	....	....	....
....	....	d 1	d 25
d 20	....	....	....
....	....	d 5	d 205
80	....	d 1	d 80
d 39	....	d 9	d 1,738

TABLE IV.—Net Gains in

DENOMINATIONS.	Gains in Ten Years Ministers.	Churches.
Congregationalists........................	567	756
Disciples of Christ:		
1. Disciples of Christ......................	2,575	3,282
2. Churches of Christ......................	....	....
Total...............................	2,575	3,282
Evangelical Bodies:		
1. Evangelical Association...................	*d* 358	*d* 693
2. United Evangelical Church...............	478	985
Total...............................	120	292
Faith Associations:		
1. Apostolic Faith Movement...............	....	....
2. Peniel Missions..........................	....	....
3. Metropolitan Church Association.........	....	....
4. Hepzibah Faith Association..............	....	....
5. Missionary Church Association...........	....	....
6. Heavenly Recruit Church................	....	....
7. Apostolic Christian Church.............	....	....
8. Christian Congregation...................	....	....
9. Voluntary Missionary Society (Colored)...	....	....
Total...............................	....	....
Free Christian Zion Church (Colored)	....	....
Friends:		
1. Orthodox.............................	166	36
2. "Hicksite".............................	....	....
3. "Wilburite".............................	....	1
4. Primitive...............................	....	....
Total...............................	166	37
Friends of the Temple.....................	....	....
German Evangelical Protestant............	1	3

d Decrease.

TWO DECADES.—*Continued*.

Ending in 1900. Communicants.	Ministers.	Gains in Ten Years Ending in 1910. Churches.	Communicants.
118,589	420	426	104,040
508,931	d 378	302	158,134
....	2,100	2,649	156,658
508,931	1,722	2,951	314,792
d 36,968	103	40	12,321
60,993	31	12	12,406
24,025	134	52	24,727
....	....	6	538
....	30	11	703
....	29	6	466
....	36	10	293
....	35	32	1,256
....	55	27	938
....	19	42	4,558
....	26	9	395
....	11	3	425
....	241	146	9,572
....	20	15	1,835
11,813	23	....	7,604
....	d 18	10	d 2,397
139	9	d 5	d 588
....	d 1	d 1	d 61
11,952	13	4	4,558
....	d 1	d 2	36
344	14	11	d 1,796

TABLE IV.—Net Gains in

DENOMINATIONS.	Gains in Ten Years Ministers.	Gains in Ten Years Churches.
GERMAN EVANGELICAL SYNOD................	229	259
JEWISH CONGREGATIONS.....................	101	37
LATTER-DAY SAINTS:		
1. Utah branch..........................	157	371
2. Reorganized branch....................	d 300	169
Total..............................	d 143	540
LUTHERANS:		
1. General Synod.........................	250	152
2. United Synod, South...................	13	d 24
3. General Council.......................	52	d 162
4. Synodical Conference..................	747	716
5. United Norwegian......................	252	d 1
INDEPENDENT SYNODS:		
6. Ohio.................................	160	183
7. Buffalo..............................	6	9
8. Hauge's..............................	37	37
9. Eielsen's (1)........................	9	52
10. Texas (1)...........................	11	14
11. Iowa (2)............................	433	824
12. Norwegian...........................	58	250
13. Michigan (3)........................	16	13
14. Danish in America...................	d 61	d 65
15. Icelandic...........................	7	13
16. Immanuel............................	24	29
17. German Augsburg (4).................	d 49	d 23
18. Suomai, Finnish.....................	3	35
19. Finnish Apostolic (5)...............	....	....
20. Finnish National (5)................	....	....
21. Norwegian Free......................	112	300
22. Danish United.......................	48	100
23. Slovakian (5).......................	....	....
24. Church of the Lutheran Brethren (5)......	....	....
25. Jehovah.............................	6	6
Independent Congregations..............	38	d 31
Total..............................	2,172	2,427

d Decrease.   (1) Not in existence in 1890.   (2) Included in General Council in 1890.

Two Decades.—*Continued.*

Ending in 1900. Communicants.	Gains in Ten Years Ending in 1910.		
	Ministers.	Churches.	Communicants.
16,142	115	185	33,041
12,504	783	1,199	....
155,648	523	d 16	50,000
22,051	60	d 30	6,826
177,699	583	d 46	56,826
34,949	117	209	102,851
1,182	34	78	10,282
31,555	302	416	102,823
223,876	684	706	185,252
10,028	189	343	31,964
7,857	128	180	50,068
758	2	6	200
d 2,190	55	135	23,817
2,800	d 3	d 26	d 1,670
1,700	10	18	1,100
74,058	94	116	32,535
11,475	130	261	33,073
d 1,935	d 53	d 78	d 9,547
d 181	11	53	3,052
3,568	5	13	d 859
538	d 33	d 44	d 3,618
d 7,010	....	....	....
9,663	21	124	6,452
....	62	73	11,000
....	20	40	6,000
38,000	63	75	d 18,000
5,007	26	26	3,494
....	17	30	9,500
....	12	16	1,800
350	3	5	750
d 16,953	....	5	1,000
429,095	1,896	2,780	583,319

(3) Dissolved after 1900.   (4) Dissolved before 1900.   (5) New bodies.

TABLE IV.—Net Gains in

DENOMINATIONS.	Gains in Ten Years Ministers.	Churches.
Scandinavian Evangelical Bodies:		
1. Swedish Evangelical Mission Covenant (1)..	265	270
2. Swedish Evangelical Free Mission (1)......	....	....
3. Norwegian Evangelical Free (2).........	....	....
Total............................	265	270
Mennonites:		
1. Mennonite............................	82	42
2. Bruederhoef..........................	....	....
3. Amish................................	37	27
4. Old Amish............................	4	3
5. Apostolic.............................	....	....
6. Reformed.............................	....	....
7. General Conference....................	33	31
8. Churches of God in Christ..............	....	....
9. Old (Wisler)..........................	....	....
10. Bundes Conference....................	4	4
11. Defenceless..........................	2	2
12. Brethren in Christ....................	45	14
Separate Conferences (3)...............	....	....
Total............................	207	123
Methodist:		
1. Methodist Episcopal....................	1,368	3,388
2. Union American Methodist Episcopal.....	93	120
3. African Methodist Episcopal............	2,531	1,506
4. African Union Methodist Protestant......	66	61
5. African Methodist Episcopal Zion.........	1,590	319
6. Methodist Protestant...................	188	470
7. Wesleyan Methodist....................	d 5	164
8. Methodist Episcopal, South.............	1,188	1,524
9. Congregational Methodist..............	175	180
10. Congregational Methodist (Colored)*.....	....	....
11. New Congregational Methodist...........	172	349
12. Zion Union Apostolic....................	....	....
13. Colored Methodist Episcopal.............	261	d 220
14. Primitive.............................	14	12
15. Free.................................	265	324
16. Reformed Methodist Union Episcopal.....	....	....
17. Independent Methodist.................	....	....
18. Evangelist Missionary*.................	1	10
Total............................	7,907	8,207

(1) Not reported in 1890.   (2) New bodies.   (3) Included in General

Two Decades.—*Continued.*

Ending in 1900. Communicants.	Ministers.	Gains in Ten Years Ending in 1910. Churches.	Communicants.
30,000	112	20	10,000
....	151	133	18,000
....	65	150	4,000
30,000	328	303	32,000
5,365	*d* 72	*d* 68	*d* 3,769
....	....	3	*d* 77
2,950	*d* 134	*d* 67	*d* 5,411
400	66	21	2,605
....	*d* 2	*d* 2	*d* 209
25	*d* 9	....	399
4,725	15	14	1,266
....	*d* 1	....	91
....	1	*d* 6	45
1,562	*d* 5	3	*d* 417
320	6	3	*d* 209
1,840	*d* 6	9	*d* 152
....	35	21	1,908
17,187	*d* 106	*d* 69	*d* 3,930
505,837	1,489	2,204	440,671
13,221	13	100	3,000
222,737	501	*d* 103	*d* 175,462
148	94	37	437
186,483	333	1,392	10,945
41,725	*d* 236	38	4,723
709	3	65	1,977
258,414	622	2,120	382,759
11,235	12	3	*d* 4,471
....	*d* 5	*d* 5	*d* 319
2,941	*d* 133	*d* 331	*d* 2,218
....	3	18	713
75,589	840	1,424	29,749
1,785	....	11	797
5,182	197	219	4,820
....	40	58	4,000
....	*d* 6	*d* 12	*d* 1,408
1,059	*d* 48	*d* 13	*d* 2,010
1,327,065	3,719	7,225	698,703

Council in 1890.   *d* Decrease.   * Dissolved after 1900.

TABLE IV.—Net Gains in

DENOMINATIONS.	Gains in Ten Years Ministers.	Churches.
Moravian Bodies:		
1. Moravian	3	28
2. Union Bohemians and Moravians*	....	....
Total	3	28
Non-Sectarian Bible Faith Churches*	....	....
Pentecostal Bodies:		
1. Pentecostal Church*	....	....
2. Other Pentecostal Associations*	....	....
Total	....	....
Presbyterians:		
1. Northern	1,236	742
2. Cumberland	d 265	166
3. Cumberland (Colored)	57	176
4. Welsh Calvinistic	d 11	d 29
5. United	187	45
6. Southern	332	568
7. Associate	....	....
8. Associate Reformed, South	d 29	15
9. Reformed (Synod)	....	d 2
10. Reformed (General Synod)	4	3
11. Reformed (Covenanted)	....	d 3
12. Reformed in United States and Canada	....	....
Total	1,511	1,681
Protestant Episcopal:		
1. Protestant Episcopal	665	1,402
2. Reformed Episcopal	22	d 5
Total	687	1,397
Reformed:		
1. Reformed (Dutch)	132	47
2. Reformed (German)	194	143
3. Christian Reformed	28	46
4. Hungarian Reformed	....	....
Total	354	236

* Not in existence in 1900.

Two Decades.—*Continued*.

Ending in 1900. Communicants.	Gains in Ten Years Ending in 1910.		
	Ministers.	Churches.	Communicants.
3,036	16	*d* 1	3,123
....	3	15	771
3,036	19	14	3,894
....	50	204	6,396
....	700	428	20,000
....	115	30	1,420
....	815	458	21,420
195,209	1,810	2,467	345,281
15,252	*d* 679	*d* 1,387	*d* 65,192
17,044	*d* 75	*d* 204	*d* 11,934
d 570	2	*d* 10	1,607
21,499	94	79	19,109
46,169	233	365	56,030
....	....	*d* 9	*d* 267
2,843	2	11	2,673
d 784	12	2	*d* 335
398	*d* 16	*d* 17	*d* 1,600
....	*d* 1	....	3
8	1	2	*d* 10
297,068	1,383	1,299	345,365
178,302	475	1,151	218,424
827	*d* 6	2	328
179,129	469	1,153	218,752
14,624	38	65	9,221
38,813	152	77	54,285
5,626	42	44	10,910
....	18	16	5,253
59,063	250	202	79,669

d Decrease.

TABLE IV.—Net Gains in

DENOMINATIONS.	Gains in Ten Years	
	Ministers.	Churches.
SALVATIONISTS:		
1. Salvation Army	2,361	334
2. American Salvation Army	....	....
Total	2,361	334
Schwenkfelders	....	....
Social Brethren	....	....
Society for Ethical Culture	....	1
Spiritualists	....	....
Theosophical Society	....	82
Unitarians	29	32
UNITED BRETHREN:		
1. United Brethren	d 434	435
2. United Brethren (Old Constitution)	88	d 9
Total	d 346	426
Universalists	22	d 186
Independent Congregations	....	....
Grand total	32,365	30,859

TABLE V.—Summary of Net

DENOMINATIONS.	Ministers.	Gains in Ten Years Churches.
Adventists	141	529
Baptists	9,925	7,402
Brethren (Dunkards)	900	92
Brethren (Plymouth)	....	....
Brethren (River)	24	....
Buddhists	....	....
Catholic Apostolic	....	....
Catholic, Eastern Orthodox	39	38
Catholic, Western	2,701	2,035
Christadelphians	....	....
Christians	d 284	93
Christian Catholic (Dowie)	55	50

d Decrease.

Two Decades.—*Continued.*

Ending in 1900. Communicants.	Gains in Ten Years Ending in 1910. Ministers.	Churches.	Communicants.
10,748	776	233	6,349
. . . .	59	20	436
10,748	835	253	6,785
. . . .	3	4	544
. . . .	d 2	d 3	349
236	7	1	1,150
. . . .	. . . .	666	104,970
2,305	. . . .	d 8	100
3,251	14	29	d 458
37,165	57	d 445	44,043
3,489	d 316	d 241	d 6,659
40,654	d 259	d 686	37,384
3,545	. . . .	111	d 589
. . . .	213	723	34,547
6,765,497	27,098	27,702	7,861,492

Gains for Two Decades.

Ending in 1900. Communicants.	Gains in Ten Years Ending in 1910. Ministers.	Churches.	Communicants.
28,214	d 352	202	6,941
815,283	6,594	5,887	1,069,885
38,399	441	107	10,653
. . . . . .	. . . . .	89	3,905
1,312	41	d 9	108
. . . . . .	15	27	3,165
97	d 62	14	3,436
39,561	173	183	331,500
2,468,651	5,239	1,199	3,730,937
. . . . . .	. . . . .	7	135
5,556	d 158	d 188	d 21,800
40,000	d 20	d 33	d 34,135

TABLE V.—SUMMARY OF NET GAINS

DENOMINATIONS.	Ministers.	Gains in Ten Years Churches.
Christian Missionary Association....	....	....
Christian Scientists.................	914	249
Christian Union....................	....	....
Church of God (Winnebrennerian)...	d 62	101
Churches of the Living God........	....	....
Church Triumphant (Schweinfurth)..	....	d 12
Churches of the New Jerusalem.....	24	19
Communistic Societies.............	....	d 1
Congregationalists.................	567	756
Disciples of Christ.................	2,575	3,282
Evangelical Bodies.................	120	292
Faith Associations.................	....	....
Free Christian Zion Church (Colored)	....	....
Friends...........................	166	37
Friends of the Temple.............	....	....
German Evangelical Protestant.....	1	3
German Evangelical Synod.........	229	259
Jewish Congregations..............	101	37
Latter-Day Saints.................	d 143	540
Lutherans.........................	2,172	2,427
Scandinavian Evangelical bodies....	265	270
Mennonites.......................	207	123
Methodists........................	7,907	8,207
Moravians........................	3	28
Non-Sectarian Bible Faith Churches.	....	....
Pentacostal bodies................	....	....
Presbyterians.....................	1,511	1,681
Protestant Episcopal..............	687	1,397
Reformed.........................	354	236
Salvationists......................	2,361	334
Schwenkfelders....................	....	....
Social Brethren...................	....	....
Society for Ethical Culture........	....	1
Spiritualists......................	....	....
Theosophical Society..............	....	82
Unitarians........................	29	32
United Brethren...................	d 346	426
Universalists......................	22	d 186
Independent Congregations........	....	....
Total......................	32,365	30,859

d Decrease.

FOR TWO DECADES.—*Continued.*

Ending in 1900. Communicants.	Gains in Ten Years Ending in 1910.		
	Ministers.	Churches.	Communicants.
. . . . . .	*d* 10	*d* 13	*d* 754
40,206	1,268	634	36,166
. . . . . .	112	*d* 57	*d* 4,309
15,489	49	15	3,475
. . . . . .	101	68	4,286
d 384	. . .	. . . .	. . . .
584	*d* 11	*d* 21	1,635
d 39	. . . . .	*d* 9	*d* 1,738
118,589	420	426	104,040
508,931	1,722	2,951	314,792
24,025	134	52	24,727
. . . . . .	241	146	9,572
. . . . . .	20	15	1,835
11,952	13	4	4,558
. . . . . .	*d* 1	*d* 2	36
344	14	11	*d* 1,796
16,142	115	185	33,041
12,504	783	1,199	. . . . . .
177,699	583	*d* 46	56,826
429,095	1,896	2,780	583,319
30,000	328	303	32,000
17,187	*d* 106	*d* 69	*d* 3,930
1,327,065	3,719	7,225	698,703
3,036	19	14	3,894
. . . . . .	50	204	6,396
. . . . . .	815	458	21,420
297,068	1,383	1,299	345,365
179,129	469	1,153	218,752
59,063	250	202	79,669
10,748	835	253	6,785
. . . . . .	3	4	544
. . . . . .	*d* 2	*d* 3	349
236	7	1	1,150
. . . . . .	. . . .	666	104,970
2,305	. . . .	*d* 8	100
3,251	14	29	*d* 458
40,654	*d* 259	*d* 686	37,384
3,545	. . . .	111	*d* 589
. . . . . .	213	723	34,547
6,765,497	27,098	27.702	7,861,492

TABLE VI.—Showing Net Gains in Communicants in the Twenty Years, 1890–1910, in the Order of Increase, 5,000 and Upward.

DENOMINATIONS.	Net Gain.	Per Cent.
1. Roman Catholic..................	6,183,680	99
2. Southern Baptist.................	1,003,000	78
3. Methodist Episcopal..............	946,508	42
4. Disciples of Christ...............	(1) 667,065	104
5. Methodist Episcopal, South.......	641,173	53
6. Presbyterian (Northern)..........	540,490	69
7. Colored Baptist..................	441,176	33
8. Northern Baptist.................	410,263	51
9. Lutheran Synodical Conference.....	409,128	115
10. Protestant Episcopal..............	396,726	75
11. Congregational...................	222,629	43
12. Latter-Day Saints (Utah branch)...	205,648	142
13. African Methodist Episcopal Zion...	197,428	44
14. Greek Orthodox..................	159,900	..
15. Churches of Christ, Disciples.......	(2) 156,658	..
16. Lutheran General Synod...........	137,800	84
17. Lutheran General Council..........	(3) 134,378	41
18. Lutheran Synod of Iowa...........	(4) 106,593	..
19. Colored Methodist Episcopal.......	105,338	81
20. Spiritualist......................	104,970	233
21. Presbyterian (Southern)...........	102,199	56
22. Reformed (German)...............	93,098	46
23. United Brethren.................	81,208	40
24. Christian Scientist...............	76,372	875
25. United Evangelical................	(5) 73,399	..
26. Lutheran Synod of Ohio...........	57,925	83
27. Armenian Apostolic...............	49,665	..
28. German Evangelical Synod.........	49,183	26
29. African Methodist Episcopal.......	47,275	10
30. Russian Orthodox................	46,496	344
31. Methodist Protestant..............	46,448	33
32. Lutheran Norwegian Synod........	44,548	80
33. Lutheran United Norwegian Synod..	41,992	35
34. United Presbyterian..............	40,608	43

(1) Not including the newer branch.   (3) Included Iowa Synod in 1890.
(2) Total number reported in 1906.   (4) Total number reported in 1910.
(5) Total number reported in 1910. Body not in existence in 1890.

TABLE VI.—SHOWING NET GAINS IN COMMUNICANTS IN THE
TWENTY YEARS, 1890–1910, IN THE ORDER OF INCREASE, 5,000
AND UPWARD.—*Continued.*

DENOMINATIONS.	Net Gain.	Per Cent.
35. Syrian Orthodox................	(1) 40,000	..
36. Swedish Evangelical Covenant......	(1) 40,000	..
37. Conservative Dunkards...........	38,899	64
38. Seventh-Day Adventist...........	36,131	125
39. Primitive Baptist Colored.........	(1) 35,076	..
40. Servian Orthodox................	(1) 35,000	..
41. Independent Congregations........	34,547	..
42. Latter-Day Saints, Reorganized....	28,877	133
43. Freewill Baptists.................	28,714	242
44. Hauge's Lutheran Synod...........	(1) 21,627	..
45. Norwegian Free Lutheran Synod....	20,000	136
46. Roumanian Orthodox.............	(1) 20,000	..
47. Bulgarian Orthodox..............	(1) 20,000	..
48. Pentecostal.....................	(1) 20,000	..
49. Orthodox Friends................	19,417	24
50. Churches of God (Winnebrennerian)	18,964	84
51. Swedish Evangelical Free..........	(1) 18,000	..
52. Salvation Army..................	17,097	200
53. Christian Reformed..............	16,536	133
54. Union American Methodist Episcopal	16,221	712
55. Suomai, Finnish Lutheran.........	(1) 16,115	..
56. Polish Catholic..................	(1) 15,473	..
57. Jewish.........................	(2) 12,504	..
58. General Baptist..................	12,238	57
59. Lutheran United Synod, South.....	11,464	31
60. Finnish Apostolic, Lutheran.......	(1) 11,000	..
61. Progressive Dunkards.............	10,518	173
62. Free Methodist..................	10,002	45
63. Slovakian Synod, Lutheran........	(1) 9,500	..
64. Danish United Synod, Lutheran....	8,501	243
65. Congregational Methodist.........	6,764	77
66. Non-Sectarian Bible Faith........	(3) 6,396	..
67. Moravian.......................	6,159	52
68. Finnish National, Lutheran.......	(4) 6,000	..
69. General Conference, Mennonite.....	5,991	106
70. Christian Catholic (Dowie)........	(3) 5,865	..

(1) Not in existence or not reported in 1890. Total number in 1910.
(2) Represents only heads of families.
(3) Not in existence or not reported in 1890. Total number in 1906.
(4) Not in existence or not reported in 1890.

TABLE VI.—Showing Net Gains in Communicants in the Twenty Years, 1890–1910, in the Order of Increase, 5,000 and Upward.—*Continued.*

DENOMINATIONS.		Net Gain.	Per Cent.
71. Associate Reformed Synod, South, Presbyterian...................		5,516	65
72. Hungarian Reformed..............	(1)	5,253	..
73. Cumberland Presbyterian, Colored..		5,110	39
74. Apostolic Christian................	(1)	4,558	..
75. Separate Baptist..................		3,581	224
76. Japanese Buddhist................	(1)	3,165	..
77. Old Amish, Mennonite............		3,005	147
78. Universalist.....................		2,956	6
79. Danish in America, Lutheran Synod..		2,871	25
80. Texas Synod, Lutheran...........	(2)	2,800	..
81. Unitarian.......................		2,793	4
82. Icelandic Synod, Lutheran.........		2,709	136
83. Wesleyan Methodist..............		2,686	16
84. Christian Workers (Colored)........	(1)	2,676	..
85. Primitive Methodist..............		2,582	54
86. Theosophist......................		2,405	..
87. Plymouth Brethren II.............		2,333	..
88. New Catholic Apostolic............	(1)	2,020	..
89. Separate Mennonite Conferences....	(1)	1,908	..
90. Saints of Christ, Baptist (Colored)..	(1)	1,823	..
91. Synod of Lutheran Brethren.......	(3)	1,800	..
92. Brethren in Christ, Mennonite.....		1,688	..
93. Mennonite......................		1,596	..
94. Catholic Apostolic................		1,513	..
95. Pentecostal Associations...........	(1)	1,420	..
96. New Jerusalem, General Convention		1,405	..
97. Ethical Culture..................		1,386	..
98. Missionary Church Association, Faith	(1)	1,256	..
99. Reformed Episcopal...............		1,155	..
100. Bundes Conference, Mennonite.....		1,145	..
101. Eielsen's Lutheran Synod..........		1,130	..
102. Jehovah Synod, Lutheran..........	(2)	1,100	..
103. Reformed Catholic................		1,100	..
104. Welsh Calvinistic Presbyterian.....		1,037	..
105. Brethren in Christ (River Brethren).		987	..

(1) Not in existence or not reported in 1890.   Total number in 1906.
(2) Not in existence or not reported in 1890.
(3) A new body.

TABLE VI.—Showing Net Gains in Communicants in the
Twenty Years, 1890–1910, in the Order of Increase, 5,000
and Upward.—*Continued.*

DENOMINATIONS.	Net Gain.	Per Cent.
106. Advent Christians.................	983	..
107. Buffalo Synod, Lutheran...........	958	..
108. Heavenly Recruit (Faith Association)	(1) 938	..
109. Church of Christ in God (Colored)..	(1) 858	..
110. General Church (New Jerusalem)...	(1) 814	..
111. Bohemian and Moravian Union.....	(1) 771	..
112. Apostolic (Churches of Living God).	(1) 752	..
113. New Congregational Methodist.....	723	..
114. Zion Union Apostolic (Methodist)...	713	..
115. Peniel Mission, Faith..............	(1) 703	..
116. Plymouth Brethren I..............	644	..
117. African Union Methodist Protestant	585	..
118. Schwenkfelders...................	544	..
119. Apostolic Faith Movement.........	(1) 538	..
120. United Baptist...................	489	..
121. Plymouth Brethren III............	489	..
122. Metropolitan Church Association...	(1) 466	..
123. Plymouth Brethren IV.............	439	..
124. American Salvation Army..........	(1) 436	..
125. Voluntary Missionary (Colored)....	(1) 425	..
126. Reformed Mennonite..............	424	..
127. Christian Congregation, Faith......	(1) 395	..
128. Social Brethren..................	349	..
129. Hepzibah Faith...................	(1) 293	..
130. United Zion's Children, River Brethren............................	224	..
131. Old Order, River Brethren..........	209	..
132. Amana Society....................	156	..
133. Christadelphian..................	135	..
134. Defenceless Mennonite............	111	..
135. Churches of God in Christ, Mennonite........................	91	..
136. Seventh-Day German Dunkards....	46	..
137. Old, Mennonite...................	45	..
138. Friends of Temple................	36	..
139. Reformed Presbyterian Covenanted.	3	..

(1) Reported since 1890.   Census returns of 1906.

TABLE VII.—SHOWING NET LOSSES IN THE TWENTY YEARS, 1890–1910, BY DECREASE AND BY DISSOLUTION.

BY DISSOLUTION:

1.	Michigan Synod, Lutheran..................	11,482
2.	German Augsburg Synod, Lutheran..........	7,010
3.	Evangelist Missionary (Methodist)............	2,010
4.	Christian Missionary Association.............	754
5.	Old Catholic...............................	665
6.	Church Triumphant (Schweinfurth)...........	384
7.	Congregational Methodist (Colored)..........	319
8.	Harmony (Communistic)....................	250
9.	Apostolic, Mennonite......................	209
10.	Church Triumphant (Communistic)...........	205
11.	Separatist (Communistic)...................	200
12.	Christian Commonwealth (Communistic)......	80
13.	Altruist (Communistic).....................	25
14.	New Icaria (Communistic)..................	21
15.	Adonai Shomo.............................	20

BY DECREASE:

1.	Cumberland Presbyterian...................	(1) 46,940
2.	Evangelical Association.....................	(2) 24,647
3.	Primitive Baptist..........................	(3) 19,036
4.	Free Baptist..............................	17,018
5.	Christian.................................	16,244
6.	Independent Congregations, Lutheran........	15,953
7.	Old Two-Seed-in-the-Spirit Baptist...........	12,070
8.	Christian Union...........................	4,309
9.	United Brethren (Old Constitution)..........	3,170
10.	Immanuel Synod, Lutheran.................	3,080
11.	Amish, Mennonite.........................	2,461
12.	"Hicksite," Friends........................	2,397
13.	Baptist Church of Christ...................	1,838
14.	German Evangelical Protestant..............	1,452
15.	Independent Methodist.....................	1,408
16.	Shakers (Communistic).....................	1,212
17.	Reformed Presbyterian (General Synod).......	1,202
18.	Reformed Presbyterian (Synod)..............	1,119
19.	Seventh-Day Baptist.......................	1,024
20.	Churches of God in Jesus Christ (Adventist)...	748
21.	Evangelical Adventists.....................	666
22.	Life and Advent Union, Adventist...........	509
23.	"Wilburite" Friends.......................	449

(1) Many united with Northern Presbyterian Church, 1906–7.   (2) Due to division.

(3) Due to separate report of Colored Primitive Baptists.

TABLE VII.—Showing Net Losses in the Twenty Years, 1890–1910, by Decrease and by Dissolution.—*Continued.*

24.	Old Order Dunkards	411
25.	Associate Presbyterian	267
26.	Six Principle Baptist	206
27.	Bruederhoef, Mennonite	77
28.	Primitive Friends	61
29.	Church of God, Adventist	36
30.	Reformed Presbyterian in U. S. and Canada	2

TABLE VIII.—Showing Gains in Communicants by Denominational Families or Groups in the Twenty Years, 1890–1910.

DENOMINATIONS.	Gain.	Percentage.
1. Adventist	35,155	58
2. Baptist	1,885,168	51
3. Brethren (Dunkards)	49,052	66
4. Brethren (Plymouth)	3,905	59
5. Brethren (River)	1,420	41
6. Buddhists	(1) 3,165	...
7. Catholic Apostolic	3,533	253
8. Catholic, Eastern Orthodox	(1) 371,061	...
9. Catholic, Western	6,199,588	99
10. Church of the Living God (Colored)	(1) 4,286	...
11. Churches of the New Jerusalem	2,219	31
12. Communistic Societies	d 1,777	...
13. Disciples of Christ	823,723	128
14. Evangelical bodies	48,752	37
15. Faith Associations	(1) 9,572	...
16. Friends	16,510	15
17. Latter-Day Saints	234,525	141
18. Lutherans	1,012,414	82
19. Scandinavian Evangelical	(1) 62,000	...
20. Mennonite	13,257	32
21. Methodist	2,025,768	44
22. Moravian	6,930	60
23. Pentecostal bodies	(1) 21,420	...
24. Presbyterian	642,433	50
25. Protestant Episcopal	397,881	74
26. Reformed	138,732	45
27. Salvationists	17,533	201
28. United Brethren	78,038	35

(1) Either entirely new or of such large growth by recent immigration as to give percentage no significance.   *d.* Decrease.

TABLE IX.—New Bodies not in Existence or not Reported in 1890.

DENOMINATIONS.	Communicants in 1910.
1. Primitive Baptist Colored probably included in Primitive Baptists (White) in 1890..............	35,076
2. Churches of God and Saints in Christ (Colored), Baptist, 1896.................................	1,823
3. Japanese Buddhists.............................	3,165
4. New Apostolic, 1862 (in Germany)...............	2,020
5. Syrian Orthodox, by immigration.................	40,000
6. Servian Orthodox, by immigration................	35,000
7. Roumanian Orthodox, by immigration.............	20,000
8. Bulgarian Orthodox, by immigration..............	20,000
9. Polish National Catholic, out of Roman Catholic, 1904	15,473
10. Christian Catholic (Dowie), 1896.................	5,865
11. Christian Workers for Friendship (Colored), 1899...	2,676
12. Apostolic Church of the Living God (Colored)......	752
13. Church of Christ, Living God (Colored)............	858
14. General Church, New Jerusalem, 1892.............	814
15. Churches of Christ, by division of Disciples of Christ	156,658
16. United Evangelical Church, by division of Evangelical Association, 1894.............................	73,399
17. Apostolic Faith Movement, 1900.................	538
18. Peniel Missions................................	703
19. Metropolitan Church Association, 1894............	466
20. Hepzibah Faith Association, 1892................	293
21. Missionary Church Association, 1898..............	1,256
22. Heavenly Recruit Church, 1885..................	938
23. Apostolic Christian Church......................	4,558
24. Christian Congregation, 1899....................	395
25. Voluntary Missionary Society (Colored), 1900......	425
26. Free Christian Zion Church (Colored), 1905........	1,835
27. Eielsen's Lutheran Synod, 1846..................	1,130
28. Texas Lutheran Synod, 1895....................	2,800
29. Finnish Apostolic Lutheran Synod................	11,000
30. Finnish National Lutheran Synod, 1900............	6,000
31. Slovakian Lutheran Synod, 1901.................	9,500
32. Church of the Lutheran Brethren, 1900...........	1,800
33. Lutheran Jehovah Conference....................	1,100
34. Swedish Evangelical Mission Covenant, by immigration and withdrawal from Lutheran bodies, 1885..	40,000

TABLE IX.—New Bodies not in Existence or not Reported in 1890.—*Continued.*

DENOMINATIONS.	Communicants in 1910.
35. Swedish Evangelical Free Mission, by immigration and withdrawal from Lutheran bodies, 1885	18,000
36. Norwegian Evangelical Free, very recent	4,000
37. Reformed Methodist Union Episcopal Church, 1896.	4,000
38. Union of Bohemian and Moravian Brethren, by immigration, 1903	771
39. Non-Sectarian Churches of Bible Faith	6,396
40. Pentecostal Church of the Nazarene, 1907	20,000
41. Hungarian Reformed, by withdrawals from German Reformed, Presbyterian, Congregational Churches, 1904	5,253
42. American Salvation Army, by division, 1884	436

GROWTH OF COLORED ORGANIZATIONS.

TABLE X.—Summary of Colored Bodies and Churches.

COLORED DENOMINATIONS.	Ministers.	Churches.	Communicants.
Colored Baptist	12,637	17,323	1,790,165
Colored Primitive Baptist *c*	1,480	797	35,076
United American Freewill Baptists *c*	136	247	14,489
Church of God and Saints of Christ *c*	75	48	1,823
Churches of the Living God *c*	101	68	4,286
Voluntary Missionary Society *c*	11	3	425
Free Christian Zion *c*	20	15	1,835
Union American Methodist Episcopal	138	255	18,500
African Methodist Episcopal	6,353	5,527	500,000
African Union Methodist Protestant	200	125	4,000
African Methodist Episcopal Zion *c*	3,488	3,298	547,216
Colored Methodist Episcopal	2,901	2,857	234,721
Zion Union Apostolic *c*	33	45	3,059
Reformed Methodist Union Episcopal *c*	40	58	4,000
Cumberland Presbyterian Colored *c*	450	400	30,000
Total colored denominations	28,063	31,066	3,189,595

c Census of 1906.

TABLE X.—Summary of Colored Bodies and Churches.—
Continued.

COLORED CHURCHES IN OTHER DENOMINATIONS.	Ministers.	Churches.	Communicants.
Adventist bodies....................	10	31	364
Northern Baptist....................	753	905	112,874
Free Baptist........................	69	195	10,876
Christians..........................	30	91	7,545
Churches of God....................	5	14	329
Congregational.....................	72	170	11,233
Disciples of Christ..................	71	129	9,705
Churches of Christ..................	20	41	1,528
Lutheran bodies....................	3	7	239
Methodist Episcopal.................	2,179	4,438	299,402
Methodist Protestant................	91	65	3,144
Wesleyan Methodist.................	9	19	1,258
Presbyterian Northern...............	279	417	27,799
Presbyterian Southern...............	29	40	1,183
Protestant Episcopal................	98	193	19,098
Reformed Episcopal.................	21	38	2,252
Roman Catholic.....................	20	36	35,235
Miscellaneous......................	19	31	1,670
Total colored churches in other denominations.............	*3,778	†6,860	†545,734

SUMMARY.	Ministers.	Churches.	Communicants.
Colored denominations...............	28,063	31,066	3,189,595
Colored churches in other denominations	3,778	6,860	545,734
Total......................	31,841	37,926	3,735,329

Compared with the returns of the census of 1890, those of 1910
show increases as follows:

	Churches.	Communicants.
Colored denominations, 1910..............	31,066	3,189,595
Colored denominations, 1890..............	19,631	2,303,351
Increase........................	11,435	886,244
Colored churches in other denominations, 1910	6,860	545,734
Colored churches in other denominations, 1890	4,139	370,826
Increase........................	2,721	174,908
Colored denominations, increase...........	11,435	886,244
Colored churches in other denominations, increase...........................	2,721	174,908
Total increase in twenty years.....	14,156	1,061,152

* Many figures in this column are estimates.
† Many of the entries are from the census of 1906.

MEMBERSHIP OF THE LEADING RELIGIOUS BODIES IN THE UNITED STATES ACCORD- ING TO THE LATEST CENSUS.

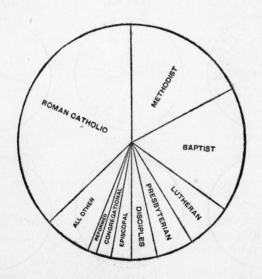

THE AREA OF THE CIRCLE REPRESENTS THE CHURCH MEMBERSHIP OF THE COUNTRY, THE SEVERAL SECTORS THE PROPORTIONAL STRENGTH OF THE SEVERAL DENOMINATIONS.

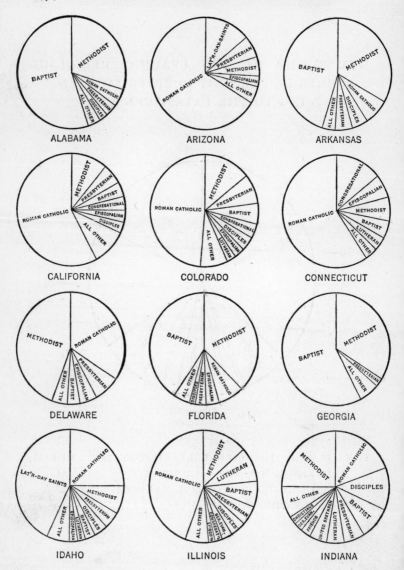

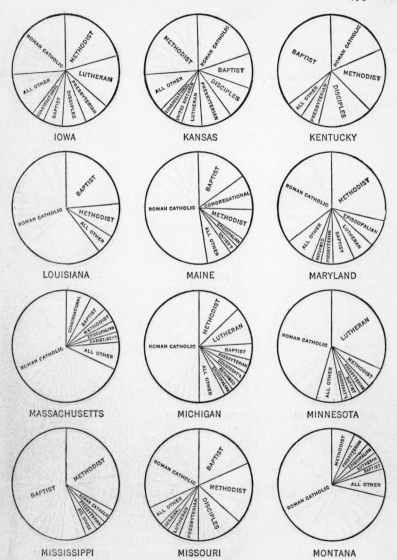

IOWA KANSAS KENTUCKY

LOUISIANA MAINE MARYLAND

MASSACHUSETTS MICHIGAN MINNESOTA

MISSISSIPPI MISSOURI MONTANA

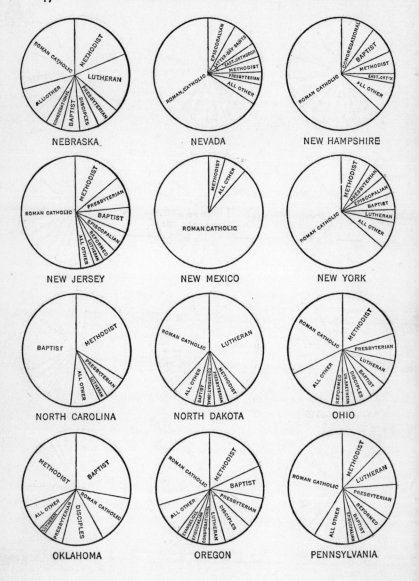

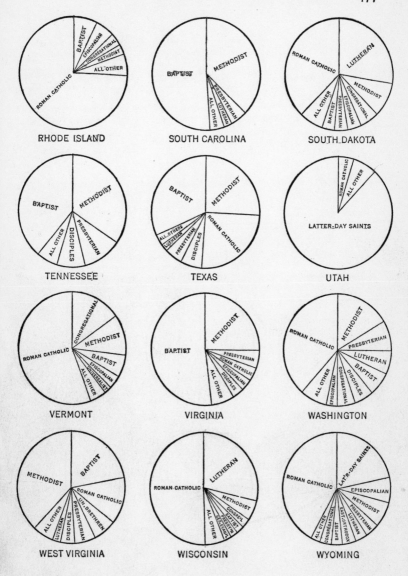

INDEX.

Adler, Felix, 348.
Adonai Shomo, 111, 117.
Advent Christians, 5.
Adventists. History and Polity, 1–4.
     Relation to Freewill Baptists, 33.
     Relation to the Adonai Shomo, 117.
     Divisions, 4.
     Summary Statistics, 14.
Adventists, Age-to-Come, 13.
Adventists, Evangelical, 4.
Adventists, Seventh-Day, 8.
Adventists, The Church of God, 11.
Adventists, The Churches of God in Christ Jesus, 13.
Advent Union, Life and, 12.
Albright, John, 139.
Albrights, The. The Albright People, 139.
Allen, Richard, 237.
Altruists, 111, 116.
Amana Society, 111, 113.
American Christian Convention, 92.
American National Convention, 28.
Amish (Mennonite), 213.
Amish, The Old (Mennonite), 214.
Ammen, Jacob, 213.
Anabaptists, 17.
Ann Lee, 111.
Apostolic, The (Mennonite), 215.
Armenian Church, 81.
Asbury, Francis, 227.
Associate Church of North America (Presbyterian), 305.
Associate Reformed Synod of the South (Presbyterian), 306.
Ballou, Hosea, 369.
Baltimore Association, 45.
Baptist Church of Christ, 43.
Baptists. History and General Characteristics, 16–18.
    Relation to Other Bodies, 16.
    Divisions, 18.

Baptists.   Summary Statistics, 53.
Baptists, Anti-Mission, 45.
Baptists (Colored), Regular, 27–29.
Baptists, Free Communion, 33.
Baptists, Freewill, 33–36.
Baptists, General, 38–40.
Baptists, General Six-Principle, 30.
Baptists, Missionary, 42.
Baptists (North), Regular, 22–24.
Baptists, Old School, 45.
Baptists, Old Two-Seed-in-the-Spirit Predestinarian, 48–54.
Baptists, Original Freewill, 37.
Baptists, Primitive, 45–48.
Baptists, Regular, 17, 18.
Baptists, Regular, General Characteristics and Principles, 18–22.
Baptists, Regular Predestinarian, 50.
Baptists, Regular Two-Seed Predestinarian Primitive, 50.
Baptists, Sabbatarian, 31.
Baptists, Separate, 41.
Baptists, Seventh-Day, 31.
Baptists (South), Regular, 25–27.
Baptists, United, 41.
Bible Bigots, 221.
Bishop Andrew, 254.
Book of Covenants, 171.
Book of Mormon, 165.
Book of Worship, 109.
Brethren in Christ, 55.
Brethren, Old Order of Yorker, 57.
Brethren (Plymouth) I., 60.
Brethren (Plymouth) II., 61.
Brethren (Plymouth) III., 62.
Brethren (Plymouth) IV., 64.
Brethren, The River.   General History, 55.
                              Summary Statistics, 58.
Brethren, Yorker, 57.
Brigham Young, 166.
Brothers of Christ, 89.
Brueder Gemeinde (Mennonite), 218.
Bruederhoef (Mennonite), 213.
Burial Hill Declaration, 120.
Catholic Apostolic Church, 84.
Catholic Church, The Greek, 79.
Catholic Church, The Old, 82.
Catholic Church, The Reformed, 82.

Catholic Church, The Roman, Statistics in the United States, 76–79.
Catholics, General Definition, 66.
Channing, William Ellery, 366.
Chemung Association, 45.
Chinese Temples, 86.
Christadelphians, 89.
Christian Church, South, 93, 94.
Christian Connection, The, 91.
Christian Missionary Association, 95.
Christian Science Journal, The, 96.
Christian Scientists, 96.
Christians, The. Origin and General Characteristics, 91–93.
　　　　　　　　　Statistics, 93.
　　　　　　　　　Withdrawal of the Christian Church, South, 93.
Christian Union Churches, 99.
Churches of God in Christ Jesus (Adventist), 13.
Church of God (Adventist), 11.
Church of God in Christ (Mennonite), 217.
Church of God, The (Winebrenner), 102.
Church Triumphant (Koreshan Ecclesia), 111, 117.
Church Triumphant, The (Schweinfurth), 105.
Coke, Thomas, 223, 227.
Communistic Societies. Definitions and Divisions, 111.
　　　　　　　　　　　Summary Statistics, 118.
Conference, The General (Mennonite), 216.
Conference, The Synodical (Lutheran), 190.
Congregational Churches. History, Polity, Relation to Presbyterians, 119–
　　　　　　　　　　　　123.
　　　　　　　　　　　　Summary Statistics, 123, 124.
Conservative Brethren, 133.
Consolidated American Missionary Convention, 28.
Council, The General (Lutheran), 184.
Cyrus Teed, 117.
Danish Association in America, The (Lutheran), 201.
Danish Church in America, The (Lutheran), 199.
Declaration of Christian Doctrine, 145.
Defenseless, The (Mennonite), 219.
Disciples of Christ, 125–127.
　　　　　　　　　Relation to Other Bodies, 91, 125.
　　　　　　　　　Principles, 126.
　　　　　　　　　Statistics, 127.
Dunkards. History and General Characteristics, 130–133.
　　　　　　Divisions, 133.
　　　　　　Summary Statistics, 138.
Eddy, Mrs. Mary Baker G., 96.

Embury, Philip, 226.

Engle, Jacob, 55.

Episcopal Church, The Protestant. History, 317–321.
  Doctrine, 319.
  Statistics, 322.

Episcopal Church, The Reformed, Origin, Principles, and Statistics, 325–327.

Ethical Culture, The Society for, 348.

Evangelical Association, 139.

Evangelist Missionary Church, The, (Methodist), 270.

Evidence from Scripture and History of the Second Coming of Christ about the year 1843, 2.

Falckner, Justus, 176.

Fee, John G., 95.

Flack, Elder J. V. B., 99.

Foreign Mission Convention of the United States, 28.

Fox, George, 143.

Friends. General Description, 143, 144.
  Divisions, 144.
  Summary Statistics, 152.

Friends (Hicksite), 147.

Friends of the Temple, 153.

Friends (Orthodox), 145.

Friends (Primitive), 150.

Friends (Wilburite), 149.

General Association of the Western States and Territories, 28.

German Baptists, 129.

German Evangelical Protestant Church, 155.

German Evangelical Synod of North America, 156.

Goetwater, John Ernest, 175.

Greek Orthodox Church, 81.

Harmony Society, 111, 114.

Hauge's Synod (Lutheran), 196.

Herrnhut, 272, 273.

Herr, John, 215.

Herrites, 216.

Hicks, Elias, 147.

Hoffmann, Christopher, 153.

Hoffmannites, 153.

Holdeman, John, 217.

Holliman, Ezekiel, 17.

Holy Club, 221.

Hookers, 214.

Huter, Jacob, 213.

Independent Churches of Christ in Christian Union, 99.

Irving, Edward, 84.

Jews. History in the United States, 159–161.
    Summary Statistics, 164.
Jones, Abner, 91.
Joseph Smith, 165.
Judicial Testimony, 299.
Koreshan Ecclesia, 111, 117.
Latter-Day Saints. History, 165, 166.
              Divisions, 166.
              Summary Statistics, 173.
Latter-Day Saints, Church of Jesus Christ of, 167.
Latter-Day Saints, Reorganized Church of Jesus Christ of, 170.
Lecturing Brethren, 90.
Lutheran Congregations, Independent, 204.
Lutherans. General Survey, 175–177.
      Summary Statistics, 205.
Lutheran Synods, Independent, 193.
Mack, Alexander, 129.
Makemie, Francis, 279.
Massachusetts Metaphysical College, 96.
McKendree, William, 228.
Mennonite Church, 212.
Mennonites. History, 206–212.
      Protest against Slavery, 207.
      Articles of Faith, 208.
      Polity, 210.
      Divisions, 212.
      Summary Statistics, 220.
Menno Simons, 206.
Methodists. History, 221–225.
      Peculiarities, 223.
      Conferences, 224.
      Articles of Religion, 225.
      Divisions, 225.
      Summary Statistics, 271.
Methodists, Colored, The Congregational, 261.
Methodist Connection of America, The Wesleyan, 250.
Methodist Episcopal Church, 226–236.
Methodist Episcopal Church, South, 252.
Methodist Episcopal Church, The African, 237.
Methodist Episcopal Church, The Colored, 262.
Methodist Episcopal Church, The Union American, 236.
Methodist Episcopal Zion Church, The African, 242.
Methodist Protestant Church, The, 246.
Methodist Protestant Church, The African Union, 242.
Methodist Church, The Primitive, 265.

Methodists, The Congregational, 259.

Methodists, The Free, 267.

Methodists, The Independent, 269.

Methodists, The New Congregational, 261.

Midnight Cry, The, 2.

Millennial Church or United Society of Believers, 111.

Miller, William, 1.

Missourians, 191.

Moravians.   History, 272–275.

              Government, 273.

              Doctrine, 274.

              Statistics, 276.

Mother Lee, 112.

Muhlenberg, Henry M., 176.

National Christian Scientist Association, 96.

New England Missionary Convention, 28.

New Hampshire Confession, 19, 20.

New Icaria Society, 111–116.

New Jerusalem, The Church of, 107.

New Lights, 312.

New Mennonites, 216.

Norwegian Church in America (Lutheran), 197.

Norwegian Church, The United (Lutheran), 203.

Oberholzer, John, 216.

O'Kelley, James, 91.

Old Order Brethren, 136.

Old (Wisler), The (Mennonite), 218.

Open Brethren, 61.

Orthodox Jews, 161.

Parker, Daniel, 49.

Philadelphia Confession, 19, 20.

Plymouth Brethren.   History and Doctrine, 59.

              Divisions, 60.

              Summary Statistics, 65.

Presbyterian Church, Colored, The Cumberland, 294.

Presbyterian Church (Covenanted), The Reformed, 314.

Presbyterian Church in the United States and Canada, The Reformed, 314.

Presbyterian Church in the United States of America.   History, 279–283.

                        Statistics, 283–288.

Presbyterian Church in the United States (Southern), 302.

Presbyterian Church, The Cumberland.   History and Doctrine, 289–291.

                        Statistics, 291–294.

Presbyterian Church, The General Synod of the Reformed, 312.

Presbyterian Church, The Synod of the Reformed, 310.

Presbyterians, Definition, Polity, Divisions, 277–279.

Presbyterians, The Reformed, History and Polity, 308.

Presbyterians, The United, 298.

Presbytery of Philadelphia, 280.

Profession of Belief, 370.

Progressive Brethren, 135.

Protestant Episcopal Bodies, 317.

Quakers, 143.

Randall, Benjamin, 33.

Rapp, George, 114.

Reformed Bodies, General Description, 329.

Reformed Church in America, 330–333.

Reformed Church of the United States, 333–337.

Reformed Church, The Christian, 337.

Reformed Jews, The, 162.

Reformed, The (Mennonite), 215.

Russian Orthodox Church, 80.

Salvation Army, Origin, Character, Government, Statistics, 340–343.

Schweinfurth, George Jacob, 105.

Schwenkfeldians, The, 344.

Second Dose of the Doctrine of Two Seeds, 49.

Separatists, 111–115.

Serving Brethren, 90.

Seventh-Day Baptists, German, 137.

Shakers, 111.

Signs of the Times, The, 2.

Social Brethren Church, The, 346.

Spiritualists, The, 350.

Statistical Summaries for 1895, 441.

Stone, Barton W., 91.

Summary Statistics by Denominational Families, 392–393.

Summary Statistics by Denominations, 380–391.

Summary Statistics by States of all Denominations, 378–381.

Summary Statistics of Churches in Cities, 404–440.

Summary Statistics of Colored Organizations, 400–403.

Summary Statistics of Denominations according to Number of Communicants, 394–397.

Summary Statistics of Denominations according to Polity, 398–400.

Summary Statistics of Denominational Families according to Number of Communicants, 397.

Swedenborg, Emmanuel, 107.

Synod of Ohio and other States, The Joint (Lutheran), 194.

Synod in the South, The United (Lutheran), 182.

Synod, The Buffalo (Lutheran), 195.

Synod, The General (Lutheran), 178.

Synod, The German Augsburg (Lutheran), 200.

Synod, The Icelandic (Lutheran), 201.

Synod, The Michigan (Lutheran), 198.
Synod, The Suomai (Lutheran), 202.
Temple Society, 153.
Theosophical Society, 353.
Thomas, John, 89.
Time Brethren, 3.
Touro, Abraham and Isaac, 159.
True Inspiration Congregations, 113.
Trumpet of Alarm, The, 2.
Uniates, 79.
Unitarians, 365.
Unitas Fratrum, 272.
United Brethren in Christ, 357.
United Brethren in Christ (Old Constitution), 361.
United Brethren, Origin and General Description, 355–357.
United Zion's Children, 57.
Unity of Brethren as Distinguished from United Brethren in Christ, 272.
Universalists, 369.
Warwick Association, 45.
Welsh Calvinistic Methodist Church (Presbyterian), 296.
Westminster Confession, Revision of, 282.
White, Mrs. Ellen G., 11.
Wilbur, John, 149.
Williams, Roger, 17.
Winebrenner, John, 102.
Woman-preachers, 34.
Woodruff, Wilford, 167.
Zion Union Apostolic Church (Methodist), 245.

Index to Introduction.

PART I.—RESULTS OF THE CENSUS OF 1890.

1. The Sources of Information and the Plan, ix–xi.
       Relation to the Census of 1890.
       Alphabetical Order of the Denominations and Historical Order
           of the Denomination of Families.
2. The Scope and Method of the Census, xi–xiii.
       The Census of 1880 and the Census of 1890.
       Exhaustive List of Denominations.
3. Variety in Religion, xiii–xv.
       Wide Range of Choice.
       Many Denominations Differ Only in Name.

4. Classification of the Churches, xv–xviii.
 The Principle of Classification.
 The Difficulty in the Nomenclature.
5. Denominational Titles, xviii–xxiii.
 Geographical, Racial, Historical, etc.
6. The Causes of Division, xxiii–xxviii.
 Controversies over Doctrine.
 Controversies over Administration and Discipline.
 Controversies over Moral Questions.
 Controversies of a Personal Character.
7. Analysis of Religious Forces of the United States, xxviii–xxxiii.
 Christians and Non-Christians.
 Ministers.
 Organizations.
 Services.
 Values.
 Communicants.
8. Religious Population, xxxiii–xxxv.
 Methods of Computation.
9. The Growth of the Churches, xxxv–xxxviii.
 The Normal Condition.
 The Net Increase.
 Statistical Proofs of the Advance of Protestant Christianity.
10. How the Religious Forces are Distributed, xxxviii–xliii.
 With respect to Number of Communicants, Value of Property, Number of Organizations or Congregations.
11. The Evangelical and Non-Evangelical Elements, xliii–xlv.
 Classification according to Definition.
12. The General Statistical Summaries, xlvi–l.
 Classification according to Polity, and of Churches in the Cities, new Features.
 Difficulties with respect to Lutherans.
 Opinions of Representative Men.
13. The Negro in his Relations to the Church, l–lv.

PART II.—THE GOVERNMENT CENSUS OF 1906.

1. Sex in Membership, lvii–lix.
2. Value of Church Property, lix–lx.
3. Average of Members to Church Edifices, lxi.
4. Tendency of Population to the Cities, lxi–lxii.
5. Communicants in the Cities, lxii–lxiii.
6. Value of Church Property in the Cities, lxiii–lxiv.

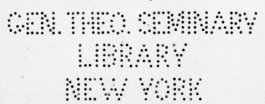

7. Growth by States in Communicants, lxiv–lxv.
8. The Rate of Growth in the South, lxv–lxvi.
9. The Largest Absolute Increases, lxvii–lxviii.
10. Effect of Migration, lxviii.

PART III.—THE RETURNS FOR 1900 AND 1910 AND WHAT THEY SHOW.

1. Growth of the Churches in the Past Twenty Years, lxix–lxx.
2. The Largest Absolute Increases, lxxi.
3. Growth of the Roman Catholic Church, lxxi–lxxii.
4. Religious Population in 1910, lxxii–lxxiii.
5. Changes of Twenty Years, lxxiii–lxxv.
6. Order According to Denominational Families or Groups, lxxv–lxxvi.

PART IV.—DOMINANT RELIGIOUS ELEMENTS.

1. The Characteristics of American Christianity, lxxvii–lxxx.
   The Phenomenal Growth of the Church of Rome and its Relation
   to Protestant America.
2. Evangelical Christianity Dominant, lxxx–lxxxi.
3. Evangelical Christianity Systematically Organized, lxxxi–lxxxii.
   Opportunity for Work in Foreign Countries.
   Opportunity for Work at Home.
   Development of Work among the Young People.
4. Evangelical Christianity Evangelistic, lxxxiii–lxxxiv.
   Importance of Christian Character and of Christian Work.
   The Church of To-day is a Gospel Church.
   The Age of Higher Biblical Criticism.
   Educational Evangelism.
5. Co-operation, Federation and Union, lxxxiv–lxxxvi.
6. How the Church Affects Society, lxxxvi–lxxxvii.
   As a Property-holder, Corporation, Public Institution, etc.